Black Art of Visual Basic Game Programming

Mark Pruett

WAITE GROUP PRESS™
Corte Madera, CA

PUBLISHER Mitchell Waite
EDITOR-IN-CHIEF Charles Drucker
ACQUISITIONS EDITOR Jill Pisoni
EDITORIAL DIRECTOR John Crudo
CONTENT EDITOR Heidi Brumbaugh
TECHNICAL REVIEWER Jeff Bankston
COPY EDITOR Judith Brown
PRODUCTION DIRECTOR Julianne Ososke
PRODUCTION MANAGER Cecile Kaufman
PRODUCTION TRAFFIC COORDINATOR Ingrid Owen
DESIGN Sestina Quarequio, Christi Fryday
PRODUCTION Christi Fryday
COVER ILLUSTRATION James Dowlen

Waite Group Press™ is distributed to bookstores and book wholesalers by Publishers Group West, Box 8843, Emeryville, CA 94662, 1-800-788-3123 (in California 1-510-658-3453).

Printed in the United States of America

95 96 97 98 • 10 9 8 7 6 5 4 3 2 1

Library of Congress Cataloging-in-Publication Data

Pruett, Mark.
Black art of Visual Basic game programming / Mark Pruett.
p. cm.
Includes index.
ISBN 1-57169-005-0
1. Computer games--Programming. 2. Microsoft Visual Basic. I. Title.
QA76.76.C672P78 1995
794.8'15265--dc20 95-32926
CIP

Dedication

For Amy and Billy

Message from the

Publisher

Welcome to Our Nervous System

Some people say that the World Wide Web is a graphical extension of the information superhighway, just a network of humans and machines sending each other long lists of the equivalent of digital junk mail.

I think it is much more than that. To me the Web is nothing less than the nervous system of the entire planet—not just a collection of computer brains connected together, but more like a billion silicon neurons entangled and recirculating electro-chemical signals of information and data, each contributing to the birth of another CPU and another Web site.

Think of each person's hard disk connected at once to every other hard disk on earth, driven by human navigators searching like Columbus for the New World. Seen this way the Web is more of a super entity, a growing, living thing, controlled by the universal human will to expand, to be more. Yet unlike a purposeful business plan with rigid rules, the Web expands in a nonlinear, unpredictable, creative way that echoes natural evolution.

We created our Web site not just to extend the reach of our computer book products but to be part of this synaptic neural network, to experience, like a nerve in the body, the flow of ideas and then to pass those ideas up the food chain of the mind. Your mind. Even more, we wanted to pump some of our own creative juices into this rich wine of technology.

Taste our Digital Wine

And so we ask you to taste our wine by visiting the body of our business. Begin by understanding the metaphor we have created for our Web site—a universal learning center, situated in outer space in the form of a space station. A place where you can journey to study any topic from the convenience of your own screen. Right now we are focusing on computer topics, but the stars are the limit on the Web.

If you are interested in discussing this Web site, or finding out more about the Waite Group, please send me email with your comments and I will be happy to respond. Being a programmer myself, I love to talk about technology and find out what our readers are looking for.

Sincerely,

Mitchell Waite

Mitchell Waite, C.E.O. and Publisher

200 Tamal Plaza
Corte Madera CA 94925
415 924 2575
415 924 2576 fax

Internet email:
mwaite@waite.com

CompuServe email:
75146,3515

Website:
http://www.waite.com/waite

Creating the Highest Quality Computer Books in the Industry

Waite Group Press
Waite Group New Media

About the Author

Mark Pruett is a programmer and writer living in rustic central Virginia. He has worked on a variety of computers and with a variety of languages over the past 12 years. He received a B.S. in Mathematics from Virginia Commonwealth University in 1985. Mark is coauthor of *Visual Basic Controls Desk Reference* (Waite Group Press, 1995).

Table of Contents

Contents

Acknowledgments

Thanks first to all the people at Waite Group Press, and especially to Mitch Waite, John Crudo, and Heidi Brumbaugh. Special thanks to James Shields, who wrote two great games especially for this book, and to Matt Tagliaferri for his wonderful game, Raytraced Reversi for Windows.

Thanks to Vance and Terry for helping me maintain my perspective. Thanks to Liz and Gregg for a much needed eleventh hour reality check. Many, many thanks to Maggie, Amy, and Billy, for their patience, support, and love.

Foreword

I've worked with developers for over five years and found they share several common traits. In fact, if I didn't know better, I'd swear that every software developer hails from the great "Show Me" state of Missouri, because they all want the same things: Good sample code, practical answers, extra references, and tips from the masters. Once shown how it's done, they want you out of their way as they build the next great application. In fact, almost all outstanding software can be traced to a passionate developer with an idea, a compiler, and a pile of reference information. (You'll also find cases of soda, empty pizza boxes, and broken chopsticks.)

At Microsoft, we spend an enormous amount of time and resources servicing the programming community. From world class conferences to our popular Microsoft Developer Network, we understand the importance of getting technical information to programmers, and recognize the developer community as a cornerstone of Microsoft's success. That's why Microsoft is always particularly pleased to see a new VB title from Waite Group Press, because we know that thousands of programmers will be obtaining another excellent tool that will help them exploit the power of Visual Basic.

Mark Pruett's *Black Art of Visual Basic Game Programming* lives up to the superior standards Waite Group Press has set for programming books. Developers will be amazed by what they will be able to do in a very short amount of time. In less than 50 pages, readers build a game in VB and are well on their way to understanding the programmatic aspects of game development. That alone is remarkable, but as this is a Waite Group book, there is much more. Going beyond the straight code, *Black Art of Visual Basic Game Programming* provides tips and tricks on topics such as score keeping, increasing difficulty, psychological issues behind "high score," the art of creating terrain and backgrounds, and much more. Readers using Visual Basic to create high-quality software of all kinds will find this book an outstanding VB resource.

From all of us at Microsoft, thanks for using Visual Basic and good luck with your game programming. In purchasing this book, you've picked up an excellent companion publication from one of the best in the business.

Cameron Myhrvold
Director, Developer Division Marketing
Microsoft Corporation

Introduction

To me, writing programs is a lot like playing a game. The object of the game is to take an idea, nothing more than an idea, and turn it into something real, a program. My "score" depends on how close the final program matches the idea I started with. Sometimes the act of programming yields new possibilities that make the end result better than the original idea. And sometimes the result is something completely unexpected. But, like any other game, most of the kick is derived from the playing.

If you think writing a game program is at least as much fun as playing a game, then I think you'll enjoy this book. If you enjoy the ease with which Visual Basic lets you build programs, but want to squeeze a bit more out of it, then this book is for you.

Who You Are

This book is aimed mainly at programmers who are already comfortable with Visual Basic. You certainly don't need to be an expert, but a basic knowledge of how to put controls onto Visual Basic forms, and how to write event subroutines for simple controls like command buttons is assumed. If you've never dealt with game logic or bitmaps or wave audio files, that's OK. I try to cover the rudiments of a topic, then ramp up to the more in-depth areas.

How This Book is Organized

This book is arranged in three sections. The first section, Chapter 1, serves as an introduction to the elements of a Visual Basic game. In Chapter 1, we build an entire game from start to finish. The game, called *BREAK-THRU!*, is not as complex as the games you'll find later in the book, but it serves to introduce bitmap manipulation, sound effects, game logic, and scoring. If you have never written a game program before, Chapter 1 is the place to start.

Section 2 consists of Chapters 2 through 9. Each of these chapters concentrates on a single element of game programming.

- Chapter 2, *Keeping Score and Increasing Difficulty*, looks at the need to give the game player a purpose, a goal, a reason to play the game. The chapter looks at simple programming methods that let you ramp up the difficulty of game play. This chapter also presents a complete High Score module that you can easily plug into any of your VB games.

- Chapter 3, *Bitmaps,* takes an in-depth look at the most visually-important aspect of games. If you want exciting and fast games, you must be able to create moving pictures on the screen. I'll show you how to exploit the Windows API to create animated sprites and bitmap masks. And you'll learn how to handle smooth and continous background scrolling.
- Chapter 4, *Multiple Players,* looks at different techniques for allowing more than one player to compete. This chapter also introduces methods for saving the *state* of a game using Visual Basic user-defined types.
- Chapter 5, *Input Devices,* provides details on how to program the three common gaming input devices: the keyboard, the mouse, and the joystick. I'll show you how to use the Windows API to adjust the keyboard repeat rate, increasing keyboard response during game play. I'll also show how to use the Windows Multimedia API to control a joystick.
- Chapter 6, *Sound and Fury,* looks at ways to add wave audio and MIDI sounds to your games. I'll demonstrate how to play .WAV files using simple Windows API calls, and how to play both .WAV and .MID files using the Media Control Interface (MCI) API. Then we'll have some major fun playing with Microsoft's WaveMix Dynamic Links Library. WaveMix lets you add layered .WAV sounds to your games, and it's a seriously wild gaming tool.
- Chapter 7, *Video and Frame Animation* introduces techniques for adding frame animation and video clips to your games. You'll learn how to create your own animation frame-by-frame, and how to display Microsoft's Video for Windows .AVI files.
- Chapter 8, *Creating Backgrounds and Terrain,* shows how to add realistic background images to your games. This chapter also demonstrates how to use Virtual Reality Laboratories *VistaPro* to create computer-generated photorealistic three-dimensional backgrounds.
- Chapter 9, *Working With Color Palettes*, covers the often ignored subject of Windows color palettes. Windows 256-color video drivers make it easy to display 256-color bitmaps. Displaying them *correctly* often requires a bit more effort. I'll show you how to use three Microsoft tools, BitEdit, PalEdit, and VidEdit, that make the job easier.

In the third and final section of the book, Chapters 10 through 16, I'll present seven complete games written entirely in Visual Basic. Each reflects a different game genre, and helps to illustrate techniques introduced in the first two sections.

- Chapter 10, *Action Arcade Games,* introduces *Space Hunt*, an arcade-style space shoot-em-up that demonstrates sprite animation, large scale bit masking to present a realistic cockpit view of the action, and layered wave audio using Microsoft's WaveMix.

- Chapter 11, *Simulations,* presents *Lunar Lander,* a game that requires the player to smoothly and accurately land an experimental spacecraft on the moon.
- Chapter 12, *Sports Games,* presents *Golf,* a game where the player can not only play a round of golf, but design their own golf course as well.
- Chapter 13, *Strategy Games,* develops *Raytraced Reversi for Windows,* which shows how to incorporate sound, animation, and imagery to create a multimedia board game.
- Chapter 14, *War Games,* shows how to create a board game, *Blue and Gray,* that pits the player against a computer opponent on the field of battle.
- Chapter 15, *Adventure Games,* introduces *VB Adventure,* a descendent of the venerable text adventure games first created two decades ago. Unlike its progenitors, this game features both sound and images. This is the first of two games written especially for this book by programmer James Shields.
- Chapter 16, *Role-playing Games,* presents *VB-RPG*, the second game created by James Shields. In this game, the player becomes an adventurer in search of hidden treasures. Along the way, the player finds mysteries, danger, and monsters.

I hope you enjoy this book. I think you'll find many of the techniques described are also useful outside of games programming. The multimedia techniques, such as playing video and audio files, are a good example. These programming methods are in demand more now than ever before.

I feel that programming games can be more fun than playing games. The challenges, the pitfalls, and the rewards are all there, just like in any good game. The adventure awaits.

Installation

The included CD-ROM contains 100MB of source code, utilities, and other goodies. There are five subdirectories on the CD: \BAVBG, \ALCHEMY, \POVRAY, \VFW, and \VRLI.

Black Art of Visual Basic Games and Source Code

The project files and source for the projects and games built in the book can be found in \BAVBG, and they are organized by chapters. For example, you'll find the first project of chapter 4 in the directory \BAVBG\CHAP04\PROJ01.

You can view the project files and play the compiled games directly from the CD, but if you want to modify the games, you'll need to copy them to your computer's hard drive. You can do this using the DOS xcopy command, Windows File Manager, or Windows 95 Explorer.

Changing CD-ROM File Attributes

Because files copied from CD-ROMs always have their attribute bit set to read-only (which prevents you from changing or deleting them), you should clear the read-only bit. You can use the DOS attrib command to do this; at the DOS prompt, type:

```
attrib /s -r c:\bavbg\chap04\*.*
```

Video for Windows Run-Time

Chapter 7 discusses the display of Audio-Video Interleave (.AVI) files using Microsoft's Video for Windows. If you don't have Video for Windows, a run-time-only version can be installed:

1. Select the Run... command from the Windows Program Manager File menu.
2. Press the Browse... button to display the Browse dialog window.
3. Select your CD-ROM's drive in the Drive combo box.
4. Select the \VFW directory in the Directories list box.
5. Select SETUP.EXE from the Files list box, then press the OK button.
6. Press the OK button from the Run dialog window.
7. Follow the instructions presented by the Video for Windows installation program.

Other Tools

The CD also includes additional tools and updated versions of the book projects.

VistaPro Demo

The \VRLI directory includes several programs from Virtual Reality Laboratories, Inc., including a demo version of the VistaPro for Windows program discussed in Chapter 8, Terrains and Backgrounds. VistaPro was also used to create the landscape flybys in Chapter 7, Video and Frame Animation.

POV-Ray and Image Alchemy

The incredible animations used by Matt Tagliaferri in his Raytraced Reversi for Windows game (Chapter 13) were created using two programs: POV-Ray and Image Alchemy. Shareware versions of these programs are found on the CD in the \POVRAY and \ALCHEMY directories.

VB4 Code

The games and utilities built in this book are also available on the CD in the newest version of Visual Basic. See the READ.ME file for details.

Part I

Getting Started

Aequator
Horizont
Aequinoctiums
Ekliptik
Wende
Solstitz

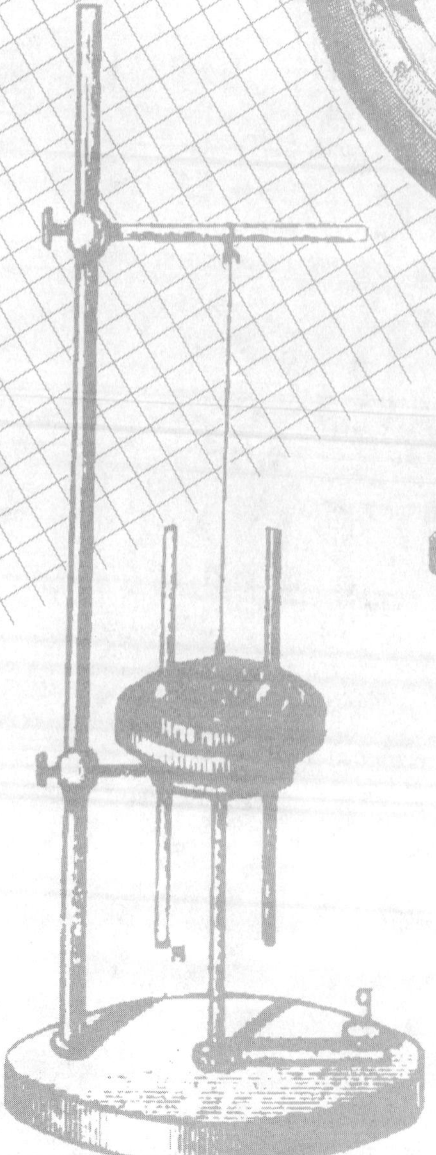

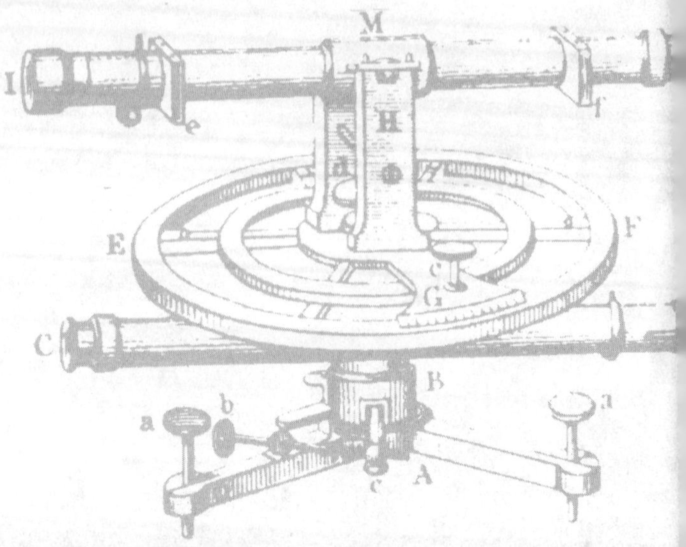
M
I
H
E
F
G
C
B
a
b
c
A

1

Your First Game: BREAK-THRU!

1

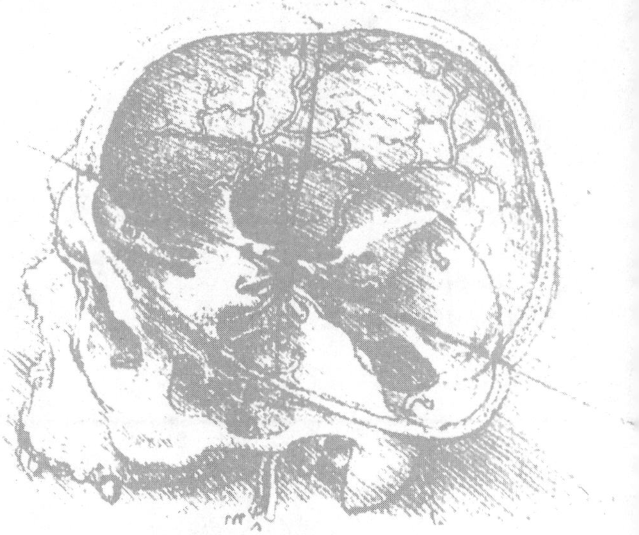

Your First Game: BREAK-THRU!

Think of this chapter as Games 101. The best way to learn how to do something is by actually doing it, so you're going to start right off by building a game. The game won't be trivial. It will contain all the basic elements you would expect to find in an arcade-style game: fast, smooth motion; support for keyboard and joystick; high-score tracking; and the ability to pause a game in progress. I won't cover every topic in detail in this chapter. The main purpose is to look at the overall construction of a game, how all the pieces fit together.

Description of the Game

The game is called BREAK-THRU!, and the concept should be fairly familiar. The player controls a paddle at the bottom of the game's rectangular playing field. The player uses the paddle to hit a ball that moves around the playing field. The ball bounces off the sides and top of the playing field, but if it misses the paddle it escapes off the bottom and the player loses that ball. When the player loses four balls, the game is over. At the top of the field are two rows of blocks; the player gets points for each block the ball hits. Look at Figure 1-1 to see the game in action.

FIGURE 1-1

The BREAK-THRU! game

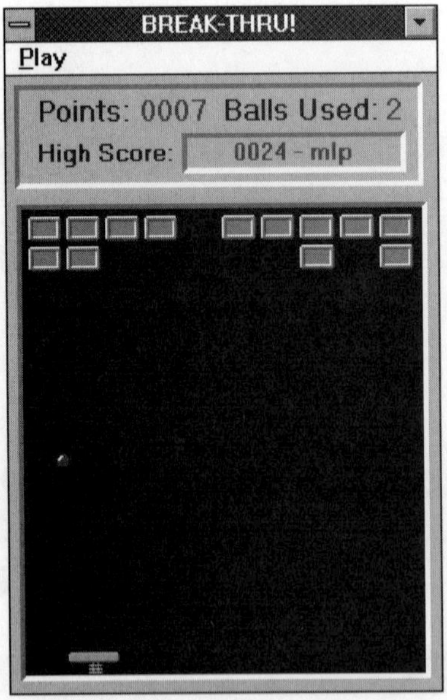

To add to the realism of the game and to make it a bit tougher, you'll add some "physics" to the interaction between the paddle and the ball. For example, the player can change the velocity of the ball by quickly moving the paddle to the left or right.

Sound effects provide an added dimension of excitement to a game, so you'll add some brief wave audio files using simple calls to the Windows API. To make the game more visually interesting, you'll use a bitmap editor to create colorful game pieces. A simple Visual Basic routine will add three-dimensional depth to the game.

Building the Game

Once you've decided on a game concept, you need to begin work on the mechanics of the game. This includes the graphics, sound, scoring, and other implementation details. In practice, it's usually good to start by designing the game's main form and the playing field within that form. The *playing field* is the area within the form where most of the action and movement takes place.

Creating a Playing Field in a PictureBox Control

In most action games, a PictureBox control makes an excellent playing field. In case you aren't familiar with the PictureBox control, I'll review it now. This control is used widely throughout the book, so you should be aware of what you can do with it.

The PictureBox is one of Visual Basic's standard controls. On the surface, it appears to be a relatively simple object. When you place it on a form, it's an unassuming white rectangle. As its name implies, you can display a picture, or *bitmap,* by assigning a bitmap file's name to the PictureBox's Picture property. The bitmap is then displayed in the upper-left corner of the PictureBox. If the bitmap is larger than the PictureBox, the bitmap is clipped to the size of the PictureBox, unless the control's AutoSize property is set to True. In this case, Visual Basic automatically resizes the PictureBox to fit the size of the bitmap exactly.

On the surface, this seems to be the extent of PictureBox's abilities. But PictureBox has two other qualities that make it perfect for game designers. The first quality is that it has an hWnd property. The second quality is that it is a *container* control.

When designing programs in Visual Basic, people usually talk in terms of forms, controls, and events. Controls are placed on forms. These controls trigger events in response to certain stimuli: Click the mouse on a Command Button control and a Click event is triggered. You write the code that goes "inside" the Click event.

At the Windows level, people talk in different terms. Forms and controls become windows, and windows are identified by a unique integer value called a window *handle.* Windows receive *messages* that tell them what to do. This world is usually hidden from you by Visual Basic, but sometimes you need to peel away the Visual Basic layer to get at some of Windows' hidden power.

That's where the PictureBox's hWnd property comes in. This property is the PictureBox's window handle. As you'll see shortly, this little property opens the PictureBox to a world of possibilities.

The second special quality of the PictureBox is that it's a *container* control. This means that you can put other controls—buttons, labels, other PictureBoxes, whatever—inside a PictureBox. I don't mean *on top of* (although you can do that too) but *inside.* These other controls become children of the PictureBox, confined within its borders. Move the PictureBox, and all its children come along for the ride. Delete the PictureBox from a form, and all its children are deleted with it.

In BREAK-THRU! you'll use a PictureBox as the playing field. Let's start building the game.

Creating the BREAK-THRU! Project

First, create a new Visual Basic project and save it as BREAK.MAK. It's a good idea to save this project in its own subdirectory, so you should actually create that first. By putting it in its own separate subdirectory, you will be able to keep track of all the associated files more easily as you build the game.

> Programming Tip: One of Visual Basic's environment options, called Require Variable Declarations, is set to False by default. I recommend setting this option to True. Declaring variables is good programming practice, as it can reduce bugs that can be caused when you accidentally misspell a variable name. A misspelled variable looks like a new variable to Visual Basic, and this can introduce insidious and unwanted side effects that can be *very* difficult to track down.

Next, create a new form, and save it as BREAK.FRM. Add a PictureBox control to the form so that it looks like Figure 1-2. Set the form and PictureBox's properties as shown in Table 1-1.

TABLE 1-1

Property settings for BREAK.FRM and the playing field PictureBox

Object	Property	Setting
Form	FormName	frmBreakThru
	BackColor	&H00C0C0C0&
	BorderStyle	1 'Fixed Single
	Caption	"BREAK-THRU!"
	ClipControls	0 'False
	ForeColor	&H00000000&
	Height	6705
	KeyPreview	-1 'True
	MaxButton	0 'False
	Width	3930
PictureBox	Name	picField
	BackColor	&H00000000&
	ClipControls	0 'False
	Height	3975
	Left	135
	ScaleMode	3 'Pixel
	Tag	"/3d/"
	Top	1140
	Width	3540

FIGURE 1-2
◉◉◉◉◉◉
Starting to build the BREAK-THRU! playing field

You're leaving room above and below the picField PictureBox for other game elements that will be added later. You'll notice that I've given both the form and the control names different than the defaults. When developing programs of any complexity, you should try to use meaningful variable names. Because controls and forms are referred to in the program by their Name property, try to call them something you'll be likely to remember.

Designing the Playing Pieces

Now that you have the playing field, you need to design some of the playing pieces. In this game, there are three basic game pieces. The blocks are arranged in two rows at the top of the field. The paddle is controlled by the player, who moves it left and right at the bottom of the playing field. Finally, the ball bounces around the playing field, knocking out blocks and bouncing off the walls and the paddle.

These game pieces are bitmaps, and a variety of tools exists for creating and manipulating them. Windows even comes with one, the accessory program called Paintbrush. Let's use it to build one of the game pieces.

Start Paintbrush by double-clicking its icon in the Windows Program Manager Accessories program group. If the icon isn't there, you can also start Paintbrush by selecting the *Run...* command from the Program Manager File menu, typing in the name *PBRUSH*, and pressing the ENTER key. After a moment, the Paintbrush program (Figure 1-3) should appear.

When drawing a bitmap with a tool such as Paintbrush, your first decision should be how big the picture is going to be. Let's draw one of the blocks first. Let's say you want about 10 blocks per row, across the width of the playing field. The playing field is 234 pixels wide (you can tell this by looking at the picField control's ScaleWidth property in the Visual Basic Properties window). That would mean that the blocks should be no more than 23 pixels wide (234 divided by 10, ignoring the remainder—you can't have fractions of pixels!). Round that number down to an even 20 pixels wide, so that you can leave a little space between each block. The height of the blocks is arbitrary, but they'll probably look better if they're wider than they are tall, so make them 14 pixels tall.

In Paintbrush, select the *Image Attributes...* command from the Options menu. Change the units to pels (these are the same as pixels) and then enter in a new width, 20, and a new height, 14. Click on OK, and the drawing area should be reduced to these new dimensions. Now you can use the editing tools to draw your block.

Paintbrush has a zoom feature (select *Zoom In* or *Zoom Out* from the View menu) that lets you magnify a section of the bitmap, letting you more precisely edit the image. This feature displays the image with fatter pixels, making it much easier to do detailed editing, particularly of small bitmaps like those used in this game.

FIGURE 1-3

The Windows Paintbrush bitmap editing program

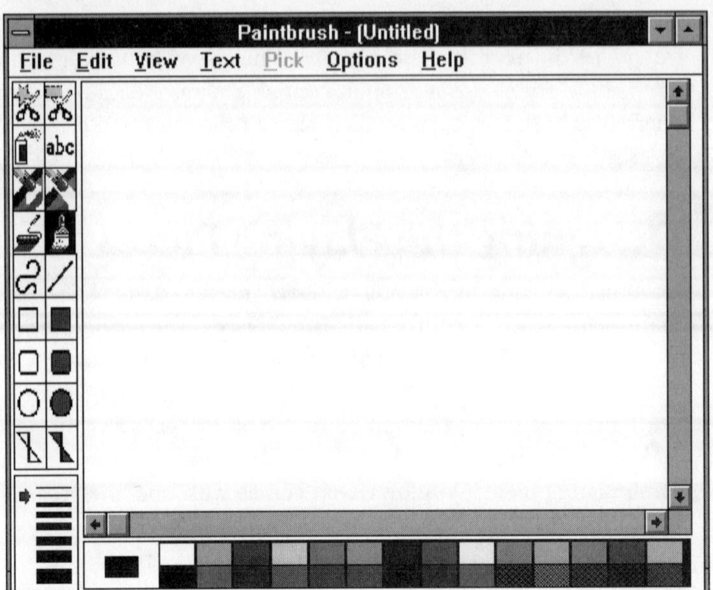

FIGURE 1-4
The game piece images

Figure 1-4 shows zoomed-in pictures of each of the game pieces. Save these images as PADDLE.BMP, BALL.BMP, and BLOCK.BMP. Store these bitmaps in the directory where your other project files are stored.

Don't Reinvent the Wheel—Writing Reusable Code

Before going further, let's add a new Basic module, called GAMESTUF.BAS. Put routines that are generic enough that you might want to use them again in another project in this module.

> Programming Tip: By putting general purpose code in a separate module, you can use it later in other games by simply adding it to the new project using the *Add File...* command from Visual Basic's File menu.

The GAMESTUF.BAS module will contain three routines, two that will let you play wave audio files to add sound effects to the game, and a third that gives Visual Basic controls a three-dimensional effect by drawing inset or raised borders around them. (For more information on wave audio files, see Chapter 6.)

Add the code in Listing 1-1 to the GAMESTUF.BAS module. The first section should be entered into the module's Declarations section. This section declares some global constants you'll use in the program, as well as some Windows API functions. Windows API functions are subroutines that are not part of Visual Basic, but rather part of the Windows operating environment itself. Many of these routines can be called by Visual Basic, and can be very useful in extending the language's abilities.

Listing 1-1 The GAMESTUF.BAS module

```
Option Explicit
'---------------------------------------------------
' Global variables, constants and declaration.
'---------------------------------------------------

' Functions and constants used to play sounds.
```

continued on next page

continued from previous page

```
Declare Function sndPlaySound Lib "MMSystem" (ByVal lpsound As String, ByVal flag As
Integer) As Integer
Declare Function sndStopSound Lib "MMSystem" Alias "sndPlaySound" (ByVal lpszNull As
Long, ByVal flags As Integer) As Integer

Global Const SND_SYNC = &H0
Global Const SND_ASYNC = &H1
Global Const SND_MEMORY = &H4
Global Const SND_LOOP = &H8
Global Const SND_NOSTOP = &H10

' Color Constants
Global Const DARK_GRAY = &H808080
Global Const WHITE = &HFFFFFF
Global Const BLACK = &H0

' KeyCode constants
Global Const KEY_LEFT = &H25
Global Const KEY_RIGHT = &H27

' 3D effect constants
Global Const BORDER_INSET = 0
Global Const BORDER_RAISED = 1

' A general purpose data structure used for tracking bitmaps.
' This structure can also be passed to Windows API calls requiring
' a RECT (rectangle structure).
Type tBitMap
    Left As Integer
    Top As Integer
    Right As Integer
    Bottom As Integer
    Width As Integer
    Height As Integer
End Type

' Windows GDI Bitmap API constants and functions
Global Const SRCCOPY = &HCC0020
Global Const SRCINVERT = &H660046
Declare Function BitBlt Lib "GDI" (ByVal hDestDC As Integer, ByVal X As Integer, ByVal
Y As Integer, ByVal nWidth As Integer, ByVal nHeight As Integer, ByVal hSrcDC As
Integer, ByVal XSrc As Integer, ByVal YSrc As Integer, ByVal dwRop As Long) As Integer

' Windows API rectangle functions
Declare Function IntersectRect Lib "User" (ResultRect As tBitMap, Rect1 As tBitMap,
Rect2 As tBitMap) As Integer

Sub Make3D (pic As Form, ctl As Control, ByVal BorderStyle As Integer)
'--------------------------------------------------
' Wrap a 3D effect around a control on a form.
'--------------------------------------------------
Dim AdjustX As Integer, AdjustY As Integer
```

```
Dim RightSide As Single
Dim BW As Integer, BorderWidth As Integer
Dim LeftTopColor As Long, RightBottomColor As Long
Dim i As Integer

    If Not ctl.Visible Then Exit Sub

    AdjustX = Screen.TwipsPerPixelX
    AdjustY = Screen.TwipsPerPixelY

    BorderWidth = 3

    Select Case BorderStyle
    Case 0: ' Inset
        LeftTopColor = DARK_GRAY
        RightBottomColor = WHITE
    Case 1: ' Raised
        LeftTopColor = WHITE
        RightBottomColor = DARK_GRAY
    End Select


    ' Set the top shading line.
    For BW = 1 To BorderWidth
        ' Top
        pic.CurrentX = ctl.Left - (AdjustX * BW)
        pic.CurrentY = ctl.Top - (AdjustY * BW)
        pic.Line -(ctl.Left + ctl.Width + (AdjustX * (BW - 1)), ctl.Top - (AdjustY *
        BW)), LeftTopColor
        ' Right
        pic.Line -(ctl.Left + ctl.Width + (AdjustX * (BW - 1)), ctl.Top + ctl.Height +
        (AdjustY * (BW - 1))), RightBottomColor
        ' Bottom
        pic.Line -(ctl.Left - (AdjustX * BW), ctl.Top + ctl.Height + (AdjustY *
        (BW - 1))), RightBottomColor
        ' Left
        pic.Line -(ctl.Left - (AdjustX * BW), ctl.Top - (AdjustY * BW)), LeftTopColor
    Next
End Sub

Function NoiseGet (ByVal FileName) As String
'-------------------------------------------------------------
' Load a sound file into a string variable.
'-------------------------------------------------------------
Dim buffer As String
Dim f As Integer
Dim SoundBuffer As String

    On Error GoTo NoiseGet_Error

    buffer = Space$(1024)
    SoundBuffer = ""
```

continued on next page

continued from previous page

```
    f = FreeFile
    Open FileName For Binary As f
    Do While Not EOF(f)
        Get #f, , buffer     ' Load in 1K chunks
        SoundBuffer = SoundBuffer & buffer
    Loop
    Close f
    NoiseGet = Trim$(SoundBuffer)
Exit Function

NoiseGet_Error:
    SoundBuffer = ""
    Exit Function
End Function

Sub NoisePlay (SoundBuffer As String, ByVal PlayMode As Integer)
'------------------------------------------------------------
' Plays a sound previously loaded into memory with function
' NoiseGet().
'------------------------------------------------------------
Dim retcode As Integer

    If SoundBuffer = "" Then Exit Sub

    ' Stop any sound that may currently be playing.
    retcode = sndStopSound(0, SND_ASYNC)

    ' PlayMode should be SND_SYNC or SND_ASYNC
    retcode = sndPlaySound(ByVal SoundBuffer, PlayMode Or SND_MEMORY)
End Sub
```

Adding a Reusable Joystick Module

To give the user the ability to control the paddle with a joystick as well as the keyboard, create another basic module, called JOYSTICK.BAS. I'll cover the joystick in depth in Chapter 5. For now, you only need to know that the routines in this module let players use an IBM-compatible joystick if one is attached to their system, shown in Listing 1-2.

Listing 1-2 The JOYSTICK.BAS module

```
Option Explicit
'-------------------------------------------------------
' JOYSTICK.BAS - Joystick support routines for
'               Visual Basic.
'-------------------------------------------------------

' Joystick Device ID
Global Const JOYSTICK1 = 0
Global Const JOYSTICK2 = 1
```

```
' Joystick error return values
Global Const JOYERR_NOERROR = 0
Global Const JOYERR_PARMS = 165
Global Const MMSYSERR_NODRIVER = 6
Global Const JOYERR_UNPLUGGED = 167

' Joystick button bit-flags used by tJoyInfo.ButtonStates
Global Const JOY_BUTTON1 = &H1
Global Const JOY_BUTTON2 = &H2
Global Const JOY_BUTTON3 = &H4
Global Const JOY_BUTTON4 = &H8


' Joystick Position
Type tJoyInfo
    Xin As Integer
    Yin As Integer
    Zin As Integer
    ButtonStates As Integer

    ' These values are determined by the fields above.
    X As Long
    Y As Long
    Z As Long
    ButtonDown(1 To 4) As Integer
End Type

' Joystick Capabilities

Const MAXPNAMELEN = 32

Type tJoyCaps
    Mid As Integer
    Pid As Integer
    Pname As String * MAXPNAMELEN
    XminIn As Integer
    XmaxIn As Integer
    YminIn As Integer
    YmaxIn As Integer
    ZminIn As Integer
    ZmaxIn As Integer
    NumButtons As Integer
    PeriodMin As Integer
    PeriodMax As Integer

    Xmin As Long
    Xmax As Long
    Ymin As Long
    Ymax As Long
    Zmin As Long
    Zmax As Long
End Type
```

continued on next page

continued from previous page

```
Global JoyCaps As tJoyCaps

' Joystick API Calls
Declare Function joyGetDevCaps Lib "MMSystem" (ByVal IDDevice As Integer, JCaps As
tJoyCaps, ByVal CapSize As Integer) As Integer
Declare Function joyGetPos Lib "MMSystem" (ByVal IDDevice As Integer, JPos As
tJoyInfo) As Integer

Function GetJoyStickPos (IDDevice As Integer, JoyInfo As tJoyInfo) As Integer
'-------------------------------------------------------
' This function is a wrapper around the joyGetPos API
' call. That call returns coordinates as unsigned
' long integers, which VB doesn't support. We move
' these coordinates into long values so that they
' can be easily evaluated.
'-------------------------------------------------------
Dim rc As Integer
Static NotFirstTime As Integer

    If Not NotFirstTime Then
        NotFirstTime = False
        rc = joyGetDevCaps(IDDevice, JoyCaps, Len(JoyCaps))

        If rc <> 0 Then
            GetJoyStickPos = rc
            Exit Function
        End If

        JoyCaps.Xmax = uint_to_long(JoyCaps.XmaxIn)
        JoyCaps.Xmin = uint_to_long(JoyCaps.XminIn)
        JoyCaps.Ymax = uint_to_long(JoyCaps.YmaxIn)
        JoyCaps.Ymin = uint_to_long(JoyCaps.YminIn)
        JoyCaps.Zmax = uint_to_long(JoyCaps.ZmaxIn)
        JoyCaps.Zmin = uint_to_long(JoyCaps.ZminIn)

    End If

    rc = joyGetPos(IDDevice, JoyInfo)
    GetJoyStickPos = rc

    If rc <> 0 Then Exit Function

    JoyInfo.X = uint_to_long(JoyInfo.Xin)
    JoyInfo.Y = uint_to_long(JoyInfo.Yin)
    JoyInfo.Z = uint_to_long(JoyInfo.Zin)

    JoyInfo.ButtonDown(1) = (JoyInfo.ButtonStates And JOY_BUTTON1) = JOY_BUTTON1
    JoyInfo.ButtonDown(2) = (JoyInfo.ButtonStates And JOY_BUTTON2) = JOY_BUTTON2
    JoyInfo.ButtonDown(3) = (JoyInfo.ButtonStates And JOY_BUTTON3) = JOY_BUTTON3
    JoyInfo.ButtonDown(4) = (JoyInfo.ButtonStates And JOY_BUTTON4) = JOY_BUTTON4

End Function
```

```
Function uint_to_long (uint As Integer) As Long
'-------------------------------------------------------
' Convert an unsigned integer into a long integer.
'-------------------------------------------------------

    uint_to_long = (CLng(uint) And &HFFFF&)
End Function
```

Building the Main Form—BREAK.FRM

With the two support modules, GAMESTUF.BAS and JOYSTICK.BAS, safely out of the way, you can get back to building the game. You have the main form and a PictureBox control, picField, to serve as the playing field. Now let's add the other controls you'll need.

First, add some controls inside the playing field. I mentioned earlier that a PictureBox can be a container control; it can hold other controls. That's what you'll do here. When adding the controls listed in Table 1-2, make sure to select the picField control first by clicking on it (you can tell it's selected if its resizing handles are displayed on picField's sides and corners). Then drop each of the new controls inside picField. To be sure that the new control is actually inside picField and not merely on top of it, try dragging the new control outside the borders of picField. A contained control can't be dragged outside of its parent control.

TABLE 1-2

Controls contained inside the picField PictureBox control

Object	Property	Setting
Image	Name	imgBlock
	Index	0
	Picture	(set at design time in Properties window)
	Visible	0 'False
Label	Name	lblPaused
	Alignment	2 'Center
	BackStyle	0 'Transparent
	Caption	"PAUSED"
	FontBold	0 'False
	FontSize	12
	ForeColor	&H000000FF&
	Visible	0 'False

continued on next page

continued from previous page

Object	Property	Setting
Label	Name	lblGameOver
	Alignment	2 'Center
	BackStyle	0 'Transparent
	Caption	"GAME OVER"
	FontBold	0 'False
	FontSize	12
	ForeColor	&H000000FF&
	Visible	0 'False

The first control, imgBlock, is an Image control. Image controls are somewhat similar to PictureBox controls, but they don't have an hWnd window handle property and they can't serve as container controls. Their advantage is that they are so-called lightweight controls: controls that eat up only a small amount of Windows' resources.

Assign the block bitmap you created earlier to the Picture property of imgBlock. To do this, select imgBlock's Picture property from the Visual Basic Properties window, then select the BLOCK.BMP file from the provided dialog box. The block bitmap will appear in the Image control.

The other two controls are just labels. The first, lblGameOver, is displayed at the end of a game. The second, lblPaused, is displayed when the player has paused the game. Notice from Table 1-2 that both labels are initially invisible; that is, their Visible properties are set to False.

After adding these controls, your form should look like Figure 1-5.

Remember that the game will display two rows of 10 blocks each; so why did you create just one? As you will see later, you can use the *control array* feature of Visual Basic to create and arrange duplicates of the imgBlock control when you need them. Note that the Index property of imgBlock is set to 0 (by default, the Index property is blank). This 0 Index is necessary if you want to create a control array later.

Adding a Menu

Next, let's give the form a menu. This will give the player an easy way to start a new game, pause the current game, or exit the program. Using the Visual Basic Menu Design window, create a menu as described in Table 1-3.

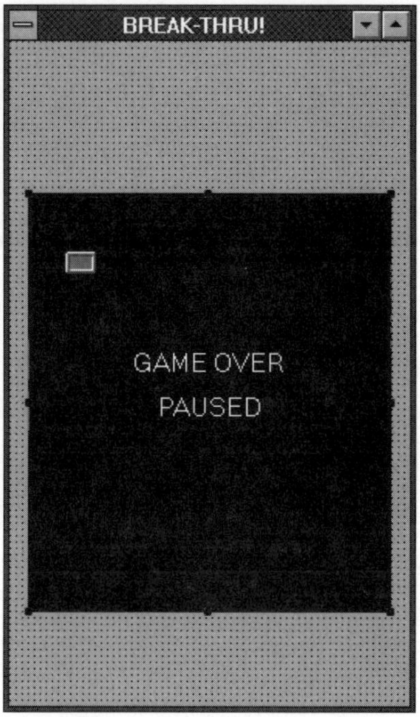

FIGURE 1-5 *BREAK.FRM with labels and image controls in picField*

TABLE 1-3 *The BREAK.FRM menu*

Caption	Name	Shortcut Key
&Play	mnuPlay	
----&New Game	mnuNewGame	F2
----&Pause	mnuPause	F3
----	mnuPlaySep1	
----E&xit	mnuPlayExit	Ctrl-X

Adding the Playing Piece Bitmaps to the Form

You still need to add the other two game pieces, the ball and the paddle, to the form. You probably think that you'll add these controls to the picField control, as you did with the block Image control. Actually, you're going to add them to the bottom of the form, below picField. Add the controls described in Table 1-4 to the BREAK.FRM form.

TABLE 1-4

Game pieces for BREAK.FRM

Object	Property	Setting
PictureBox	Name	picBall
	AutoRedraw	-1 'True
	AutoSize	-1 'True
	BorderStyle	0 'None
	Picture	(set at design time in Properties window)
	ScaleMode	3 'Pixel
	Visible	0 'False
PictureBox	Name	picPaddle
	AutoRedraw	-1 'True
	AutoSize	-1 'True
	BorderStyle	0 'None
	Picture	(set at design time in Properties window)
	ScaleMode	3 'Pixel
	Visible	0 'False
PictureBox	Name	picBlack
	AutoRedraw	-1 'True
	BackColor	&H00000000&
	FillStyle	0 'Solid
	Visible	0 'False

You should now assign the BALL.BMP bitmap to the picBall control's Picture property and the PADDLE.BMP bitmap to picPaddle, in the same way you assigned imgBlock's bitmap. In both cases, the bitmap should appear in the control, and the form should now look like Figure 1-6.

Why did you put the paddle and ball in PictureBox *outside* the playing field PictureBox, picField? Well, you could have put them inside picField and simply

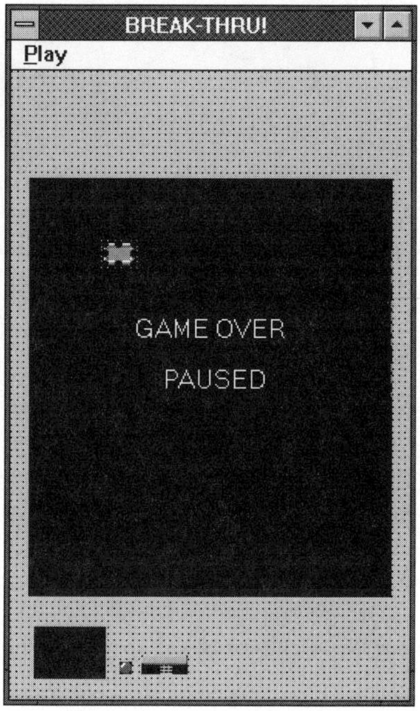

FIGURE 1-6

The BREAK.FRM form with added game pieces

moved the ball and paddle by changing their Left and Top properties. This technique works, and it's very easy to program. It's also *slow.* Moving Visual Basic controls around the screen won't provide the smooth motion players expect in action games. Instead, you can use the PictureBox controls to store the bitmaps, but use a fast Windows API routine, called *BitBlt*, to copy the bitmap images onto the playing field. Thus, picBall and picPaddle are just used to hold the bitmap images. Notice that their Visible properties are set to False. At runtime, the players won't even see the PictureBox controls, but they'll see the images the controls contain when they're copied onto the playing field.

The use of BitBlt is just one example of the trade-offs you need to consider when programming games in Visual Basic. Visual Basic provides Image and PictureBox controls that can simplify manipulation of bitmaps. That simplicity comes at the price of speed. You can use the Image control to display the rows of blocks at the top of the playing field. That's because these blocks don't move. How fast they can be displayed on the screen is not a real issue. But the ball and paddle are in almost constant motion. If you can't display them quickly, their motion will appear jerky and the game will seem unresponsive to the player. I'll cover bitmaps in depth in Chapter 3, including more uses for the BitBlt function.

Adding the Timer Controls

Let's finish adding controls to the form. Next add two Timer controls. Timer controls can trigger a Timer event at regular intervals. Use one timer to control the action during normal game play. The other timer will independently handle moving the paddle when the player moves the joystick right or left. Add these controls anywhere on the form; they are always invisible at runtime. Set their properties as shown in Table 1-5.

TABLE 1-5

Timer controls for BREAK.FRM

Object	Property	Setting
Timer	Name	Timer1
	Enabled	0 'False
	Interval	5
Timer	Name	JoyTimer
	Interval	22

The Timer1 control, which controls the actual game action, is initally disabled. Its Enabled property is set to True at the start of a new game.

Adding Labels to Show Scores

Finally, let's add some labels to the upper section of the form, above the playing field. These labels will be used to display the current score, the high score, and how many balls the player has left. Table 1-6 describes the settings for each label. Use Figure 1-6 as a guide for placing them on the form.

TABLE 1-6

Label controls for BREAK.FRM

Object	Property	Setting
Label	Name	lblPoints
	Alignment	1 'Right Justify
	BackStyle	0 'Transparent
	Caption	"0000"
	FontSize	12
	ForeColor	&H000000FF&

Object	Property	Setting
Label	Name	lblMisses
	Alignment	1 'Right Justify
	BackStyle	0 'Transparent
	Caption	"0"
	FontSize	12
	ForeColor	&H000000FF&
Label	Name	lblHiScore
	Alignment	2 'Center
	BackStyle	0 'Transparent
	Caption	"0000"
	FontSize	9.75
	ForeColor	&H000000FF&
	Tag	"/3d/"
Label	Name	Label1
	Alignment	1 'Right Justify
	BackStyle	0 'Transparent
	Caption	"Balls Used:"
	FontSize	12
	ForeColor	&H00FF0000&
Label	Name	Label2
	Alignment	1 'Right Justify
	BackStyle	0 'Transparent
	Caption	"Points:"
	FontSize	12
	ForeColor	&H00FF0000&
Label	Name	Label3
	BackStyle	0 'Transparent
	Tag	"/3d/"

continued on next page

continued from previous page

Object	Property	Setting
Label	Name	Label4
	Alignment	1 'Right Justify
	BackStyle	0 'Transparent
	Caption	"High Score:"
	FontSize	9.75
	ForeColor	&H00FF0000&

Notice that in Figure 1-7, Label3 is the selected control whose resizing handles can be seen surrounding the other labels. Label3 is used solely to make it easy to draw a three-dimensional panel around the other labels. You'll see how this is done a little later.

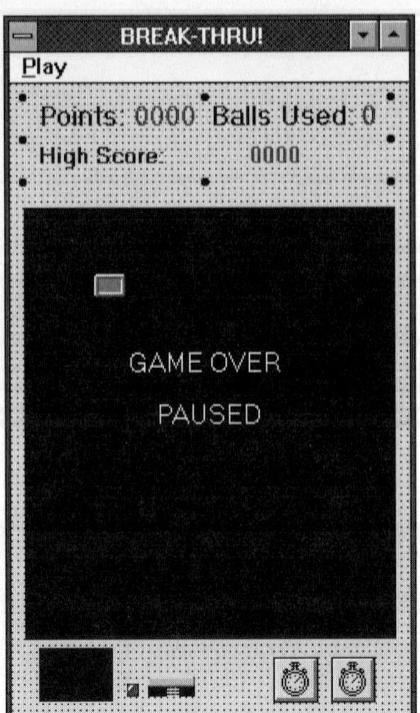

FIGURE 1-7

The BREAK.FRM form at design time, with all controls in place

Adding the Game Logic

Now that the form is completed, you can start on the program code itself. First, declare all the variables you'll be using in the form. Add the code from Listing 1-3 to the Declarations section of BREAK.FRM.

Listing 1-3 Declaring Variables in BREAK.FRM

```
Option Explicit
'-------------------------------------------------
' Global constants and variables used within the
' game's main form.
'-------------------------------------------------

' Ball Information ------------------------------
Dim bmpBall As tBitMap

' The current ball speed
Dim XSpeed As Integer
Dim YSpeed As Integer

' The slowest allowable ball speed
Dim MinXSpeed As Integer
Dim MinYSpeed As Integer

' The units at which the ball speed can change
Dim SpeedUnit As Integer

' Either +1 or -1, determines the direction
' that the ball is moving
Dim Xdir As Integer
Dim YDir As Integer

' The starting position of the ball.
Dim XStartBall As Integer
Dim YStartBall As Integer

Dim NumBalls As Integer

' Paddle Information ----------------------------
Dim bmpPaddle As tBitMap

' The starting position of the paddle
Dim XStartPaddle As Integer
Dim YStartPaddle As Integer

' The current amount of "english" that the paddle
' will apply to the ball.
Dim PaddleEnglish As Integer

' The amount that the paddle will move.
```

continued on next page

continued from previous page

```
Dim PaddleIncrement As Integer

' Block Information -------------------------------
Const BLOCKS_IN_ROW = 10
Const NUM_ROWS = 2
Const BLOCK_GAP = 3

' Strings that store game wave audio files in memory.
Dim wavPaddleHit As String
Dim wavBlockHit As String
Dim wavWall As String
Dim wavMissed As String
Dim wavSetup As String
Dim wavNewLevel As String

' Joystick Information
Dim JoyInfo As tJoyInfo
Dim JoyAtRestMin As Long
Dim JoyAtRestMax As Long

' Used when calling the two API functions below.
Const SECTION = "HiScore"
Const ENTRY = "Score"
Const INI_FILE = "BREAKTHR.INI"

' Two Windows API calls used to read and write private .INI files.
Declare Function GetPrivateProfileString Lib "Kernel" (ByVal lpSectionName As String,
ByVal lpKeyName As String, ByVal lpDefault As String, ByVal lpReturnedString As
String, ByVal nSize As Integer, ByVal lpFileName As String) As Integer

Declare Function WritePrivateProfileString Lib "Kernel" (ByVal lpSectionName As
String, ByVal lpKeyName As String, ByVal lpString As String, ByVal lplFileName As
String) As Integer

Dim HiScore As Integer
Dim HiPlayer As String

' Boolean (True/False) value that indicates if game
' has been paused.
Dim Paused As Integer
```

The first thing to notice in this section are the bmpBall and bmpPaddle variables, which have been declared as type tBitMap. What's tBitMap? This is a data type that you declared in the GAMESTUF.BAS module. Its structure looks like this:

```
Type tBitMap
    Left As Integer
    Top As Integer
    Right As Integer
    Bottom As Integer
    Width As Integer
    Height As Integer
End Type
```

This data structure contains information similar to that stored for controls: left, top, width, and height. It also stores the coordinates for the right and bottom of the bitmap. This structure will be used later to detect when two game objects collide.

Setting Up the Game Board

When you're playing a board game like Monopoly, the first thing you do is set up the board and organize and arrange the pieces. A game program is no different. When a program like this is run, with only one form, the first thing Visual Basic does is call the form's Load event. This is the perfect place to get everything ready for the player.

Enter the Load event in Listing 1-4 for BREAK.FRM.

Listing 1-4 The Load event for BREAK.FRM

```
Sub Form_Load ()
'-----------------------------------------------------
' Position the game form and initialize all game
' values
'-----------------------------------------------------
Dim JoyXRange As Long
Dim JoyXCenter As Long
Dim rc As Integer
Dim ScoreStr As String

      ' Center the form on the screen.
    Me.Move (Screen.Width - Me.Width) \ 2, (Screen.Height - Me.Height) \ 2

    ' Display the form.
    Me.Show

    InitGeneralGameData

    CreateBlocks

    ' Read the current High Score.
    HiScore = 0
    HiPlayer = "???"
    ScoreStr = Space$(25)
    rc = GetPrivateProfileString(SECTION, ENTRY, "", ScoreStr, Len(ScoreStr), INI_FILE)
    If rc > 0 Then
        ScoreStr = Left$(ScoreStr, rc)
        If IsNumeric(ScoreStr) Then HiScore = Val(ScoreStr)
        HiPlayer = Space$(255)
        rc = GetPrivateProfileString(SECTION, "Player", "", HiPlayer, Len(HiPlayer), INI_FILE)
        If rc > 0 Then
            HiPlayer = Left$(HiPlayer, rc)
        Else
            HiPlayer = "???"
```

continued on next page

continued from previous page

```
        End If
    End If

    ' Set up the Joystick
    rc = GetJoystickPos(JOYSTICK1, JoyInfo)
    JoyXRange = (JoyCaps.Xmax - JoyCaps.Xmin)
    JoyXCenter = JoyCaps.Xmin + (JoyXRange / 2)
    JoyAtRestMin = JoyXCenter - (JoyXRange * .08)
    JoyAtRestMax = JoyXCenter + (JoyXRange * .08)

    ' Boolean (True/False) value that indicates if game
    ' has been paused.
    Paused = False
End Sub
```

There's a lot going on here. First, center the form on the player's screen using the form's Move method. Next call the subroutine InitGeneralGameData. Add this routine to the form. This subroutine initializes several variables that are used during the course of a game, but whose values never change. This subroutine is only called once, from the form's Load event. So why didn't you stick this code into the Load event itself, rather than bother with a separate subroutine? Because this code has a certain cohesiveness. By separating the code from the Load event and giving it a single descriptive name, InitGeneralGameData, you can tell at a glance the purpose of the subroutine and not clutter up the Load event.

> **Programming Tip: Breaking your program code into cohesive subroutines can make it easier to change and easier to comprehend.**

Listing 1-5 The InitGeneralGameData subroutine

```
Sub InitGeneralGameData ()
'--------------------------------------------------------
' Set up variables that don't change during game play.
'--------------------------------------------------------

    ' Determine the ball's start position based on game board dimensions.
    XStartBall = (picField.ScaleWidth - picBall.ScaleWidth) / 2
    YStartBall = (picField.ScaleHeight) / 4

    ' Determine the paddle's start position based on game board dimensions.
    XStartPaddle = (picField.ScaleWidth - picPaddle.ScaleWidth) / 2
    YStartPaddle = picField.ScaleHeight - picPaddle.ScaleHeight

    ' Load all the Game sounds into memory.
    wavSetup = NoiseGet(app.Path & "\" & "setup.wav")
    wavPaddleHit = NoiseGet(app.Path & "\" & "paddle.wav")
```

```
    wavBlockHit = NoiseGet(app.Path & "\" & "blockhit.wav")
    wavWall = NoiseGet(app.Path & "\" & "wallhit.wav")
    wavMissed = NoiseGet(app.Path & "\" & "missed.wav")
    wavNewLevel = NoiseGet(app.Path & "\" & "newlevel.wav")

    ' Get Ball dimensions from the picBall control
    bmpBall.Left = XStartBall
    bmpBall.Top = YStartBall
    bmpBall.Width = picBall.ScaleWidth
    bmpBall.Height = picBall.ScaleHeight

    ' Get Paddle dimensions from the picPaddle control
    bmpPaddle.Left = XStartPaddle
    bmpPaddle.Top = YStartPaddle
    bmpPaddle.Width = picPaddle.ScaleWidth
    bmpPaddle.Height = picPaddle.ScaleHeight

    ' Number of balls the user gets during the game.
    NumBalls = 4
End Sub
```

The next routine called by the Load event is CreateBlocks. Enter this subroutine as shown in Listing 1-6.

Listing 1-6 The CreateBlocks subroutine

```
Sub CreateBlocks ()
'--------------------------------------------------
' Create all the imgBlock elements that we need.
'--------------------------------------------------
Dim i As Integer

    For i = 1 To (NUM_ROWS * BLOCKS_IN_ROW)
        Load imgBlock(i)
    Next
End Sub
```

This subroutine creates 20 imgBlock Image controls. Remember that you created a single imgBlock control and placed it inside the playing field. You set its Index property to 0 at design time; this made it the first element in a *control array.* A control array is similar to a conventional Visual Basic array, except that each element of the array is a control. You used the Load function inside a For loop to create 20 clones of the original imgBlock. When created this way, the new controls are invisible. You'll make them visible, and place them where you want them on the playing field.

The remaining code in the form's Load event handles retrieving the previous high score from a Windows *initialization file,* setting up some variables needed to move the paddle via the joystick, and setting the Paused flag. You can learn more about initialization files in Chapter 2, and you'll learn about the intricacies of the joystick in Chapter 5.

Starting a New Game

When you built the BREAK-THRU! form, you added a menu option to start a new game and called the option mnuPlayNewGame. Add some code to this menu's Click event, which handles starting up a new game.

Listing 1-7 The mnuPlayNewGame_Click subroutine

```
Sub mnuPlayNewGame_Click ()
'--------------------------------------------------
' When this menu item is selected, the program
' initializes and sets up a new game.
'--------------------------------------------------
Dim retcode As Integer

    ' Disable this menu option so a new game can't
    ' be started when one is in progress.
    mnuPlayNewGame.Enabled = False

    ' Initialize the data needed for a new game.
    InitNewGameData

    ' Set up the game for the first level.
    SetupNextLevel
End Sub
```

The first thing this event routine does is disable the menu option that caused it to be called in the first place. By setting mnuPlayNewGame's Enabled property to False, you "gray-out" the menu option. This will prevent the player from starting a new game until this one is completed.

Getting the Program Ready for a New Game

Next, call two subroutines. The first is InitNewGameData. You've already seen a routine called InitGeneralGameData that initializes variables that never change from game to game. This new routine (Listing 1-8) initializes game data that must be reset at the beginning of each new game—variables that will change during the course of a game.

Listing 1-8 The InitNewGameData subroutine

```
Sub InitNewGameData ()
'--------------------------------------------------
' Set up all the variables we need for a new game.
'--------------------------------------------------
```

```
    ' Reset the score counting labels.
    lblHiScore = Format$(HiScore, "0000") & " - " & Trim$(HiPlayer)
    lblMisses = 0
    lblPoints = "0000"

    ' Turn off the "Game Over" sign.
    lblGameOver.Visible = False

    ' The slowest speed increment is one pixel.
    SpeedUnit = 1

    ' Set the minimum speed.
    MinXSpeed = SpeedUnit * 6
    MinYSpeed = MinXSpeed

    ' Initial Speed is as slow as allowable.
    XSpeed = MinXSpeed
    YSpeed = MinYSpeed

    ' Move ball to starting position.
    ResetBall

    ' Make sure the playing field is clear.
    picField.Cls

    ' Draw the paddle on the playing field.
    Bitmap_Move bmpPaddle, bmpPaddle.Left, bmpPaddle.Top, picPaddle

    ' Set up the initial state of the paddle.
    PaddleEnglish = 0
    PaddleIncrement = 7
End Sub
```

InitNewGameData also introduces two new subroutines, ResetBall and Bitmap_Move. These routines are called not just at the beginning of the game, but during the course of game play as well. That's another good reason to collect code that performs some specific task into a subroutine: It's easier to reuse elsewhere in the program and it cuts down on the total amount of code you have to maintain. I'll look at ResetBall now and save Bitmap_Move for a little later. Enter the ResetBall routine as shown in Listing 1-9.

Listing 1-9 The ResetBall subroutine

```
Sub ResetBall ()
'-------------------------------------------------
' Move the ball back to its starting position,
' and reset the starting ball direction.
'-------------------------------------------------

    ' The ball always starts out going down and right.
```

continued on next page

continued from previous page

```
    Xdir = 1
    YDir = 1

    ' Move the ball to the starting position.
    bmpBall.Left = XStartBall
    bmpBall.Top = YStartBall
End Sub
```

When you start a new game, you need to place the ball somewhere on the playing field. You also need to tell the ball what direction it should be going in. Because you always want to start the ball at the same location, you precalculated this position back in the InitGeneralGameData routine and stored the values as XStartBall and YStartBall. This places the ball at the center of the playing field, about one-fourth of the way down from the top. You'll need to call this routine at the beginning of each game; you'll also call it to reset the ball when the player misses it with the paddle.

The other routine in mnuPlayNewGame's Click event is SetupNextLevel. Add this routine to BREAK.FRM as shown in Listing 1-10.

Listing 1-10 The SetupNextLevel subroutine

```
Sub SetupNextLevel ()
'----------------------------------------------------
' Each time the user moves to a new level (after
' clearing all the blocks at the current level)
' the blocks must be replaced and the balls return
'----------------------------------------------------
Dim retcode As Integer

    ' Suspend game play.
    Timer1.Enabled = False

    ' Hide the ball.
    retcode = BitBlt(picField.hDC, bmpBall.Left, bmpBall.Top,
            bmpBall.Width, bmpBall.Height, picBlack.hDC, 0, 0, SRCCOPY)

    ' Put a fresh set of blocks on the screen.
    retcode = sndPlaySound(app.Path & "\" & "newlevel.wav", SND_SYNC)
    SetupBlocks

    ' Put the ball back at its starting position.
    ResetBall

    ' Resume game play.
    Timer1.Enabled = True
End Sub
```

There are two times when this routine might be called: at the beginning of a new game, as in this case, or when the player has cleared all the blocks from the playing field. In either case, you need to suspend game play, display a fresh set of blocks, and resume game play. Because the game play is controlled by the the main Timer control, Timer1, the first thing to do is disable it.

Next hide the ball using a function called BitBlt, which you can use to copy a bitmap from one PictureBox into an area of another PictureBox. When you were building the form, you added a PictureBox control, picBlack, whose BackColor property was set to black. If the ball is currently visible on the screen (I'll show you how the ball is displayed in a moment), the BitBlt function will make it disappear. By copying a piece of picBlack, which is the same color as the playing field, over the top of the ball's image, you can effectively "blot out" the ball.

Putting the Blocks on the Playing Field

Now you need to place the blocks on the playing field. You do this with the subroutine SetupBlocks, shown in Listing 1-11. Remember that you've already created a control array containing 20 blocks in the routine CreateBlocks. Now add the SetupBlocks routine to the form.

Listing 1-11 The SetupBlocks subroutine

```
Sub SetupBlocks ()
'-------------------------------------------------
' Setup the blocks between each round of game play.
'-------------------------------------------------
Dim XIncr As Integer
Dim i As Integer
Dim j As Integer
Dim ArrPos As Integer

    ' Make sure any visible blocks are hidden.
    For j = 1 To (NUM_ROWS * BLOCKS_IN_ROW)
        imgBlock(j).Visible = False
        DoEvents
    Next

    XIncr = imgBlock(0).Width + BLOCK_GAP
    imgBlock(0).Top = BLOCK_GAP

    For j = 1 To NUM_ROWS
        For i = 1 To BLOCKS_IN_ROW
            ' Translate a 2-dimensional position to a 1-D array index.
            ArrPos = ((j - 1) * BLOCKS_IN_ROW) + i

            ' Place the block...
            imgBlock(ArrPos).Move BLOCK_GAP + ((i - 1) * XIncr), imgBlock(0).Top
            ' and make it visible.
```

continued on next page

continued from previous page

```
            imgBlock(ArrPos).Visible = True

            ' Make a noise each time a block is displayed.
            NoisePlay wavSetup, SND_SYNC

            ' DoEvents makes sure that the screen has a chance to update
            ' between sounds.
            DoEvents
        Next

        ' Calculate the new row position
        imgBlock(0).Top = imgBlock(0).Top + imgBlock(0).Height + BLOCK_GAP
    Next
End Sub
```

This routine places the 20 blocks, in two rows of 10, at the top of the playing field. But notice that you don't see the numbers 20, 10, or 2 anywhere in this routine. Instead, you see constants like NUM_ROWS and BLOCKS_IN_ROW. This is another programming technique that can make changing your code easier. By avoiding *magic numbers,* numbers that are hard-coded throughout your program, you can make a program more adaptable. For example, say you wanted to display three rows of blocks instead of two. Had you hard-coded the number 2 everywhere, then you'd need to track down and change every occurrence. By using the NUM_ROWS constant, all you need to do is change the constant's value in the form's Declarations section and you'd see three rows of blocks on the playing field. No other program code would need to be changed!

Setting It All in Motion—The Main Timer Event

Now let's get back to the SetupNextLevel routine. Make a call to ResetBall, the subroutine that puts the ball at its starting position. Finally, start the main Timer control, Timer1, by setting its Enabled property to True. This will cause Visual Basic to begin generating Timer events, and Timer events are at the core of this game. Listing 1-12 shows Timer1's Timer event.

Listing 1-12 The Timer1 event

```
Sub Timer1_Timer ()
'---------------------------------------------------
' This event handles most of the game action, with
' the exception of paddle movement, which is
' handled by the form's Key_Down event.
'---------------------------------------------------
Dim Xinc As Integer
```

```
Dim Yinc As Integer
Dim i As Integer
Dim PaddleCollision As Integer
Static MoreBlocks As Integer
Static PrevPaddleCollision As Integer

    If Paused Then Exit Sub

    ' Determine how much, and in which direction, to move the ball.
    Xinc = Xdir * XSpeed
    Yinc = YDir * YSpeed

    ' Ball will hit the left wall
    If (bmpBall.Left + bmpBall.Width + Xinc) > picField.ScaleWidth Then
        Xdir = -Xdir
        Xinc = Xdir * XSpeed
        NoisePlay wavWall, SND_ASYNC
    End If
    ' Ball will hit the right wall
    If (bmpBall.Left + Xinc) < 0 Then
        Xdir = -Xdir
        Xinc = Xdir * XSpeed
        NoisePlay wavWall, SND_ASYNC
    End If

    ' Ball got past paddle (at the bottom of playing field)
    If (bmpBall.Top) > picField.ScaleHeight Then
        MissedBall
    End If

    ' Ball hit the back (top) wall
    If (bmpBall.Top + Yinc) < 0 Then
        YDir = -YDir
        Yinc = YDir * YSpeed
        NoisePlay wavWall, SND_ASYNC
    End If

    ' Check if the paddle and ball collided.
    PaddleCollision = Collided(bmpBall, bmpPaddle)

    ' Move the ball to its new position
    Bitmap_Move bmpBall, bmpBall.Left + Xinc, bmpBall.Top + Yinc, picBall

    ' If the paddle is hit, then redraw the paddle.
    If PaddleCollision Then
        Bitmap_Move bmpPaddle, bmpPaddle.Left, bmpPaddle.Top, picPaddle
    End If

    ' See if we've hit the paddle...
    If PaddleCollision And (Not PrevPaddleCollision) Then
        YDir = -Abs(YDir)
```

continued on next page

continued from previous page

```
            ' Adjust ball dynamics for paddle english
            If Abs(PaddleEnglish) > 0 Then
                If PaddleEnglish > 0 Then
                    If Xdir > 0 Then
                        ' Speed it up.
                        XSpeed = XSpeed + SpeedUnit
                    Else
                        ' Slow it down.
                        XSpeed = XSpeed - SpeedUnit
                        ' Reverse the ball's X direction.
                        Xdir = -Xdir
                    End If
                ElseIf PaddleEnglish < 0 Then
                    If Xdir < 0 Then
                        ' Speed it up.
                        XSpeed = XSpeed + SpeedUnit
                    Else
                        ' Slow it down.
                        XSpeed = XSpeed - SpeedUnit
                        ' Reverse the ball's X direction.
                        Xdir = -Xdir
                    End If
                End If

                ' Don't let the ball go too slow
                If XSpeed < MinXSpeed Then XSpeed = MinXSpeed
            End If

            ' Play the paddle hit noise.
            NoisePlay wavPaddleHit, SND_ASYNC

        ' See if the ball collided with the blocks.
        ElseIf bmpBall.Top < ((NUM_ROWS + 1) * imgBlock(0).Height) Then
            MoreBlocks = False
            For i = 1 To (NUM_ROWS * BLOCKS_IN_ROW)
                If imgBlock(i).Visible Then
                    MoreBlocks = True
                    If BlockCollided(bmpBall, imgBlock(i)) Then
                        ' "Turn off", or hide, this block.
                        imgBlock(i).Visible = False
                        ' If we hit a block, send the ball back down.
                        YDir = Abs(YDir)
                        ' Play the block hit noise.
                        NoisePlay wavBlockHit, SND_ASYNC
                        ' The player gets a point for each block hit.
                        lblPoints = Format$(Val(lblPoints) + 1, "0000")
                    End If
                End If
            Next
            ' Out of blocks and we've still got more balls,
            ' so rack 'em up again.
```

```
        If (Not MoreBlocks) And (lblMisses < NumBalls) Then
            SetupNextLevel
        End If
    End If

    ' This is used to avoid multiple collision detections
    ' for a single hit.
    PrevPaddleCollision = PaddleCollision
End Sub
```

The very first thing to do in the Timer event is check the Paused flag. If this flag is set to True, then the player has paused the game, so immediately exit the Timer routine. This effectively short-circuits game play. Visual Basic will continue to generate Timer events, but no game action can occur while the Paused flag is on.

The Mechanics of the Game

Let's review the mechanics of the BREAK-THRU! game. There are four basic game objects: the playing field, the blocks, the ball, and the paddle. The ball moves across the playing field and can bounce off the paddle and side walls of the playing field. If the ball collides with a block, that block disappears and the player receives a point. If the player doesn't hit the ball with the paddle, the ball flies off the bottom of the playing field, and the player loses that ball. A game ends when a player loses all four balls.

You'll be creating all this game action within the Timer routine and a few additional support subroutines.

The playing field, which is really the PictureBox control picField, can be thought of as a rectangle with an X-Y coordinate system. An object's (a ball, paddle, or block) position on the playing field is determined by the object's X and Y coordinates relative to the upper-left corner of the field.

You can think of each Timer event as a game "move": the program will move the ball once, then evaluate the repercussions of that move. Did the ball hit a wall? Did it collide with a block? Did it run into the player's paddle? Each of these questions must be answered.

The ball has a current X and Y position on the playing field. The program tracks the speed and direction at which the ball is currently traveling. The ball's direction is tracked by two variables, Xdir and Ydir. These variables have a value of either -1 or 1. If Xdir is -1, then the ball is currently moving left across the playing field. If Xdir is 1, then the ball is moving right. These same values for Ydir indicate whether the ball is moving up or down the playing field.

The variables XSpeed and YSpeed determine the current speed of the ball. This is actually the number of pixels the ball moves. The higher the value, the faster the ball appears to move. By multiplying Xdir by XSpeed, and Ydir by YSpeed, you get XInc and YInc. These variables, when added to the current X and Y locations of the ball, give the new position for the ball.

But before the player can move the ball, you need to make sure that the ball hasn't collided with some other object. The first thing you check is if the ball has collided with the left or right walls. Do this by checking whether the ball has gone beyond the X-boundaries of the playing field. If it has, you need to reverse its X-direction, which is stored in the Xdir variable. Because Xdir is either -1 (for left) or 1 (for right), you need only reverse the sign of the value, like this,

```
Xdir = -Xdir
```

to change the ball's direction.

Oops! You Missed!

Next, check if the ball has passed the player's paddle. You'll know that it did if the top of the ball has gone beyond the bottom of the playing field. If the ball got past the paddle, you call a new subroutine, MissedBall. Enter the MissedBall routine as shown in Listing 1-13.

Listing 1-13 The MissedBall subroutine

```
Sub MissedBall ()
'-----------------------------------------------------
' Move the ball back to its starting position.
'-----------------------------------------------------
Dim answer As String
Dim rc As Integer

    ' Suspend game play
    Timer1.Enabled = False

    ' Play the "Missed Ball" sound.
    NoisePlay wavMissed, SND_SYNC

    ' Update the number of balls missed.
    lblMisses = lblMisses + 1

    ' If there are more balls left, continue playing.
    If lblMisses < NumBalls Then
        ResetBall
        Timer1.Enabled = True
    ' if no balls left, the game is over.
    Else
        lblGameOver.Visible = True
        mnuPlayNewGame.Enabled = True

        If IsNumeric(lblPoints) Then
            If lblPoints > HiScore Then
```

```
            answer = InputBox$("Congratulations! This is a new HIGH SCORE! Enter Your
                   Name:", "Great Game!")
            rc = WritePrivateProfileString(SECTION, "Player", answer, INI_FILE)
            rc = WritePrivateProfileString(SECTION, ENTRY, Format$(lblPoints), INI_FILE)
            HiScore = lblPoints
            HiPlayer = Trim$(answer)
            lblHiScore = Format$(HiScore, "0000") & " - " & Trim$(HiPlayer)
        End If
    End If
End If
          End Sub
```

The MissedBall routine first disables Timer1, so that no new Timer events are generated as this subroutine goes about its business. Next it plays an obnoxious little sound, via a wave audio file, to let the player know he or she missed the ball. Then the routine updates the label that tracks the total number of balls the player has missed so far. Remember that the player only gets four balls per game. So the MissedBall routine checks if the player has any remaining balls. If there are more balls, then the routine calls the ResetBall routine (to move the ball back to its starting position) and reenables the Timer.

If there are no balls left, then the game is over. Make the lblGameOver label visible, displaying a bright red "Game Over" in the middle of the playing field. Also reenable the *New Game* menu option, so the player can start a new game from the menu.

Finally, compare the player's score with the high score that was loaded when the program started. If the new score exceeds the high score, invite the player to enter his or her name, then save both the name and new high score to the Windows initialization file. For more information on initialization files and tracking high scores, see Chapter 2.

When Bitmaps Collide—Detecting Game Piece Collisions

Now back to the Timer event. You need to determine if the paddle and the ball have collided. To do this, I'll introduce a function, Collided, that determines whether two objects have run into each other.

Listing 1-14 Collision detection

```
Function Collided (A As tBitMap, B As tBitMap) As Integer
'-----------------------------------------------
' Check if the two rectangles (bitmaps) intersect,
' using the IntersectRect API call.
'-----------------------------------------------

' Although we won't use it, we need a result
```

continued on next page

continued from previous page

```
' rectangle to pass to the API routine.
Dim ResultRect As tBitMap

    ' Calculate the right and bottoms of rectangles needed by the API call.
    A.Right = A.Left + A.Width - 1
    A.Bottom = A.Top + A.Height - 1

    B.Right = B.Left + B.Width - 1
    B.Bottom = B.Top + B.Height - 1

    ' IntersectRect will only return 0 (false) if the
    ' two rectangles do NOT intersect.
    Collided = IntersectRect(ResultRect, A, B)
End Function
```

Notice that the Collided function takes two parameters of type tBitMap. This is the data type defined earlier in the GAMESTUF.BAS module. The tBitMap data type is defined like this:

```
Type tBitMap
    Left As Integer
    Top As Integer
    Right As Integer
    Bottom As Integer
    Width As Integer
    Height As Integer
End Type
```

Earlier you created two variables of type tBitMap, bmpBall and bmpPaddle. Use these variables to keep track of the locations and sizes of these two game objects. The Collided function uses this structure and a Windows API function called IntersectRect to determine if two objects have collided. Actually, it determines if the two objects have overlapped, or *intersected.* The IntersectRect function returns a 0 if two rectangles *do not* overlap, so it's the perfect function for detecting simple collisions. The IntersectRect function actually takes as parameters data types called TRECTs, not the tBitMap data types that we use.

A TRECT structure is identical to the tBitMap structure, except that it lacks the Width and Height fields. Luckily, the IntersectRect function ignores this extra baggage and just looks at the first four fields. You need the Width and Height fields in other parts of the program, so rather than create two different data types, create a single, hybrid type, tBitMap, that can serve a dual purpose.

Fast-Moving Bitmaps

Meanwhile, back in the Timer event, store the value returned by Collided in the Boolean PaddleCollision variable. Earlier you calculated the new position for the ball, and now it's time to redraw the ball at its new position. I'll now explain the Bitmap_Move function. Add the code from Listing 1-15 to create the Bitmap_Move subroutine.

Listing 1-15 The Bitmap_Move subroutine

```
Sub Bitmap_Move (ABitMap As tBitMap, ByVal NewLeft As Integer, ByVal NewTop As
Integer, SourcePicture As PictureBox)
'-----------------------------------------------
' This routine uses the BitBlt API function to
' first remove a bitmap from its original location
' (by simply BitBlting a black rectangle over its
' current position), then BitBlting the picture
' to its new location.
'-----------------------------------------------
Dim retcode As Integer

    ' Cover the image with a black rectangle, erasing it.
    retcode = BitBlt(picField.hDC, ABitMap.Left, ABitMap.Top, ABitMap.Width,
             ABitMap.Height, picBlack.hDC, 0, 0, SRCCOPY)

    ' Update the image's location in its data structure.
    ABitMap.Left = NewLeft
    ABitMap.Top = NewTop

    ' Redisplay it at its new location.
    retcode = BitBlt(picField.hDC, ABitMap.Left, ABitMap.Top, ABitMap.Width,
             ABitMap.Height, SourcePicture.hDC, 0, 0, SRCCOPY)
End Sub
```

This routine is one of the most important in the entire game. It handles "erasing" bitmaps at their old location and redrawing them at a new location. To perform this erasing and redrawing, rely on the BitBlt function. As I mentioned earlier, this Windows API routine can quickly copy all or part of a bitmap from one PictureBox to a location inside another PictureBox. You're using it here to move the ball, but you'll also use it to move the paddle back and forth later. Remember that the ball's image is being stored in an invisible PictureBox, picBall, outside the playing field. All you do here is make a copy of that image and "paint" it onto the picField PictureBox. Before you draw it, make sure to erase the previous ball by using BitBlt to paint a black rectangle (courtesy of the picBlack PictureBox) over it. Look at Chapter 3 for more information on the BitBlt function.

In the Timer event, the program redraws the paddle if it has collided with the ball. This is so that the ball appears to go behind the paddle, rather than in front of it. Because the ball is actually a square bitmap (a ball surrounded by black), if you draw it on top of the blue paddle, the player will see the black part of the ball. Redrawing the paddle makes the ball appear to move a bit behind the paddle, and this looks much better.

Putting a Little English on the Ball

You already determined if the ball has hit the paddle; now you need to do something about it. This is when you get into issues of physics. In real-life games like tennis or ping-pong, a player can put a spin on the ball by hitting it with the paddle at a particular speed and angle. This is sometimes called "putting English" on the ball. Using a little arithmetic, you can do the same in this game. First, you'll use the integer variable PaddleEnglish to track how much English to apply to the ball. You'll set this variable when you move the paddle using the keyboard or joystick. If PaddleEnglish is a negative number, then when the paddle strikes, the ball will tend to move to the left. This means that if the ball was previously traveling left, it will continue traveling left, only faster. If it was traveling right, the English will send it toward the left, making it travel a little more slowly than before.

Another Look at Collisions

One of the final things you do in the Timer event is check if the ball has collided with one or more of the blocks. You could use the Collided function introduced earlier, but remember that the blocks are actually Image controls, so they have no associated tBitMap structure. So you'll create your own routine to check for collisions between a block and the ball. This routine, called BlockCollided, outwardly works very much like the Collided function. The only difference is that, instead of taking two tBitmap variables as parameters, the routine is passed a tBitMap variable and an Image control. You'll need to call this routine once for each block that's still visible on the playing field. BlockCollided, like its cousin Collided, returns True if the block overlaps the ball bitmap. If a collision is detected, the score is bumped up by one (remember, the player gets points for each block hit). The block control's Visible property is set to False, rendering it invisible. Finally, a wave audio file is played to give the player feedback.

Let's take a look at the BlockCollided function. Enter the code as shown in Listing 1-16.

Listing 1-16 The BlockCollided function

```
Function BlockCollided (A As tBitMap, B As Image) As Integer
'--------------------------------------------------
' Check if the bitmap, A, and the image control, B,
' overlap each other.
'--------------------------------------------------
```

```
Dim ACenterY As Integer
Dim BCenterY As Integer

Dim ACenterX As Integer
Dim BCenterX As Integer

    ACenterY = (A.Height \ 2) + A.Top
    BCenterY = (B.Height \ 2) + B.Top

    ACenterX = (A.Width \ 2) + A.Left
    BCenterX = (B.Width \ 2) + B.Left

    BlockCollided = False

    ' See if they intersect in the same Y range
    If Abs(ACenterY - BCenterY) < ((A.Height + B.Height) \ 2) Then
        ' See if they intersect in the same X range
        If Abs(ACenterX - BCenterX) < ((A.Width + B.Width) \ 2) Then
            BlockCollided = True
        End If
    End If

End Function
```

This function detects collision, or actually intersection, of two rectangles by comparing the distance between the centers of the two objects. If the distance is short enough, then the two objects must overlap. You could have adapted the Collided routine to do the same thing; you could have just loaded a block's coordinates into a tBitmap structure and called the Collided function. But using BlockCollided shows that there are often numerous approaches to tackling the same problem.

In the Timer event, the last important thing you need to worry about is whether the collisions in this "move" have wiped out all the blocks. If all the blocks are gone, you need to call the SetupNextLevel routine to put a new set of blocks on the playing field.

Moving the Paddle—Two Ways to Handle User Input

That pretty much covers the part of the game play handled by the main Timer, Timer1. But you've still got some work to do. You know what happens when the ball and paddle collide, but how does the player move the paddle? You said at the beginning that you wanted the player to be able to use either the keyboard or the joystick.

Visual Basic has built-in support for the keyboard. Several events are provided to notify the program when a key has been pressed. By setting the form's KeyPreview property to True when you build the form, you can intercept any keys pressed while the game is in progress. Use the form's KeyDown event to handle paddle movement via the keyboard. Add the KeyDown event shown in Listing 1-17 to BREAK.FRM.

Listing 1-17 The KeyDown event

```
Sub Form_KeyDown (KeyCode As Integer, Shift As Integer)
'-------------------------------------------------
' All game play input is handled through the
' keyboard (left and right arrow keys).
'-------------------------------------------------
    Select Case KeyCode
        Case KEY_LEFT:
            ' Make sure we're not off the left side
            If (bmpPaddle.Left - PaddleIncrement) > 0 Then
                ' Move the paddle to the left.
                Bitmap_Move bmpPaddle, bmpPaddle.Left - PaddleIncrement, bmpPaddle.Top, picPaddle

                ' Discard any english the paddle might have had from the opposite direction.
                If PaddleEnglish > 0 Then PaddleEnglish = 0
                PaddleEnglish = PaddleEnglish - 1
            End If
        Case KEY_RIGHT:
            ' Make sure we're not off the right side.
            If (bmpPaddle.Left + bmpPaddle.Width + PaddleIncrement) < picField.ScaleWidth Then
                ' Move the paddle to the right.
                Bitmap_Move bmpPaddle, bmpPaddle.Left + PaddleIncrement, bmpPaddle.Top, picPaddle

                ' Discard any english the paddle might have had from the opposite direction.
                If PaddleEnglish < 0 Then PaddleEnglish = 0
                PaddleEnglish = PaddleEnglish + 1
            End If
    End Select
End Sub
```

The KeyDown event is simple. Any time the player hits a key, the KeyDown event is triggered. The KeyCode parameter tells it which key was pressed. You only want to react to two possible keys, the left and right arrows. So build a Visual Basic Select-Case structure to look at these two keys. Any other keys are ignored. If the left arrow is pressed, use the Bitmap_Move routine to move the paddle left, checking first that the player hasn't hit the left side of the playing field. Remember that Bitmap_Move works by first "erasing" the paddle at its current location by copying a section of the black picBlack image over the top of it. Another call to BitBlt copies the paddle image in picPaddle onto the playing field at its new location. Also adjust the amount of paddle English. The longer the paddle has been traveling in the same direction (either right or left), the larger an amount of paddle English is accumulated in the PaddleEnglish variable. Actions are virtually identical when the right arrow key is pressed, except that the actions are oriented in the opposite direction.

Handling the joystick is identical in concept. You want to move the paddle left when the player moves the joystick left, and right when the player moves the joystick right. But unlike the keyboard, for which Visual Basic provides built-in support, the joystick doesn't automatically trigger events. You have to extract information about the state of the joystick by calling the Windows API. How can you tell, at frequent intervals, whether the joystick has moved left or right? Why not set up a new Timer control to keep track of the joystick? You may remember that you did just that when you built the form: You added a second timer called JoyTimer. Now add a Timer event to it, as shown in Listing 1-18.

Listing 1-18 The JoyTimer event

```
Sub JoyTimer_Timer ()
'--------------------------------------------------
'--------------------------------------------------
Dim rc As Integer

    rc = GetJoystickPos(JOYSTICK1, JoyInfo)

    If JoyInfo.X < JoyAtRestMin Then
        ' Make sure we're not off the left side
        If (bmpPaddle.Left - PaddleIncrement) > 0 Then
            ' Move the paddle to the left.
            Bitmap_Move bmpPaddle, bmpPaddle.Left - PaddleIncrement, bmpPaddle.Top, picPaddle

            ' Discard any english the paddle might have had from the opposite direction.
            If PaddleEnglish > 0 Then PaddleEnglish = 0
            PaddleEnglish = PaddleEnglish - 1
        End If
    ElseIf JoyInfo.X > JoyAtRestMax Then
        ' Make sure we're not off the right side.
        If (bmpPaddle.Left + bmpPaddle.Width + PaddleIncrement) < picField.ScaleWidth Then
            ' Move the paddle to the right.
            Bitmap_Move bmpPaddle, bmpPaddle.Left + PaddleIncrement, bmpPaddle.Top, picPaddle

            ' Discard any english the paddle might have had from the opposite direction.
            If PaddleEnglish < 0 Then PaddleEnglish = 0
            PaddleEnglish = PaddleEnglish + 1
        End If
    End If

End Sub
```

If this routine looks suspiciously like the form's KeyDown event, that's because it is. You get the current coordinates of the joystick and use these to determine if the joystick is currently being moved to the left or right. Joysticks can be rather sensitive devices, so check the current X position, JoyInfo.X, against two values you calculated when the program started: JoyAtRestMin and JoyAtRestMax. These two values are used to determine when the joystick moves beyond 8 percent left or right of its dead-center "at rest" position. Joysticks can be slightly miscalibrated, so these little "fudge factors" help ensure that the paddle only moves when the player actually moves it. How did I arrive at 8 percent? Through the scientific method of trial and error. Until I raised these values to 8 percent, I got random, ghostlike fluctuations, even when I wasn't touching the joystick.

Odds and Ends

All that remains to this game are a few minor odds and ends. To give the form a more polished, three-dimensional look, you want to draw some borders around the playing field and some labels. You already have a routine, Make3D, in the GAMESTUF.BAS module to do this. Now you need to tell it which controls to make three dimensional. Do this by adding a Paint event to the form, shown in Listing 1-19.

Listing 1-19 The Form_Paint subroutine

```
Sub Form_Paint ()
'-------------------------------------------------
' Draw 3D effect around selected controls on form.
'-------------------------------------------------
Dim i As Integer

    On Error Resume Next
    ' Look at the tag fields of all controls
    For i = 0 To Me.Controls.Count - 1
        If InStr(UCase$(Me.Controls(i).Tag), "/3D/") Then
            Make3D Me, Me.Controls(i), BORDER_INSET
        ElseIf InStr(UCase$(Me.Controls(i).Tag), "/3DUP/") Then
            Make3D Me, Me.Controls(i), BORDER_RAISED
        End If
    Next
End Sub
```

There are a couple of little tricks in this routine. First, notice that you don't refer to any control by its actual name. Controls are referred to as Me.Controls(i). Visual Basic automatically builds a *control collection* that contains every control on a form. This control collection provides an alternate method for referencing controls. The second trick is the use of a control's Tag property. The Tag property is a sort of general purpose property that can be assigned a text string. You can use the Tag field for any purpose. When you were building the form, you set the Tag property of certain controls to the string "/3D/". The Paint event looks at all the controls on the form, and if it finds either this Tag value or the Tag value "/3DUP", it will draw an inset or a raised border around that control. The nice thing about this technique is that you don't have to change the Paint event to make a control three dimensional or change it from raised to inset. All you need to do is change its Tag property value. The Paint event, which is called whenever Visual Basic needs to redraw the form, handles the rest of the work.

Two more simple events, and you're done. You handled the menu option that lets you start a new game, but now you need to handle the other two menu options. The mnuPauseGame option should let the player temporarily suspend game play. I already introduced the Paused Boolean variable that determines whether or not the game is paused. You used this variable to bail out of the main Timer event. The mnuPauseGame Click event sets this variable:

```
Sub mnuPauseGame_Click ()
'-----------------------------------------------------
' Pause the Game.
'-----------------------------------------------------
    Paused = Not Paused

    If Paused Then
        lblPaused.Visible = True
    Else
        lblPaused.Visible = False
    End If
End Sub
```

The first thing this routine does is toggle the current value of the Paused variable. If Paused was True, now it's False, and vice versa. Then it either turns on or turns off the Paused label that tells the player if the game has been paused. It does this by setting the label's Visible property.

Finally, you have a menu option that lets the player exit the game. This routine simply unloads the main form:

```
Sub mnuPlayExit_Click ()
'-----------------------------------------------------
' Exit the program.
'-----------------------------------------------------
    Unload Me
End Sub
```

Running the BREAK-THRU! Game

Now the game is complete. When you run it and select New Game from the Play menu, you should see something like Figure 1-8.

There's no such thing as a perfect game. Games are highly subjective things at best, and what one person finds exciting may irritate someone else. Even so, once you've completed a game, it's helpful to look for ways to improve it, even though you can never make it perfect. BREAK-THRU! is no exception. Let me suggest some excercises you might undertake to improve it.

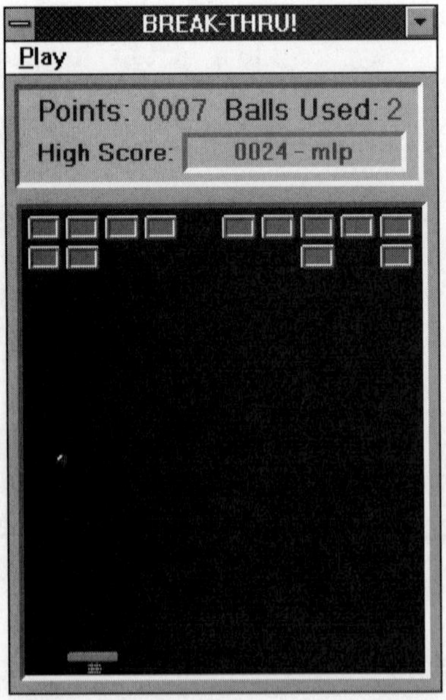

FIGURE 1-8

The completed BREAK-THRU! game in action

- BREAK-THRU! can only make sounds if the player's computer is equipped with a sound card that can play wave audio files. Change the game so that it can also make sounds from the PC speaker.
- On slower PCs, there might be a slight pause when the ball collides with a block. You might initially suspect that the pause is caused when the program is checking for collisions with all the blocks. But the delay is actually coming from a rather unexpected source. When a block is hit, the user receives a point, and the lblPoints label control is updated to reflect the new score. Updating this label causes most of the delay! Verify this by commenting out the line of code in Timer1's Timer event that updates lblPoints. Try to change the program to avoid this delay.

This chapter presented the anatomy of an entire game. You've covered a lot of different topics and have a feel for all the elements needed to master game design. Now, we'll examine each of these elements, and more, in greater depth.

Part II

Game Development

Aequator
Aequator
Krebses
West
M
I
H
E
F
G
C
B
A
a
b
a

2

Keeping Score and Increasing Difficulty

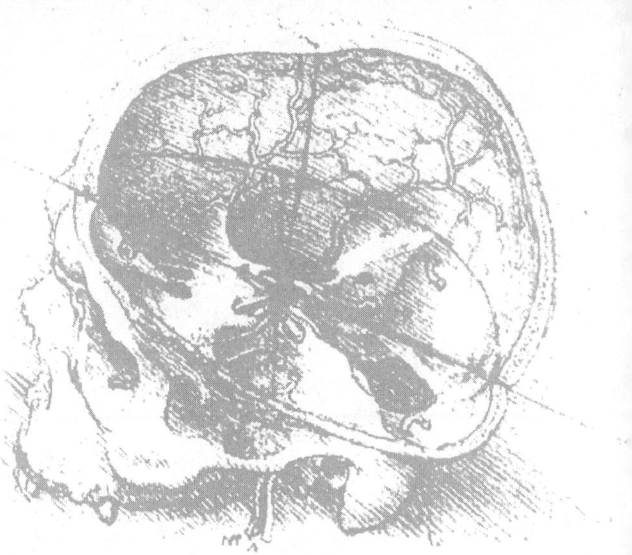

2

Keeping Score and Increasing Difficulty

You're in your car driving to work. You're driving down a four-lane interstate, and traffic is packed. It's a nightmare trying to change from one lane to the next. You arrive at work and you feel physically and mentally drained.

Now back up a minute. Let's say we've equipped your car with a little black box with a digital readout on the dashboard that gives you a point every time you pass another car. You loose a point every time someone else passes you. The readout is reset to zero when you enter the freeway. It also displays your previous high score.

Now your drive to work takes on a new perspective. You think, "Yeah, I can just squeeze in between those two cars," and "Hey, that guy's not getting past me!" You weave your way between other cars, the readout clicking slowly upward. "Just three more cars and I can beat last Tuesday's high score!" Suddenly, the off-ramp looms a quarter mile ahead. You make your move, sliding between a Buick land yacht and that little Hyundai, gracefully aiming your car onto the exit ramp.

You only tied your previous high score, but your blood is pumping and you feel *great.* You know you'll beat that score on the way home, unless the police stop you again. There's a 25 point penalty for that.

Of course, although a fantasy like this is fun to ponder, in real life it would be impractical. Imagine if everybody on a freeway had the little black box. It would be anarchy, it would be bedlam, it would be… uh, Los Angeles? Oh, never mind.

What's the difference between the two scenarios I just described? It's perspective. In the first scenario, driving is a chore. In the second, it's a game. The difference is in keeping score, making it a *competition*.

In this chapter, we'll first take a look at general scoring strategies that apply to any game. Then we'll build a reusable High Score module that you can easily plug in to any of your Visual Basic games.

Scoring Strategies and Game Lives

Scoring should develop as a natural outgrowth of the game design process. As you build the concept for a game, whether it's a simple game like BREAK-THRU! or a more complex game like Doom, you should build a scoring system that serves a few basic purposes.

- The scoring system should give players continuous feedback on their progress. Players should know, at any given time, whether they're doing well or about to buy the farm. This knowledge feeds a player's emotional involvement, that adrenaline rush when victory or defeat seems just a button's click away.
- The scoring system should be easy for the player to understand. The player is partaking in entertainment, not a math quiz. Players should be able to tell, at a brief glance, how they are doing. This must be absolutely true of action games, where the player may be caught up in the frenzy of the game.
- The scoring system should try to be consistent with the "world" of the game. In the Lunar Lander game presented in Part III, players receive a final score at the end of the game based on how well they landed their simulated lander. There's no numeric score presented. Rather, the players are given a rank—Freighter Pilot, Ensign, Commander, and so on—that lets them know how well they did. This is consistent with the simulated world you're trying to create, and reinforces the illusion.

Beyond these simple guidelines, you'll also need to make some decisions about how your scoring system relates to the overall game. The main question becomes, how does the game end? Many action games have a limited number of lives. Once the lives are used up, the game is over. This is by far the most popular way to end arcade games. Look at classics like Centipede, Asteroids, Space Invaders, or BattleZone. All these games share the same core strategy: Points are accumulated for destroying the enemy, and lives are lost when the bad guy gets the player.

With these games you'll also notice that it is impossible to win. The player will invariably run out of lives. For arcade-style games, I recommend adhering to this strategy because it is so well understood by players.

This strategy is easy to implement. Just maintain program variables for the current number of lives and the current score for each player. Each "enemy" is assigned a point value. When the enemy is destroyed, his associated point value is added to the score. When the player is "killed," a life is subtracted from the associated variable.

Other types of games may require more complex scoring strategies. In a battle strategy simulation, where two players marshall military resources to oppose one another, the scoring and the victor may be somewhat inconclusive. In these games, each side arranges resources: people, supplies, and equipment on a playing field. The game is then set in motion. In a game like this, determining when the game is over may not be quite as clear as in an arcade shoot-em-up. The battle may progress to the point where neither side has sufficient resources to continue the fight, so a game like this may have no clear winner.

Increasing Difficulty

Practice makes perfect. As players become more adept at a game, they need ever-increasing challenges. Otherwise, boredom sets in. By increasing the difficulty level as the game progresses, you give the players a goal to strive for: to do a little better than last time, to get to the next level, to kill a few more bad guys, to live a few seconds longer.

There are many strategies for increasing difficulty; really engaging games have a subtle mix of these strategies. The list I present here covers a wide range of techniques, but is by no means comprehensive.

1. The Bad Guy Gets Faster

In the classic arcade game Space Invaders, rows and columns of alien ships slowly descend as the player blasts away with a cannon from the bottom of the screen. The player's goal is to destroy them all. There are only so many aliens, so it should be a cinch, right? The catch is, as the number of aliens decreases and as they get lower on the screen, they move faster. Aliens that a minute ago were slowly creeping down the screen are suddenly scampering frenetically—and they're coming straight for the player!

Space Invaders is also an example of the use of sound to increase the sense of urgency and as a side-effect to make the game more difficult. When the game begins, the aliens make a slow "dee-dum . . . dee-dum" noise as they move. As the game progresses, the speed of the sound increases with the alien's speed—until, near the end, it becomes a frantic "DEEDUM!DEEDUM!DEEDUM!" sound. The human brain finds it hard to stay calm with that kind of noise going on.

2. The Player Gets Slower

This is the flip side of the previous technique. The player is in control of some game objects—like the cannon in Space Invaders. By slowly increasing the sluggishness of the player's control over an object, you can make it more difficult to accomplish the player's goal.

3. The Player Gets Faster

You'd think this would be a *good* thing. The controls suddenly become more responsive or a vehicle the player controls suddenly moves twice as fast. The problem is, nobody bothered to make the player twice as coordinated. Oops! The car just ended up in a ditch! Uh-Oh! The twice-as-responsive jet fighter corkscrewed into Interstate 95!

4. The Enemy Gets Reinforcements

This simple and frequently used technique simply gives the player more things to shoot at—or vice versa. In the Microsoft game JezzBall (Figure 2-1), the object is to

FIGURE 2-1

Microsoft's JezzBall game

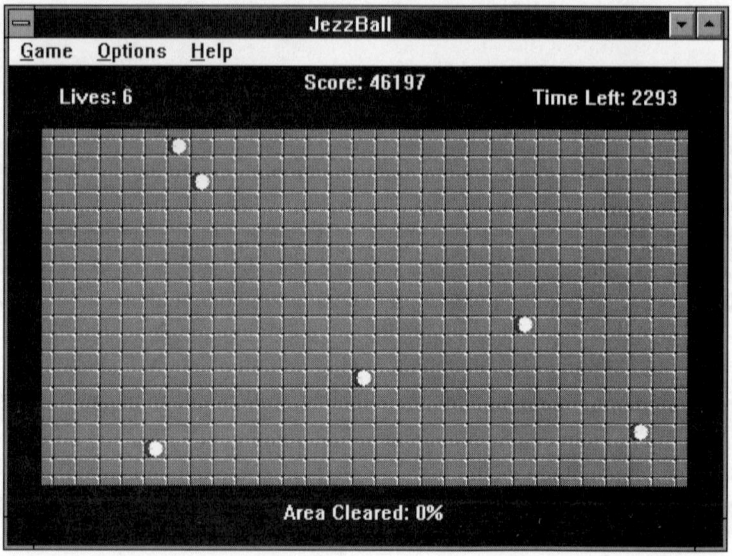

reduce the size of the playing field by dividing it into ever-smaller pieces. The problem here is that the playing field is populated by bouncing balls. The player moves the mouse pointer over an area of the playing field and presses the mouse button. The playing field begins to divide either vertically or horizontally from the position of the mouse pointer. If a divided section of the field contains no balls, the entire section disappears. To move to the next level of the game, the player has to clear 75 percent of the playing field. But if a ball hits a new divider wall as it's being created, the player loses a life. The game is simple at first, with just two balls. But by the time the player gets to the fifth level, with six balls, it's a nightmare.

5. The Player's Life Gets Shorter

This is a simple technique for making the game more difficult. As the player moves to a higher level, you make it easier for the player to be killed. If the enemy needed six shots to kill you in level 1, at level 2 it only needs 5. In a space battle game, you might deplete the player's energy shields 50 percent faster in the second level than in the first.

6. Life Just Got a Lot More Complex

The arcade game Asteroids is a classic example of this technique. The player's spaceship is stuck in the middle of an asteroid field, and four large asteroids are drifting around it. If they hit it, the player's history. The good news is, the ship is equipped with a laser cannon that can blow up a large asteroid. The bad news is, the big asteroid blows up into several little asteroids. And because they're smaller, they're harder to hit! Only the smallest of asteroids can be obliterated completely. The player spends a good portion of the game creating more targets! Finally, as the player begins to clear the field of asteriods, the game starts sending in enemy space ships—and they're shooting at the player.

This is one of the most common and popular methods of increasing difficulty, and there are many good examples of it. In Centipede, when the player kills a segment of a centipede, it turns into a mushroom, which clutters up the playing field and makes it harder to hit the other targets.

7. The Enemy Seems a Lot Smarter than It Was a Second Ago

You'll see this technique used most often in games of strategy. In most computer chess games, the player can choose the skill level of the computerized opponent. Most chess games analyze the best next move by looking several moves ahead. They simulate possible sequences of moves for both players, and decide on the move that will leave them in the best situation later. It's a brute force method, and it takes time for the computer to simulate the moves. One way to adjust the difficulty level in a strategy game is to limit the number of moves that the computer is allowed to think ahead.

8. The Enemy Gets Harder To Kill

This is another common method for increasing difficulty. The enemy spaceships that would blow up with one good shot in level 1 now require three shots, and they have to be dead center shots at that!

9. Hey! Who Moved the Finish Line?

In level 1 of a road race game, the player has to drive five miles down a twisting course. The player does it in record time and figures this game is a cinch. On to level 2. The player's approaching the five-mile mark and—Hey! Where's the finish line? Sorry, but at level 2 the finish line is another three miles down the road. And did we forget to mention the oil slicks?

10. The Player Is Getting Tired (The Enemy Is Relentless)

This is an often-overlooked aspect of game design. You don't explicitly build this into the game, it's an inevitable aspect of life: fatigue. As the game marches forward, over time the player will get tired. The electronic opponent doesn't have this problem. The enemy is relentless.

If you don't allow the player any respite from the onslaught of the bad guys, eventually he or she will make mistakes.

Tracking High Scores

Game players want immortality. They play for hours with their favorite games, trying to get to the next level, to surpass their personal best. They want those achievements to be remembered. You can help them on their quest for fame.

Most of the best games will have a "winners' gallery," a list of previous high scores alongside the names of the players who achieved them. This feature may seem extraneous to the programmer. After all, what more could the player want beyond the simple joy of playing a game you designed? But don't underestimate the importance of letting the players keep a record of their victories. That list of scores gives impetus to play your game more in the hopes of doing just a little better next time.

Luckily, you can build a high score module that can be plugged, unchanged, into any game that scores with numbers. There's no need to write a new high score module for each game. In fact, we'll simplify the process so much that you'll only need to call a single subroutine to handle the entire process.

The great thing about high scores is that they're remembered between games. When the players finish a game, the score is compared to a list of previous high scores, and if the score is "worthy," the players are invited to add their names to the list of notables. The catch is, there's a limited number of slots on the list, so it soon becomes necessary to make the list by bumping a "not-quite-so-worthy" player off.

This high score module will remember the five best scores, along with the players who achieved them. When a player achieves a new high score, he or she is presented with a window like the one shown in Figure 2-2.

The first problem to overcome is how does the game remember high scores between games? Clearly, you'll need to store the players' names and their scores. Windows provides a simple way to store information like this in *initialization files.* These files are simple text files with a rigid format that Windows programs often use to store various bits of information. These files are recognized by their .INI file extension. Windows itself uses two major initialization files, WIN.INI and SYSTEM.INI, to track a variety of information.

You could store high scores inside WIN.INI. Many programs do this, but over time this can cause WIN.INI to get very large. A better approach is to create a separate .INI file for your game and store the high scores in it. The .INI file can be given the same

FIGURE 2-2

The High Score window

file name as your game, with the exception of its .INI extension. Later, if the player wants to move or delete the game, this separate .INI file will be easier to find than an entry buried deep within the Windows WIN.INI file.

Windows provides API calls that let you read and write from .INI files. Initialization files always have a format like the sample shown here:

```
[A Section Name]
Entry1=some text
Entry2=some more text

[Another Section Name]
Entry1=some text
AnotherEntry=more text
```

In an .INI file, section names are always enclosed within square brackets ([ ]). Within a section, entry names are separated from entry values by an equal sign (=). Although you can edit these files with any text editor, such as Windows Notepad, they are generally accessed from within a program using one of the two API calls shown below.

```
' Two Windows API calls used to read and write private .INI files.

Declare Function GetPrivateProfileString Lib "Kernel" (ByVal lpSectionName As String, _
        ByVal lpEntryName As String, ByVal lpDefault As String, _
        ByVal lpReturnedString As String, ByVal nSize As Integer, _
        ByVal lpINIFileName As String) As Integer

Declare Function WritePrivateProfileString Lib "Kernel" (ByVal lpSectionName As String, _
        ByVal lpEntryName As String, ByVal lpString As String, _
        ByVal lpINIFileName As String) As Integer
```

The first function, GetPrivateProfileString, is used to read information from an .INI file. You provide this function with a section name (omitting the square brackets), an entry name, and a default string to return to if the entry can't be found in the file. You also provide the maximum allowed size of the returned string and the name of the .INI file itself. The function passes back the string itself in the lpReturnedString parameter. GetPrivateProfileString returns an integer that specifies the actual length of the returned string.

The second function is WritePrivateProfileString. Like the first function, this function is passed a section name, an entry name, and an .INI file name. It also receives a string value that replaces any existing value for the specified entry in that section of the .INI file. If the entry or section doesn't exist in the file, a new section or entry is created as needed. For that matter, if the .INI file itself doesn't exist, Windows will create it automatically.

For the high score module, you'll have an .INI file in this format:

```
[HiScores]
Score1=15113;Jeff
Score2=13125;George
Score3=13001;Jim
Score4=10436;Mark
Score5=10009;mlp
```

The scores and players' names are stored together in a single entry, separated by a semicolon. The GetPrivateProfileString API call will pass back the entire entry value (everything to the right of the equal sign); the module will handle splitting this string into a player name and score.

Let's go ahead and build the Visual Basic module and form needed for the high score component.

Steps

1. First, create a new project called SCORE1.MAK. The pieces of this project (the .FRM and .BAS files) will be included directly into the game.
2. Add a new module, SCORE1.BAS, to this project. This module contains support routines to assist in reading and writing the .INI files as well as a data structure, tScores, used to retain the current list of high scores and players. The focal point for this module is the ShowHiScores subroutine. This is the only routine the game will need to call to add or display a high score.

```
Option Explicit
'----------------------------------------------------------
' SCORE1.BAS
'----------------------------------------------------------

' Constant used to display the form modally.
Const MODAL = 1

' The maximum number of High Scores tracked.
Const MAX_HISCORES = 5

' Used when calling the two API functions below.
Const SECTION = "HiScores"
Const ENTRY = "Score"

' Two Windows API calls used to read and write private .INI files.
Declare Function GetPrivateProfileString Lib "Kernel" (ByVal lpSectionName As String, ByVal
lpKeyName As String, ByVal lpDefault As String, ByVal lpReturnedString As String, ByVal
nSize As Integer, ByVal lpFileName As String) As Integer
Declare Function WritePrivateProfileString Lib "Kernel" (ByVal lpSectionName As String,
ByVal lpKeyName As String, ByVal lpString As String, ByVal lplFileName As String) As Integer
```

continued on next page

continued from previous page

```
' The data structure that stores high scores.
Type tScores
    Name As String
    Score As Long
End Type

' This should ALWAYS be set to MAX_HISCORES + 1.
Global Hi(1 To 6) As tScores

' The current number of high scores stored in Hi() array.
Global Num_HiScores As Integer

' The new score to test.
Global gNewScore As Long

' The .INI file to store scoring information.
Global gINIFile As String

' This global Boolean tells the form to just display
' the high scores (no player name data entry).
Global gDisplayOnly As Integer

' The game title displayed as the form caption
' of the High Score window.
Global gGameTitle As String

Sub AddScoreAndSave (ByVal NewName As String, ByVal NewScore As Long)
'-------------------------------------------------------------
' Add this new score to the list of high scores and save
' everything back to the .INI file.
'-------------------------------------------------------------
Dim i As Integer
Dim j As Integer
Dim temp As tScores

    ' Add the new score to the end of the Hi() array.
    Hi(Num_HiScores + 1).Name = NewName
    Hi(Num_HiScores + 1).Score = NewScore

    ' Bubble-sort the scores in descending order (highest first) ...
    For j = 1 To Num_HiScores + 1
        For i = 2 To Num_HiScores + 1
            If Hi(i).Score > Hi(i - 1).Score Then
                temp = Hi(i - 1)
                Hi(i - 1) = Hi(i)
                Hi(i) = temp
            End If
        Next
    Next

    If Num_HiScores < MAX_HISCORES Then Num_HiScores = Num_HiScores + 1
```

```
    ' Write the scores back to the .INI file.
    For i = 1 To Num_HiScores
        WriteScore gINIFile, i, Format$(Hi(i).Score) & ";" & Trim$(Hi(i).Name)
    Next

End Sub

Sub GetScores (INIFile As String)
'-------------------------------------------------------------
' Read scores from the .INI file and store them in the Hi()
' array. In the .INI file, the score and player's name are
' stored together, separated by a semicolon like this:
'
' ENTRY1=9999;name
'
' We separate the two pieces of data after reading them in.
'-------------------------------------------------------------
Dim i As Integer
Dim rc As Integer
Dim pos As Integer
Dim AString As String
Dim DefValue As String


    For i = 1 To MAX_HISCORES
        AString = Space$(255)

        ' Windows API call to retrieve data from an .INI file.
        rc = GetPrivateProfileString(SECTION, ENTRY & Format$(i), "", AString, 255, INIFile)

        If rc > 0 Then
            ' rc tells us the length of the returned string,
            ' so we truncate the string at that length.
            AString = Left$(AString, rc)

            ' Separate the player's name and score.
            pos = InStr(AString, ";")
            If pos > 0 Then
                Hi(i).Score = Left(AString, pos - 1)
                Hi(i).Name = Mid$(AString, pos + 1)
            End If
        Else
            Num_HiScores = i - 1
            Exit Sub
        End If
    Next
    Num_HiScores = MAX_HISCORES
End Sub

Function IsAHiScore (NewScore As Long) As Integer
```

continued on next page

continued from previous page

```
    '------------------------------------------------------------
    ' Returns True if NewScore is a High Score, False otherwise.
    '------------------------------------------------------------
    Dim i As Integer

        ' Assume that it's not a high score.
        IsAHiScore = False

        If Num_HiScores > 0 Then
            ' If we've only equalled the lowest high score,
            ' then don't bother...
            If Num_HiScores = MAX_HISCORES And (NewScore = Hi(Num_HiScores).Score) Then
                Exit Function
            End If
        End If

        ' If we haven't filled up the High Scores table,
        ' then this must be a new high score.
        If Num_HiScores < MAX_HISCORES Then
            IsAHiScore = True
            Exit Function
        End If

        ' Compare this new score to the existing high scores.
        For i = 1 To Num_HiScores
            If Hi(i).Score <= NewScore Then
                IsAHiScore = True
                Exit For
            End If
        Next

    End Function

    Sub Main ()
    '------------------------------------------------------------
    ' This test procedure should be removed when using this
    ' module in your programs. It's included to show the proper
    ' way to call the ShowHiScores routine.
    '------------------------------------------------------------

        ShowHiScores CLng(Command$), "My Game", "MYAPP2.INI", False
        End
    End Sub

    Sub ShowHiScores (ByVal NewScore As Long, ByVal GameTitle As String, ByVal INIFile As
    String, ByVal DisplayOnly As Integer)
    '------------------------------------------------------------
    ' Call this routine after a game is completed, passing it
    ' the score of the game and the .INI file where your game's
    ' high scores are stored. If the new score is a new high,
    ' then a form is displayed where the players can enter their
    ' names. This information is then stored back in the .INI file.
    '------------------------------------------------------------
```

```
    gINIFile = INIFile
    gGameTitle = GameTitle

    ' Get the current high scores from the .INI file.
    GetScores gINIFile

    If DisplayOnly Then
        gDisplayOnly = True
        frmScores.Show MODAL
    Else
        ' If this is a new high, then display the High Score form.
        If IsAHiScore(NewScore) Then
            gNewScore = NewScore
            frmScores.Show MODAL
        End If
    End If
End Sub

Sub WriteScore (ByVal FileName As String, EntryNum As Integer, ByVal AString As String)
'-------------------------------------------------------------
' Write a high score back to the .INI file.
'-------------------------------------------------------------
Dim rc As Integer

    ' Windows API call to write to a private .INI file.
    rc = WritePrivateProfileString(SECTION, ENTRY & Format$(EntryNum), AString, FileName)
End Sub
```

3. Next, create a new form, SCORE1.FRM. Add the controls shown in Table 2-1 to this form. At design time, the form should look like Figure 2-3.

TABLE 2-1

Objects and properties for the SCORE1 form

Object	Property	Setting
Form	FormName	frmScores
	BackColor	&H00C0C0C0&
	BorderStyle	3 'Fixed Double
	Caption	"High Scores"
	ControlBox	0 'False
	MaxButton	0 'False
	MinButton	0 'False
Image	Name	imgMain
	Picture	(set at design time in Properties window)

continued on next page

continued from previous page

Object	Property	Setting
Label	Name	lblInfo
	Alignment	2 'Center
	BackStyle	0 'Transparent
	Caption	"Congratulations! You've just achieved a New High Score! Enter your name below:"
	ForeColor	&H00FF0000&
Image	Name	Image2
	Picture	(set at design time in Properties window)
Image	Name	Image1
	Picture	(set at design time in Properties window)
Image	Name	Image3
	Picture	(set at design time in Properties window)
Label	Name	Label1
	Alignment	2 'Center
	BackStyle	0 'Transparent
	Caption	"PLAYERS"
	FontSize	9.75
Label	Name	Label2
	Alignment	2 'Center
	BackStyle	0 'Transparent
	Caption	"SCORES"
	FontSize	9.75
ListBox	Name	lstNames
	BackColor	&H00C0C0C0&
	FontSize	9.75
	ForeColor	&H000000FF&
	TabStop	0 'False

Object	Property	Setting
ListBox	Name	lstScores
	BackColor	&H00C0C0C0&
	FontSize	9.75
	ForeColor	&H000000FF&
	TabStop	0 'False
TextBox	Name	txtName
	FontSize	9.75
	Text	"Text1"
CommandButton	Name	btnOK
	Caption	"&OK"
	Default	-1 'True
TextBox	Name	txtScore
	FontSize	9.75
	TabStop	0 'False
	Text	"Text2"
CommandButton	Name	btnNewScore
	Caption	"&OK"
Timer	Name	Timer1
	Interval	3000

Note that there are four image controls in this form. The bottom three images, Image1, Image2, and Image3, are storage areas for three bitmaps. These three bitmaps are copied one by one into the top imgMain bitmap on cue from the Timer control. This creates an animating twinkle effect on the gold trophy. The three lower images should be hidden by resizing the form so that they are "below" the bottom of the form.

Also note that there are two OK buttons. The upper one, btnNewScore, is displayed only when the user is entering a new player name.

4. Now add the following code to SCORE1.FRM. In use, this form can be displayed in one of two ways: as a display-only high score form or as a combination data entry and high score display form that allows the player to enter his or her name when he or she achieves a new high score.

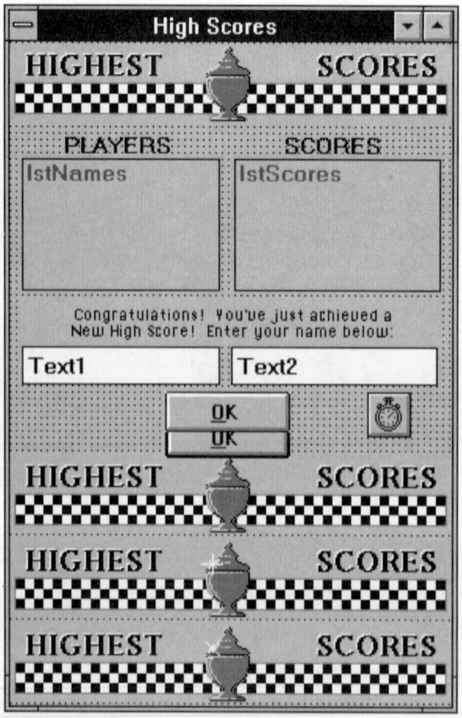

FIGURE 2-3

The High Scores form at design time

```
Option Explicit
'--------------------------------------------------------------
' SCORE1.FRM
' This form is dependent on file SCORE1.BAS.
'--------------------------------------------------------------

' Windows API call used to send a message to a window. In
' our case, we use it to send a message to a text box control
' that it should be read-only.
Declare Function SendMessage Lib "User" (ByVal hWnd As Integer, ByVal wMsg As Integer,
ByVal wParam As Integer, lParam As Any) As Long

' Constants used to make a text box read-only.
Const WM_USER = &H400
Const EM_SETREADONLY = (WM_USER + 31)

Sub btnNewScore_Click ()
'--------------------------------------------------------------
' When this button is pressed, save the new player name and
' score, then hide the text boxes and button used to enter
' the player's name, and resize the form.
'--------------------------------------------------------------
```

```
    ' Save all high scores back to the .INI file.
    AddScoreAndSave txtName, txtScore

    DisplayScores

    SetForDisplay
End Sub

Sub btnOK_Click ()
'-------------------------------------------------------------
' Close the frmScores window when this button is pushed.
'-------------------------------------------------------------

    Timer1.Enabled = False
    Timer1.Interval = 0
    DoEvents

    Unload Me
End Sub

Sub DisplayScores ()
'-------------------------------------------------------------
' Display the scores and player names from the Hi() array
' into the form's list controls.
'-------------------------------------------------------------
Dim i As Integer

    If Num_HiScores > 0 Then
     ' Empty the lists.
     lstNames.Clear
     lstScores.Clear

     ' Display the high scores in the list boxes.
     For i = 1 To Num_HiScores
         lstNames.AddItem Hi(i).Name
         lstScores.AddItem Format$(Hi(i).Score)
     Next
    End If

End Sub

Sub Form_Load ()
'-------------------------------------------------------------
' When the form is loaded, center it and display the current
' high scores.
'-------------------------------------------------------------
Dim rc As Long

    ' Center the form on the screen.
    Me.Left = (Screen.Width - Me.Width) \ 2
    Me.Top = (Screen.Height - Me.Height) \ 2
```

continued on next page

continued from previous page

```
    Me.Caption = gGameTitle

    ' Display current high scores.
    DisplayScores

    If gDisplayOnly Then
      SetForDisplay
    Else

      btnOK.Visible = False
      btnNewScore.Default = True

      ' Clear text field to let player enter his or her name.
      txtName = ""
      txtName.MaxLength = 15
      txtScore = Format$(gNewScore)

      rc = SendMessage(txtScore.hWnd, EM_SETREADONLY, 1, 0)
    End If
End Sub

Sub Form_Paint ()
' Draw 3D effect around selected controls.
    Make3D Me, lstNames, 1
    Make3D Me, lstScores, 1
    If txtName.Visible Then
      Make3D Me, txtName, 0
      Make3D Me, txtScore, 0
    End If
End Sub

Sub Make3D (pic As Form, ctl As Control, ByVal BorderStyle As Integer)
'-----------------------------------------------------
' Wrap a 3D effect around a control on a form.
'-----------------------------------------------------
Dim AdjustX As Integer, AdjustY As Integer
Dim RightSide As Single
Dim BW As Integer, BorderWidth As Integer
Dim LeftTopColor As Long, RightBottomColor As Long
Dim i As Integer
' Color Constants
Const DARK_GRAY = &H808080
Const WHITE = &HFFFFFF
Const BLACK = &H0


    If Not ctl.Visible Then Exit Sub

    AdjustX = Screen.TwipsPerPixelX
    AdjustY = Screen.TwipsPerPixelY
```

```
    BorderWidth = 1

    Select Case BorderStyle
     Case 0: ' Inset
         LeftTopColor = DARK_GRAY
         RightBottomColor = WHITE
     Case 1: ' Raised
         LeftTopColor = WHITE
         RightBottomColor = DARK_GRAY
    End Select


    ' Set the top shading line.
    For BW = 1 To BorderWidth
     ' Top
     pic.CurrentX = ctl.Left - (AdjustX * BW)
     pic.CurrentY = ctl.Top - (AdjustY * BW)
     pic.Line -(ctl.Left + ctl.Width + (AdjustX * (BW - 1)), ctl.Top - (AdjustY *
     BW)), LeftTopColor
     ' Right
     pic.Line -(ctl.Left + ctl.Width + (AdjustX * (BW - 1)), ctl.Top + ctl.Height +
     (AdjustY * (BW - 1))), RightBottomColor
     ' Bottom
     pic.Line -(ctl.Left - (AdjustX * BW), ctl.Top + ctl.Height + (AdjustY * (BW -
     1))), RightBottomColor
     ' Left
     pic.Line -(ctl.Left - (AdjustX * BW), ctl.Top - (AdjustY * BW)), LeftTopColor
    Next
End Sub

Sub SetForDisplay ()
' Rearrange the form as a "display-only" form.

    ' Hide "New Hi" controls...
    lblInfo.Visible = False
    txtName.Visible = False
    txtScore.Visible = False
    btnNewScore.Visible = False

    ' Adjust the OK button position and Window Height.
    btnOK.Visible = True
    btnOK.Top = lblInfo.Top
    btnOK.Default = True
    Me.Height = btnNewScore.Top + 45
    Me.Refresh

End Sub

Sub Timer1_Timer ()
' Animate the trophy bitmap to add a twinkle effect.
Static InSub As Integer
```

continued on next page

continued from previous page

```
Dim StartTime As Single
Dim i As Integer

    If InSub Then Exit Sub
    InSub = True

    For i = 1 To 4
     imgMain.Picture = Image2.Picture
     StartTime = Timer
     Do While (Timer - StartTime) < .1
         DoEvents
     Loop

     imgMain.Picture = Image3.Picture
     StartTime = Timer
     Do While (Timer - StartTime) < .1
         DoEvents
     Loop
    Next

    imgMain.Picture = Image1.Picture
    InSub = False
End Sub
```

Running the High Score Example Program

After building the example program as described in the steps above, save the project. The main subroutine shows how to call the ShowHiScores routine. ShowHiScores is the heart of the high score component. Before running the example program, select the Project command from the Visual Basic Options menu and set the Command Line Argument to some integer value, such as 1249. Now run the example program. The High Score form should appear, the score 1249 should be displayed in the lower-right text box, and you should be prompted to enter your name in the lower-left text box. After entering your name, click the OK button. The two text boxes should disappear, and you should see only the high score lists and an OK button.

The SendMessage Function—Making a Text Control Read-Only

One thing you may notice in the high score example program is that the new high score is displayed in a text control, alongside the text control where the player enters his or her name. This may seem odd, because text boxes are editable, and you certainly don't want the users to be able to edit their scores. A more logical choice would seem to be a Label control.

The problem turns out to be the way labels and text controls justify the text they display. They both can left-justify text within their borders, but the Label control tends to adjust text closer to the top of the border, and the Edit control justifies text near the bottom border. Display a Label and a Text control next to each other, and they can appear vertically askew.

An easy solution for this is to use two Text controls, but don't allow data to be changed in one of them. You might consider doing this by simply setting the text control's Enabled property to False. This will prevent data entry, but it also has the unfortunate side effect of turning the displayed text gray.

Another solution, and the one used in this program, is to resort to the Windows API again. This time use a versatile routine called SendMessage. Visual Basic hides much of the inner workings of Windows from the programmer. For example, when you click on a Command Button control in Visual Basic, a Click event is generated by Visual Basic. Visual Basic programmers become accustomed to this event-driven paradigm. At the Windows level, things happen a bit differently. Components, such as buttons or text controls, are all considered windows. Each window has a unique identifier, called a *window handle*. Through these window handles, components can be sent *messages*. These messages can affect the way a window behaves, and this is what SendMessage is used for.

The SendMessage API function is declared like this:

```
Declare Function SendMessage Lib "User" (ByVal hWnd As Integer, ByVal wMsg As Integer, _
        ByVal wParam As Integer, lParam As Any) As Long
```

The first parameter is the window handle, hWnd. Most Visual Basic controls, such as the Text control in this example, have an hWnd property, so this parameter is easy to get. The second parameter is a constant that determines the actual message to be sent to the window. Windows defines hundreds of these messages as constants, and different types of windows (Text controls, buttons, list boxes) react to their own unique subset of these messages. The last two parameters allow you to send additional information that the window may need to process the message correctly.

In this example, you use the EM_SETREADONLY message. The EM_ prefix indicates that this message is only valid with Edit controls; other types of windows have their own prefixes. The message name is fairly self-explanatory. You want to tell the text control to change itself into a read-only control. You also need to set the wParam parameter to 1, for True. The SendMessage call is made as shown below:

```
rc = SendMessage(txtScore.hWnd, EM_SETREADONLY, 1, 0)
```

Call this routine in the form's Load event, so that when the txtScore control is first displayed, no data entry is possible. If at some later time you want to reenable data entry, you would simply call SendMessage a second time, this time setting wParam to 0, for False.

The SendMessage function is a versatile routine that can extend the native abilities of Visual Basic. To learn more about the types of messages that can be sent, you may want to explore the Windows SDK help file WIN31WH.HLP, which is installed in your Visual Basic WINAPI directory. This file contains a wealth of information on SendMessage and other Windows API calls.

The Make3D Routine—Adding Depth to Your Controls

The Make3D subroutine presented in the SCORE1 form produces a 3D raised or inset appearance to a Visual Basic control. This effect can add depth to what otherwise may be a drab and flat form. The routine is completely self-contained, so you can pluck it out of the example program and put it in any of your programs that need that three-dimensional appearance.

Let's take a look at how the function is used. In the form's Paint event, you'll see several calls similar to the one shown below:

```
Make3D Me, lstNames, 1
```

The function is passed three parameters: a form variable, a control variable, and a style flag. The form variable indicates the form on which the target control resides. The control variable refers to the control to be made 3D. The style variable is an integer, 0 or 1, used to indicate whether the control will be drawn with an inset or raised border.

The Make3D routine works by drawing white and dark gray lines onto the form itself, around the edges of the specified control. White lines drawn outside a control's top and left edges and gray lines around its bottom and right edges make a control appear sunken or inset into the form. Reverse those colors and the control appears to rise up off the form.

Using the High Score Component

To plug the high score component into your games, add the form and .BAS module from the SCORE1.MAK project into your project. Then call the ShowHiScores subroutine from within the program. You may also find it necessary to remove the subroutine called *main* from the SCORE1.BAS module.

A call to this subroutine should look like this:

```
DisplayOnly = False
ShowHiScores Score, "My Game", "MYGAME.INI", DisplayOnly
```

FIGURE 2-4 *The High Scores Form in Display-Only Mode*

There are two occasions when you might want to call ShowHiScores. The first is immediately after a game has completed. Pass the score, game title, name of the .INI file, and the DisplayOnly Boolean flag. You don't need to determine if a high score was achieved, the ShowHiScores routine will do this for you. If the player has reached a new high score, then the High Score form will be displayed, with the caption specified ("My Game," in the example above). The players can then enter their names in a text box. And the new high score list is saved back to the .INI file (MYGAME.INI in the example above). If no file path is specified for the .INI file, it is stored in the player's Windows directory.

The second occasion when you might call ShowHiScores is to allow the player to view the current high scores. To do this, call the ShowHiScores routine with its DisplayOnly parameter set to True. The High Scores form is resized and rearranged as shown in Figure 2-4.

Little Things Count

So many tiny details can contribute to, or detract from, enjoyment of a game. A well thought-out scoring strategy, a clever game design that slowly but relentlessly increases the difficulty level, or a simple mechanism for remembering the player's earlier victories—all these little things, when done well, can make your game an addictive pastime.

In the next chapter, we'll look at the most important visual aspect of games programming: creating and manipulating bitmaps. You'll learn how to display, move, and scroll these Windows objects and how to create game sprites using Windows API functions.

3

Bitmaps

3

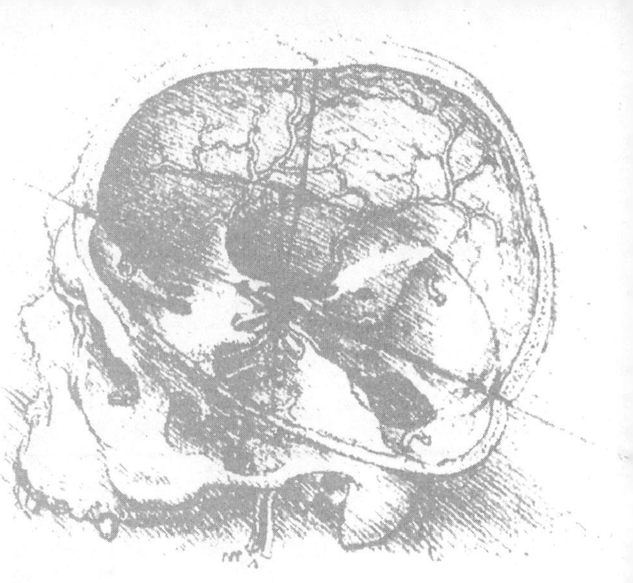

Bitmaps

The first impression your game makes will be its visual style. Are the images the player sees exciting and compelling, or do they more closely resemble a three-year-old's attempts at coloring? Do the game elements look flat and boxlike, or do they seem real and three dimensional? Do objects move smoothly around the screen, or do they jerk haphazardly? To create visually exciting games, you have to master the basics of bitmaps.

Basics of Bitmaps

A *bitmap* is a digitized picture. It's a rendering composed of thousands of tiny colored dots, or pixels. These pictures are most commonly stored in Windows files that have a .BMP file extension.

There are many ways to display a bitmap using Visual Basic. For example, the Form object has a Picture property that can display a bitmap. This property can be set at either design time or runtime, and will display the selected bitmap in the upper-left corner of the form. Figure 3-1 shows a form whose Picture property has been set at design time. The bitmap is WINLOGO.BMP, one of the wallpaper bitmaps that Windows 3.1 installs in the Windows directory.

FIGURE 3-1

Displaying a bitmap using the form's Picture property

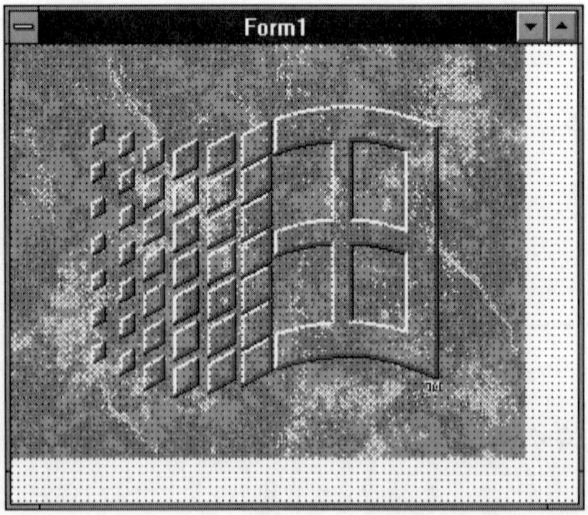

Two standard Visual Basic controls, Image and PictureBox, can also be used to display bitmaps. These controls give more flexibility, as they can be placed anywhere on a form and they can be resized and repositioned at runtime.

You might wonder why Visual Basic provides two controls that seem to serve the same purpose: displaying bitmaps. These controls are not as similar as they first appear; each embodies a set of design trade-offs that the game programmer must understand.

The Image control is quite good at *displaying* bitmaps. It has a Stretch property that can be used to resize a bitmap automatically to the size of its Image control.

One of the most important differences to note is that the PictureBox uses considerably more Windows resources than the Image control. In particular, the PictureBox is a graphics resource hog. Unrestrained use of the PictureBox can deplete Windows resources to the point where a game, or other programs, will fail to run.

So why would you use the PictureBox control? Because it can do many things an Image control can't. The PictureBox control has a special property, hDC, that the Image control lacks. This property lets you unleash the power of the Windows graphics API in your Visual Basic programs.

Visual Basic hides much of the internals of Windows from the programmer. This greatly simplifies most programming tasks, letting you worry more about the problem at hand than the intricacies of Windows itself. But the designers of Visual Basic knew there would be times when you needed to go a level deeper to perform tasks that couldn't be handled by simply setting properties or calling methods. So they added trap doors within Visual Basic to let you use the power of the Windows API when you need it.

That's what the PictureBox's hDC property is. In Windows parlance, the hDC is a *handle* to a *device context*. A handle is a generic term used by Windows programmers. It refers to a 16-bit number that uniquely identifies some object. That object might be a window or an icon or a mouse pointer. A device context is an internal data structure in which Windows keeps information about a graphics display device. In this case, that display device is a PictureBox control.

The Graphics Device Interface, or GDI, is the part of the Windows API that handles most graphics tasks. The GDI is a set of external function calls that can be included in a Visual Basic program using the Declares statement. Most GDI functions require a device context handle as a parameter.

A device context is like a canvas onto which you will draw graphics. The GDI provides a set of tools, brushes, and paints that you can use to create pictures.

BitBlt

The *BitBlt* function is by far the most versatile GDI function for game programmers. It is most often used to copy a bitmap from one device context to another, but it can also be used to combine two bitmaps in interesting ways. BitBlt stands for *Bit Block Transfer.*

Before using BitBlt, you must first declare it in the Declarations section of a Visual Basic form, class, or module, as shown below.

```
Declare Function BitBlt Lib "GDI" (ByVal hDestDC As Integer, _
                                   ByVal X As Integer, ByVal y As Integer, _
                                   ByVal nWidth As Integer, ByVal nHeight As Integer, _
                                   ByVal hSrcDC As Integer, _
                                   ByVal XSrc As Integer, ByVal YSrc As Integer, _
                                   ByVal dwRop As Long) As Integer
```

At first, BitBlt looks pretty daunting, with its nine parameters. But it actually turns out to be quite easy once you break it down. Let's create a very small Visual Basic project to see how this works. In Visual Basic, create a new project. In Form1, add two picture boxes, Picture1 and Picture2, and a command button, Command1. Size Picture1 so that it is considerably larger than Picture2. Set the Picture property of Picture2 so that it displays a bitmap. The Windows directory is a good place to look for bitmaps. Your form should look something like the one shown in Figure 3-2.

Now you need to add the BitBlt code. First, add the BitBlt declaration, as shown at the beginning of this section, to Form1's Declarations section. Then create a Click event for the Command1 button, as shown below. This event routine will copy the bitmap shown in Picture2 into the Picture1 control.

FIGURE 3-2

A simple BitBlt example at design time

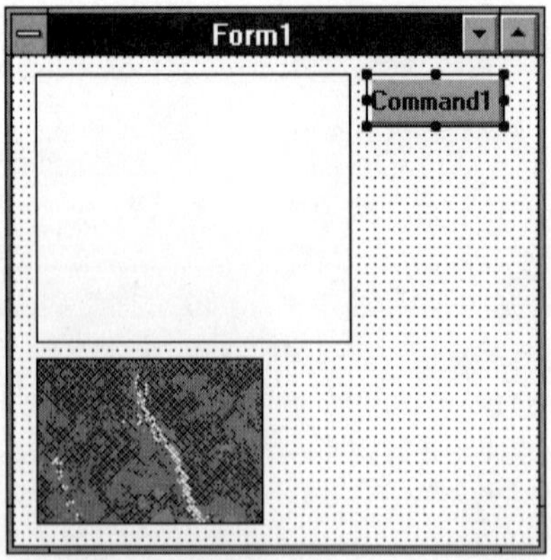


```
Sub Command1_Click ()
Const SRCCOPY = &HCC0020
Const PIXELS = 3
Dim rc As Integer


    Picture1.ScaleMode = PIXELS
    Picture2.ScaleMode = PIXELS
    rc = BitBlt(Picture1.hDC, 10, 10, Picture2.ScaleWidth, Picture2.ScaleHeight, _
                Picture2.hDC, 0, 0, SRCCOPY)
End Sub
```

Notice that you set the ScaleMode property of both PictureBox controls to pixels. The PictureBox control has several properties that define a coordinate system inside the boundaries of the PictureBox. These properties are ScaleLeft, ScaleTop, ScaleWidth, ScaleHeight, and ScaleMode. The first four properties determine the dimensions inside the PictureBox. The ScaleMode property determines the units those dimensions are measured in. Valid units include twips (which are the default), pixels, points, inches, millimeters, centimeters, and user-defined units. The BitBlt function expects units in pixels, so you set the ScaleMode property accordingly.

Now let's look at the BitBlt itself. The first parameter is the device context handle, or hDC, of the destination PictureBox, Picture1. The next two parameters are X and Y coordinates within Picture1. These coordinates represent the upper-left corner of the rectangular area into which the bitmap will be copied. In this example, the bitmap will be copied to a position starting 10 pixels from the top and left of Picture1.

The next two parameters define the width and height of the bitmap to be copied. In this case, these values are set to Picture2's ScaleWidth and ScaleHeight properties. This means that the entire visible area of Picture2 will be copied.

The next parameter is the hDC of the source bitmap; in this case, that's Picture1.hDC. Following that parameter are X and Y coordinates of the source bitmap. These define the upper-left corner of the rectangular area from which BitBlt will

FIGURE 3-3

The BitBlt example at runtime

copy. These coordinates give you the freedom to clip any portion of one bitmap and copy it into another bitmap.

Finally, the last parameter is a constant that defines how the source bitmap is to be combined with the destination bitmap. This is called a *raster operation*. In this case, you use the constant SRCCOPY. This tells BitBlt to replace the destination region with the source bitmap. The section on sprite animation will show how to use BitBlt with other raster operations to create game objects that can move independently over a bitmapped background.

Run the example program and press the command button. The result should look something like Figure 3-3.

This program shows the simplest use of BitBlt: copying one bitmap over another. Now let's expand this idea to reveal techniques you can use in games.

Smooth Scrolling Backgrounds

Many computer games let the player move through a virtual universe. That universe might be an alien landscape or a World War II battlefield or the labyrinthine caverns of some forgotten civilization.

Let's say you wanted to create a game in which the player guided a submarine through an underwater world. As the submarine moved through the water, the underwater background would appear to scroll past smoothly. How can you create that scrolling background?

The trick is to create a background bitmap that wraps around on itself. Imagine taking a piece of paper and wrapping it around a coffee can, cutting the paper so that its left and right edges just touch each other. Now draw your background picture on the paper. Make the picture continuous, ignoring the seam where the paper edges meet. When you're finished, the result should be a picture that appears complete when viewed from any side of the coffee can. If the paper is removed from the can, you'd have a picture where the right edge is a continuation of the left edge. We're going to translate that same idea to bitmaps.

The bitmap in Figure 3-4 is an example of a continuous bitmap, where the left edge matches up with the right edge. This type of bitmap can be used as the starting point for a smooth scrolling background. This example will show how to scroll horizontally, but the technique can be expanded to perform smooth scrolling in any direction.

The trick to scrolling is to use the BitBlt function to display only a section of the background bitmap. By slowly shifting the section that's displayed, the background appears to scroll past. In this example, the value of the X axis of the source bitmap is increased, so the background will appear to scroll to the left (Figure 3-5).

Let's build another example project to see how this works. Before starting the new project, you'll need to draw a background bitmap similar to the one shown in Figure 3-5. That bitmap is 500 pixels wide and 130 pixels high. The left and right edges of the picture should match up.

Once that's done, create a new project called UNDRSEA1.MAK. The project will only have one form, UNDRSEA1.FRM. In UNDRSEA1.FRM, add two PictureBox controls, a Timer control, and a Horizontal Scroll Bar control. Set the Picture property of the second PictureBox (Picture2) to the bitmap you've created. Arrange the controls as shown in Figure 3-6.

Next, add the following code to the form's Declarations section.

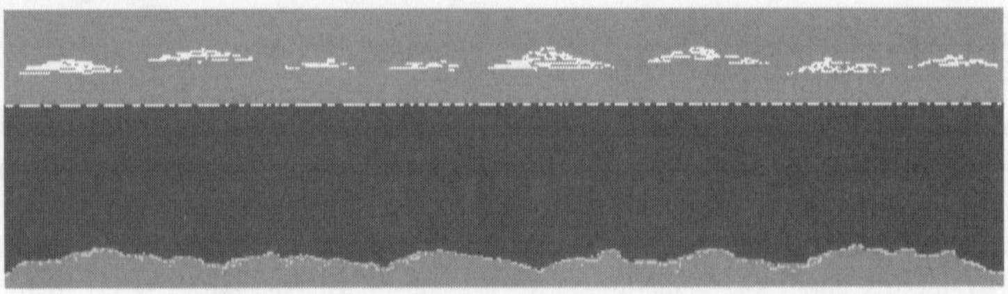

FIGURE 3-4

A continuous background bitmap

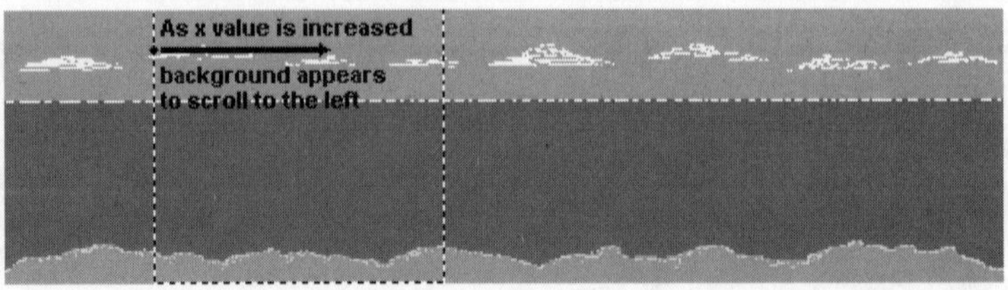

FIGURE 3-5

BitBlting a section of the background bitmap to create scrolling

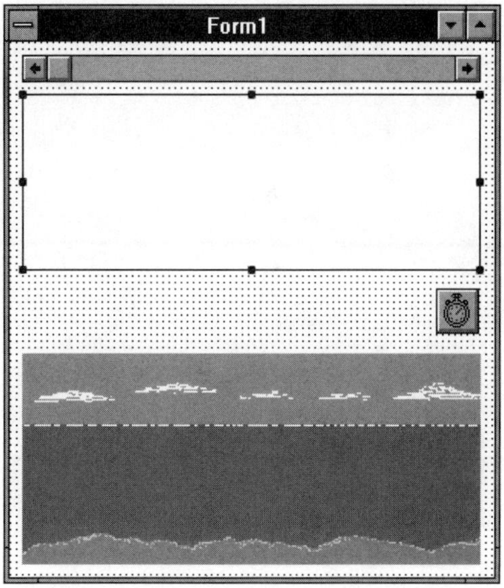

FIGURE 3-6

The scrolling background example at design time

```
Option Explicit

Const SRCCOPY = &HCC0020
Const PIXELS = 3

Declare Function BitBlt Lib "GDI" (ByVal hDestDC As Integer, _
                              ByVal x As Integer, ByVal y As Integer, _
                              ByVal nWidth As Integer, ByVal nHeight As Integer, _
                              ByVal hSrcDC As Integer, _
                              ByVal XSrc As Integer, ByVal YSrc As Integer, _
                              ByVal dwRop As Long) As Integer
```

This code declares some constants and the BitBlt function that are used later. The PIXELS constant is used to set the ScaleMode property of the two PictureBoxes, as discussed in the earlier BitBlt example. The SRCCOPY constant is used as the raster operation parameter when calling the BitBlt function.

Next, add the following code to the form's Load event.

```
Sub Form_Load ()

    ' Set the ScaleMode of both PictureBox controls to
    ' pixels, the units expected by the BitBlt function.
    Picture1.ScaleMode = PIXELS
    Picture2.ScaleMode = PIXELS

    ' Picture2 holds the entire background bitmap. Setting
    ' AutoSize lets the control resize itself to the same
```

continued on next page

continued from previous page

```
    ' dimensions as the bitmap it contains.
    Picture2.AutoSize = True

    ' Setting AutoRedraw to true creates a persistent bitmap,
    ' which can be BitBlted even if it's not visible in the
    ' window.
    Picture2.AutoRedraw = True

    ' Make sure Picture1 is the same height as Picture2.
    Picture1.Height = Picture2.Height

    ' The maximum scrolling rate will be 20 pixels at a time.
    HScroll1.Max = 20
    HScroll1.LargeChange = 2

    ' Resize the window to hide Picture2.
    Me.Height = (Me.Height - Me.ScaleHeight) + Picture1.Top + Picture1.Height + HScroll1.Top

    ' Setting the timer interval causes timer events to begin.
    Timer1.Interval = 55
End Sub
```

In this subroutine, you set the ScaleMode properties of the two PictureBoxes to pixel units, because this is what the BitBlt function requires. Because Picture2 contains the entire background bitmap, you set its AutoSize property to True so that the control will automatically resize itself to the bitmap's dimensions. You also set its AutoRedraw property to True. This creates a *persistent bitmap.* A persistent bitmap can be copied using BitBlt even if it is not visible on the screen, because a copy of the bitmap is maintained in memory. You need to make Picture2 persistent because you will be resizing the form to hide Picture2 completely.

The last thing you do in the Load event is set the Interval property of the Timer control. Now Visual Basic will begin to trigger Timer events, and this is where most of the work of this program takes place. Add the following code to the Timer1 control's Timer event.

```
Sub Timer1_Timer ()
Static x As Integer
Dim AWidth As Integer
Dim rc As Integer

    ' Calculate the next x position for Picture2.
    x = x + HScroll1
    If x > Picture2.ScaleWidth Then x = 0

    If x > (Picture2.ScaleWidth - Picture1.ScaleWidth) Then
        AWidth = Picture2.ScaleWidth - x
        ' When x gets close to the right edge of Picture2's bitmap,
        ' two sections of Picture2 need to be copied into Picture1.
        ' The first BitBlt copies whatever remains to the right of
```

```
        ' position x in Picture2. The second BitBlt will copy from
        ' the far left side of Picture2 to fill in the remaining
        ' area to the right of Picture1.
        rc = BitBlt(Picture1.hDC, 0, 0, AWidth, Picture2.ScaleHeight, Picture2.hDC, x, 0, SRCCOPY)
        rc = BitBlt(Picture1.hDC, AWidth, 0, Picture1.ScaleWidth - AWidth, Picture2.ScaleHeight, _
                Picture2.hDC, 0, 0, SRCCOPY)
    Else
        ' Normally, only one BitBlt is required to copy the section
        ' of Picture2 into Picture1.
        rc = BitBlt(Picture1.hDC, 0, 0, Picture1.ScaleWidth, Picture2.ScaleHeight, _
                Picture2.hDC, x, 0, SRCCOPY)
    End If
End Sub
```

This routine is actually very simple. You maintain a static variable X, which tells you at what X position to begin copying from Picture2. Static variables retain their value between subroutine calls, so X always contains the previous X position at the start of each Timer event.

The position of the horizontal scroll bar control, HScroll1, determines the speed at which the background scrolls. The value of HScroll1 is added to X in each Timer event. This new value of X is used to calculate what section of Picture2 to copy. Normally, you only need to perform a single BitBlt, copying Picture2 starting at position X for a width equal to Picture1's width.

The one problem arises when X nears the right edge of Picture2. You don't have enough bitmap remaining on the right side of Picture2 to fill the entire width of Picture1 completely (see Figure 3-7). But because the left side of Picture2 is a

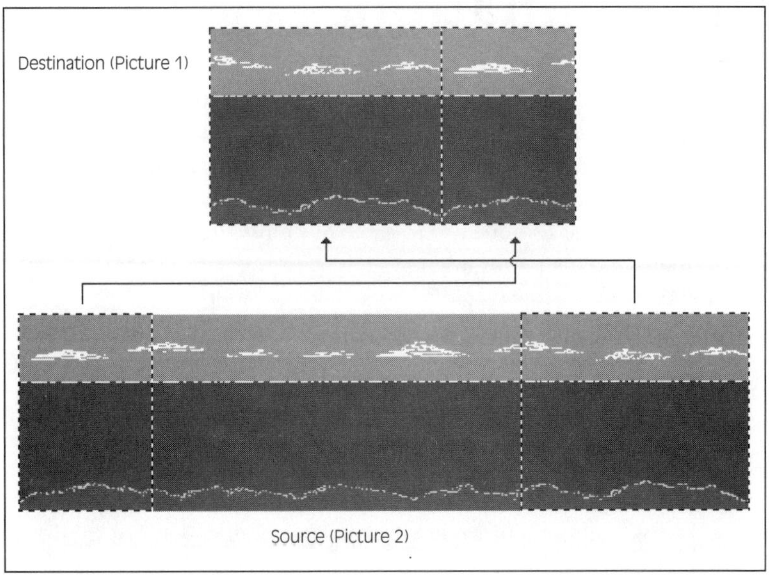

FIGURE 3-7

Wrapping around the edges to create continuous scrolling

FIGURE 3-8

The scrolling background example at runtime

continuation of its right side, you can simply BitBlt a piece of Picture2's left side to fill in the remaining blank right section of Picture1. This seamlessly completes the picture. Of course, X will eventually increase beyond the right edge of Picture2. When this happens, merely reset X to 0 and the whole process continues. Using this technique, you can create a background that appears to scroll endlessly.

Save and run this project. The form should look something like Figure 3-8. Initially the background will be motionless. Click on the right arrow of the horizontal scroll bar to increase the scroll speed and set the background into motion. You can play with different scroll speeds and see their effects on the smoothness of the movement.

Sprite Animation

You've undoubtedly seen sprites in video and computer games, though you may not have heard the term before. A *sprite* is an independently moving game element. In a game like Atari's Centipede, there are many different sprites: Each section of the centipede, the spiders, the snails, and the moving cannon used by the player are all sprites. In Mario Bros., Mario is a sprite.

On some computers and game machines, the ability to display and move sprites is built into the hardware or system software. Such is not the case with Windows. The good news is that it's fairly easy to use the BitBlt function to create and move your own sprites.

Simple Sprite Animation

I've already shown that BitBlt can be used to copy one rectangular bitmap over another. If sprites were always rectangles, you'd have no problem; you could simply BitBlt them onto a game's background bitmap. Unfortunately, sprites can have any shape. Does that mean you have to abandon the BitBlt function? No, you just need to do a little extra work.

Look at the three bitmaps in Figure 3-9. The first one, on the left, is the background bitmap. This is the surface onto which you will draw the sprite. The middle bitmap is the sprite itself, in this case a simple red ball. The last bitmap is a *sprite mask*. A sprite mask is a separate bitmap that looks like a silhouette of the sprite. The sprite mask is used to define the area of the background that will be obscured by the sprite. The best way to understand this is to look at the process step by step.

Earlier, I showed that the last parameter of the BitBlt function defines a raster operation. The raster operation defines how the source and destination bitmaps are combined. Usually the SRCCOPY raster operation is used. SRCCOPY causes the source bitmap to replace the destination region completely.

But there are many other raster operations. In the first step of the sprite-drawing process, you will BitBlt the sprite mask bitmap onto the background bitmap using a new raster operation: SRCAND. As its name implies, the SRCAND operation combines each pixel of the source bitmap with the corresponding pixel of the destination bitmap using a bitwise AND operation. The actual function call looks like this:

```
rc = BitBlt(picBackground.hDC, 5, 5, picMask.ScaleWidth, picMask.ScaleHeight, _
          picMask.hDC, 0, 0, SRCAND)
```

Figure 3-10 shows the result of this function. The black part of the mask has been overlayed onto the background, but the white area of the mask has no effect on the background. Why is that?

FIGURE 3-9

The background, sprite, and sprite mask bitmaps

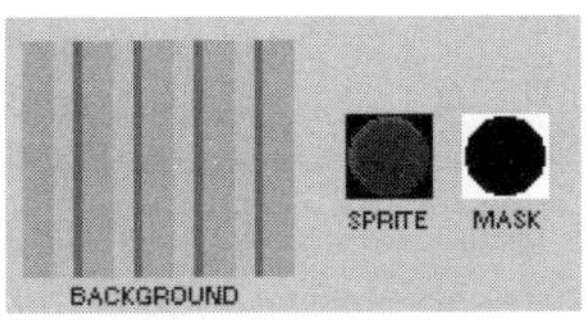

FIGURE 3-10

The background bitmap with sprite mask overlayed

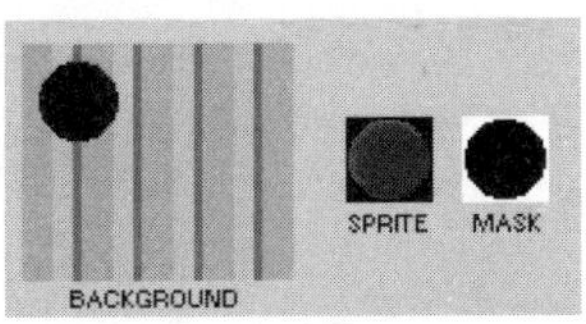

Every pixel of a bitmap has a corresponding integer value that represents its color. How big this integer value can get depends on your video driver. If your driver supports only 16 colors, then it requires only a 4-bit integer to store those 16 color combinations. By comparison, a 256-color video driver would require a full 8 bits to cover all the possible color combinations. The mask has only two colors: black and white. Black is always represented as 0. White is always represented as the highest possible integer value that the video driver supports. So with 4-bit color, white would be 15, and with 8-bit color, white would be 255. In both cases, white is a value with all its bits set to 1.

When a pixel in the black area of the mask is combined with a pixel from the background, each bit is ANDed together. Anything ANDed with 0 results in a 0, so any black areas in the mask become black in the resulting background bitmap.

When a pixel in the white area of the mask is combined with a pixel from the background, each bit is again ANDed together. In this case, you're ANDing some bit value from the background with a 1 (all white bits are 1). If the background bit is a 1, then the resulting bit will also be 1 (1 AND 1 = 1). Likewise, if the background bit is a 0, the resulting bit will remain 0 (0 AND 1 = 0). In other words, any color ANDed with white remains unchanged.

The second step in drawing the sprite onto the background involves another BitBlt. This time you'll BitBlt our sprite bitmap onto the "masked" background, using the SRCPAINT raster operation:

```
rc = BitBlt(picBackground.hDC, 5, 5, picSprite.ScaleWidth, picSprite.ScaleHeight, _
            picSprite.hDC, 0, 0, SRCPAINT)
```

Figure 3-11 shows the results of the operation. The background around the sprite is still unchanged, but the sprite has been painted into the previously black area. How did this happen? Like SRCAND, the SRCPAINT raster operation performs a bitwise combination of the source and destination bitmaps. This time, the operation is a bitwise OR operation. The background of the sprite bitmap was all black, which you'll recall has a value of 0. Likewise, the area of the background where the ball will go has been changed to black by the previous BitBlt of the sprite mask. In a bitwise OR operation, 1 OR 0 = 1 and 0 OR 0 = 0. In other words, any time you OR a color with 0,

FIGURE 3-11

The background bitmap after the sprite has been painted

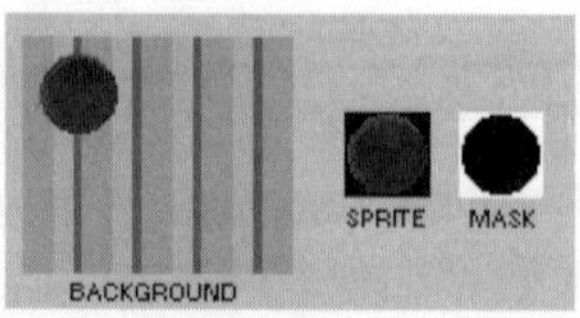

or black, the result is that original color. So you end up with our background intact and the sprite image painted onto its silhouette.

These two operations are all that's needed to draw a sprite onto a background, but what about moving it? The illusion of sprite movement is achieved by adjusting the sprite's position on the background. You can do this by slightly changing the sprite's X and Y positions and BitBlting it again onto the background bitmap, but this presents a problem. You've messed up the background when you drew the sprite the first time. How do you get rid of the original sprite?

One simple way to do this is to remember what the background looked like under the sprite before you drew the sprite onto the background. To do this, set up a save area to hold this section of the background. The save area, which is just another PictureBox control, only needs to be as big as the sprite. SRCCOPY the area of the background into the save area PictureBox before you draw the sprite. Then, when you're ready to draw the sprite in its next position, simply SRCCOPY the save area back onto the background, restoring the background to its original appearance. The save area PictureBox is never seen by the game player. This PictureBox either can have its Visible property set to False or can be positioned outside the visible region of the form. In either case, the save area's AutoRedraw property should be set to True so that the bitmap image can be stored in memory.

There is one problem with this technique. Because you are basically erasing the previous sprite before redrawing it at its new position, the sprite appears to flicker as it is rapidly drawn and then removed and then redrawn again. Let's look at one way to avoid this flicker problem.

Flickerless Sprite Animation

Because the problem is that the game player sees the sprite being removed from the background, you need to avoid having the sprite visibly removed. You'll use another PictureBox control, similar to the save area just described. Let's call this new PictureBox a *work area*. You'll also store a duplicate copy of the original background either off screen or in an invisible PictureBox. This original bitmap will always provide a "clean" copy of the background.

Each time you move the sprite, you increment its X and Y positions on the background by some amount. Let's call this amount *delta*. The work area PictureBox must be larger than the sprite. In fact, it must be the size of the sprite plus a delta-width margin around it. If the sprite is 32 pixels square and the delta is 5 (meaning you move the sprite by 5 pixels each time) then the work area must be 42 pixels square. This gives a 5 pixel margin around the work area.

Let's look at the steps you'll need to move the sprite without flicker.

1. Use BitBlt to SRCCOPY a section of the duplicate, pristine background into the work area PictureBox.
2. Draw the sprite into the work area using the two-step SRCAND/SRCPAINT technique described earlier. Place the sprite in the center of the work area, leaving a delta-width border all around it.
3. SRCCOPY the work area onto the on-screen background. The sprite is now visible to the game player.

To move the sprite to a new location, simply repeat these three steps for a new X and Y position. The only time you BitBlt to the screen is in Step 3. The reason this works is that you always have that margin around the work area. The margin contains the original background, and it is always just wide enough to wipe out the previous sprite.

There are other variations of this technique. If the background of the game is constantly moving, you'll probably be BitBlting an entire new background to the screen for each frame. In this case, you can use a work area the size of the entire visible background, simply BitBlt the sprites into it, and then BitBlt the entire work area onto the screen.

Multiple Frame Sprites

You've looked at how to move a sprite around the background, but not at how to animate the sprite. Animation of the sprite is the articulation of the sprite itself. So far, I've shown you how to move a creature around the screen, but I haven't shown you how to make that creature's eyes blink or hand wave.

In movie or television animation, the illusion of movement is achieved by drawing individual pictures of a character, each in a slightly different position. When these frames are displayed rapidly, the character seems to move. We'll use exactly the same idea to create animated sprites.

Actually, I've already shown you all the techniques you'll need. But instead of creating just one image for each sprite, you'll need to create several. Each image corresponds to an animation frame, and so it will require its own sprite mask. The easiest way to keep track of these frames is by creating a *control array* of PictureBoxes. A control array is a collection of controls that share the same name but, like an array, have different numeric indexes. You can create an array of sprites, where each subsequent frame has a higher index value. By incrementing the index value each time the sprite is displayed, you can easily step through the animation sequence.

Another technique is to pack all the sprites into a single PictureBox and then pull them out in sequence. The example program that follows demonstrates this technique.

Example

I've put together an example program that demonstrates everything covered in this chapter: scrolling backgrounds, sprite display, and sprite animation. The example was designed to illustrate the basics of bitmap manipulation without getting bogged down in the complexities of game logic. Figure 3-12 shows how the example program looks at runtime.

Figure 3-12 shows a large picture box dominating the center of the form (let's call this the viewer picture box), with two scroll bars attached to its left and bottom sides. These are standard scroll bar controls that have been aligned to the sides of a simple picture box control. Run the program and then press the scroll buttons. The bitmap displayed in the viewer picture box appears to scroll in all directions under control of these scroll bars. How is this done? To understand this, it's helpful to see what the form looked like at design time, because several things are hidden from the user at runtime. Figure 3-13 shows the form at design time.

Notice the large picture box at the lower right of the form. This picture box, which is hidden from the user at runtime, contains a large bitmap of a star field. This

FIGURE 3-12

The bitmap demonstration program at runtime

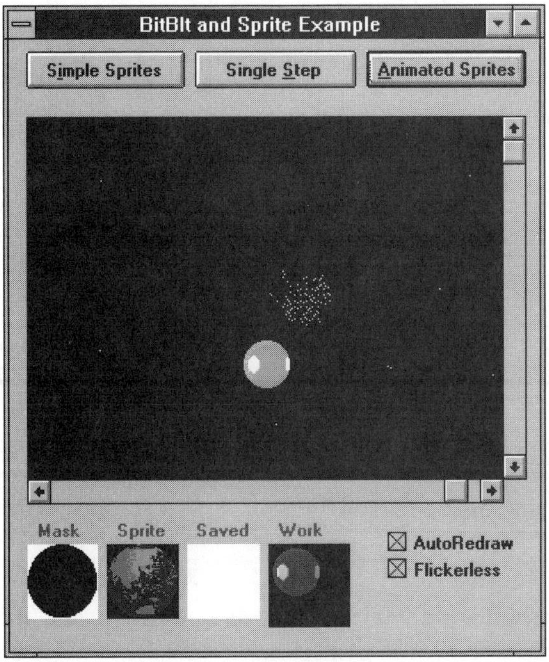

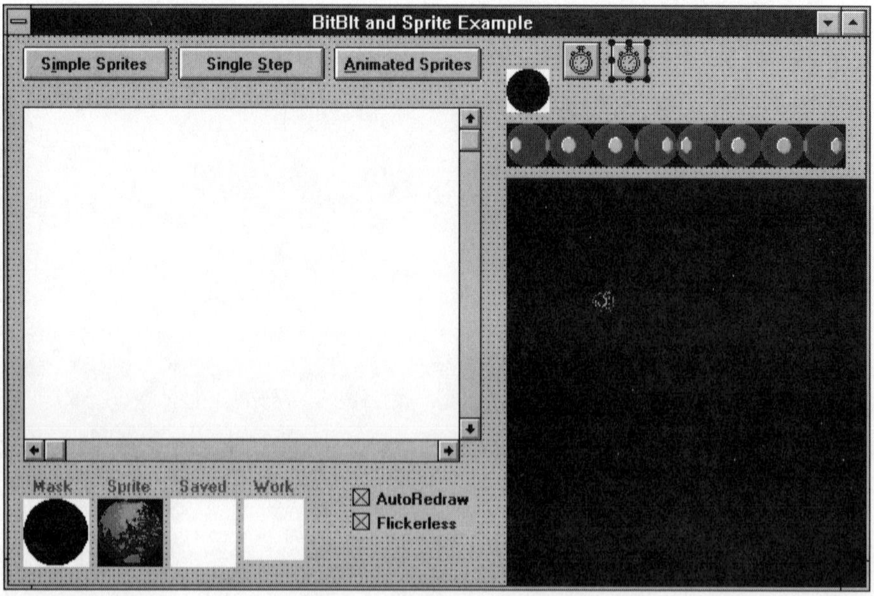

FIGURE 3-13

The bitmap demonstration program at design time

picture box is well over four times the size of the viewer picture box the user sees; you can only see a corner of it in the figure. At runtime, the program BitBlts a section of the hidden star field bitmap into the viewer picture box.

The scroll bars are used to determine what section of the star field bitmap to copy. You'll recall that the BitBlt function needs to know the X and Y coordinates of the upper-left corner in the source bitmap from which to start copying. The Value property of the horizontal scroller provides the X coordinate within the source bitmap from which to start the bitmap copy. Likewise, the Value property of the vertical scroller provides the Y coordinate.

To make sure that you don't copy beyond the right or bottom edges of the source bitmap, the Max property of each scroll bar is set to the width of the star field minus the width of the viewer picture box. That way, when the scroll bars are set to the far right and bottom, the viewer will display the lower-right corner of the starfield bitmap.

Steps

1. Create a new project called BITDEMO1.MAK. Then create a new form called BITDEMO1.FRM. Add the controls listed in Table 3-1 to the form. Use Figure 3-13 as a guide for the placement of the controls on the form.

TABLE 3-1
Objects and properties for BITDEMO1.FRM

Object	Property	Setting
Form	FormName	Form1
	BackColor	&H00C0C0C0&
	Caption	"BitBlt and Sprite Example"
Label	Name	lblStep
	Alignment	2 'Center
	BackStyle	0 'Transparent
Label	Name	Label1
	Alignment	2 'Center
	BackStyle	0 'Transparent
	Caption	"Mask"
	ForeColor	&H000000C0&
	Index	0
Label	Name	Label1
	Alignment	2 'Center
	BackStyle	0 'Transparent
	Caption	"Sprite"
	ForeColor	&H000000C0&
	Index	1
Label	Name	Label1
	Alignment	2 'Center
	BackStyle	0 'Transparent
	Caption	"Saved"
	ForeColor	&H000000C0&
	Index	2
Label	Name	Label1
	Alignment	2 'Center
	BackStyle	0 'Transparent
	Caption	"Work"
	ForeColor	&H000000C0&
	Index	3

continued on next page

continued from previous page

Object	Property	Setting
Timer	Name	Timer2
	Enabled	0 'False
	Interval	55
PictureBox	Name	picBackground
	BackColor	&H00FFFFFF&
	ScaleMode	3 'Pixel
PictureBox	Name	picMask
	AutoRedraw	-1 'True
	AutoSize	-1 'True
	BorderStyle	0 'None
	Picture	(set at design time in Properties window)
	ScaleMode	3 'Pixel
PictureBox	Name	PicImage
	AutoRedraw	-1 'True
	AutoSize	-1 'True
	BorderStyle	0 'None
	Picture	(set at design time in Properties window)
	ScaleMode	3 'Pixel
Timer	Name	Timer1
	Enabled	0 'False
	Interval	55
PictureBox	Name	picSave
	AutoSize	-1 'True
	BorderStyle	0 'None
	ScaleMode	3 'Pixel
CommandButton	Name	btnGo
	Caption	"&S&imple Sprites"
CommandButton	Name	btnStep
	Caption	"Single &Step"

Object	Property	Setting
PictureBox	Name	picBMP
	AutoRedraw	-1 'True
	AutoSize	-1 'True
	Picture	(set at design time in Properties window)
	ScaleMode	3 'Pixel
VScrollBar	Name	VScroll1
	LargeChange	12
HScrollBar	Name	HScroll1
	LargeChange	12
PictureBox	Name	picWork
	AutoSize	-1 'True
	BorderStyle	0 'None
	ScaleMode	3 'Pixel
CheckBox	Name	chkAutoRedraw
	BackColor	&H00C0C0C0&
	Caption	"AutoRedraw"
	Value	1 'Checked
CheckBox	Name	chkFlickerless
	BackColor	&H00C0C0C0&
	Caption	"Flickerless"
	Value	1 'Checked
PictureBox	Name	picEarthSprites
	AutoRedraw	-1 'True
	AutoSize	-1 'True
	BorderStyle	0 'None
	Picture	(set at design time in Properties window)
	ScaleMode	3 'Pixel
PictureBox	Name	picEarthMask
	AutoRedraw	-1 'True

continued on next page

continued from previous page

Object	Property	Setting
	AutoSize	-1 'True
	BorderStyle	0 'None
	Picture	(set at design time in Properties window)
	ScaleMode	3 'Pixel
CommandButton	Name	btnSprites
	Caption	" &Animated Sprites"

2. If you want to create your own sprites, you'll need to use a bitmap editor (such as Windows Paintbrush) to create sprite and mask images, then assign them to the picture box controls at design time. Likewise, you can create your own background bitmap and assign it to the picBMP bitmap at design time.
3. Next, add the code in Listing 3-1 to the BITDEMO form.

Listing 3-1 BITDEMO1.FRM

```
Option Explicit
'----------------------------------------------------
' BITDEMO1.FRM
' This program demonstrates some of the methods used
' to display bitmaps and sprites.
'----------------------------------------------------

' The number of pixels to offset the sprite
' each time it is moved.
Const INCREMENT = 3

' Constants for Raster Operations used by BitBlt function.
Const SRCAND = &H8800C6      ' dest = source AND dest
Const SRCCOPY = &HCC0020     ' dest = source
Const SRCPAINT = &HEE0086    ' dest = source OR dest

' The BitBlt Windows API call.
Declare Function BitBlt Lib "GDI" (ByVal hDestDC As Integer, ByVal X As Integer,
ByVal y As Integer, ByVal nWidth As Integer, ByVal nHeight As Integer, ByVal hSrcDC As
Integer, ByVal XSrc As Integer, ByVal YSrc As Integer, ByVal dwRop As Long) As Integer

' The x and y coordinates for the Sprite
```

```
Dim SpriteX As Integer
Dim SpriteY As Integer

' The x and y coordinates for the upper left corner
' of the large bitmap (picBMP).
Dim BackgroundX As Integer
Dim BackgroundY As Integer

' The width and height of the work area bitmap (picWork).
Dim WorkWidth As Integer
Dim WorkHeight As Integer

Sub AnimatedSpriteMove ()
'------------------------------------------------------
' Move the animated sprite to its next position.
'------------------------------------------------------
Dim rc As Integer
Static SpriteNum As Integer

    ' Calculate the next position for the sprite, and any
    ' necessary direction changes.
    GetNextPos picEarthMask.ScaleWidth, picEarthMask.ScaleHeight

    ' Copy a section of the large bitmap into the work area.
    rc = BitBlt(picWork.hDC, 0, 0, WorkWidth, WorkHeight, picBMP.hDC, (BackgroundX +
         SpriteX) - INCREMENT, (BackgroundY + SpriteY) - INCREMENT, SRCCOPY)

    ' Draw the sprite mask into the work area.
    rc = BitBlt(picWork.hDC, INCREMENT, INCREMENT, picEarthMask.ScaleWidth,
         picEarthMask.ScaleHeight, picEarthMask.hDC, 0, 0, SRCAND)

    ' The picEarthSprites bitmap contains 8 "frames".  Each frame
    ' is displayed in sequence to animate the object.
    rc = BitBlt(picWork.hDC, INCREMENT, INCREMENT, picEarthMask.ScaleWidth,
         picEarthMask.ScaleHeight, picEarthSprites.hDC, (SpriteNum \ 2) * 32, 0,
         SRCPAINT)

    ' Increment the Sprite Frame number.
    SpriteNum = (SpriteNum + 1) Mod 16

    ' Copy the work area onto the background.
    rc = BitBlt(picBackground.hDC, SpriteX - INCREMENT, SpriteY - INCREMENT,
         WorkWidth, WorkHeight, picWork.hDC, 0, 0, SRCCOPY)

    DoEvents
End Sub

Sub btnGo_Click ()
'------------------------------------------------------
' Start the simple sprite demonstration when this
' button is pushed.
'------------------------------------------------------
```

continued on next page

continued from previous page

```
Dim rc As Integer

    ' We're running.
    If Timer1.Enabled Then
     Timer1.Enabled = False
     ' Restore BG
     If chkFlickerless = 0 Then
        rc = BitBlt(picBackground.hDC, SpriteX, SpriteY, picSave.ScaleWidth,
            picSave.ScaleHeight, picSave.hDC, 0, 0, SRCCOPY)
     Else
        VScroll1_Change
     End If
    ' We're stopped.
    Else
     ' Save BG
     If chkFlickerless = 0 Then rc = BitBlt(picSave.hDC, 0, 0, picSave.ScaleWidth,
     picSave.ScaleHeight, picBackground.hDC, SpriteX, SpriteY, SRCCOPY)
     Timer1.Enabled = True
    End If

End Sub

Sub btnSprites_Click ()
'-----------------------------------------------------
' Start the animated sprite demonstration.
'-----------------------------------------------------

    ' We're running.
    If Timer2.Enabled Then
     Timer2.Enabled = False

     ' This makes sure the background is refreshed.
     VScroll1_Change
    ' We're stopped.
    Else
     Timer2.Enabled = True
    End If

End Sub

Sub btnStep_Click ()
'-----------------------------------------------------
' Run the next step of the Single Step demonstration
' when this button is pushed.
'-----------------------------------------------------
    SingleStep
End Sub

Sub chkAutoRedraw_Click ()
'-----------------------------------------------------
' Show the effects of the AutoRedraw property on
' the sprite work and save areas.
'-----------------------------------------------------
```

```
    picSave.AutoRedraw = (chkAutoRedraw = 1)
    If picSave.AutoRedraw Then picSave.Cls

    picWork.AutoRedraw = (chkAutoRedraw = 1)
    If picWork.AutoRedraw Then picWork.Cls

    picSave.Refresh
    picWork.Refresh
End Sub

Sub FlickerlessSpriteMove ()
'-------------------------------------------------------
' Moving a sprite without flicker requires the use
' of an off-screen work area into which we copy a
' section of the background and sprite.
'-------------------------------------------------------
Dim rc As Integer


    ' Calculate the next position for the sprite, and any
    ' necessary direction changes.
    GetNextPos picImage.ScaleWidth, picImage.ScaleHeight

    ' Copy a section of the large bitmap into the work area.
    rc = BitBlt(picWork.hDC, 0, 0, WorkWidth, WorkHeight, picBMP.hDC, (BackgroundX +
         SpriteX) - INCREMENT, (BackgroundY + SpriteY) - INCREMENT, SRCCOPY)

    ' Draw the mask and sprite bitmaps into the work area.
    rc = BitBlt(picWork.hDC, INCREMENT, INCREMENT, picMask.ScaleWidth,
         picMask.ScaleHeight, picMask.hDC, 0, 0, SRCAND)
    rc = BitBlt(picWork.hDC, INCREMENT, INCREMENT, picImage.ScaleWidth,
         picImage.ScaleHeight, picImage.hDC, 0, 0, SRCPAINT)

    ' Copy the work area onto the background.
    rc = BitBlt(picBackground.hDC, SpriteX - INCREMENT, SpriteY - INCREMENT,
         WorkWidth, WorkHeight, picWork.hDC, 0, 0, SRCCOPY)

    DoEvents
End Sub

Sub Form_Load ()
'-------------------------------------------------------
'
'-------------------------------------------------------
Dim rc As Integer

    Me.Show

    chkAutoRedraw.Value = 1

    ' Set the limits of the scroll bars.
    HScroll1.Max = picBMP.ScaleWidth - picBackground.ScaleWidth
    VScroll1.Max = picBMP.ScaleHeight - picBackground.ScaleHeight
```

continued on next page

continued from previous page

```
    ' Only enable the scrollers if picBMP is larger than
    ' the picBackground bitmap.
    If picBMP.ScaleWidth <= picBackground.ScaleWidth Then HScroll1.Enabled = False
    If picBMP.ScaleHeight <= picBackground.ScaleHeight Then VScroll1.Enabled = False

    ' Save this initial section of the background. It may be
    ' needed for the flickering sprite demo.
    rc = BitBlt(picBackground.hDC, 0, 0, picBackground.ScaleWidth,
         picBackground.ScaleHeight, picBMP.hDC, HScroll1, VScroll1, SRCCOPY)

    ' Set the dimensions of the work bitmap.
    WorkWidth = (picImage.Width / 15) + (INCREMENT * 2)
    WorkHeight = (picImage.Height / 15) + (INCREMENT * 2)
    picWork.Width = WorkWidth * 15
    picWork.Height = WorkHeight * 15

    Me.Refresh
End Sub

Sub GetNextPos (ByVal AWidth As Integer, ByVal AHeight As Integer)
'-----------------------------------------------------
' Calculate the next position for the sprite, and
' make any necessary direction changes.
'-----------------------------------------------------
Static xdir As Integer
Static ydir As Integer

    ' If this is the first time into the routine,
    ' then initialize the x and y direction indicators.
    If xdir = 0 Then
     xdir = 1
     ydir = 1
    End If

    ' Calculate the new position for the sprite.
    SpriteX = SpriteX + (INCREMENT * xdir)
    SpriteY = SpriteY + (INCREMENT * ydir)

    ' Change direction of the sprite if it reaches the edge
    ' of the background bitmap.
    If (SpriteX + AWidth) >= picBackground.ScaleWidth Then
     xdir = -1
    End If

    If SpriteX <= 0 Then
     xdir = 1
    End If

    If (SpriteY + AHeight) >= picBackground.ScaleHeight Then
     ydir = -1
    End If
```

```
    If SpriteY <= 0 Then
     ydir = 1
    End If
End Sub

Sub HScroll1_Change ()
'---------------------------------------------------------
' Move the background horizontally under scroller
' control.
'---------------------------------------------------------
Dim rc As Integer

    BackgroundX = HScroll1
    rc = BitBlt(picBackground.hDC, 0, 0, picBackground.ScaleWidth,
         picBackground.ScaleHeight, picBMP.hDC, BackgroundX, BackgroundY, SRCCOPY)
End Sub

Sub SingleStep ()
'---------------------------------------------------------
' Single step through the process of displaying a
' sprite.
'---------------------------------------------------------
Dim rc As Integer
Static cstep As Integer

    ' Perform the current step.
    Select Case cstep
     Case 0:
        lblStep = "1: Copy BG to Save Area"
        rc = BitBlt(picSave.hDC, 0, 0, picSave.ScaleWidth, picSave.ScaleHeight,
             picBackground.hDC, SpriteX, SpriteY, SRCCOPY)
        btnGo.Enabled = False
     Case 1:
        lblStep = "2: Bitwise AND Mask to BG"
        rc = BitBlt(picBackground.hDC, SpriteX, SpriteY, picMask.ScaleWidth,
             picMask.ScaleHeight, picMask.hDC, 0, 0, SRCAND)
     Case 2:
        lblStep = "3: Bitwise OR Sprite to BG"
        rc = BitBlt(picBackground.hDC, SpriteX, SpriteY, picImage.ScaleWidth,
             picImage.ScaleHeight, picImage.hDC, 0, 0, SRCPAINT)
     Case 3:
        lblStep = "4: Copy Save Area to BG"
        rc = BitBlt(picBackground.hDC, SpriteX, SpriteY, picSave.ScaleWidth,
             picSave.ScaleHeight, picSave.hDC, 0, 0, SRCCOPY)
        btnGo.Enabled = True
        cstep = -1
        GetNextPos picImage.ScaleWidth, picImage.ScaleHeight
    End Select

    ' Get ready for the next step.
    cstep = cstep + 1
```

continued on next page

continued from previous page

```
End Sub

Sub SpriteMove ()
'--------------------------------------------------------
' A simple method for displaying a sprite.
'--------------------------------------------------------
Dim rc As Integer

    ' Replace the background saved when sprite was
    ' last displayed.
    rc = BitBlt(picBackground.hDC, SpriteX, SpriteY, picSave.ScaleWidth,
        picSave.ScaleHeight, picSave.hDC, 0, 0, SRCCOPY)

    ' Calculate the next position for the sprite, and any
    ' necessary direction changes.
    GetNextPos picImage.ScaleWidth, picImage.ScaleHeight

    ' Save the area of the background where the sprite is
    ' about to be drawn.  This saved area will be used to
    ' "erase" the sprite before it is displayed at a new
    ' position.
    rc = BitBlt(picSave.hDC, 0, 0, picSave.ScaleWidth, picSave.ScaleHeight,
        picBackground.hDC, SpriteX, SpriteY, SRCCOPY)

    ' Draw the sprite mask directly onto the background.
    rc = BitBlt(picBackground.hDC, SpriteX, SpriteY, picMask.ScaleWidth,
        picMask.ScaleHeight, picMask.hDC, 0, 0, SRCAND)

    ' Draw the sprite over top of the mask.
    rc = BitBlt(picBackground.hDC, SpriteX, SpriteY, picImage.ScaleWidth,
        picImage.ScaleHeight, picImage.hDC, 0, 0, SRCPAINT)
    DoEvents
End Sub

Sub Timer1_Timer ()
'--------------------------------------------------------
' Depending on the value of the Flickerless check
' box, run one of the simple sprite move subroutines.
'--------------------------------------------------------

    If chkFlickerless = 1 Then
      FlickerlessSpriteMove
    Else
      SpriteMove
    End If
End Sub

Sub Timer2_Timer ()
'--------------------------------------------------------
' Move the animated sprite to its next position.
'--------------------------------------------------------
```

```
    AnimatedSpriteMove
End Sub

Sub VScroll1_Change ()
'--------------------------------------------------------
' Move the background vertically under scroller
' control.
'--------------------------------------------------------
Dim rc As Integer

    BackgroundY = VScroll1
    rc = BitBlt(picBackground.hDC, 0, 0, picBackground.ScaleWidth,
         picBackground.ScaleHeight, picBMP.hDC, BackgroundX, BackgroundY, SRCCOPY)
End Sub
```

4. Save the BITDEMO1.MAK project. You are now ready to run the program.

Problems and Pitfalls

When working with bitmaps, be aware of some of the trade-offs involved. First, large bitmaps eat up memory. The larger the bitmap and the larger the number of colors, the worse the bite.

You can reduce the number of bitmaps you store in memory by storing them on disk as .BMP files and loading them as needed. But this introduces another trade-off: disk access. Loading a bitmap from disk can be time consuming, so you'll need to plan the best times to load new bitmaps. For example, a good time to load a new background bitmap is when the player moves to a new game level. But the players wouldn't want constant pauses while they're in the middle of game play.

Also, although BitBlting is a fairly fast operation, you should avoid unnecessary BitBlts and BitBlt as small a region as possible. It takes longer to BitBlt larger regions. Faster computers and computers with faster video cards can BitBlt much faster, so it is a good idea to test your games out on both slower and faster machines. This way you can suggest to the user a minimal acceptable computer configuration for the game.

In the next chapter, we'll look at some techniques for letting more than one player take part in a game.

4

Multiple Players

4

Multiple Players

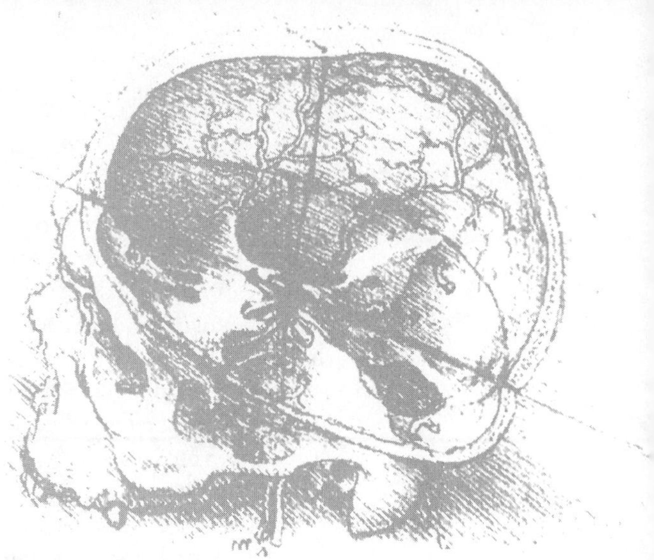

Most action-style games are multiple player games. The catch is, the other player is the computer. Although the computer can be a daunting opponent, sometimes it is much more satisfying to see an actual, living, breathing, person, someone the player cares about, beaten mercilessly on the electronic field of battle.

There are two basic techniques for handling a game with more than one player. Each player can take a separate turn, giving the active player complete control of the game. This alternative clearly won't work in cases where you want to match two players head-to-head as opponents. In that situation, you need to give each player his or her own set of controls, be it joystick, mouse, keyboard, or whatever.

We'll take a look at both techniques, starting with the problem of tracking separate players when they're taking alternate turns.

Handling Multiple Players Alternately

In those games where each player gets a separate turn, you need to devise a technique to "remember" a player's status between turns. What do I mean by game *status*? Well, if two players are exploring some dungeon in a role-playing game, the program might need to remember information about their locations in the dungeon, what items they are carrying, and so on. If two players are playing a Space Invaders-style arcade game, the program would need to remember how many aliens were remaining and at what positions.

Generally speaking, a player's game state or status is all the pertinent information the program must retain while the player is inactive. Although saving this information is sufficient, you'd also like to be able to save it in an organized fashion. Rather than save a player's state information as a hodge-podge of variables strewn throughout the program, it would be preferable to tuck all that information into a neat package.

Luckily, Visual Basic lets you do just that. You can create your own data types (called *user-defined types* in Visual Basic), which are collections of variables that are stored together with the same name. Here's an example of a Visual Basic user-defined type.

```
' structure that holds a single x-y coordinate
Type tPoint
    X As Integer
    Y As Integer
End Type

MyPoint as tPoint
```

In this example, you define a new user-defined type, tPoint, as consisting of two integers, X and Y. Once you've defined a type, you can declare a variable of that type, as you do with the variable MyPoint. You can now refer to X and Y as you would other variables, as long as you preface it with MyPoint.

```
MyPoint.X = 3
MyPoint.Y = 5
```

Using user-defined types, you can neatly package all the information about a player you need to track. Let's build a short example program that shows how.

In this example, we'll build a form that contains three icons and a text box. The user can drag the icons around the form using the mouse. By clicking on an icon, the user can add or remove a single-line border from the icon. The text box can contain any text the user cares to enter. The form will also contain a button that allows the user to toggle between Player 1 and Player 2. Each player can move the icons anywhere he or she wants, set any icon borders, and type any text into the text box. The program's job is to remember a player's icon positions, border styles, and text information. For example, if Player 1 is currently displayed, pressing the toggle button will display Player 2 with his or her associated icon positions, border styles, and text. Figure 4-1 shows what the form will look like.

To create this program, create a new project called STATE.MAK. First build the user-defined types you'll need for remembering each player's game state. One restriction with user-defined types in Visual Basic 3.0 and earlier is that they must be

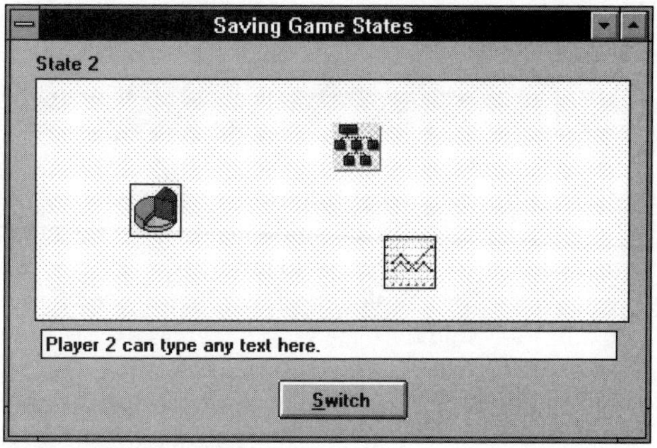

FIGURE 4-1

The Game State example program

declared in a .BAS module; they cannot be declared in a form. So create a new module called STATE.BAS, and add the code shown in Listing 4-1 to its Declarations section.

Listing 4-1 The STATE.BAS module

```
Option Explicit
'--------------------------------------------------
' STATE.BAS
'--------------------------------------------------

' Maximum number of objects we're tracking
Global Const MAX_OBJECTS = 3
' Actual number of objects we're tracking
Global Const NUM_OBJECTS = 3

' structure that holds a single x-y coordinate
Type tPoint
    X As Integer
    Y As Integer
End Type

' structure that holds information about a single game object.
Type tObject
    Pos As tPoint
    BorderStyle As Integer
End Type

' structure that holds information about a single player's
' game state.
Type tState
    Object(0 To MAX_OBJECTS)  As tObject
    TextData As String
End Type
```

This module actually defines three separate user-defined types, as well as two global constants. Notice that the second user-defined type contains a field Pos of type tPoint; tPoint is the first user-defined type. This illustrates that the fields of a user-defined type need not be a simple type such as a string or integer. And the third type, tState, contains an array of tObject, the second user-defined type!

Let's consider what these types will be used for. The example program needs to track three basic pieces of information: the position of each icon, each icon's border style, and the contents of the text box. The text box is easy, just store this in the TextData field of tState. The position and border style of each icon is a little trickier. Ideally, you'd like an arbitrary number of icons, or at least you'd like to make the number of icons easy to change within the program. You created an array of tObjects, each array element representing a separate icon. If you add an icon to the form, then you'll only need to increase the upper boundary of the Object array.

A tObject consists of two fields: an integer that indicates the associated icon's border style and a field that indicates the icon's position on the form. This field, Pos, is of type tPosition, which itself consists of two integers, X and Y. These fields hold the actual X-Y screen coordinates for an icon.

Now you have a data type, tState, that can hold all the information the program needs about each player's game state. There are many different ways you could have designed user-defined type. For example, you could have packed everything into a single type like this:

```
Type tBigUglyState
        BorderStyle0 As Integer
        X0 As Integer
        Y0 As Integer
        BorderStyle1 As Integer
        X1 As Integer
        Y1 As Integer
        BorderStyle2 As Integer
        X2 As Integer
        Y2 As Integer
        TextData As String
End Type
```

The problem with this user-defined type is that it can't treat each icon generically; the first icon is bound tightly to the fields X0, Y0, and BorderStyle0. By contrast, in the original tState data type, the field Object(i).X could refer to any of the icons, depending on the value of i. Careful planning in the design of data types can drastically reduce the amount of code you'll need to write later.

Now let's create our example program's form. Add a new form to the STATE.MAK project, and call it STATE.FRM. Add the objects and properties described in Table 4-1 to this new form.

TABLE 4-1
Objects and properties of the STATE.FRM form

Object	Property	Setting
Form	FormName	Form1
	BackColor	&H00C0C0C0&
	Caption	"Saving Game States"
TextBox	Name	txtStringData
	Text	"Enter some text here."
Label	Name	lblCurrentState
	BackStyle	0 'Transparent
	Caption	"Label1"
CommandButton	Name	btnSwitch
	Caption	"&Switch"
PictureBox	Name	picField
	BackColor	&H00E0FFFF&

Inside the picField PictureBox control, add the three Image controls described in Table 4-2. These Image controls should be contained inside the picField control. To do this, first select the picField control by clicking on it once. Its resizing handles should appear around its border. Now select an Image control from the Visual Basic Toolbox and drop it into the picField PictureBox. Repeat this process for each Image control. You'll know that the Image control is actually contained by the picField control if you cannot drag the Image control outside the borders of picField.

Programming Tip: Some controls, such as Frames and PictureBox's, can actually contain other controls. These controls are often even called *container controls*. When you move a container control, all the controls inside it move with it. A control placed within a container control can't be moved outside the container's borders.

TABLE 4-2

The Image controls placed inside the picField control

Object	Property	Setting
Image	Name	imgObject
	Index	0
	Picture	(set at design time in Properties window)
Image	Name	imgObject
	Index	1
	Picture	(set at design time in Properties window)
Image	Name	imgObject
	Index	2
	Picture	(set at design time in Properties window)

Notice that the three Image controls have the same Name property. Each Image is an element of a control array. As you'll see, creating a control array will simplify some programming chores later. Now you can assign an icon for each of the Image controls. Set each Image's Picture property, selecting an icon from your Visual Basic ICONS directory (it doesn't matter which icons you choose). The completed form should look like Figure 4-2.

FIGURE 4-2

STATE.FRM at design time

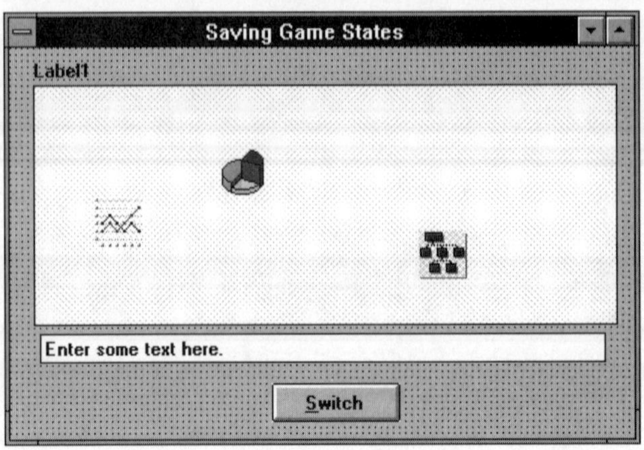

Now you're ready to start adding our program code. First you'll need to declare some variables to be used throughout the form. Add the code shown in Listing 4-2 to STATE.FRM's Declarations section.

Listing 4-2 STATE.FRM

```
Option Explicit
'-----------------------------------------------
' STATE.FRM
'-----------------------------------------------

' Number of states we're tracking in this program.
Const NUM_STATES = 2

' Boolean indicating if we're currently dragging
' an object.
Dim Dragging(0 To NUM_OBJECTS) As Integer

' Used while dragging an object.
Dim Ofs As tPoint

' Boolean that indicates if we are allowed to
' change the border style of an object.
Dim ChangeStyle As Integer

' An array of state structures. In practice, each
' element corresponds to a player.
Dim State(1 To NUM_STATES) As tState

' The state (or player, if you will) that is currently
' active.
Dim CurrentState As Integer
```

The first thing you declare is a constant, NUM_STATES, that determines the number of states (i.e., players) the program will be tracking. The Dragging and Ofs variables are used when you are dragging icon images around the form. ChangeStyle is used to help determine when to change an icon's border style.

The State array is where you'll be tracking the state of each player's icons and text string. This is an array of user-defined type tState. The variable CurrentState will track which player is currently displayed on the form.

Add a Load event to the form. Here's the code for it:

```
Sub Form_Load ()
'-----------------------------------------------
' Set the initial active state to Player 1.
'-----------------------------------------------

    CurrentState = 1
    lblCurrentState = "State " & Format$(CurrentState)
End Sub
```

All you do in the Load event is set the initial player to Player 1. You also reflect this in the Label control that is displayed in the upper-left corner of the form.

Next, create a subroutine that will save the current player's state in that player's data structure. What this really means is that the program will look at the position of the player's icons on the form, the icon's border styles, and the contents of the TextBox control, and copy that information back into the State structure. Add the subroutine SaveState, as shown in Listing 4-3.

Listing 4-3 SaveState routine

```
Sub SaveState (StateNum As Integer)
'-----------------------------------------------
' Save information about the current screen back
' into a state structure.
'-----------------------------------------------
Dim i As Integer

    For i = 0 To NUM_OBJECTS - 1
        State(StateNum).Object(i).Pos.X = imgObject(i).Left
        State(StateNum).Object(i).Pos.Y = imgObject(i).Top
        State(StateNum).Object(i).BorderStyle = imgObject(i).BorderStyle
    Next

    State(StateNum).TextData = txtStringData
End Sub
```

Notice that this routine simply assigns the values of each Image control's Left, Top, and BorderStyle property into a player's corresponding State fields. This is also an illustration of the usefulness of the imgObject control array and the Object array within the tState data type. By using arrays, you can save all three icon states within a single For loop. This may not seem like a big savings until you consider that you could add another 5 or 20 or 100 imgObject controls and not have to change a line of code in SaveState.

Now that you can save the state, you need a way of retrieving a previously saved state and displaying it on the form. This is essentially the reverse of the SaveState routine. Add this new routine, LoadState, to the form, as shown in Listing 4-4.

Listing 4-4 LoadState routine

```
Sub LoadState (StateNum As Integer)
'-----------------------------------------------
' Take information for a particular state (i.e., player)
' and display it on the screen, in effect activating
' the player.
'-----------------------------------------------
Dim i As Integer
```

```
    For i = 0 To NUM_OBJECTS - 1
        imgObject(i).Left = State(StateNum).Object(i).Pos.X
        imgObject(i).Top = State(StateNum).Object(i).Pos:Y
        imgObject(i).BorderStyle = State(StateNum).Object(i).BorderStyle
    Next

    txtStringData = State(StateNum).TextData

End Sub
```

Now you can add a way to toggle between the two players. Do this by pressing the Switch button, btnSwitch. Add the following Click event for this button.

```
Sub btnSwitch_Click ()
'--------------------------------------------------
' Switch between the two game states (Players 1 and 2).
'--------------------------------------------------

    If CurrentState = 1 Then
        SaveState 1
        LoadState 2
        CurrentState = 2
    Else
        SaveState 2
        LoadState 1
        CurrentState = 1
    End If
    lblCurrentState = "State " & Format$(CurrentState)
End Sub
```

In this event, simply look at the CurrentState variable to determine who the current player is. Then save the current player's state with a call to SaveState. Next, load the inactive player's state information back into the form with a call to LoadState. Then set the CurrentState variable to reflect the new active player.

Now you need to add some code to handle dragging the icons around the form. Do this with three imgObject mouse events, MouseDown, MouseMove, and MouseUp. You want to be able to move the mouse pointer over an icon, press and hold down the mouse button, then drag the mouse, moving the icon in the process. Doing this is a little tricky, but the technique is quite useful. First, add the following imgObject MouseDown event subroutine to the form.

```
Sub imgObject_MouseDown (Index As Integer, Button As Integer, Shift As
Integer, X As Single, Y As Single)
'--------------------------------------------------
' If the mouse is held down over an object, prepare
' to drag that object.
'--------------------------------------------------
```

continued on next page

continued from previous page

```
    Dragging(Index) = True
    Ofs.X = X
    Ofs.Y = Y
End Sub
```

Again in this routine, you see the benefit of creating icons as a control array. The event routine automatically receives an Index parameter, indicating which Image control it will be dragging. This means you can write a single set of event routines that will move any of the icons. Set the Dragging Boolean value to let you know that you are beginning to drag an icon. Also save the starting X-Y coordinates.

Next, add an imgObject MouseMove event. This event will handle moving the icon to a new location as the mouse moves.

```
Sub imgObject_MouseMove (Index As Integer, Button As Integer, Shift As
Integer, X As Single, Y As Single)
'-----------------------------------------------------
' Drag an object if the mouse is clicked and
' dragged over it.
'-----------------------------------------------------

    If Dragging(Index) Then
        imgObject(Index).Move imgObject(Index).Left + (X - Ofs.X),
        imgObject(Index).Top + (Y - Ofs.Y)
        ChangeStyle = False
    End If
End Sub
```

Here you move the object using the Move method. But you only move it if the Dragging Boolean is set to True. The MouseMove event is generated any time the mouse moves over an object, regardless of whether the mouse button has been pressed down. You don't want to move the icon any time the mouse just happens to pass over it, so check the Dragging variable to ensure that you've started a drag process.

Finally, you need to know when the drag process ends. This is when the user releases the mouse button. Add the following imgBlock MouseUp event to the form.

```
Sub imgObject_MouseUp (Index As Integer, Button As Integer, Shift As
Integer, X As Single, Y As Single)
'-----------------------------------------------------
' End the drag process.
'-----------------------------------------------------

    Dragging(Index) = False

End Sub
```

Here you simply set the Dragging Boolean flag back to False, indicating the end of the dragging process.

Now that you've seen how to handle two players separately, let's look at a technique to let two players take part in the action at the same time.

Handling Two Players at the Same Time

Probably the best method for handling two players simultaneously is to program your game to support two joysticks. The programming isn't that difficult; it's mainly a variation on the joystick/timer control method shown in Chapter 1. The only real difference is that you'll need a second Timer control to support the second joystick.

The problem, though, is that many people do not have a joystick. What do you do then? You might consider letting the two players share the keyboard. Perhaps you could let player 1 use the Q, A, and Z keys, located on the left side of the keyboard, while player 2 could use P, L and M on the right side. Such a set-up might work except for one thing: One player could monopolize the keyboard simply by holding a key down.

The way Visual Basic keyboard events are processed, if Player 1 presses and holds down key Q, Visual Basic will begin to trigger multiple KeyDown events for the Q key. If during this time Player 2 presses the P key, Visual Basic won't be able to "see" it until Player 1 releases the Q key. So you need another way to let both players have game input without unfairly hogging the game.

One way is to let one player control the game through the keyboard while the other controls it through the mouse. Depending on the type of game, this technique may be limiting, due to the limitations of the mouse. But as we'll see, you can implement a two-player game in this manner.

A Simple Western Shoot-Out Game

To illustrate this two-player technique, we'll create a simple "mini-game" where one player uses the keyboard while the other controls the mouse. The game is a simple shoot-out. Because this game is designed to illustrate this two-player technique, I've pared it down to a bare minimum. The game sprites are simply icons in Image controls, and the game action is pretty simple.

Each player will move his or her gunslinger up and down the playing field, as shown in Figure 4-3. Cacti move between the two players to provide cover and get in the way. Player 1, on the left, controls her gunslinger using the up arrow, down arrow, and space bar to move up, move down, and shoot the gun, respectively. Player 2 uses the right mouse button, left mouse button, and left mouse double-click to perform the same tasks.

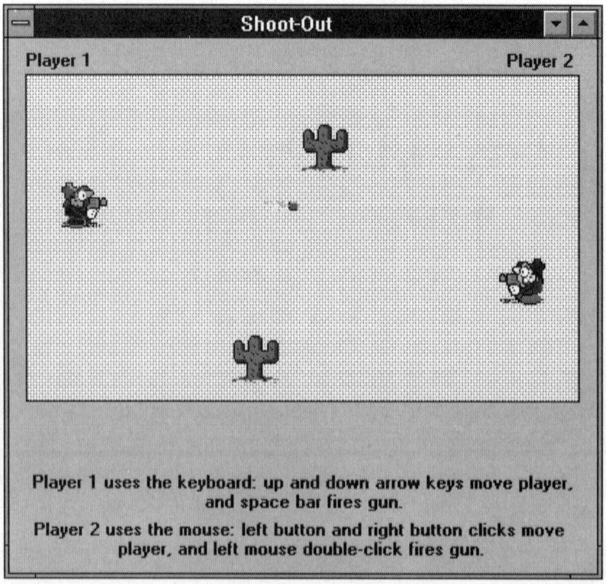

FIGURE 4-3
The Shoot-Out game at runtime

Building the Game

Start by building a new project called SHOOTOUT.MAK. To this project add a new .BAS module, SHOOTOUT.BAS. Add the code shown in Listing 4-5 to this module's Declarations section.

Listing 4-5 SHOOTOUT.BAS

```
Option Explicit
'-----------------------------------------------------------
' SHOOTOUT.BAS
'-----------------------------------------------------------

' Data type required by the IntersectRect function
Type tRect
    Left As Integer
    Top As Integer
    Right As Integer
    Bottom As Integer
End Type

' Windows API rectangle functions
Declare Function IntersectRect Lib "User" (ResultRect As tRect, Rect1 As tRect, Rect2
As tRect) As Integer
```

```
' Functions and constants used to play sounds.
Declare Function sndPlaySound Lib "MMSystem" (ByVal lpsound As String, ByVal flag As
Integer) As Integer

' Constant used with sndPlaySound function
Global Const SND_ASYNC = &H1
```

These declarations include a Windows API function and user-defined type to detect collisions, and another function to play wave audio files.

Next, build the game's form. Create a new form called SHOOTOUT.FRM. Add the objects and controls descibed in Table 4-3 to this form.

TABLE 4-3

Objects and properties of the SHOOTOUT.FRM form

Object	Property	Setting
Form	FormName	frmShootOut
	BackColor	&H00C0C0C0&
	Caption	"Shoot-Out"
	KeyPreview	-1 'True
Image	Name	imgRIP
	Picture	(set at design time in Properties window)
	Visible	0 'False
Label	Name	Label1
	BackStyle	0 'Transparent
	Caption	"Player 1"
Label	Name	Label2
	Alignment	1 'Right Justify
	BackStyle	0 'Transparent
	Caption	"Player 2"
Label	Name	Label3
	Alignment	2 'Center
	BackStyle	0 'Transparent
	Caption	"Player 1 uses the keyboard: up and down arrow keys move player, and spacebar fires gun."

continued on next page

continued from previous page

Object	Property	Setting
Label	Name	Label4
	Alignment	2 'Center
	BackStyle	0 'Transparent
	Caption	"Player 2 uses the mouse: left button and right button clicks move player, and left mouse double-click fires gun."
PictureBox	Name	picDesert
	BackColor	&H00C0FFC0&
Timer	Name	Timer1
CommandButton	Name	btnStart
	Caption	"&Start"
Timer	Name	tmrMouseCntl
	Interval	22

The picDesert PictureBox control described in Figure 4-3 will be used as the game's playing field. You'll now need to add the playing pieces. These will be Image controls placed inside the picDesert control. Add the controls described in Table 4-4 to the form, making sure that they are placed inside the picDesert control.

TABLE 4-4
Image controls placed inside the picDesert PictureBox control

Object	Property	Setting
Image	Name	imgPlayer
	Index	0
	Picture	(set at design time in Properties window)
Image	Name	imgPlayer
	Index	1
	Picture	(set at design time in Properties window)

Object	Property	Setting
Image	Name	imgCactus
	Index	0
	Picture	(set at design time in Properties window)
Image	Name	imgCactus
	Index	1
	Picture	(set at design time in Properties window)
Image	Name	imgLBullet
	Index	0
	Picture	(set at design time in Properties window)
	Visible	0 'False
Image	Name	imgRBullet
	Index	0
	Picture	(set at design time in Properties window)
	Visible	0 'False

The finished form should look similar to Figure 4-4. You can design your own icons using an icon-editing tool such as IconWorks, the sample program that comes with Visual Basic 3.0.

Now you can start adding the code for the game itself. First, add a Load event to the form as shown in Listing 4-6. This event will set up the main game timer's Interval property and will create five more bullet images for each player. These bullets are simply Image control arrays and are initially invisible.

Listing 4-6 The Shoot-Out Load event

```
Sub Form_Load ()
'-----------------------------------------------------------
' Set the main timer's interval and make sure it's disabled.
' Load 5 more bullets for each player from the bullet images
' created at design time.
'-----------------------------------------------------------
```

continued on next page

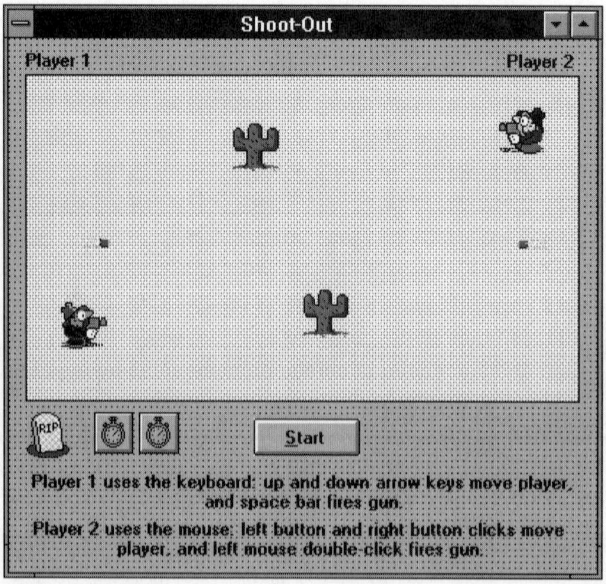

FIGURE 4-4 *The Shoot-Out game at design time*

continued from previous page

```
Dim i As Integer

    Timer1.Interval = 22
    Timer1.Enabled = False
    MouseButtonDown = NO_BUTTON

    For i = 1 To NUM_BULLETS - 1
        Load imgLBullet(i)
        Load imgRBullet(i)
    Next
End Sub
```

Next, let's add a simple subroutine to detect collisions. When a player fires his or her gun, one of the bullet images will be made visible and will move toward the opposing player. The program needs to detect collisions with either the player or a cactus. The Collided function takes two Image controls as parameters and returns True if they have collided. It does this by calling the IntersectRect Windows API call after loading each Image's rectangle coordinates into a tRect data structure as shown in Listing 4-7.

Listing 4-7 Collided function

```
Function Collided (imgA As Image, imgB As Image) As Integer
'-------------------------------------------------
' Check if the two Images intersect, using the
' IntersectRect API call.
'-------------------------------------------------
```

```
Dim A As tRect
Dim B As tRect
Dim ResultRect As tRect

    ' Copy information into tRect structure
    A.Left = imgA.Left
    A.Top = imgA.Top
    B.Left = imgB.Left
    B.Top = imgB.Top

    ' Calculate the right and bottoms of rectangles needed by the API call.
    A.Right = A.Left + imgA.Width - 1
    A.Bottom = A.Top + imgA.Height - 1

    B.Right = B.Left + imgB.Width - 1
    B.Bottom = B.Top + imgB.Height - 1

    ' IntersectRect will only return 0 (false) if the
    ' two rectangles do NOT intersect.
    Collided = IntersectRect(ResultRect, A, B)
End Function
```

Next, add the code that starts the game. The btnStart button gets everything rolling by enabling the main game timer, Timer1, in btnStart's Click event.

```
Sub btnStart_Click ()
'----------------------------------------------------------
' Start the game by enabling the main timer and hiding
' the start button.
'----------------------------------------------------------

    Timer1.Enabled = True
    btnStart.Visible = False
End Sub
```

Player 1 controls her gunslinger using the keyboard. To handle her actions, build a form-level KeyDown event that is triggered for each keystroke. You're only interested in three possible keys: up arrow, down arrow, and space bar. Handle these within the main Select-Case statement. The player's up and down movement is handled directly, inside the KeyDown event (shown in Listing 4-8), by simply moving the player's icon. Firing the gun (via the space bar) is handled by setting a Boolean, GunFired, which is then processed in the game's main Timer event.

Listing 4-8 The KeyDown event for Shoot-Out

```
Sub Form_KeyDown (KeyCode As Integer, Shift As Integer)
'----------------------------------------------------------
' This event handles Player 1's game action via the
' keyboard.
'----------------------------------------------------------
Dim rc As Integer
Static InKeyDown As Integer
```

continued on next page

continued from previous page

```
    If Not Timer1.Enabled Then Exit Sub

    If InKeyDown Then Exit Sub
    InKeyDown = True

    ' Don't hog the cycles...
    DoEvents

    Select Case KeyCode
        Case KEY_UP
            imgPlayer(0).Top = imgPlayer(0).Top - PlayerIncrement
            If imgPlayer(0).Top < 0 Then imgPlayer(0).Top = 0
        Case KEY_SPACE
            GunFired(0) = True
            rc = sndPlaySound(App.Path & "\BANG.WAV", SND_ASYNC)
        Case KEY_DOWN
            imgPlayer(0).Top = imgPlayer(0).Top + PlayerIncrement
            If imgPlayer(0).Top > (picDesert.ScaleHeight - imgPlayer(0).Height) Then
                imgPlayer(0).Top = picDesert.ScaleHeight - imgPlayer(0).Height
            End If
    End Select

    InKeyDown = False
End Sub
```

Now you need to handle Player 2's game action. Player 2 will use the mouse, which presents an interesting problem. When you press and hold down a key on the keyboard, multiple KeyDown events are generated. So, for example, when Player 1 wants to move down, she merely holds down the down arrow key and multiple KeyDown events are automatically generated, allowing her to move smoothly down the screen. Unfortunately, the MouseDown event doesn't work the same way. When you press and hold down a mouse button, one, and only one, MouseDown event is generated. If you wanted to move the player using only the MouseDown event, then the player would have to press the mouse button repeatedly. This is hardly a desirable requirement.

Luckily, you can emulate behavior similar to the keyboard's automatic repetition using a Timer control in conjuction with the MouseDown and MouseUp events. Add the event routines shown in Listing 4-9 to the program.

Listing 4-9 MouseDown and MouseUp Events

```
Sub Form_MouseDown (Button As Integer, Shift As Integer, X As Single, Y As Single)
'-----------------------------------------------------------
' Set the module-level MouseButtonDown variable, so that
' the Mouse Control timer knows a button was pushed.
'-----------------------------------------------------------

    MouseButtonDown = Button
End Sub
```

```
Sub Form_MouseUp (Button As Integer, Shift As Integer, X As Single, Y As Single)
'------------------------------------------------------------
' Let the Mouse Control timer know the button has been
' released.
'------------------------------------------------------------

    MouseButtonDown = NO_BUTTON
End Sub

Sub tmrMouseCntl_Timer ()
'------------------------------------------------------------
' Handle Player 2's movement (up and down).
'------------------------------------------------------------

    If Not Timer1.Enabled Then Exit Sub

    Select Case MouseButtonDown
        Case RBUTTON
            imgPlayer(1).Top = imgPlayer(1).Top - PlayerIncrement
            If imgPlayer(1).Top < 0 Then imgPlayer(1).Top = 0
        Case LBUTTON
            imgPlayer(1).Top = imgPlayer(1).Top + PlayerIncrement
            If imgPlayer(1).Top > (picDesert.ScaleHeight - imgPlayer(1).Height) Then
                imgPlayer(1).Top = picDesert.ScaleHeight - imgPlayer(1).Height
            End If
    End Select

End Sub
```

The MouseDown and MouseUp events set a global variable that indicates which mouse button (if any) was pressed. The tmrMouseCntl Timer event handles the actual evaluation of the buttons, using a Select-Case statement similar to the one used in the keyboard handler.

How does this work? Say Player 2 wants to move his gunslinger down by holding down the left mouse button. He holds the left mouse button down, generating a single MouseDown event. In this event, the MouseButtonDown variable is set to the value LBUTTON. A few milliseconds later, the tmrMouseCntl Timer event is triggered, as it is every few milliseconds. Because the MouseButtonDown variable is set to LBUTTON, the appropriate section of the Timer event's Select-Case statement is executed, moving the player's icon down. The Timer event is called again a few milliseconds later, again moving the icon down. Eventually the player releases the mouse button, generating a MouseUp event that sets MouseButtonDown to the value NO_BUTTON. A few milliseconds later, when the Timer event is triggered, the icon will not move, as there is no section in the Select-Case statement for the value NO_BUTTON.

You may have noticed that you didn't handle firing the gun from within the tmrMouseCntl Timer event. This can be handled directly via a form-level double-click event, as shown below.

```
Sub Form_DblClick ()
'-----------------------------------------------------------
' Double-clicking the mouse fires Player 1's gun.
'-----------------------------------------------------------
Dim rc As Integer

    If Not Timer1.Enabled Then Exit Sub

    GunFired(1) = True
    rc = sndPlaySound(App.Path & "\BANG.WAV", SND_ASYNC)
End Sub
```

Again, the gunfire is not handled directly, only the Boolean GunFired variable is set. The actual gunfire motion, as well as other game processing such as the movement of the cacti and collision detection, is handled in the main Timer event, shown in Listing 4-10.

Listing 4-10 The Shoot-Out Main Timer event

```
Sub Timer1_Timer ()
'-----------------------------------------------------------
' The main game timer.
'-----------------------------------------------------------
Const CactusIncrement = 30
Const BulletIncrement = 300
Const NumCacti = 2

Dim i As Integer
Dim rc As Integer

    ' Move the roving cacti.
    For i = 0 To NumCacti - 1
        imgCactus(i).Top = imgCactus(i).Top - CactusIncrement
        If imgCactus(i).Top < -imgCactus(i).Height Then
            imgCactus(i).Top = picDesert.Height
        End If
    Next

    ' Did player 1 fire a bullet?
    If GunFired(0) Then
        GunFired(0) = False

        ' Find a spare (invisible) bullet.
        For i = 0 To NUM_BULLETS - 1
            If Not imgLBullet(i).Visible Then
                imgLBullet(i).Top = imgPlayer(0).Top
                imgLBullet(i).Left = imgPlayer(0).Left + (imgPlayer(0).Width / 2)
                imgLBullet(i).Visible = True
                Exit For
            End If
        Next
```

```
    End If
    ' Did player 2 fire a bullet?
    If GunFired(1) Then
        GunFired(1) = False

        ' Find a spare (invisible) bullet.
        For i = 0 To NUM_BULLETS - 1
            If Not imgRBullet(i).Visible Then
                imgRBullet(i).Top = imgPlayer(1).Top
                imgRBullet(i).Left = imgPlayer(1).Left - (imgPlayer(1).Width / 2)
                imgRBullet(i).Visible = True
                Exit For
            End If
        Next
    End If

    ' Move Visible Bullets
    For i = 0 To NUM_BULLETS - 1
        ' Move player 0's bullets.
        If imgLBullet(i).Visible Then
            imgLBullet(i).Left = imgLBullet(i).Left + BulletIncrement
            If Collided(imgLBullet(i), imgCactus(0)) Then
                imgLBullet(i).Visible = False
            ElseIf Collided(imgLBullet(i), imgCactus(1)) Then
                imgLBullet(i).Visible = False
            ElseIf imgLBullet(i).Left > picDesert.ScaleWidth Then
                imgLBullet(i).Visible = False
            ElseIf Collided(imgLBullet(i), imgPlayer(1)) Then
                imgLBullet(i).Visible = False
                imgPlayer(1).Picture = imgRIP.Picture
                Timer1.Enabled = False
                rc = sndPlaySound(App.Path & "\OH!!.WAV", SND_ASYNC)
            End If
        End If
        ' Move player 1's bullets.
        If imgRBullet(i).Visible Then
            imgRBullet(i).Left = imgRBullet(i).Left - BulletIncrement
            If Collided(imgRBullet(i), imgCactus(0)) Then
                imgRBullet(i).Visible = False
            ElseIf Collided(imgRBullet(i), imgCactus(1)) Then
                imgRBullet(i).Visible = False
            ElseIf imgRBullet(i).Left < -imgRBullet(i).Width Then
                imgRBullet(i).Visible = False
            ElseIf Collided(imgRBullet(i), imgPlayer(0)) Then
                imgRBullet(i).Visible = False
                imgPlayer(0).Picture = imgRIP.Picture
                Timer1.Enabled = False
                rc = sndPlaySound(App.Path & "\OH!!.WAV", SND_ASYNC)
            End If
        End If
    Next
End Sub
```

Now you are ready to save the project and run the game. You'll see that both players can move and shoot simultaneously. This provides a workable solution for games that can't practically provide support for two joysticks.

In the next chapter, we'll take an in-depth look at joysticks and keyboards and mice. Each of these input devices has its own strengths and drawbacks. Proper handling of these devices is crucial to creating smooth game play.

5

Input Devices

5

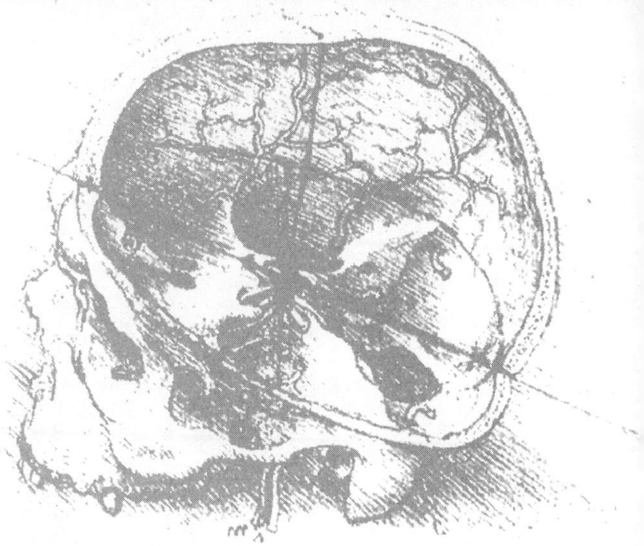

Input Devices

One of the most important aspects of game design is how the player interacts with the game. In the Microsoft Windows version of Tetris (Figure 5-1), the player rotates and moves collections of blocks as they descend one by one into a well. The player can use the left and right arrow keys of the keyboard to move the falling blocks in those directions. The up arrow key is used to rotate the falling block, and the down arrow key is used to push the block quickly to the bottom of the well. This interaction is very simple: Four keys are all that are required to master the game, and the keys that were chosen are all fairly intuitive. Beyond that, the keys are also geographically close on the keyboard. By contrast, imagine if the game designer had decided to use the L, R, D, and S, keys to move left, right, and down, and to spin the block—the resulting game would be more difficult and more aggravating for the player. These keys are widely spread over the keyboard, increasing the player's chance of hitting the wrong key.

In Windows Solitaire (Figure 5-2), you can move the playing cards by placing the mouse pointer over a card, pressing and holding down the left mouse button, and then dragging the card to its destination. Easy, right? But what many people don't realize is that Solitaire can be played without a mouse. Using the TAB, arrow, and ENTER keys, it is possible to perform all the moves needed to play the game. Is it as quick and intuitive as using the mouse? No, but the game designers did provide the player with that alternative.

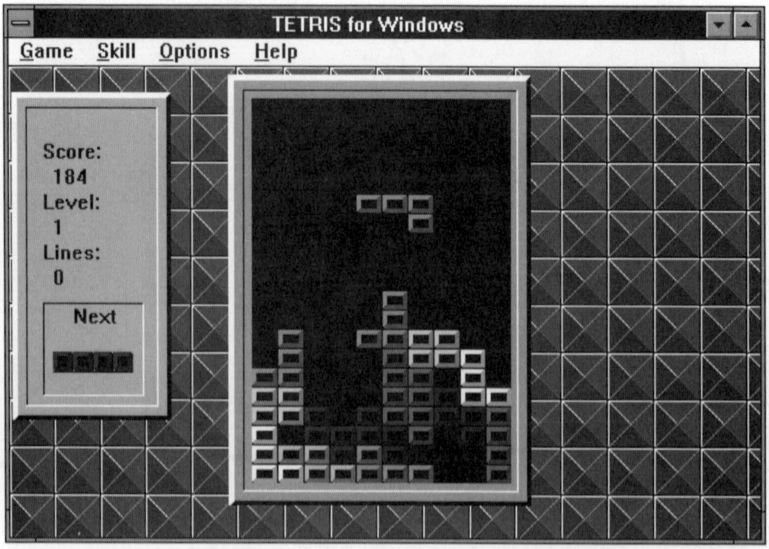

FIGURE 5-1

Microsoft's Tetris for Windows

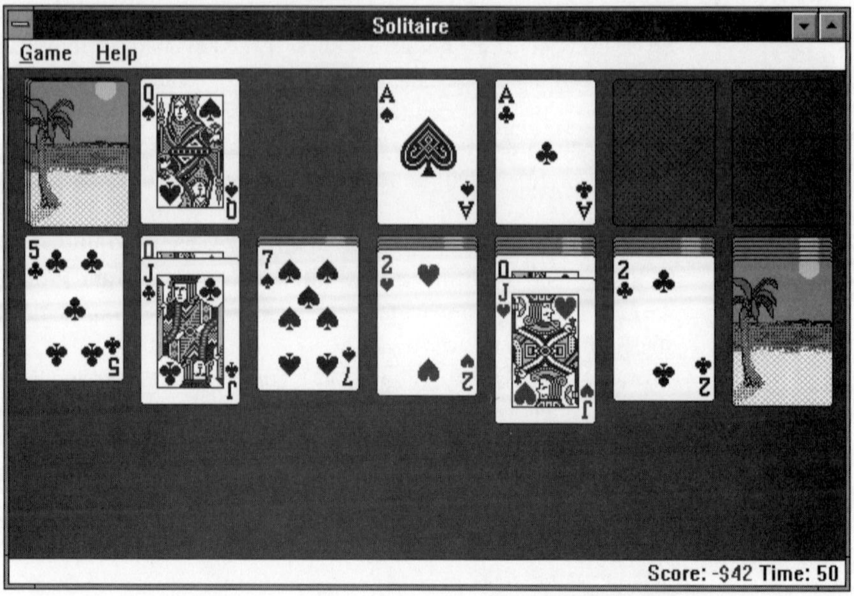

FIGURE 5-2

Microsoft's Solitaire can be played using only the keyboard

Choosing a Device

Your choice of which input devices to support should be based on many factors that may seem conflicting. How the game is played will often dictate what input device—keyboard, mouse, or joystick—is supported. The Microsoft Windows version of Tetris only supports the keyboard. But when you think about it, how could Tetris be played with a mouse? You could use the left and right mouse buttons to move left and right, but then how would you handle rotation and descent?

Each of the three input devices has its own strengths. The keyboard is good for discrete, one-time commands, such as "move one block left" in Tetris. The mouse is better for continuous motion and pinpointing a location on the screen. You pinpoint a playing card and drag it continuously to a new location in Solitaire. Unlike the mouse, for which Windows automatically provides an on-screen mouse pointer, the joystick does not automatically display anything on the screen. Even so, as I'll show later, it can be used as a pointing device that is similar to a mouse.

The dynamics of the joystick are different from the mouse in an important but somewhat subtle way. The joystick is *self-centering*. The joystick returns X and Y coordinates that you can use to move game objects. When the joystick is moved left, the returned X value gets smaller. Move the joystick right, and the X value gets larger. When the user releases the joystick, it returns to its center position, and the X value returns to an "at rest" number that should be about half-way between the minimum and maximum ranges of X. By comparison, a mouse can return X and Y values as it moves, but when the user releases the mouse, these values do not change.

This can make a difference in the way a game is played. If you're building a flight simulator game where you want the user to be able to bank the airplane to the left or right as the X value is changed, then the ability for X to self-center is very important. With a joystick, moving the stick left would bank the plane to the left, and releasing the joystick would cause the plane to fly straight again. This action is difficult to mimic with a mouse. Sure, you can move the mouse to the left, but how far to the left? And how would you straighten the plane out again? Move to the right?

This points to another difference in the dynamics of mice and joysticks. Joysticks have a limited range (left, right, up, and down) and they provide immediate tactile feedback when those limits have been reached. The players know exactly when they've moved the joystick to the far left because it stops. They can't move it any further. But the range of the mouse is limited to the size of the player's desk top and the length of the mouse's cord. The only feedback the player gets about the limits of the mouse is visual feedback: the position of the mouse pointer on the screen.

The different strengths of each of these devices must be weighed when designing your game. You may want to support all three devices, or you may decide that only one is right for your game. Choosing the right one, and then designing the player's interaction with it wisely, will in large part determine the success of your game.

Keyboard Input

The keyboard is the lowest common denominator input device for Windows programmers. It's a good bet that, except in very unusual circumstances, your user will have access to a keyboard. Visual Basic has good built-in support for the keyboard in the form of Key events. From a game designer's perspective, there is one obstacle, key repeat rate, that requires some help from the Windows API to overcome, but I'll start by looking at what Visual Basic provides.

Key Events in Visual Basic

The Visual Basic form object supports three Key events: subroutines that are triggered automatically when the user presses or releases a key. The first is KeyPress, which is fired whenever the user presses and releases a key. This event has one fatal problem for game designers: It doesn't get fired if the key is an extended key, such as the arrow and function keys.

A better choice for game control is often the KeyDown event, which can receive the extended characters. This event is actually fired before the KeyPress event. The final event in this trio is KeyUp, which is fired, as you might have guessed, when the key is released.

Pressing a key and quickly releasing it fires the three events in this order:

KeyDown

KeyPress

KeyUp

If the key is an extended key, such as a left arrow, only the KeyDown and KeyUp events are fired.

If a key is pressed and held down, the KeyDown and KeyPress events are fired repeatedly. This is controlled by the *key repeat rate,* which I'll cover in more depth shortly. Pressing the M key for a few seconds and then releasing it results in a sequence of Key events that look like this:

KeyDown

KeyPress

KeyDown

KeyPress

....

KeyDown

KeyPress

KeyUp

FIGURE 5-3
The simple keyboard example form at design time

Notice that the KeyUp event is called only once, when the key is finally released.

Let's look at a simple example that shows how you might move an object, in this case an icon, around a form using only the arrow keys. Create a new project with a single form, called Form1. On that form place a standard Image control. It doesn't matter where. Now set the Image's Picture property to an icon from the Visual Basic ICONS directory. Your form should look something like the one shown in Figure 5-3.

Next, add the following code to the Declarations section of Form1.

```
Option Explicit

' Keycodes used by the KeyDown Event.
Const KEY_LEFT = &H25
Const KEY_UP = &H26
Const KEY_RIGHT = &H27
Const KEY_DOWN = &H28

Dim IncrementX As Integer
Dim IncrementY As Integer
```

The constants will be used in the form's KeyDown event to determine when one of the arrow keys has been pressed. IncrementX and IncrementY determine how far the icon is moved on each keystroke.

> **Programming Tip: Many commonly used constants (including the four KEY_ constants above) are included with Visual Basic in a file called CONSTANT.TXT. You'll find it in the Visual Basic directory.**

Next, add the following Load event to Form1.

```
Sub Form_Load ()
    ' We want to create the form to see any keystrokes first.
    Form1.KeyPreview = True

    ' This is how much we'll move the image each time.
    IncrementX = Screen.TwipsPerPixelX
    IncrementY = Screen.TwipsPerPixelY
End Sub
```

This routine will be called when the form is first loaded. Setting the form's KeyPreview property to True ensures that any keystrokes are received by the form first, and then by any controls on the form. In this example, which only has one Image control, this distinction is not very important, but you'll see in a later example why this is often necessary.

Also in the Load event, you set the IncrementX and IncrementY values to 1 pixel each. By default, a Visual Basic form is measured in twips, and these are usually smaller than pixels. For example, using a standard VGA driver, 1 pixel is equal to 15 twips. The handy Screen properties, TwipsPerPixelX and TwipsPerPixelY, provide an easy way to set up desired increments.

Finally, add the following KeyDown event routine to the form.

```
Sub Form_KeyDown (KeyCode As Integer, Shift As Integer)

    Select Case KeyCode
        Case KEY_LEFT:
            If Image1.Left > 0 Then Image1.Left = Image1.Left - IncrementX
        Case KEY_RIGHT:
            If Image1.Left < (Form1.ScaleWidth - Image1.Width) Then
                Image1.Left = Image1.Left + IncrementX
            End If
        Case KEY_UP:
            If Image1.Top > 0 Then Image1.Top = Image1.Top - IncrementY
        Case KEY_DOWN:
            If Image1.Top < (Form1.ScaleHeight - Image1.Height) Then
                Image1.Top = Image1.Top + IncrementY
            End If
    End Select
End Sub
```

This routine is fired whenever the key is pressed down, and is called repeatedly if that key is held down. It ignores all the keys except the four arrow keys. If the KeyDown routine receives one of these through its KeyCode parameter, then the icon moves 1 pixel in the direction of the arrow. The program checks before the move to ensure that the icon hasn't reached a screen edge.

Save the project, then run this program. The screen should look similar to Figure 5-4. Now, use the arrow keys to move the icon around the screen. Several things are worth noting here. First, press and hold down an arrow key. The icon will move a little (1 pixel, actually), then pause for a moment, then begin to move smoothly in the direction of the arrow. That slight delay between the time the key is pressed and when the icon begins to move continuously is called the *keyboard delay rate*, and I'll examine it in a moment. Now press and hold down both the left and down arrows at the same time. Notice that the icon moves either down or left, but does not move diagonally, as you might expect. If you need to move smoothly on a diagonal, you are better off defining a separate key for that task. It's the nature of the Windows key-

FIGURE 5-4

The simple keyboard example at runtime

board driver to see only one key at a time when keys are pressed simultaneously in this manner.

Key Repeat and Delay Rates

The Windows Control Panel application has an applet that lets the user set the keyboard's behavior (see Figure 5-5). In particular, the user can set the keyboard's delay and repeat rates. The *delay rate* is the time it takes for Windows to begin repeating keys after the user presses and holds down a key.

The *repeat rate* determines how fast the key events are generated once a key is pressed and held down. Though this is great for the Windows user, it presents a problem for the game programmer. Ideally, you would like very little delay and a very fast repeat rate, because this makes game motion appear more fluid. Slow repeat rates mean that KeyDown events are generated less frequently; this can make game motion appear jerky.

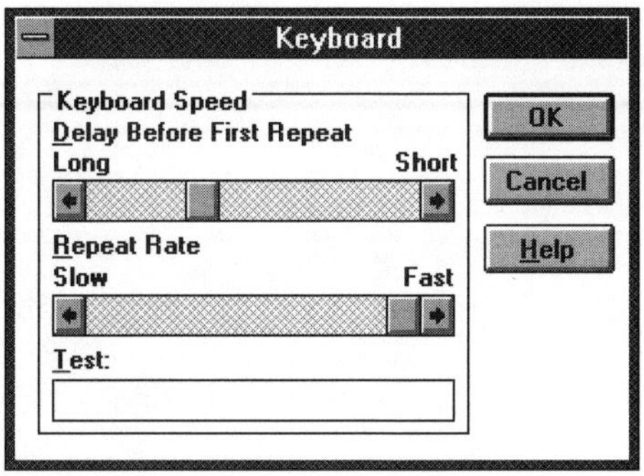

FIGURE 5-5

The Windows Control Panel keyboard applet

The good news is that the Windows API provides a way for you to change both the delay and the repeat rates at runtime. The SystemParametersInfo function lets you retrieve and set a wide range of Windows parameters, from determining whether icon titles wrap to setting the Windows desktop wallpaper bitmap file. Here you're interested in SystemParametersInfo's ability to retrieve and set the keyboard's repeat and delay rates.

As with any Windows API call, you must first declare it in the Declarations section of a form, module, or class file, as shown here:

```
Declare Function SystemParametersInfo _
        Lib "User" (ByVal uAction As Integer, _
        ByVal uParam As Integer, lpvParam As Any, _
        ByVal fuWinIni As Integer) As Integer
```

The first parameter, uAction, is a constant that tells the function what kind of information to retrieve or set. In this case, you're interested in only these four constants:

```
Const SPI_GETKEYBOARDDELAY = 22
Const SPI_GETKEYBOARDSPEED = 10
Const SPI_SETKEYBOARDDELAY = 23  ' Range 3 (long delay) to 0 (short delay).
Const SPI_SETKEYBOARDSPEED = 11  ' Range 0 (slow) to 31 (fast).
```

Their names are quite descriptive of their purposes. The first two constants retrieve the current system settings for keyboard delay and repeat rate, while the last two constants change those settings to new values.

The uParam parameter is used when setting a new value, and the lpvParam parameter is used when retrieving an existing system value. The last parameter, fuWinIni, determines if a changed setting is written to the WIN.INI file.

To see what effect these settings can have on the responsiveness of a keyboard, let's build another short example program.

The first step is to create a new Visual Basic project and name it KEYBOARD.MAK. This project will have one form, called Form1. Add the controls shown in Table 5-1, so that the form looks similar to the one shown in Figure 5-6.

TABLE 5-1

Objects and properties for Form1

Object	Property	Setting
Label	Name	Label1
	Alignment	2 'Center
	BackStyle	0 'Transparent
	Caption	"Keyboard Delay"
Label	Name	Label2
	Alignment	2 'Center

Object	Property	Setting
	BackStyle	0 'Transparent
	Caption	"Keyboard Speed"
Label	Name	lblSpeed
	Alignment	2 'Center
	BackStyle	0 'Transparent
	ForeColor	&H00FF0000&
Label	Name	lblDelay
	Alignment	2 'Center
	BackStyle	0 'Transparent
	ForeColor	&H00FF0000&
Label	Name	Label3
	BackStyle	0 'Transparent
	Caption	"slower"
Label	Name	Label4
	BackStyle	0 'Transparent
	Caption	"shorter"
Label	Name	Label5
	Alignment	1 'Right Justify
	BackStyle	0 'Transparent
	Caption	"faster"
Label	Name	Label6
	Alignment	1 'Right Justify
	BackStyle	0 'Transparent
	Caption	"longer"
Label	Name	lblStats
	Alignment	2 'Center
	BackStyle	0 'Transparent
	Caption	"0 frames per second"
	ForeColor	&H000000FF&

continued on next page

continued from previous page

Object	Property	Setting
Label	Name	Label7
	Alignment	2 'Center
	BackStyle	0 'Transparent
	Caption	"Press and hold down the left or right arrow key. Note the frame rate. Change the Keyboard speed and repeat the process."
	FontBold	0 'False
	ForeColor	&H00FF0000&
HScrollBar	Name	hscrDelay
HScrollBar	Name	hscrSpeed
PictureBox	Name	Picture1
	BackColor	&H0000C000&
Form	FormName	Form1
	BackColor	&H00C0C0C0&
	Caption	"Keyboard Example"
	KeyPreview	-1 'True

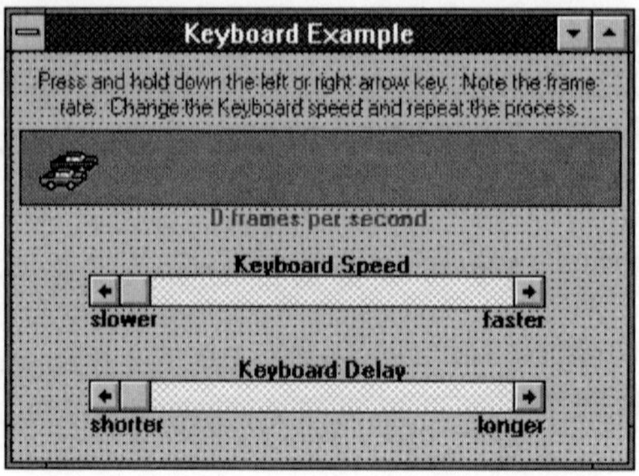

FIGURE 5-6

The keyboard repeat and delay rate example at design time

Now add the Image control described in Table 5-2. This control should be placed inside the Picture1 PictureBox control. You can assign the Picture property of imgIcon to CARS.ICO, an icon that can be found in your Visual Basic ICONS\INDUSTRY directory.

TABLE 5-2

The Image control placed inside Picture1

Object	Property	Setting
Image	Name	imgIcon
	Picture	(set at design time in Properties window)

Next, add the code in Listing 5-1 to the Declarations section of Form1. Here you declare the SystemParametersInfo function and the constants needed to use it. You also declare the key code constants you'll use when processing the form's KeyDown event. The INCREMENT constant determines how much the cars are moved when a key is pressed.

Listing 5-1 The SystemParametersInfo function

```
Option Explicit

Declare Function SystemParametersInfo Lib "User" (ByVal uAction As Integer, ByVal
uParam As Integer, lpvParam As Any, ByVal fuWinIni As Integer) As Integer

Const SPI_GETKEYBOARDDELAY = 22
Const SPI_GETKEYBOARDSPEED = 10
Const SPI_SETKEYBOARDDELAY = 23   ' Range 3 (long delay) to 0 (short delay).
Const SPI_SETKEYBOARDSPEED = 11   ' Range 0 (slow) to 31 (fast).

Const KEY_LEFT = &H25
Const KEY_RIGHT = &H27

Const INCREMENT = 50

Dim SavedSpeed As Integer
Dim SavedDelay As Integer

Dim EventStart As Integer
```

Next, add the following Load event to Form1. In this subroutine shown in Listing 5-2, you'll set the range for the two scroll bars. The keyboard repeat rate range is 0 to 31, while the keyboard delay rate is 0 to 3. You'll also use SystemParametersInfo to retrieve the current system repeat and delay rates. These values are used for the initial scroll bar settings, and you also save them so that you can restore system values before you end the program.

Listing 5-2 Setting the scroll bar range

```
Sub Form_Load ()
Dim rc As Integer
Dim lParam As Long

    Me.Show

    hscrSpeed.Max = 31
    rc = SystemParametersInfo(SPI_GETKEYBOARDSPEED, 0, lParam, 0)
    hscrSpeed = lParam
    lblSpeed = lParam
    SavedSpeed = lParam

    hscrDelay.Max = 3
    rc = SystemParametersInfo(SPI_GETKEYBOARDDELAY, 0, lParam, 0)
    hscrDelay = lParam
    lblDelay = lParam
    SavedDelay = lParam
End Sub
```

Next, add Change events for the two scroll bars, hscrSpeed and hscrDelay (as shown in Listing 5-3). Use these to change the repeat and delay rates by moving the scroll bars. To do this, simply pass the scroll value into the SystemParametersInfo function whenever a Change event is triggered. Notice that the last line of each event routine is Picture1.SetFocus. Because the user presses the left and right arrow keys to move the cars back and forth, you have to be careful. The scroll bars, when they have the input focus, also use these keys to move the scroller. If the user presses a right arrow key, intending to move the cars right, and the speed scroll bar has the focus, then the car will move, but so will the scroll bar! To prevent this unwanted behavior, always move the focus away from the scroll bars each time they're used.

Listing 5-3 Adding ScrollBar Change events

```
Sub hscrSpeed_Change ()
Dim rc As Integer
Dim Param As Integer

    Param = hscrSpeed
    rc = SystemParametersInfo(SPI_SETKEYBOARDSPEED, Param, 0, 0)
    lblSpeed = hscrSpeed
    Picture1.SetFocus
End Sub
```

```
Sub hscrDelay_Change ()
Dim rc As Integer
Dim Param As Long

    Param = hscrDelay
    rc = SystemParametersInfo(SPI_SETKEYBOARDDELAY, Param, 0, 0)
    lblDelay = hscrDelay
    Picture1.SetFocus
End Sub
```

Now, add a KeyDown event to the form as shown in Listing 5-4. You're actually doing two things in this routine. First, you're keeping a running calculation of the number of moves that the cars make per second. Call this the frame rate. Second, you actually move the cars either left or right. Display the current frame rate about once per second while the user holds down either the left or right arrow keys.

Listing 5-4 Adding a KeyDown event

```
Sub Form_KeyDown (KeyCode As Integer, Shift As Integer)
Static Frames As Long
Static StartTimer As Single
Dim NowTimer As Single
Const ASecond = 1

    ' If we're not already in an event, then start a new one.
    If Not EventStart Then
        EventStart = True
        StartTimer = Timer
    End If

    ' Update the frame count about once a second.
    NowTimer = Timer
    Frames = Frames + 1
    If (NowTimer - StartTimer) >= ASecond Then
        lblStats = Format$(Frames) & " frames per second"
        Frames = 0
        StartTimer = Timer
    End If

    ' Move the cars. When they get to the left or right edge,
    ' wrap them back to the opposite edge.
    If KeyCode = KEY_RIGHT Then
        imgIcon.Left = imgIcon.Left + INCREMENT
        If imgIcon.Left > Picture1.ScaleWidth Then imgIcon.Left = -imgIcon.Width
    ElseIf KeyCode = KEY_LEFT Then
        imgIcon.Left = imgIcon.Left - INCREMENT
        If imgIcon.Left < -imgIcon.Width Then imgIcon.Left = Picture1.ScaleWidth
    End If
End Sub
```

Next, add a small KeyUp event routine to let you know when the user has released a key.

```
Sub Form_KeyUp (KeyCode As Integer, Shift As Integer)
    EventStart = False
End Sub
```

Finally, add an Unload event to the form. This subroutine ensures that the original key repeat or delay rates are restored when the program terminates. It's never a good idea to alter a system setting permanently without the user's permission.

```
Sub Form_Unload (Cancel As Integer)
Dim rc As Integer

    rc = SystemParametersInfo(SPI_SETKEYBOARDDELAY, SavedDelay, 0, 0)
    rc = SystemParametersInfo(SPI_SETKEYBOARDSPEED, SavedSpeed, 0, 0)

End Sub
```

Save these changes to the project and run the program. Notice that the scroll bars show the current system settings for repeat speed and delay rate. Press and hold down either the left or right arrow key. The cars will begin to move, and after a few seconds, the frame rate should stabilize around some value (see Figure 5-7). Try slowing the repeat speed rate to 0; again hold down an arrow key. The frame rate will now be much slower. This is because the KeyDown events are directly related to the repeat and delay rates. Change the delay rate to its maximum and hold down an arrow key. You should notice that the cars move once, then pause, then begin to move continuously. This pause is a direct result of the delay rate.

If you use the keyboard for fast game motion, you'll want to maximize the repeat rate and minimize the delay rate before you start the game play. But make sure you return the settings to their original system values when the game is over.

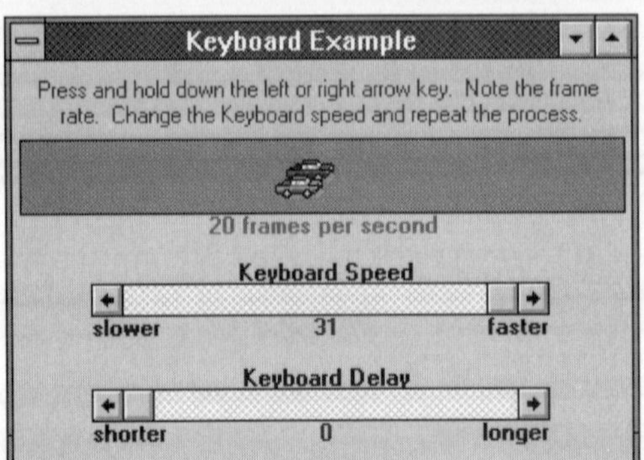

FIGURE 5-7

The key repeat speed and delay example at runtime

Mouse Input

On most Windows systems, you can expect that the user will have a mouse or some other similar type of pointing device. Mouse support, like keyboard support, is built into Windows. It's also built into Visual Basic in the form of several Mouse events. A Visual Basic program can be notified when the mouse is moved over an object, such as a form or control, and when the mouse buttons are clicked. In addition to this, the shape of the mouse pointer, the visible cursor the user sees on-screen, can be changed.

Let's dive right in and build a short example that shows how to use the Click event. Create a new project called MOUSE1.MAK, with a single form called Form1. Add a Timer control, Timer1, and two Image controls, Image1 and Image2. Set the Picture property of Image1 to the CLOUD.ICO icon in the Visual Basic ICONS\ELEMENTS directory, and set the Picture property of Image2 to SUN.ICO from the same directory. Also add a Label control, Label1, to the center of the form, and change its FontSize to 18 point. The form at design time should look like the one shown in Figure 5-8.

Now add the following code to the form's Declarations section.

```
Option Explicit

Dim SkyColor(1 To 9) As Long
Dim CurrentSky As Integer
```

These variables are used to change the sky color, which is really the form's background color.

Next, create a Load event for the form with the code as shown in Listing 5-5. This code initializes the array that holds different sky colors, and sets the form's BackColor property to the darkest color. Also set the timer's Interval property. This "starts up" the timer, triggering a Timer event every 200 milliseconds. Make Image2 invisible, as its only use is to hold the sun icon until later, when you will copy it into Image1,

FIGURE 5-8

The mouse events example at design time

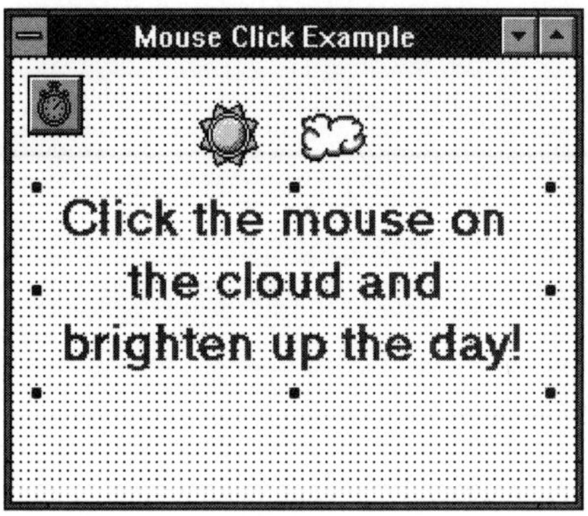

replacing the cloud icon. Also set the MousePointer property of Image1. By default, when the mouse pointer is over a Visual Basic object, it retains the default arrow shape. Setting it to one of the predefined MousePointer values changes the shape of the pointer while it's over the control. In this case, change it to the "no drop" cursor. By using a resource editor, you can design your own custom mouse pointers, which are also called *cursors*.

Listing 5-5 Creating a Load event

```
Sub Form_Load ()
    Timer1.Interval = 200

    SkyColor(9) = &H0&
    SkyColor(8) = &H404040
    SkyColor(7) = &H808080
    SkyColor(6) = &H404000
    SkyColor(5) = &H808000
    SkyColor(4) = &HC0C000
    SkyColor(3) = &HFFFFC0
    SkyColor(2) = &HFFFF80
    SkyColor(1) = &HFFFF00

    CurrentSky = 9
    Me.BackColor = SkyColor(CurrentSky)

    Image2.Visible = False

    Image1.MousePointer = 12 'No Drop Cursor

End Sub
```

Next, add Timer1's Timer event as shown in Listing 5-6. Here you randomly move the cloud around the sky. The Visual Basic Rnd function generates a random speed and direction that's used to reposition the cloud each time the Timer event is triggered. The cloud is wrapped to the other end of the form, so if it drifts off the right side of the form, it reappears on the left side.

Lisitng 5-6 Adding a Timer event

```
Sub Timer1_Timer ()
Dim IncrementX As Integer
Dim DirectionX As Integer

Dim IncrementY As Integer
Dim DirectionY As Integer

Const MAX_SPEED = 270

    IncrementX = Rnd * MAX_SPEED + 1
    IncrementY = Rnd * MAX_SPEED + 1
```

```
        DirectionX = Rnd
        If DirectionX = 0 Then DirectionX = -1
        DirectionY = Rnd
        If DirectionY = 0 Then DirectionY = -1

        Image1.Left = Image1.Left + (IncrementX * DirectionX)
        If Image1.Left > Me.ScaleWidth Then
            Image1.Left = 1
        ElseIf Image1.Left < -Image1.Width Then
            Image1.Left = Me.ScaleWidth - MAX_SPEED
        End If

        Image1.Top = Image1.Top + (IncrementY * DirectionY)
        If Image1.Top > Me.ScaleHeight Then
            Image1.Top = 1
        ElseIf Image1.Top < -Image1.Height Then
            Image1.Top = Me.ScaleHeight - MAX_SPEED
        End If

    End Sub
```

Finally, add a Click event to the Image1 control as shown in Listing 5-7. Here are the guts of the program. Whenever the user clicks the mouse while the mouse pointer is directly over the cloud, the sky gets a little brighter. Set the form's BackColor property to the next color from the SkyColor array. After repeated mouse clicks, when the sky gets completely bright, turn the cloud into the sun, center it on the form, and turn off the timer (you don't want the sun wandering about).

Listing 5-7 Adding a Click event

```
Sub Image1_Click ()

    ' Lighten up the sky each time the user hits the
    ' cloud.
    If CurrentSky > 1 Then
        CurrentSky = CurrentSky - 1
        Me.BackColor = SkyColor(CurrentSky)
    End If

    ' When the sky is at its lightest color, turn the
    ' cloud into the sun and center it on the form.
    If CurrentSky = 1 Then
        Label1.Visible = False
        Image1.Picture = Image2.Picture
        Image1.Left = (Me.ScaleWidth - Image1.Width) / 2
        Image1.Top = (Me.ScaleHeight - Image1.Height) / 2
        Image1.MousePointer = 3 'Cross Cursor

        Timer1.Enabled = False
    End If

End Sub
```

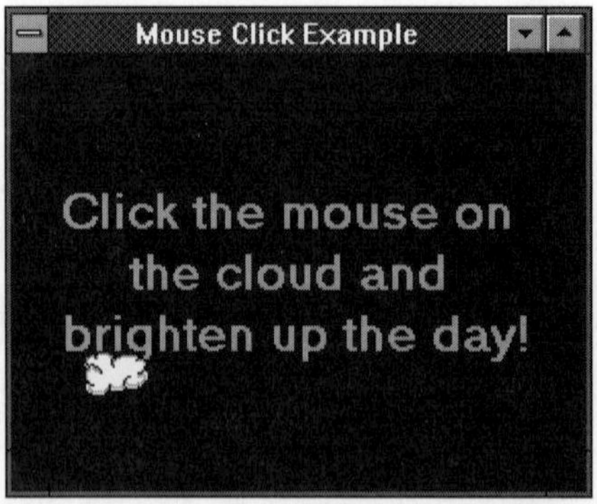

FIGURE 5-9

The mouse events example at runtime

Save this project and run the program. It should look similar to Figure 5-9. Move the mouse pointer over the cloud (if you can catch it). Notice that the mouse pointer changes from an arrow to the no drop pointer whenever it is over the cloud. Click the mouse button over the cloud and watch the sky color change.

This is a simple use of the mouse. Visual Basic also provides MouseDown and MouseUp events for forms and most controls. These are similar to the Click event, but, as their names imply, these events are triggered as soon as the mouse button is pressed down or released. These events also receive parameters telling the event at what X and Y coordinates the mouse pointer is relative to the control.

The MouseMove event detects when the mouse is simply moving over a form or control. You might use this event to create customized controls. For example, you could place a label on a form with the caption Move Left. Whenever the mouse is over this label, the label will receive a MouseMove event, and your game object could be moved left.

Although this sounds good in theory, it falls apart in practice. Add the following MouseMove event to the Label1 control in the project you just built.

```
Sub Label1_MouseMove (Button As Integer, Shift As Integer, X As Single, Y As Single)
Static AColor As Integer

    Label1.ForeColor = QBColor(AColor)
    AColor = (AColor + 1) Mod 16
End Sub
```

Save the project and run the program. Now whenever you move the mouse pointer over the label, the color of its text changes. The catch is, the mouse has to be *moving*. If you move the mouse pointer over the label, then release the mouse, the label color will stop changing. As a method for controlling game action, it's not very useful.

But, as with the keyboard repeat rate problem at the beginning of the chapter, the Windows API can provide a solution. The GetCursorPos Windows API function

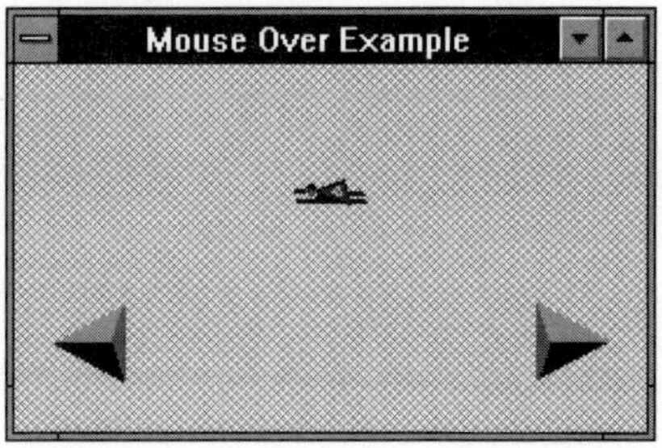

FIGURE 5-10

Creating "Mouse Over" controls using the Windows API

returns the mouse pointer's current X and Y coordinates. You can use this function to check if the mouse is over a Visual Basic control. Whereas the MouseOver event is fired for you automatically by Visual Basic, you'll have to poll GetCursorPos constantly to determine if it is over a particular control.

Let's build a program that moves an icon left or right on a form when the mouse is held over pictures of left and right arrows. This idea is illustrated in Figure 5-10. These arrow "controls" don't need to be clicked, the user merely moves the mouse pointer over them to move the icon.

First, create a new project called MOUSOVER.MAK. Add a new module and name it MOUSEPOS.BAS. Add the code in Listing 5-8 to this module.

Listing 5-8 MOUSEPOS.BAS

```
Option Explicit
'------------------------------------------------------------
' MOUSEPOS.BAS
'------------------------------------------------------------

' Data type expected by GetCursorPos.
Type POINTAPI
    X As Integer
    Y As Integer
End Type

' This Windows API call returns the cursor's absolute position
' on the screen. We can use this to determine whether the
' cursor is over a particular VB control.
Declare Sub GetCursorPos Lib "USER" (lpPoint As POINTAPI)

Function MouseIn (ACntl As Control) As Integer
'------------------------------------------------------------
' This routine returns True if the mouse pointer is currently
' inside the control ACntl.
'------------------------------------------------------------
```

continued on next page

continued from previous page

```
Const PIXEL = 3

Dim APoint As POINTAPI
Dim SaveFormMode As Integer
Dim SaveCntlMode As Integer
Dim XOffset As Integer
Dim YOffset As Integer
Dim BorderWidth As Integer
Dim TitleHeight As Integer
Dim PixX As Integer, PixY As Integer
Dim AForm As Form

    Set AForm = ACntl.Parent

    On Error Resume Next
    MouseIn = False

    GetCursorPos APoint

    ' Save the current ScaleModes for the control and form.
    SaveFormMode = AForm.ScaleMode
    SaveCntlMode = ACntl.ScaleMode

    ' Then set them to Pixels.
    AForm.ScaleMode = PIXEL
    ACntl.ScaleMode = PIXEL

    ' Store the screen Pixel resolutions.
    PixX = Screen.TwipsPerPixelX
    PixY = Screen.TwipsPerPixelY

    ' Take into account the form's border width and title height.
    BorderWidth = ((AForm.Width / PixX) - AForm.ScaleWidth) \ 2
    TitleHeight = (AForm.Height / PixY) - AForm.ScaleHeight - (BorderWidth * 2)

    ' Calculate the controls offset from the top left corner of the screen.
    XOffset = (AForm.Left / PixX) + BorderWidth + ACntl.Left
    YOffset = (AForm.Top / PixY) + BorderWidth + TitleHeight + ACntl.Top

    ' See if the point is inside the control.
    If (APoint.X > XOffset) And (APoint.X < (XOffset + ACntl.Width)) Then
        If (APoint.Y > YOffset) And (APoint.Y < (YOffset + ACntl.Height)) Then
            MouseIn = True
        End If
    End If

    ' Restore the original scale modes.
    AForm.ScaleMode = SaveFormMode
    ACntl.ScaleMode = SaveCntlMode
End Function
```

In this module, you encapsulate the GetCursorPos Windows function within the function MouseIn. MouseIn is passed a control as a parameter, and returns True if the mouse is over that control. GetCursorPos can't tell you directly whether the mouse is over the control, only the mouse's X and Y screen coordinates. But with a few calculations, you can determine the control's X and Y screen coordinates. From those, it is a simple matter to determine if the mouse is within the boundaries of the control.

Now let's build a form and see how to use this technique. Add a form called MOUSOVER.FRM to your project. Then add a Timer control, called Timer1, and three Image controls: imgLeft, imgRight, and imgMan. You can set each Image control's Picture property by selecting an appropriate icon image from the Visual Basic ICONS\ARROWS directory (I used ARW03LT.ICO and ARW03RT.ICO in this example).

Next, add the code in Listing 5-9 to this form. The Timer event is where most of the action happens. Every time the Timer is triggered, MouseIn is called to see if the mouse pointer is over either of the arrow Image controls. If it is, the program adjusts imgMan's Left property, decreasing it to go left or increasing it to move right. It also checks to see if the icon has moved off either edge of the form, and wraps around to the other edge if necessary.

Listing 5-9 The Timer event

```
Option Explicit
'-------------------------------------------------------------
' MOUSOVER.FRM
'-------------------------------------------------------------

' This is how much we'll move the imgMan image each time.
Const INCREMENT = 45

Sub Form_Load ()
'-------------------------------------------------------------
' Start up the Timer control when the program starts.
'-------------------------------------------------------------

    Timer1.Interval = 22
End Sub

Sub Timer1_Timer ()
'-------------------------------------------------------------
' Check if the mouse is inside either arrow image, then
' move imgMan accordingly, wrapping him around the left
' or right edge of the form if necessary.
'-------------------------------------------------------------

    If MouseIn(imgLeft) Then
        imgMan.Left = imgMan.Left - INCREMENT
```

continued on next page

continued from previous page

```
        If imgMan.Left <= -imgMan.Width Then imgMan.Left = Me.ScaleWidth
    ElseIf MouseIn(imgRight) Then
        imgMan.Left = imgMan.Left + INCREMENT
        If imgMan.Left >= Me.ScaleWidth Then imgMan.Left = -imgMan.Width
    End If
End Sub
```

Now save the project and run the program. You can now control a game element, in this case an Image control, just by holding the mouse over a control. This technique lets you build your own "customized" controls using nothing but pictures. For example, you could easily change the arrow images to red when they are active (that is, when the mouse is over them) and then back to gray when the mouse is moved away. Just change the Image control's Picture property to a bitmap of a red arrow when the MouseIn function tells you the pointer is over it.

Joystick Input

Of the three input devices, the joystick is the one most often associated with games. Unfortunately, it's also the least likely input device to be owned by the player. Windows has built-in support, sort of, for the joystick. There are Windows API joystick calls built into the multimedia extensions that ship with Windows 3.1. But these functions require that users first have an IBM-compatible joystick installed on their systems and an IBM joystick driver loaded properly in Windows.

For this section, I'll assume that you have a joystick and I'll show you how to install and configure the joystick driver. Luckily, the IBM joystick driver is readily available from a number of sources, and it is included on the accompanying CD as well. It only takes a few minutes to install, so I'll walk through the steps now before showing how to make your programs aware of the joystick.

First, put the CD that accompanies this book into your CD drive. Then start the Windows Control Panel program from Program Manager. Select the Drivers applet. The Drivers window is displayed, showing a list of currently installed drivers. Press the Add button, and the dialog box shown in Figure 5-11 should appear.

Select the first option, *Unlisted or Updated Driver,* and press the OK button. When you are prompted for the Driver's path, enter D:\IBMJOY, where D: is the drive letter of your CD-ROM drive. Your CD may be drive D:, E:, or something else entirely, depending on how your system is configured. Windows will copy the necessary driver files from the CD to your hard drive. You'll need to restart Windows before it recognizes the joystick driver.

Once the driver is installed, you can use the Control Panel to configure and calibrate your joystick. If Windows doesn't recognize your joystick during configuration, you may have improperly installed the driver or you may not have installed the joystick correctly.

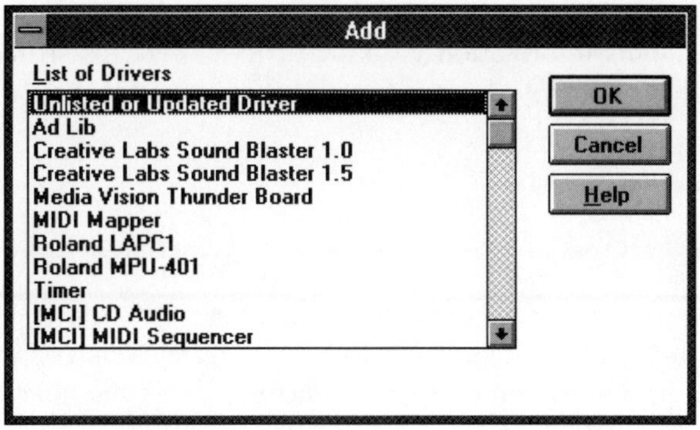

FIGURE 5-11

The Control Panel Add Driver dialog box

Once you have the joystick working correctly, you'll want to use it in your Visual Basic games. Although the Windows multimedia extensions support eight different joystick-related function calls, only two of them are useful in a Visual Basic program. This is because several of the joystick functions rely on *callbacks*, a Windows feature not supported by Visual Basic. It's a good thing for us that these two calls are all we really need.

The first call is joyGetDevCaps. This function call must be declared in your Visual Basic programs as follows:

```
Declare Function joyGetDevCaps Lib "MMSystem" (ByVal IDDevice As Integer, _
                 JCaps As tJoyCaps,
                 ByVal CapSize As Integer) As Integer
```

You'll also need to declare two constants and a Visual Basic structure that looks like this:

```
Global Const JOYSTICK1 = 0
Global Const JOYSTICK2 = 1

Type tJoyCaps
    Mid As Integer
    Pid As Integer
    Pname As String * MAXPNAMELEN
    Xmin As Integer
    Xmax As Integer
    Ymin As Integer
    Ymax As Integer
    Zmin As Integer
    Zmax As Integer
    NumButtons As Integer
    PeriodMin As Integer
    PeriodMax As Integer
End Type
```

The joyGetDevCaps function returns important information about a joystick's capabilities. This information is returned in a tJoyCaps structure like the one described above. The following code can be used to call joyGetDevCaps.

```
Dim rc As Integer
Dim JoyCaps as tJoyCaps

rc = joyGetDevCaps(JOYSTICK1, JoyCaps, Len(JoyCaps))
```

The first parameter tells the function that you want information about joystick number 1, that is, the joystick attached to the first game adapter port on the computer. The second parameter is the JoyCaps structure, where the function will return the information. The last parameter is simply the size of the JoyCaps structure.

For this purpose you only care about the maximum and minimum values and the number of buttons. For most games, you'll probably only need one button, and all joysticks should support at least that.

The minimum and maximum values are very important for proper joystick programming. Image a piece of graph paper that is numbered with increasing values along its top and left edges, forming an X and Y coordinate system. If you place your finger near the center of the paper, that represents the "at rest" coordinates of the joystick. Moving the joystick to the left is like moving your finger to the left on the graph paper. The first catch is that you can only go to the edge of the paper, in this case up to the minimum X value. The second catch is that without using the joyGetDevCaps, you can't tell where the edges, the minimum and maximum values, are.

The second call is joyGetPos. This call tells the current position within the X and Y coordinate system and which buttons if any are pushed. As with joyGetDevCaps, you'll need to declare this function, as well as a Visual Basic structure to return position information.

```
Type tJoyInfo
    X As Integer
    Y As Integer
    Z As Integer
    ButtonStates As Integer
End Type

Declare Function joyGetPos Lib "MMSystem" (ByVal IDDevice As Integer,
JPos As tJoyInfo) As Integer
```

The first parameter indicates which joystick you want to retrieve information about. The second parameter is the tJoyInfo data structure. This returns the coordinates and button positions.

Button positions are all packed into a single ButtonStates field, and you can use constants to extract the individual button states. I'll show how in the example. You might have noticed that both this function and the earlier joyGetDevCaps function support a Z coordinate. Some joysticks can support motion in three dimensions, so the Z coordinate reflects this capability. For these examples, assume that the player is using a conventional X-Y coordinate joystick.

The best way to see how these functions work is to build an example program. This one is a little more involved than the other examples in this chapter, so let's do it step by step.

1. Create a new project called JOYTEST1.MAK. Create a new module called JOYSTICK.BAS, and add the following code. The two functions in this module circumvent one of the pitfalls of using the joystick API in Visual Basic: Coordinates are returned as unsigned 16-bit integers. Visual Basic only supports *signed* 16-bit integers. This means that higher coordinate values, when returned as signed integers, are mistakenly interpreted by Visual Basic as negative numbers! Luckily, there's an easy way to fix this. The uint_to_long function, presented here, translates these values into positive long integers, returning them to their original positive values.

Listing 5-10 JOYSTICK.BAS

```
Option Explicit
'-----------------------------------------------------
' JOYSTICK.BAS - Joystick support routines for
'                Visual Basic.
'-----------------------------------------------------

' Joystick Device ID
Global Const JOYSTICK1 = 0
Global Const JOYSTICK2 = 1

' Joystick error return values
Global Const JOYERR_NOERROR = 0
Global Const JOYERR_PARMS = 165
Global Const MMSYSERR_NODRIVER = 6
Global Const JOYERR_UNPLUGGED = 167

' Joystick button bit-flags used by tJoyInfo.ButtonStates
Global Const JOY_BUTTON1 = &H1
Global Const JOY_BUTTON2 = &H2
Global Const JOY_BUTTON3 = &H4
Global Const JOY_BUTTON4 = &H8


' Joystick Position
Type tJoyInfo
    Xin As Integer
    Yin As Integer
    Zin As Integer
```

continued on next page

continued from previous page

```
    ButtonStates As Integer

    ' These values are determined by the fields above.
    X As Long
    Y As Long
    Z As Long
    ButtonDown(1 To 4) As Integer
End Type

' Joystick Capabilities

Const MAXPNAMELEN = 32

Type tJoyCaps
    Mid As Integer
    Pid As Integer
    Pname As String * MAXPNAMELEN
    XminIn As Integer
    XmaxIn As Integer
    YminIn As Integer
    YmaxIn As Integer
    ZminIn As Integer
    ZmaxIn As Integer
    NumButtons As Integer
    PeriodMin As Integer
    PeriodMax As Integer

    Xmin As Long
    Xmax As Long
    Ymin As Long
    Ymax As Long
    Zmin As Long
    Zmax As Long
End Type

Global JoyCaps As tJoyCaps

' Joystick API Calls
Declare Function joyGetDevCaps Lib "MMSystem" (ByVal IDDevice As Integer, _
                                        JCaps As tJoyCaps, ByVal CapSize As
Integer) As Integer
Declare Function joyGetPos Lib "MMSystem" (ByVal IDDevice As Integer, JPos As
tJoyInfo) As Integer

Function GetJoystickPos (IDDevice As Integer, JoyInfo As tJoyInfo) As Integer
'--------------------------------------------------------
' This function is a wrapper around the joyGetPos API
' call. That call returns coordinates as unsigned
' long integers, which VB doesn't support. We move
' these coordinates into long values so that they
' can be easily evaluated.
'--------------------------------------------------------
```

```
Dim rc As Integer
Static NotFirstTime As Integer

    If Not NotFirstTime Then
        NotFirstTime = False
        rc = joyGetDevCaps(IDDevice, JoyCaps, Len(JoyCaps))

        If rc <> 0 Then
            GetJoystickPos = rc
            Exit Function
        End If

        JoyCaps.Xmax = uint_to_long(JoyCaps.XmaxIn)
        JoyCaps.Xmin = uint_to_long(JoyCaps.XminIn)
        JoyCaps.Ymax = uint_to_long(JoyCaps.YmaxIn)
        JoyCaps.Ymin = uint_to_long(JoyCaps.YminIn)
        JoyCaps.Zmax = uint_to_long(JoyCaps.ZmaxIn)
        JoyCaps.Zmin = uint_to_long(JoyCaps.ZminIn)

    End If

    rc = joyGetPos(IDDevice, JoyInfo)
    GetJoystickPos = rc

    If rc <> 0 Then Exit Function

    JoyInfo.X = uint_to_long(JoyInfo.Xin)
    JoyInfo.Y = uint_to_long(JoyInfo.Yin)
    JoyInfo.Z = uint_to_long(JoyInfo.Zin)

    JoyInfo.ButtonDown(1) = (JoyInfo.ButtonStates And JOY_BUTTON1) = JOY_BUTTON1
    JoyInfo.ButtonDown(2) = (JoyInfo.ButtonStates And JOY_BUTTON2) = JOY_BUTTON2
    JoyInfo.ButtonDown(3) = (JoyInfo.ButtonStates And JOY_BUTTON3) = JOY_BUTTON3
    JoyInfo.ButtonDown(4) = (JoyInfo.ButtonStates And JOY_BUTTON4) = JOY_BUTTON4

End Function

Function uint_to_long (uint As Integer) As Long
'-----------------------------------------------------
' Convert an unsigned integer into a long integer.
'-----------------------------------------------------

    uint_to_long = (CLng(uint) And &HFFFF&)
End Function
```

2. Next, create a form called JOYTEST1.FRM with the objects and properties described in Table 5-3. The form should look similar to the one shown in Figure 5-12.

TABLE 5-3

Objects and properties of the JOYTEST1 form

Object	Property	Setting
Form	FormName	Form1
	BackColor	&H00C0C0C0&
	Caption	"Joystick Example"
Label	Name	Label1
	BackStyle	0 'Transparent
	Caption	"X:"
	Index	0
Label	Name	Label2
	BackStyle	0 'Transparent
	Caption	"Y:"
Label	Name	Label1
	BackStyle	0 'Transparent
	Caption	"Max X:"
	Index	1
Label	Name	Label1
	BackStyle	0 'Transparent
	Caption	"Min X:"
	Index	2
Label	Name	Label1
	BackStyle	0 'Transparent
	Caption	"Max Y:"
	Index	3
Label	Name	Label1
	BackStyle	0 'Transparent
	Caption	"Min Y:"
	Index	4
Label	Name	lblX
	BackStyle	0 'Transparent
	ForeColor	&H00800000&
Label	Name	lblY
	BackStyle	0 'Transparent

Object	Property	Setting
	ForeColor	&H00800000&
Label	Name	lblMaxX
	BackStyle	0 'Transparent
	ForeColor	&H00800000&
Label	Name	lblMinX
	BackStyle	0 'Transparent
	ForeColor	&H00800000&
Label	Name	lblMaxY
	BackStyle	0 'Transparent
	ForeColor	&H00800000&
Label	Name	lblMinY
	BackStyle	0 'Transparent
	ForeColor	&H00800000&
PictureBox	Name	picBackground
	AutoSize	-1 'True
	BackColor	&H00008000&
Timer	Name	Timer1
	Interval	22
CommandButton	Name	btnCancel
	Caption	"&Cancel"

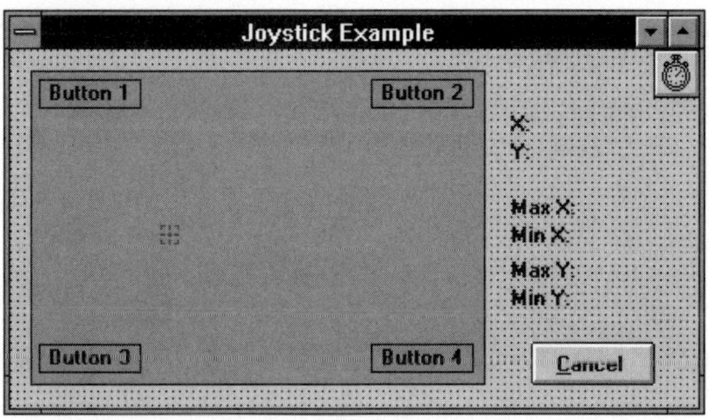

FIGURE 5-12
JOYTEST1.FRM at design time

3. The controls in Table 5-4 are placed within the picBackground PictureBox control. Make sure that the picBackground control is the currently selected control before adding these controls.

TABLE 5-4

Objects and properties placed within the picBackground control

Object	Property	Setting
Label	Name	lblButton
	Alignment	2 'Center
	BackColor	&H000000FF&
	BorderStyle	1 'Fixed Single
	Caption	"Button 1"
	Index	0
Label	Name	lblButton
	Alignment	2 'Center
	BackColor	&H000000FF&
	BorderStyle	1 'Fixed Single
	Caption	"Button 2"
	Index	1
Label	Name	lblButton
	Alignment	2 'Center
	BackColor	&H000000FF&
	BorderStyle	1 'Fixed Single
	Caption	"Button 3"
	Index	2
Label	Name	lblButton
	Alignment	2 'Center
	BackColor	&H000000FF&
	BorderStyle	1 'Fixed Single
	Caption	"Button 4"
	Index	3
Image	Name	imgJoyCursor
	Picture	(set at design time in Properties window)

4. Add the code in Listing 5-11 to the form, making sure that event routines are associated with the proper controls.

Listing 5-11 JOYTEST1.FRM

```
Option Explicit
'-----------------------------------------------------------
' Constants and module-level variables used by
' JOYTEST1.FRM.
'-----------------------------------------------------------

Dim JoyInfo As tJoyInfo

Dim RangeWidth As Integer
Dim RangeHeight As Integer

Const YELLOW = &HFFFF&
Const RED = &HFF&

Sub btnCancel_Click ()
'-----------------------------------------------------------
' Exit the program when the Cancel button is pressed.
'-----------------------------------------------------------
    Unload Me
End Sub

Sub Form_Load ()
'-----------------------------------------------------------
' Set the range for the little on-screen joystick cursor.
'-----------------------------------------------------------
    RangeWidth = picBackground.ScaleWidth - imgJoyCursor.Width
    RangeHeight = picBackground.ScaleHeight - imgJoyCursor.Height
End Sub

Sub Timer1_Timer ()
'-----------------------------------------------------------
' The timer routine constantly polls the joystick to
' determine the current positions and button states,
' and changes the screen accordingly.
'-----------------------------------------------------------
Dim rc As Integer
Dim i As Integer

    rc = GetJoystickPos(JOYSTICK1, JoyInfo)
    If rc = 0 Then
        imgJoyCursor.Left = RangeWidth * ((JoyInfo.X - JoyCaps.Xmin) / (JoyCaps.XMax - JoyCaps.Xmin))
        imgJoyCursor.Top = RangeHeight * ((JoyInfo.Y - JoyCaps.YMin) / (JoyCaps.YMax - JoyCaps.YMin))

        lblX = JoyInfo.X
        lblY = JoyInfo.Y

        lblMinX = JoyCaps.Xmin
```

continued on next page

continued from previous page

```
        lblMaxX = JoyCaps.XMax
        lblMinY = JoyCaps.YMin
        lblMaxY = JoyCaps.YMax

        For i = 0 To 3
            If JoyInfo.ButtonDown(i + 1) Then
                If lblButton(i).BackColor <> RED Then lblButton(i).BackColor = RED
            Else
                If lblButton(i).BackColor <> YELLOW Then lblButton(i).BackColor = YELLOW
            End If
        Next
    End If

End Sub
```

5. Finally, save the project and run the program.

How It Works

Assuming that your joystick is working properly, the running program should be similar to the one shown in Figure 5-13.

By moving the joystick, you should be able to move the cursor around within the large PictureBox control. Pressing a joystick button will change the color of the corresponding button label until the button is released. This program also displays the minimum and maximum X and Y coordinates for the joystick, as well as the joystick's current position.

As with many of the other examples in this chapter, a Timer control is key to the operation of this program. Here the Timer event's sole duty is to retrieve fresh joystick information and update the Visual Basic form accordingly.

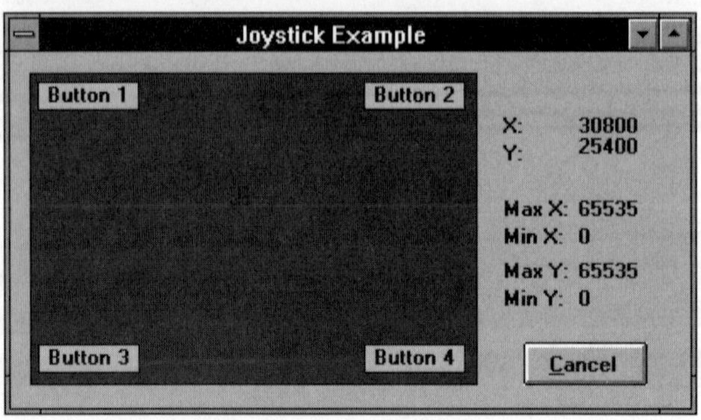

FIGURE 5-13

The Joystick example at runtime

While the joystick returns specific X and Y coordinates, you may want simply to determine whether the joystick is left of center, centered, or right of center. This would be useful, for example, in an auto-racing game to steer a car left and right. To do this, you need to save the at rest coordinates of the joystick when the game starts, then compare the current coordinates against these at rest values.

As you can see, there are many ways to get user input in your games. Now that you can make objects move based on user feedback, let's move on to a very important, and often overlooked, aspect of game programming: the soundtrack.

6

Sound and Fury

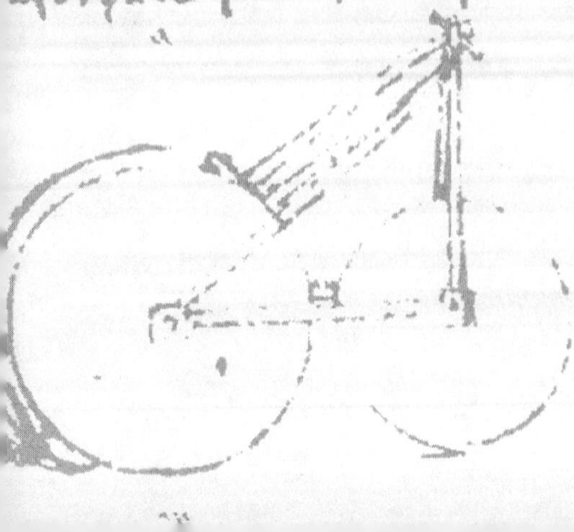

6

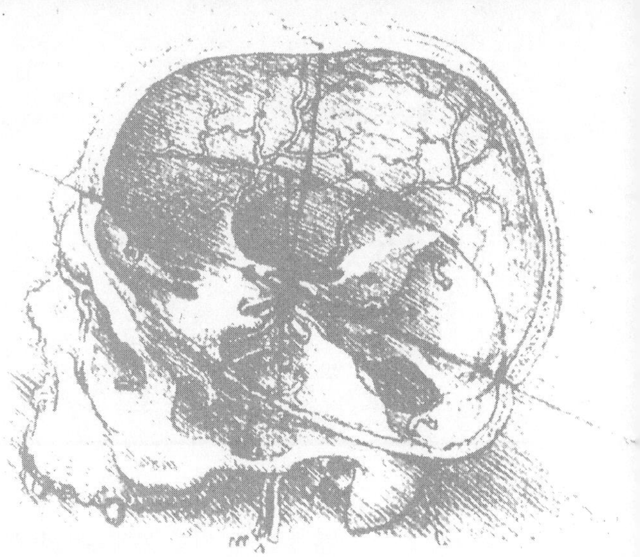

Sound and Fury

There's a scene near the end of the movie *Return of the Jedi* when Darth Vader learns that Princess Leia is Luke's sister, and Luke steps out of the darkness to engage in his final battle with Vader. Visually, the scene is nothing spectacular, but listen to the sound: The orchestra swells and over it you can hear the voices of a choir; interspersed with all of this is the hiss and crackle of light saber against light saber. The sound track provides an emotional quality that the visuals alone cannot.

As with action movies, when you think of your favorite high-powered, exciting action games, what you probably remember first are the images: monsters, space ships, creepy dungeons, and the like. But sound effects and music can heighten the sense of danger and impending peril. And Windows is quite adept at producing them.

I'll look at several techniques for adding sound effects and music to your games in this chapter. First I'll review the basics of playing wave audio files, then take a look at MIDI music. Finally, I'll show you Microsoft's WaveMix library (included on the CD), a handy tool for building layered wave audio sound to your games.

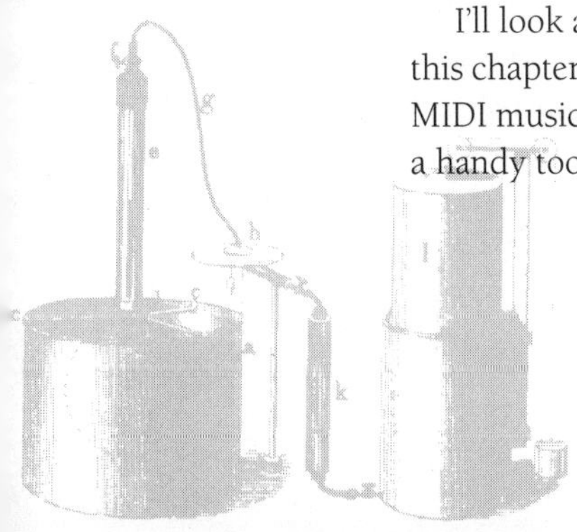

Making Waves

Windows 3.1 supports wave form audio files. These files can store sounds—voices, music, and sound effects—in much the same way a tape recorder does. These wave files, which by convention are stored with a .WAV file extension, can be played back through a sound card. A sound card is an add-in board that, when installed in your PC, provides a range of sound recording and playback abilities.

NOTE: Actually, it is possible to play back wave files without a sound card. A special Windows 3.1 device driver, the PC Speaker driver, lets you play wave files through the tiny PC speaker that's built into your PC. This sound driver is useful, but it has some serious limitations for game programmers.

A Visual Basic programmer can play wave files in several ways. The most common way is to use the sndPlaySound function. To use this API function, you must first declare it in the Declarations section of your form, module, or class.

```
Declare Function sndPlaySound Lib "MMSYSTEM.DLL" (ByVal SoundFileName As
String, ByVal Flags As Integer) As Integer
```

The function's first parameter, SoundFileName, is a string containing the full path and file name of a wave file. The second parameter, Flags, contains a combination of constant values that tells Windows *how* to play the sound.

```
Const SND_SYNC = &h0           ' Don't return until the sound ends (This is the default)
Const SND_ASYNC = &h1          ' Return immediately after the sound starts
Const SND_NODEFAULT = &h2      ' If the sound file is not found, do NOT play default sound
Const SND_MEMORY = &h4         ' Play a sound from a buffer in memory
Const SND_LOOP = &h8           ' Loop sound continuously (used with SND_ASYNC)
Const SND_NOSTOP = &h10        ' Don't stop this sound to play another one
```

Windows 3.1 installs several sample wave files in the Windows directory. These are short sound effects designed to be tied to Windows events such as error messages. One of these files is DING.WAV, which makes a dinging sound. You can play this wave file with the following line of code.

```
result = sndPlaySound ("C:\WINDOWS\DING.WAV", SND_ASYNC Or SND_NODEFAULT)
```

The first parameter should be clear; it's the name of the wave file. The second parameter sets the flags. The constants are combined into a single flag value using the bitwise OR operator. In this example, you tell Windows to play the sound asynchronously. This means that the sndPlaySound function will start the sound, then immediately return control back to the program. This lets the program continue to run, even while sound is still playing. Had you used the SND_SYNC constant, the sndPlaySound function would not have returned until the sound had ended, even if the sound lasted for several minutes.

I mentioned earlier that Microsoft provides a PC speaker driver that lets you play wave files without a sound card. The limitation of this driver is that it can *only* play sounds synchronously. This makes it less than suitable for games where a sudden pause in the action would be unacceptable.

The second flag, SND_NODEFAULT, tells Windows not to play the default sound if C:\WINDOWS\DING.WAV isn't found. The default sound can be assigned using the Sound applet in the Windows Control Panel. In most games, you don't want the default sound to play if your wave file is missing, particularly if you don't know what that default sound might be.

The SND_LOOP constant tells Windows to replay the sound continuously. You might use this constant to play a short snippet of music. By looping, you can create a continuous background music track. This constant is always used with the SND_ASYNC constant. Why? Because a wave file played synchronously doesn't return control until the sound has finished, and a wave file played with SND_LOOP technically never finishes. The wave file would play forever with no way for the program to tell it to stop.

How do you stop a wave file? The sndPlaySound function can do it, but you need to pass it a null pointer for its FileName parameter. The sndPlaySound function was designed to be called from a program written in C; unfortunately, Visual Basic does not support pointers. But you can simulate a null pointer by aliasing the sndPlaySound function.

```
Declare Function sndStopSound Lib "MMSystem" Alias "sndPlaySound" (ByVal
ANull As Long, ByVal flags As Integer) As Integer
```

This declaration lets you create the function sndStopSound in our program to stop a wave file.

```
result = sndStopSound (0,0)
```

In reality, you're still calling the same function, but you're fooling it into thinking the long integer value, 0, is a null pointer.

One problem with playing wave files is that, because they *are* files, they must be loaded from disk, and disk access takes time. Timing is everything in an action game, and you don't want distracting pauses in your game each time a wave file is played. A way around this is to use the SND_MEMORY constant. This constant tells the sndPlaySound function to play a wave file that has previously been loaded into an area of memory. When this constant is used, sndPlaySound's first parameter doesn't refer to the name of a wave file. Instead, the parameter is a string buffer that holds the contents of a previously loaded wave file.

You can load a wave file into a string buffer using the following subroutine.

Listing 6-1 The WaveGet function

```
Function WaveGet (ByVal FileName) As String
'-----------------------------------------------------------
' Load a sound file into a string buffer.
'-----------------------------------------------------------
Dim SoundBuffer As String
Dim chunk As String
Dim f As Integer

    On Error GoTo WaveGet_Error

    chunk = Space$(1024)
    SoundBuffer = ""
    f = FreeFile
    Open FileName For Binary As f
    Do While Not EOF(f)
        Get #f, , chunk      ' Load in 1K chunks
        SoundBuffer = SoundBuffer & chunk
    Loop
    Close f
    WaveGet = Trim$(SoundBuffer)

Exit Function
WaveGet_Error:
    WaveGet = ""
    Exit Function
End Function
```

You can use this function to load waves into memory, usually at the beginning of a game, then play them from memory during the course of the game.

```
' Declare buffers to hold the waves
Dim SoundLaser As String
Dim SoundExplosion As String
...
' Load Sound Effects at start of game.
SoundLaser = WaveGet ("C:\SOUNDS\LASER.WAV")
SoundExplosion = WaveGet ("C:\SOUNDS\BOOM.WAV")
...
' Later, during game play, you can play the sounds from memory.
result = sndPlaySound (SoundLaser, SND_MEMORY Or SND_ASYNC)
...
result = sndPlaySound (SoundExplosion, SND_MEMORY Or SND_ASYNC)
```

There are limitations when playing sounds from memory. Because the waves are being stored in strings, you're restricted to Visual Basic's limitations on string sizes. Using Visual Basic in Windows 3.1, variable-length strings can't exceed 64K; in practice, you'll find that the limit is considerably lower. Wave files are notorious disk hogs, so you'll want to restrict in-memory waves to a few short sound effects. Luckily, it's possible to create effective sound effects that are less than 1 second in duration.

Microsoft's own documentation recommends that you use the sndPlaySound function only with relatively small wave files, files less than about 100K. For larger files, Microsoft recommends that you use MCI services.

The Media Control Interface

The Media Control Interface, or MCI, is a set of services that gives you access not only to the sound capabilities of a PC but to a wide range of multimedia services as well. MCI can let you control devices, such as audio CDs and video laserdiscs, in addition to playing sounds and displaying animations and video.

The mciSendString function lets you control a media device, in this case a sound card, by sending the device a *command string*.

```
Declare Function mciSendString Lib "MMSYSTEM.DLL" _
        (ByVal ACommand As String, _
         ByVal AReturnString As Long, _
         ByVal AReturnLength As Integer, _
         ByVal ACallBack As Integer) As Long
```

The last three parameters to mciSendString are used for returning information from the function and for specifying a callback window handle. None of these parameters is needed for this discussion; let's concentrate on the first parameter: the command string.

Earlier, I showed how to play the Windows DING.WAV file using the sndPlaySound function. You can do the same thing with mciSendString.

```
result = mciSendString ("play C:\WINDOWS\DING.WAV", 0&, 0, 0)
```

All MCI devices recognize a *command set*. The example above uses the *play* command to play back the wave file. Table 6-1 shows a subset of the commands supported by wave audio devices.

TABLE 6-1

A subset of the WaveAudio MCI command set

Command	Arguments
close ***device_name***	
open ***device_name***	[alias ***device_alias***] [shareable] [type ***device_type***]
pause	
play ***device_name***	[from ***position***] [to ***position***]
resume ***device_name***	
seek ***device_name***	[to ***position*** | to start | to end]
stop ***device_name***	

These commands are easy to understand if you think of them as corresponding to the buttons on a cassette tape recorder. The open command is like putting a tape into the machine. The close command is like pulling the tape out. The pause command suspends a currently playing wave file, and the resume command continues a paused wave file from the position at which it was suspended.

The open command lets you alias a device name, which in this case is the name of a wave file. This can make it easier to refer to a device in subsequent commands. Let's look at a more involved example.

```
result = mciSendString("open C:\WINDOWS\DING.WAV type waveaudio alias ding", 0&, 0, 0)
result = mciSendString("play ding from 100 to 300", 0&, 0, 0)
```

Here, you are issuing two commands: open and play. The *open* command tells MCI services that you are opening a file, C:\WINDOWS\DING.WAV, as a wave audio device, and that in later commands you will refer to this device by the alias "ding." The type waveaudio argument isn't strictly necessary in this case, because MCI services would have assumed that this was a wave device by the file's .WAV extension.

In the second command, *play*, you tell MCI services to play a part of the wave file. The "from 100 to 300" arguments tell MCI services to start playing the file 100 milliseconds (1/10th of a second) from the beginning of the file, and to stop playing 300 milliseconds into the file. This shows one of the advantages of mciSendString over the sndPlaySound function: the ability to control how much of a media file is played.

Making Music with MIDI

I mentioned earlier that the mciSendString command can be used to control a variety of devices. In game play, there is another sound-producing device that you can use: the *MIDI device*. If you have a sound card, chances are good that it has MIDI capabilities in addition to its ability to play wave files. MIDI stands for Musical Instrument Digital Interface, and is a standard for controlling electronic music devices. In Windows, files with a .MID extension store MIDI information that can be used to reproduce music on a MIDI device such as a sound card.

A disadvantage of MIDI files is that they can store only synthesized music. They can't be used to produce speech or other natural sounds like a wave device can. Their big advantage, however, is their small size. MIDI files are tiny compared to wave files. Windows 3.1 comes with an example MIDI file, CANYON.MID. This file, which you can find in the Windows directory, plays for slightly more than 2 minutes, but takes up only about 33 kilobytes of disk space. By comparison, DING.WAV plays for just over half a second but takes up about 11 kilobytes.

Using mciSendString, you can play MIDI files with basically the same commands as those used for wave audio devices.

```
result = mciSendString("open C:\WINDOWS\CANYON.MID type sequencer alias canyon", 0&, 0, 0)
result = mciSendString("play canyon", 0&, 0, 0)
```

This example opens the CANYON.MID file as a MIDI sequencer device, and aliases the device as "canyon." The second command then plays the MIDI file.

MIDI files can provide an efficient way to create background music for games. This is useful in cases where you want to have background music and foreground sound effects. Wave files cannot easily be layered, or mixed, using the sndPlaySound or mciSendString functions. For example, if you begin playing one wave file using sndPlaySound, then start a second wave file, the first sound file is terminated when the second one begins. But you can layer a MIDI and a wave file using the mciSendString command. To demonstrate this, let's build a short sample project.

Resource Tip: If you're not a musician (personally, I can only carry a tune with the aid of a large bucket), the CompuServe Information Service (CIS) is a good source for public domain MIDI and wave files. In particular, the CIS forum *MIDI/Music* contains a wide variety of sounds, as well as shareware and freeware tools.

Steps

1. First, create a new project called MCIAPI1.MAK. Create a new form with the objects and properties described in Table 6-2. Save this form as MCI-API1.FRM.

TABLE 6-2
Objects and properties for MCIAPI1.FRM

Object	Property	Setting
CommandButton	Name	btnPlayMIDI
	Caption	"Play MIDI"
CommandButton	Name	btnPlayWave
	Caption	"Play Wave"
Form	Name	frmMCIAPI
	Caption	"MCI API Demo"

2. After creating MCIAPI1.FRM, add the code shown in Listing 6-2. This code handles the Click events for the two buttons and opens the MCI devices when the form is loaded. If your WINDOWS directory has a different name, then change the directory references in the Form_Load subroutine accordingly.

Listing 6-2 Handling the Click events and MCI devices

```
Option Explicit
'-----------------------------------------------------------
' MCIAPI1.FRM
' This program shows how to create layered sounds using the
' MIDI sequencer for background music, and wave audio for
' sound effects.
'-----------------------------------------------------------

Private Declare Function mciSendString Lib "MMSYSTEM.DLL" (ByVal ACommand As String, ByVal
AReturnString As Long, ByVal AReturnLength As Integer, ByVal ACallBack As Integer) As Long

Private Sub btnPlayMIDI_Click()
'-----------------------------------------------------------
' Play the MIDI file aliased as "canyon".
'-----------------------------------------------------------
Dim result As Long

    result = mciSendString("play canyon", 0&, 0, 0)
End Sub

Private Sub btnPlayWave_Click()
'-----------------------------------------------------------
' Play the Wave file aliased as "ding".
'-----------------------------------------------------------
Dim result As Long

    result = mciSendString("play ding from 100 to 300", 0&, 0, 0)
End Sub

Private Sub Form_Load()
'-----------------------------------------------------------
' Open a wave audio device and a MIDI sequencer device, and
' associate an alias for each.
'-----------------------------------------------------------
Dim result As Long

    result = mciSendString("open C:\WINDOWS\CANYON.MID type sequencer alias canyon", 0&, 0, 0)
    result = mciSendString("open C:\WINDOWS\DING.WAV type waveaudio alias ding", 0&, 0, 0)
End Sub

Private Sub Form_Unload(Cancel As Integer)
```

```
'-----------------------------------------------------------
' Close any open MCI devices, in this case the wave audio
' and MIDI sequencer devices.
'-----------------------------------------------------------
Dim result As Long

    result = mciSendString("close all", 0&, 0, 0)
End Sub
```

How It Works

This very simple program, shown in Figure 6-1, demonstrates one way to layer sounds. Run the program. You'll see two buttons, labeled Play MIDI and Play Wave. Press the Play MIDI button and the MIDI file, CANYON.MID, begins to play. The music in this MIDI file will last about 2 minutes. During that time, press the Play Wave button several times.

Programming Tip: Notice that the wave file, DING.WAV, can be heard along with, or "on top of," the MIDI music. Neither sound is disturbed or stopped by the other. This technique lets you build games that feature both background music and foreground sound effects.

Using the Visual Basic MCI Control to Create Sounds

You can also use Visual Basic's MCI control to play both wave audio and MIDI sequencer sounds. This control can be added to your toolbox in Visual Basic 4.0 by selecting the *Custom Controls...* command from the Visual Basic Tools menu, and then selecting *Microsoft Multimedia Control* from the list of available controls.

FIGURE 6-1

The MCI API demonstration program

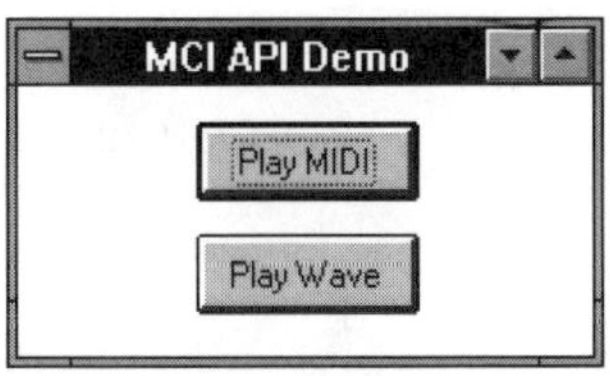

FIGURE 6-2
The Microsoft Multimedia, or MCI, Control

The MCI control encapsulates the power of the Multimedia API into a single control. When placed on a form, the control looks like VCR or tape recorder buttons, as shown in Figure 6-2.

This control provides an easy way to create looped or repeating MIDI background music. In an earlier section, I showed how MIDI music could be used as background music by using the mciSendString function call. Although it's easy to play MIDI music this way in Visual Basic, it's harder to loop the music. Looping wave files is easy; just use the SND_LOOP flag when calling the sndPlaySound function. Unfortunately, there's no similar way to loop MIDI files automatically. To overcome this, you must find a way to determine when a MIDI tune has completed and then restart it. Luckily, the MCI control lets you do this. The following short example program shows a technique for looping MIDI files.

Steps

1. Create a new project called MCICNTL1.MAK. Make sure to add the MCI control to your toolbox by selecting the *Custom Controls...* command from the Visual Basic Tools menu and then selecting *Microsoft Multimedia Control* from the list of available controls.

2. Create a new form with the objects and properties described in Table 6-3. Save this form as MCICNTL1.FRM.

TABLE 6-3
Objects and properties for MCICNTL1.FRM

Object	Property	Setting
Form	Name	Form1
	BackColor	&H00C0C0C0&
	Caption	"MCI Control Demo"
MMControl	Name	MMControl1
	Visible	0 'False
CommonDialog	Name	CMDialog1
	cancelerror	-1 'True

Object	Property	Setting
	defaultext	".mid;.rmi"
	dialogtitle	"Open an MCI File"
	filter	"MIDI Files (*.mid,*.rmi)|*.mid;*.rmi"
Label	Name	lblFileName
	BackColor	&H00C0FFFF&
	BorderStyle	1 'Fixed Single
	Caption	"[none]"
	ForeColor	&H00000000&
CheckBox	Name	chkLoopSounds
	BackColor	&H00C0C0C0&
	Caption	"Loop Sounds"
	Value	1 'Checked
CommandButton	Name	btnStart
	Caption	"Start Sound"
	Enabled	0 'False
CommandButton	Name	btnStop
	Caption	"Stop Sound"
	Enabled	0 'False

3. Add a menu to the form created in Step 2, using the Visual Basic Menu Design Window, setting the captions and names as shown in Table 6-4.

TABLE 6-4

Menu definition for MCICNTL1.FRM

Caption	Name
&File	mnuFile
----&Open	mnuFileOpen
----	mnuFileSep
----E&xit	mnuFileExit

4. Next, add the code in Listing 6-3 to the form.

Listing 6-3 MCICNTL1.FRM

```
Option Explicit
'------------------------------------------------------------
' MCICNTL1.FRM
' This program shows how to loop MIDI music using the
' MCI control.
'------------------------------------------------------------

Private Sub btnStart_Click()
'------------------------------------------------------------
' Start playing the music.
'------------------------------------------------------------
Dim Cancel As Integer

    Cancel = False
    If MMControl1.FileName <> "" Then MMControl1_PlayClick False
End Sub

Private Sub btnStop_Click()
'------------------------------------------------------------
' Stop playing the music.
'------------------------------------------------------------

    If MMControl1.FileName <> "" Then MMControl1_StopClick False
End Sub

Private Sub MMControl1_PlayClick(Cancel As Integer)
'------------------------------------------------------------
' Set the UpdateInterval, so that the StatusUpdate event
' is generated.
'------------------------------------------------------------

    MMControl1.UpdateInterval = 55
End Sub

Private Sub MMControl1_StatusUpdate()
'------------------------------------------------------------
' Check to see if the music has stopped, and if it has,
' then restart it. This is only done if the Loop Sounds
' check box is checked.
'------------------------------------------------------------

    If chkLoopSounds = 1 Then
        If MMControl1.Mode = vbMCIModeStop Then
            MMControl1.Command = "Prev"
            MMControl1.Command = "Play"
        End If
    Else
```

```
        MMControl1.UpdateInterval = 0
    End If
End Sub

Private Sub MMControl1_StopClick(Cancel As Integer)
'--------------------------------------------------------------
' Stop the music and "rewind".
'--------------------------------------------------------------

    MMControl1.UpdateInterval = 0
    MMControl1.Command = "Stop"
    MMControl1.Command = "Prev"
End Sub

Private Sub mnuFileExit_Click()
'--------------------------------------------------------------
' Exit the program.
'--------------------------------------------------------------
    Unload Me
End Sub

Private Sub mnuFileOpen_Click()
'--------------------------------------------------------------
' Open a MIDI or Wave file for use by the MCI control.
'--------------------------------------------------------------
Dim FileExtension As String

    On Error Resume Next
    CMDialog1.ShowOpen

    If Err <> 0 Then Exit Sub

    MMControl1.Wait = True
    MMControl1.UpdateInterval = 0

    ' If a device is open now, then close it.
    If Not MMControl1.Mode = vbMCIModeNotOpen Then
        MMControl1.Command = "Close"
    End If

    ' Load the file into the MCI control.
    If MMControl1.FileName <> CMDialog1.FileName Then
        MMControl1.FileName = CMDialog1.FileName
        FileExtension = UCase$(Right$(MMControl1.FileName, 4))

        ' Determine the device type from the file extension.
        If FileExtension = ".WAV" Then
            MMControl1.DeviceType = "WaveAudio"
        ElseIf (FileExtension = ".MID") Or (FileExtension = ".RMI") Then
            MMControl1.DeviceType = "Sequencer"
        End If
```

continued on next page

continued from previous page

```
        ' Open the device
        MMControl1.Command = "Open"

        ' Enable the command buttons.
        btnStart.Enabled = True
        btnStop.Enabled = True
    End If
    lblFileName = CMDialog1.FileName
End Sub
```

How It Works

In this example, the MCI control is invisible and its functions are controlled by two command buttons, btnStart and btnStop. Use the *Open* command on the File menu to select a MIDI file, then press the Start button. If the Loop Sounds check box is checked, then the MIDI file will restart automatically when the music finishes.

The program does this by monitoring the status of the MIDI device. The MCI control provides a StatusUpdate event that is triggered periodically. The program only receives this event if the MCI control's UpdateInterval property is greater than 0. In this example program, the UpdateInterval property is set to 55, causing the program to fire a StatusUpdate event every 55 milliseconds.

In the StatusUpdate event, the program checks to see if the looping option is enabled by evaluating the state of the chkLoopSound check box. If it is looping, it then checks the Mode property of the MCI control. If the Mode says the music has stopped (via the constant vbMCIModeStop), the program then "rewinds" the MIDI music and starts playing it again.

Mixing Wave Audio with WaveMix

One of the problems with wave files is that you can't layer or "mix" them using the standard API calls like mciSendString or sndPlaySound. Luckily, there is a solution to this problem.

WaveMix is a dynamic link library developed by Microsoft to assist game programmers. (It's one of Microsoft's "unsupported tools," which I suspect means it was developed in-house by Microsoft for its own use, but was so useful that Microsoft made it available to developers as well. I'll discuss two other unsupported tools, BitEdit and PalEdit, in Chapter 9.) WaveMix gives you an easy way to layer sounds, in the form of wave files, in your games. It does this by allowing you to establish separate sound channels. You can think of these as independent sound pipelines; sound from each pipeline is mixed to form a single soundtrack.

WaveMix supports up to eight channels. Each of these channels can be assigned a different wave file, with its own playback options. For example, you can specify a music wave file on one channel, specify the sound looping option, and use this channel as background music. You can use other channels for various sound effects. These sound effects will be heard over the background music, but won't interrupt it.

Using the WaveMix API

WaveMix is a collection of function calls in a DLL. You have to call some initialization functions before you can start playing sounds, and you have to call some clean-up functions when you're finished to free any Windows resources.

To initialize WaveMix, first call the function WaveMixInit. This function returns a handle that you'll need when you make other WaveMix calls. WaveMixInit configures the DLL and determines what wave playback capabilities you'll have. WaveMixInit uses settings saved in the WAVEMIX.INI initialization file.

Alternately, you can call the WaveMixConfigureInit function. This function serves the same purpose as WaveMixInit, but lets you specify configuration options such as stereo playback and sampling rate directly, rather than relying on the values in WAVEMIX.INI.

Now that WaveMix is initialized, you can associate a wave file with a particular WaveMix channel. Use two functions to do this. First, call WaveMixOpenWave to open a wave file for use by WaveMix. Then, call WaveMixOpenChannel to associate the wave with a specified WaveMix channel. Call these two functions for each wave you'll be using.

Next, make a call to WaveMixActivate. This tells WaveMix to grab the wave output device for its use.

Now you're ready to make some noise. To play a channel, use the WaveMixPlay function. This function takes as its only parameter a MIXPLAYPARAMS structure, which has the following form:

```
Type MIXPLAYPARAMS
    wSize As Integer
    hMixSession As Integer
    iChannel As Integer
    lpMixWave As Long
    hWndNotify As Integer
    dwFlags As Long
    wLoops As Integer
EndType
```

You can set the fields in this structure to specify which channel to play and how to play it. For example, you can tell WaveMix to put the wave in a queue and play it after other queued waves are played, or play it on any available channel.

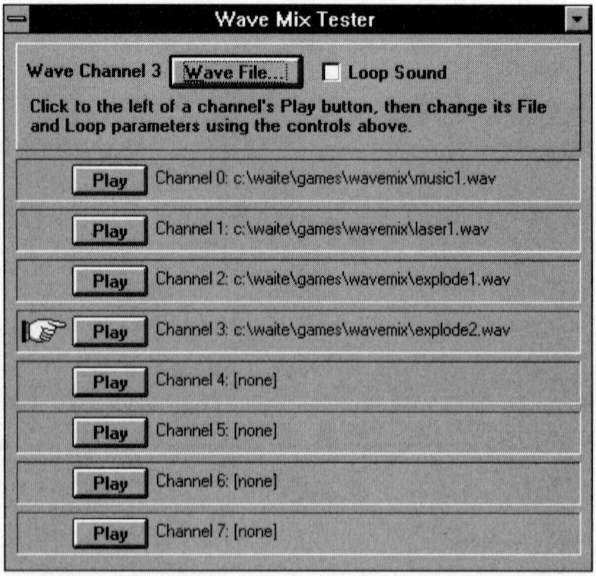

FIGURE 6-3

The WaveMix sound mixing program

When you're finished with WaveMix, usually when your program is about to end, you need to make sure you clean up. First, close all open channels using the WaveMixCloseChannel function. Next, call WaveMixFreeWave for each open wave file to free any memory held by it. Finally, terminate your WaveMix session with a call to WaveMixCloseSession.

A WaveMix Sound Mixing Program

I've built an example program to help show how WaveMix works. The program, shown in Figure 6-3, lets you assign wave files to any of WaveMix's eight channels. You can also specify whether or not to loop the sound. Play a wave file by pushing the corresponding channel's Play button.

Steps

1. Create a new Visual Basic project called WAVMIX1.MAK. Create a new module called WAVEMIX.BAS, and add the code in Listing 6-4 to it.

Listing 6-4 WAVEMIX.BAS

```
Option Explicit
'------------------------------------------------------------
' WAVEMIX.BAS
' This module contains declarations for all the functions
' in the WaveMix DLL, and provides some higher-level Basic
' functions to make using WaveMix simpler.
'------------------------------------------------------------
Dim hWaveMix As Integer
Dim lpWaveMix() As Long
Dim WaveHandle As Integer
Global WAVMIX_Quiet As Integer

Global Const WAVEMIX_MAXCHANNELS = 8

Type WAVEMIXINFO
   wSize As Integer
   bVersionMajor As String * 1
   bVersionMinor As String * 1
   szDate(12) As String
   dwFormats As Long
End Type

Type MIXCONFIG
    wSize As Integer
    dwFlags As Long
    wChannels As Integer
    wSamplingRate As Integer
End Type

Type MIXPLAYPARAMS
    wSize As Integer
    hMixSession As Integer
    iChannel As Integer
    lpMixWave As Long
    hWndNotify As Integer
    dwFlags As Long
    wLoops As Integer
End Type

' WaveMix DLL declarations.

Declare Function WaveMixInit Lib "WAVEMIX.DLL" () As Integer
Declare Function WaveMixConfigureInit Lib "WAVEMIX.DLL" (lpConfig As MIXCONFIG) As Integer
Declare Function WaveMixActivate Lib "WAVEMIX.DLL" (ByVal hMixSession As Integer, ByVal
fActivate As Integer) As Integer
Declare Function WaveMixOpenWave Lib "WAVEMIX.DLL" (ByVal hMixSession As Integer, szWaveFilename
As Any, ByVal hInst As Integer, ByVal dwFlags As Long) As Long
Declare Function WaveMixOpenChannel Lib "WAVEMIX.DLL" (ByVal hMixSession As Integer, ByVal
iChannel As Integer, ByVal dwFlags As Long) As Long
```

continued on next page

continued from previous page

```
Declare Function WaveMixPlay Lib "WAVEMIX.DLL" (lpMixPlayParams As MIXPLAYPARAMS) As Integer
Declare Function WaveMixFlushChannel Lib "WAVEMIX.DLL" (ByVal hMixSession As Integer, ByVal
iChannel As Integer, ByVal dwFlags As Long) As Integer
Declare Function WaveMixCloseChannel Lib "WAVEMIX.DLL" (ByVal hMixSession As Integer, ByVal
iChannel As Integer, ByVal dwFlags As Long) As Integer
Declare Function WaveMixFreeWave Lib "WAVEMIX.DLL" (ByVal hMixSession As Integer, ByVal
lpMixWave As Long) As Integer
Declare Function WaveMixCloseSession Lib "WAVEMIX.DLL" (ByVal hMixSession As Integer) As Integer
Declare Sub WaveMixPump Lib "WAVEMIX.DLL" ()
Declare Function WaveMixGetInfo Lib "WAVEMIX.DLL" (lpWaveMixInfo As WAVEMIXINFO) As Integer

Function WAVMIX_AddFile(FileName As String) As Integer
'------------------------------------------------------------
' Open a wave file and assign it to the next available
' channel.
'------------------------------------------------------------
Dim wRtn As Long

    WAVMIX_AddFile = False
    If WAVMIX_Quiet Then Exit Function
    If WaveHandle + 1 = WAVEMIX_MAXCHANNELS Then Exit Function

    ReDim Preserve lpWaveMix(WaveHandle)
    lpWaveMix(WaveHandle) = WaveMixOpenWave(hWaveMix, ByVal FileName, 0, 0)
    wRtn = WaveMixOpenChannel(hWaveMix, WaveHandle, 0)
    WAVMIX_AddFile = WaveHandle
    WaveHandle = WaveHandle + 1
    WAVMIX_AddFile = True
End Function

Sub WAVMIX_SetFile(FileName As String, AChannel As Integer)
'------------------------------------------------------------
' Assign a new wave file, FileName, to the specified channel,
' AChannel. If this channel is currently assigned another
' wave file, stop playing the channel and free the active
' wave file.
'------------------------------------------------------------
Dim wRtn As Long

    If WAVMIX_Quiet Then Exit Sub

    If AChannel > UBound(lpWaveMix) Then
        ReDim Preserve lpWaveMix(AChannel)
        WaveHandle = AChannel
    End If

    ' If another wave is currently assigned to this
    ' channel, free it.
    If lpWaveMix(AChannel) <> 0 Then
        WAVMIX_StopChannel AChannel
        wRtn = WaveMixFreeWave(hWaveMix, lpWaveMix(AChannel))
    End If
```

```
    ' Open the new wave and assign it to this channel.
    lpWaveMix(AChannel) = WaveMixOpenWave(hWaveMix, ByVal FileName, 0, 0)
    wRtn = WaveMixOpenChannel(hWaveMix, AChannel, 0)
End Sub


Sub WAVMIX_Close()
'-------------------------------------------------------------
' Stop playing all channels and free all wave files, then
' close down this WaveMix session.
'-------------------------------------------------------------
Dim wRtn As Long
Dim i As Integer, rc As Integer

    If WAVMIX_Quiet Then Exit Sub

    If (hWaveMix <> 0) Then
        For i = 0 To UBound(lpWaveMix)
            If lpWaveMix(i) <> 0 Then
                WAVMIX_StopChannel i
                rc = WaveMixFreeWave(hWaveMix, lpWaveMix(i))
            End If
        Next
        wRtn = WaveMixCloseSession(hWaveMix)
        hWaveMix = 0
    End If
End Sub

Function WAVMIX_InitMixer() As Integer
'-------------------------------------------------------------
' Initialize and activate the WaveMix DLL.
'-------------------------------------------------------------
Dim wRtn As Long
Dim config As MIXCONFIG

    If WAVMIX_Quiet Then Exit Function

    WaveHandle = 0
    ReDim lpWaveMix(0)
    ChDir App.Path

    config.wSize = Len(config)
    config.dwFlags = 1
    'Allow stereo sound
    config.wChannels = 2
    hWaveMix = WaveMixConfigureInit(config)
    wRtn = WaveMixActivate(hWaveMix, True)

    If (wRtn <> 0) Then
        WAVMIX_InitMixer = False
    Else
        WAVMIX_InitMixer = True
```

continued on next page

continued from previous page

```
    End If
End Function

Sub WAVMIX_StopChannel(ChannelNum As Integer)
'------------------------------------------------------------
' Stop playing the specified channel.
'------------------------------------------------------------
Dim rc As Integer

    If WAVMIX_Quiet Then Exit Sub
    If (hWaveMix = 0) Then Exit Sub

    rc = WaveMixFlushChannel(hWaveMix, ChannelNum, 0)
End Sub

Sub WAVMIX_Activate(Activate As Integer)
'------------------------------------------------------------
' Activate the WaveMix DLL.
'------------------------------------------------------------
Dim rc As Integer

    If WAVMIX_Quiet Then Exit Sub
    If (hWaveMix = 0) Then Exit Sub

    rc = WaveMixActivate(hWaveMix, Activate)
End Sub

Sub WAVMIX_PlayChannel(ChannelNum As Integer, LoopWave As Integer)
'------------------------------------------------------------
' Play a specified channel, and indicate whether the sound
' should be looped.
'------------------------------------------------------------
Dim params As MIXPLAYPARAMS
Dim wRtn As Long

    If WAVMIX_Quiet Then Exit Sub
    If ChannelNum > UBound(lpWaveMix) Then Exit Sub
    If (hWaveMix = 0) Then Exit Sub

    params.wSize = Len(params)
    params.hMixSession = hWaveMix
    params.iChannel = ChannelNum
    params.lpMixWave = lpWaveMix(ChannelNum)
    params.hWndNotify = 0
    params.dwFlags = 5
    params.wLoops = LoopWave
    wRtn = WaveMixPlay(params)
End Sub
```

2. Create a new form called WAVMIX1.FRM. Add the controls listed in Table 6-5 to the form.

TABLE 6-5
◇◇◇◇◇◇
Objects and properties for WAVMIX1.FRM

Object	Property	Setting
VB.Form	Name	frmWaveMixTest
	Auto3D	-1 'True
	BorderStyle	1 'Fixed Single
	Caption	"Wave Mix Tester"
	MaxButton	0 'False
SSPanel	Name	panMain
SSPanel	Name	panWaveFrame
	Index	0
	bevelouter	1
CommonDialog	Name	CMDialog1
	defaultext	"WAV"
	dialogtitle	"Open Wave File"
	filter	"Wave Files (*.wav)|*.wav"

3. Click on the panMain SSPanel control you just placed on the form in Step 2. Add the controls listed in Table 6-6 inside the panMain control.

TABLE 6-6
◇◇◇◇◇◇
Controls placed inside the panMain control

Object	Property	Setting
Label	Name	lblSoundNbr
	BackStyle	0 'Transparent
	Caption	"Wave Channel 0"
Label	Name	Label1
	BackStyle	0 'Transparent
	Caption	"Click to the left of a channel's Play button, then change its File and Loop parameters using the controls above."
	ForeColor	&H000000C0&

continued on next page

continued from previous page

Object	Property	Setting
CommandButton	Name	btnOpen
	BackColor	&H00C0C0C0&
	Caption	"&Wave File..."
CheckBox	Name	chkLoop
	BackColor	&H00C0C0C0&
	Caption	"Loop Sound"

4. Place the controls shown in Table 6-7 within the panWaveFrame SSPanel control.

TABLE 6-7

Controls placed inside the panWaveFrame SSPanel control

Object	Property	Setting
Label	Name	lblWaveFile
	BackStyle	0 'Transparent
	Caption	"[none]"
	Index	0
Image	Name	imgHand
	Index	0
CommandButton	Name	btnPlay
	BackColor	&H00C0C0C0&
	Caption	"Play"
	Index	0

Once you've placed these controls inside the panWaveFrame control, click on the imgHand image control. In the Visual Basic properties window, select imgHand's Picture property. The Loan Picture dialog box will let you select a bitmap or icon to be displayed in the image control. I selected the pointing hand from Visual Basic's icon collection, but you can select any appropriate picture.

5. Next, you'll need to make seven copies of the panWaveFrame control. Notice that panWaveFrame, along with all the controls inside it, was given an Index property value of 0. This lets you make copies to create a control array. To do this, just click on the panWaveFrame control to select it. Next, select the *Copy* command from Visual Basic's Edit menu. Next, click on the form itself—outside of any control—to select it. Then select the *Paste* command from the Visual Basic Edit menu. A copy of the panWaveFrame control, including the controls inside it, will appear at the top of the form. Drag the frame down and place it below the original panWaveFrame. This duplicate panWaveFrame is automatically given an index of 1. Repeat the paste process to create a total of eight panWaveFrame controls, indexed 0 through 7. Make sure that you click on the form itself before pasting. If you click on one of the frames by accident, then the *Paste* command will paste a new frame inside the selected frame, which is not what you want.

6. Finally, add the code to the form in Listing 6-5. Make sure all event procedures are associated with their corresponding controls.

Listing 6-5 WAVMIX1.FRM

```
Option Explicit
'--------------------------------------------------------------
' WAVMIX1.FRM
' This example program lets the user set multiple wave audio
' channels for simultaneous playback using the WAVEMIX DLL.
'--------------------------------------------------------------

Dim CurrentChannel As Integer
Const MAX_CHANNELS = 8

Private Type tChannelInfo
    Loops As Integer
    WaveFile As String
End Type

Dim Channel(0 To MAX_CHANNELS - 1) As tChannelInfo

Private Sub btnOpen_Click()
'--------------------------------------------------------------
' Let the user assign a wave file to the current channel.
'--------------------------------------------------------------

    On Error Resume Next

    ' Let the user select another wave file via the
    ' Open File common dialog.
```

continued on next page

continued from previous page

```
    CMDialog1.CancelError = True
    CMDialog1.ShowOpen
    If Err <> 0 Then Exit Sub

    ' If we're currently looping a sound on this
    ' channel, then stop the sound and reset the
    ' text on the button.
    If btnPlay(CurrentChannel).Caption = "Stop" Then
        WAVMIX_StopChannel CurrentChannel
        btnPlay(CurrentChannel).Caption = "Play"
    End If

    ' Set the current channel to use the new wave file.
    lblWaveFile(CurrentChannel) = "Channel " & Format$(CurrentChannel) & ": " &
                                  LCase$(CMDialog1.FileName)
    Channel(CurrentChannel).WaveFile = LCase$(CMDialog1.FileName)
    Channel(CurrentChannel).Loops = (chkLoop.Value = 1)
    WAVMIX_SetFile Channel(CurrentChannel).WaveFile, CurrentChannel
End Sub

Private Sub btnPlay_Click(Index As Integer)
'------------------------------------------------------------
' Play the wave assigned to the specified channel.
'------------------------------------------------------------
    If btnPlay(Index).Caption = "Play" Then
        If Channel(Index).Loops Then btnPlay(Index).Caption = "Stop"
        WAVMIX_PlayChannel Index, Channel(Index).Loops
    Else
        btnPlay(Index).Caption = "Play"
        WAVMIX_StopChannel Index
    End If
End Sub

Private Sub chkLoop_Click()
'------------------------------------------------------------
' Set the Boolean that determines if the current channel
' will loop the wave file when played.
'------------------------------------------------------------
    Channel(CurrentChannel).Loops = (chkLoop.Value = 1)
End Sub

Private Sub Form_Load()
'------------------------------------------------------------
' Initialize the WaveMix DLL and adjust the position of
' controls on the form.
'------------------------------------------------------------
Dim LeftMargin As Integer, TopMargin As Integer
Dim i As Integer, j As Integer

    CurrentChannel = 0
    ChDir App.Path

    ' Initialize the WaveMix DLL.
```

```
    If Not WAVMIX_InitMixer() Then
        MsgBox "Unable to Initialize WaveMix DLL", _
               vbOKOnly Or vbCritical, "WaveMix Error"
        End
    End If

    ' Adjust the channel frames on the screen.
    LeftMargin = panWaveFrame(0).Left
    TopMargin = panWaveFrame(0).Top - (panMain.Top + panMain.Height)
    lblWaveFile(0) = "Channel 0: [none]"
    For i = 1 To 7
        lblWaveFile(i) = "Channel " & Format$(i) & ": [none]"
        panWaveFrame(i).Left = LeftMargin
        panWaveFrame(i).Width = panWaveFrame(1).Width
        panWaveFrame(i).Height = panWaveFrame(1).Height
        panWaveFrame(i).Top = panWaveFrame(i - 1).Top _
                            + panWaveFrame(i - 1).Height _
                            + TopMargin
    Next
    Me.Height = (Me.Height - Me.ScaleHeight) _
                + panWaveFrame(7).Top + panWaveFrame(7).Height _
                + (TopMargin * 2)
End Sub

Private Sub Form_Unload(Cancel As Integer)
'------------------------------------------------------------
' Before the program ends, shut down the WaveMix DLL.
'------------------------------------------------------------

    WAVMIX_Close
End Sub

Private Sub panWaveFrame_Click(Index As Integer)
'------------------------------------------------------------
' Change the current channel.
'------------------------------------------------------------

    If Index = CurrentChannel Then Exit Sub
    imgHand(Index).Visible = True
    imgHand(CurrentChannel).Visible = False
    CurrentChannel = Index
    lblSoundNbr = "Wave Channel " & Format$(CurrentChannel)
    chkLoop.Value = Abs(Channel(CurrentChannel).Loops)
End Sub
```

How It Works

Run the program. You'll see a panel for each of the eight WaveMix channels. Click on the left side of one of these panels to select that channel. The hand icon will appear in the panel. Now you can set the channel's wave file and looping option using the controls at the top of the form.

Set up several channels and press their Play buttons. For the best effect, set up one channel with a background music wave file, preferably one that will last several seconds. You may want to set this channel so that the music loops as well. Next set up a few of the other channels with short sound effect wave files. Start playing the music channel, and while it's playing, play the various sound effects channels. You should be able to hear the sound effects layered over the background music.

You can use this same technique when designing sounds for games. You may even want to use this example program to test various sounds while you're building a game, to hear how well they sound together.

Now that you know the ins and outs of sound, let's take a look at another multimedia aspect of games programming: displaying video and frame animation.

7

Video and Frame Animation

7

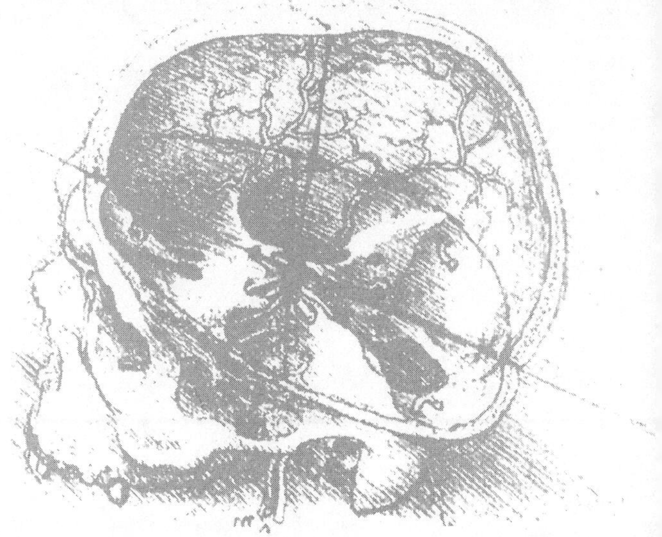

Video and Frame Animation

Persistence of vision is the term used to describe the fact that humans tend to see an image for a few short moments after it's gone. It's this phenomenon that makes inventions like motion pictures possible. Motion pictures are, after all, simply a collection of still phototgraphs displayed one after another.

Persistence of vision causes individual pictures to merge together into a smooth approximation of motion. To create an illusion of real-life motion, the images must be displayed rapidly; the minimum required speed is about 16 frames per second. If the images are displayed slower than this, the motion appears jerky and unnatural. Motion picture film is generally shot at 24 frames per second, whereas American television is standardized at a rate of 30 frames per second.

It was inevitable that video animation would eventually move to the personal computer. In this chapter we'll look at two techniques for displaying video or frame-based animation using Visual Basic.

How can you integrate video into a game? There are many possibilities. Some games use live action video sequences with real actors and sets, much like actual motion pictures, in opening sequences or bridging segues. Others use video to display moving three-dimensional backgrounds on which to stage a game. Some role-playing games are almost entirely created from video clips, with the player making choices that propel the characters into one situation or another.

Video clips don't have to be live action. You can create animated sequences using off-the-shelf software, and integrate these sequences into your games.

Frame Animation Using Bitmaps

One technique for building animated sequences provides the programmer with a high degree of control over each frame. This method calls for each frame of an animation sequence to be stored in a separate bitmap. You display each bitmap, in sequence, inside a PictureBox or Image control. This gives you both responsibility for and control of each frame.

One advantage of this technique is that it allows you to add, or superimpose, foreground objects using the sprite techniques described in Chapter 3. For example, if you have a video sequence of a lap around a race track, you could later superimpose bitmapped cars to create the illusion of a race.

There are some disadvantages to this technique. First, the individual bitmaps that make up the frames take up a lot of storage space. And of course, the bigger bitmaps and bitmaps with higher color resolutions require even more storage. This problem forces you to choose from a series of trade-offs. One way to deal with the storage problem is to store each frame on disk and only load it as needed. The downside of this technique is that it takes significantly longer to access an image on disk than one already in memory. You could load all the bitmaps into memory, but only a limited amount of Windows memory is available. And after a certain point, memory is swapped out to the Windows swap file, which brings you back to the problem of disk access. One way to decrease the disk usage is to limit the number of frames in the sequence; this will undoubtedly be at the expense of the smoothness and realism of the animation.

Let's build an animation sequence that illustrates some of these trade-offs. The project will contain a computer-generated animation of a fly-by of the Alps. The animation sequence was created using a program called VistaPro from Virtual Reality Laboratories, Inc. I'll look at this program in more detail in Chapter 8. For now, you need to know that I've created 196 frames of animation that, when viewed in sequence, provide a fly-by loop around a section of the Alps. Figure 7-1 shows the path the virtual camera took as it flew around the computer-generated Alps.

Let's take a look at the trade-offs for this particular program. To ensure that I had enough memory to display the fly-by, I loaded each bitmap from disk as it was needed. Reading from disk slows the speed, so to compensate partially, I decided to make the bitmaps fairly small, only 200 pixels wide and 160 pixels high, and I restricted the color resolution to 256 colors. Even with these restrictions, each frame still weighs in at a little more than 32 kilobytes.

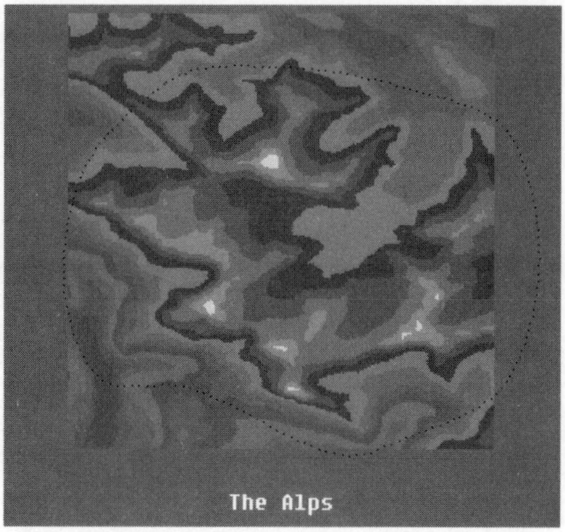

FIGURE 7-1
Overhead view of the Alps fly-by

Create a new project called BMP_ANIM.MAK. This project will require a single form, called BMP_ANIM.FRM. Add this form to the project. Add the controls described in Table 7-1 to the form.

TABLE 7-1
Objects and properties of the BMP_ANIM.FRM form

Object	Property	Setting
Form	FormName	Form1
	BackColor	&H00C0C0C0&
	Caption	"Bitmap Frame Animation"
Label	Name	Label1
	Alignment	1 'Right Justify
	BackStyle	0 'Transparent
	Caption	"Frame Delay (ms.):"
Label	Name	lblFrame
	Alignment	2 'Center
	BackStyle	0 'Transparent
	Caption	"0"

continued on next page

continued from previous page

Object	Property	Setting
Label	Name	lblAveFrames
	Alignment	2 'Center
	BackStyle	0 'Transparent
	Caption	"Average Frames: 00.0 per second"
CommandButton	Name	btnStart
	Caption	"&Start"
TextBox	Name	txtFrameDelay
	MaxLength	5
	Text	"5"
HScrollBar	Name	HScroll1
	LargeChange	5
	Max	195
PictureBox	Name	picView
	AutoRedraw	-1 'True
	AutoSize	-1 'True
	Picture	(set at design time in Properties window)
	ScaleMode	3 'Pixel
PictureBox	Name	picSprite
	AutoRedraw	-1 'True
	AutoSize	-1 'True
	BorderStyle	0 'None
	Picture	(set at design time in Properties window)
	ScaleMode	3 'Pixel
	Visible	0 'False
PictureBox	Name	picMask
	AutoRedraw	-1 'True
	AutoSize	-1 'True

Object	Property	Setting
	BorderStyle	0 'None
	Picture	(set at design time in Properties window)
	ScaleMode	3 'Pixel
	Visible	0 'False
CheckBox	Name	chkTargeting
	BackColor	&H00C0C0C0&
	Caption	"Targeting On"

The finished form at design time should look similar to Figure 7-2. The picView control will display each animation frame, so its AutoSize property has been set to True. The targeting sprite, which is composited over each frame, is created with the sprite techniques described in Chapter 3. The sprite and its mask are stored as two persistent bitmaps in the invisible PictureBox controls, picSprite and picMask. The targeting sprite will only be superimposed if the Targeting On check box control is checked.

FIGURE 7-2

The BMP_ANIM.FRM form at design time

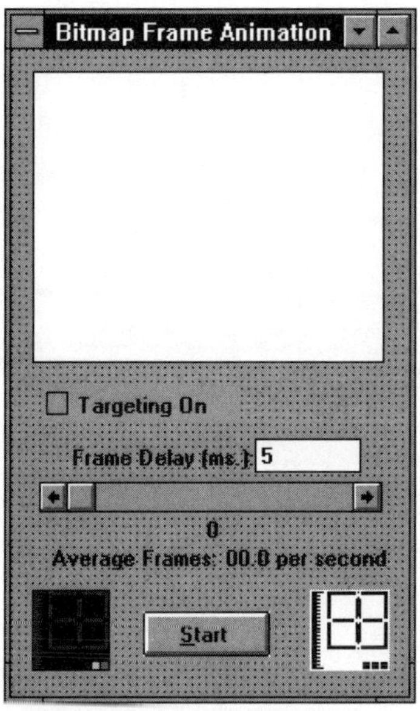

Now you'll need to start adding the code to make the program work. First, add a few variables, constants, and function declarations that will be used throughout the form. Add the code in Listing 7-1 to BMP_ANIM.FRM's Declarations section.

Listing 7-1 BMP_ANIM.FRM

```
Option Explicit
'------------------------------------------------------------
' BMP_ANIM.FRM
'------------------------------------------------------------

' Constants used in Windows API Call
Const SRCCOPY = &HCC0020
Const SRCAND = &H8800C6
Const SRCPAINT = &HEE0086

' Windows API call used to render bitmaps
Declare Function BitBlt Lib "GDI" (ByVal hDestDC As Integer, ByVal DestX As Integer,
ByVal DestY As Integer, ByVal DestWidth As Integer, ByVal DestHeight As Integer, ByVal
hSrcDC As Integer, ByVal SrcX As Integer, ByVal SrcY As Integer, ByVal RasterOp As
Long) As Integer

' Variables used to create a file name for each frame.
Dim FilePrefix As String
Dim LastBMPNum As Integer

' The x-y coordinates at which to draw the "targeting" sprite.
Dim DrawX As Integer
Dim DrawY As Integer
```

You need to initialize the variables just declared, and the most convenient place to do this is when the program starts. Add the following Load event to the form.

```
Sub Form_Load ()
'------------------------------------------------------------
' Set the values of form-level variables used by the
' program.
'------------------------------------------------------------
Dim FrameNum As Integer

    DrawX = (picView.ScaleWidth - picMask.ScaleWidth) / 2
    DrawY = (picView.ScaleHeight - picMask.ScaleHeight) / 2

    LastBMPNum = 195
    HScroll1.Max = LastBMPNum
    FilePrefix = "ALP"

End Sub
```

The Load event initializes DrawX and DrawY, which are simply the X and Y coordinates inside the picView control where the optional targeting sprite will be drawn. The other two variables, LastBMPNum and FilePrefix, help build the file names of each animation frame. One hundred ninety-six bitmap files, ALP00000.BMP through ALP00195.BMP, are used to create the animation sequence. To make it easier to use this program to display other animations, store the file prefix, in this case ALP to indicate these are pictures of the Alps, in the string variable FilePrefix. The program also needs to know when the last frame of the animation has been reached so that it can automatically jump back to the first frame. This value is stored in the LastBMPNum variable. This is especially important in the fly-by animation; because the fly-by is a loop around the Alps, the last frame brings you back to the point where you started. By jumping back to the first frame after the last frame has been displayed, the Alps fly-by appears to be one never-ending journey.

The user of this program can display the animation in one of two ways: by stepping through the animation frame by frame using the horizontal scroll bar or by cycling the animation automatically by pressing the Start button.

In either case, you need to be able to display a frame of the animation in the picView PictureBox control. Create a separate subroutine as shown in Listing 7-2, called DrawFrame, to serve this purpose.

Listing 7-2 DrawFrame

```
Sub DrawFrame (ByVal FrameNum As Integer)
'-----------------------------------------------------
' Render a frame into the picView PictureBox control and
' optionally draw the "targeting" sprite.
'-----------------------------------------------------
Dim retcode As Integer

    ' Get New Background...
    picView.Picture = LoadPicture(App.Path & "\" & FilePrefix & Format$(FrameNum,
                      "00000") & ".bmp")

    If (chkTargeting = 1) Then
        ' Draw the Mask onto the background
        retcode = BitBlt(picView.hDC, DrawX, DrawY, picMask.ScaleWidth,
                  picMask.ScaleHeight, picMask.hDC, 0, 0, SRCAND)
        ' Draw the Sprite onto the backgorund
        retcode = BitBlt(picView.hDC, DrawX, DrawY, picSprite.ScaleWidth,
                  picSprite.ScaleHeight, picSprite.hDC, 0, 0, SRCPAINT)
    End If
    DoEvents
End Sub
```

This routine uses the Visual Basic LoadPicture function to load a bitmap file and display it in picView. The routine expects the bitmap file to be in the same directory as the BMP_ANIM application. Each file name can be constructed from the file prefix and the current frame number, as described earlier.

If the chkTargeting check box is currently checked, then the DrawFrame routine also renders the targeting sprite into the picView control. The sprite is rendered over the top of the background at the coordinates specified by DrawX and DrawY. Because these coordinates never change, the targeting sprite remains stationary, whereas the Alps appear to move "underneath" it.

Because the user can move frame by frame using the horizontal scroller, the frame needs to be updated every time the scroller changes. This is easily accomplished within the HScroll1's Change event.

```
Sub HScroll1_Change ()
'---------------------------------------------------------------
' When the scroller changes, draw the corresponding new
' frame and update the frame label.
'---------------------------------------------------------------

    DrawFrame HScroll1
    lblFrame = Format$(HScroll1)
End Sub
```

This event calls the DrawFrame routine, passing it the new value of the scroller. Set the Max property of the scroller to the last frame number, so the scroller can only move within the range of valid frames. This Change event also updates the label displayed beneath the scroller, indicating the current frame number.

Now you want to add automatic animation to the program. This will allow the player to run the animation like a movie. This will be controlled by pressing the Start button, so add the Click event in Listing 7-3 to the btnStart control.

Listing 7-3 The btnStart_Click subroutine

```
Sub btnStart_Click ()
'---------------------------------------------------------------
' This routine handles starting and stopping the animation
' when the Start/Stop button is pressed.
'---------------------------------------------------------------
Static FrameNum As Integer
Static Running As Integer
Static StartTime As Single
Static TotalFrames As Long
Dim AveFrames As Single

    ' Toggle the Boolean that tells us if we're running.
    Running = Not Running

    If Running Then
        btnStart.Caption = "&Stop"
```

```
        StartTime = Timer
        TotalFrames = 0
    Else
        btnStart.Caption = "&Start"
        HScroll1 = FrameNum
        lblFrame = Format$(FrameNum)
        AveFrames = TotalFrames / (Timer - StartTime)
        lblAveFrames = "Average Frames: " & Format$(AveFrames, "#0.0") & " per second"
    End If

    On Error Resume Next

    ' This is where the actual animation takes place. We increment
    ' FrameNum
    Do While Running
        ' Draw the frame.
        DrawFrame FrameNum
        Delay txtFrameDelay

        ' Bail out if we've stopped running.
        If Not Running Then Exit Do

        ' Bump up the frame, or jump back to the first frame.
        FrameNum = (FrameNum + 1) Mod LastBMPNum

        ' Keep track of total frames displayed to calculate statistics
        ' when animation is stopped.
        TotalFrames = TotalFrames + 1
    Loop

End Sub
```

The key to this routine is the static variable Running. This Boolean tells the subroutine whether the animation is currently running. This is analogous to an on/off switch on a film projector: If Running is True, the projector is on, if Running is False, the projector is off. The value of Running is toggled each time the btnStart button is pushed.

After the value of Running is toggled, the routine checks to see if the animation should be running or not. If the animation is running, the routine initializes some variables that are used later to calculate the average number of frames that were displayed per second. If the animation has been "turned off," then the scroll bar's position and label are updated, and the average frames per second are calculated and displayed.

The real work of this routine is performed in the Do While Running loop. The program draws a frame, using the DrawFrame routine, then waits a specified number of milliseconds, increments the current frame number, and starts the process all over again. The loop is stopped when the user presses the btnStart button again (the label on the button toggles between Start and Stop). When the button is pressed while the animation is running, the Running variable is set to False and the Do While Running loop is terminated.

The delay between frames is handled by the subroutine Delay. This routine uses the built-in Visual Basic Timer function to wait a specified number of milliseconds.

```
Sub Delay (ByVal ms As Single)
'-----------------------------------------------------------
' Delay the program for a specified number of milliseconds.
'-----------------------------------------------------------
Dim StartTimer As Single

    StartTimer = Timer
    Do
        DoEvents
    Loop While (Timer - StartTimer) < (ms / 1000)

End Sub
```

Note that this program does not use a Timer control. It certainly could have, but I chose instead to cycle through the frames within a simple Do While loop and to handle the timing with the Delay routine shown above. Either technique is acceptable.

Now all that remains is to end the program. Add the following Unload event to the form.

```
Sub Form_Unload (Cancel As Integer)
'-----------------------------------------------------------
' End the program when the form is unloaded.
'-----------------------------------------------------------

    End
End Sub
```

This routine calls the Visual Basic End command to ensure that the program terminates when the form is unloaded.

Save the project. Now you can run the program. Click the horizontal scroller and you should see a frame displayed in the picView control. Press the Start button and the animation sequence should begin. Clicking the Targeting On check box should toggle the targeting sprite on and off. The program should look like Figure 7-3 at runtime.

There are a few things to note about this program. The first is that drawing the sprite significantly slows down the speed of the program. In testing, the average frames per second with the sprite displayed ran about 50 percent slower than when the sprite was not displayed. As you would expect, the smaller the sprite image, the smaller the effect on performance.

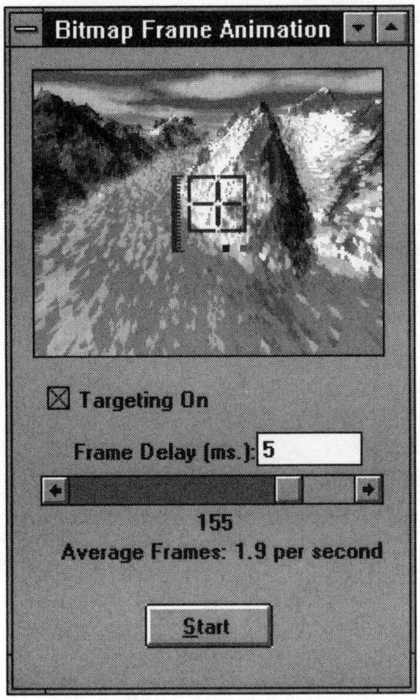

FIGURE 7-3

The Bitmap Animation example at runtime

Another important aspect of this program is that it causes a large amount of disk activity. This is to be expected from a program that must load each frame from a disk file. For shorter animation sequences, you might consider storing individual frames in an Image control array. This array could be loaded from disk at the beginning of the game, and then displayed into a PictureBox control by assigning each Image control array's Picture property to the PictureBox's Picture property.

Adding Real-Time Video

Microsoft has developed a standard for displaying real-time video under Windows. The standard, called Audio-Video Interleave format, or AVI, allows you to display actual video segments, with full synchronized sound capabilities, within an application.

The Visual Basic Professional Edition contains a special control, called the MCI control, that makes it easy to display and control these AVI files. The MCI control (MCI stands for Media Control Interface) is quite versatile; it can be used to control any device that conforms to the MCI multimedia specification. This includes devices such as audio CD players and video disc players, as well as file-oriented devices such as wave audio and MIDI files and AVI files. In this section I'll concentrate solely on MCI's abilities to display and manipulate AVI files.

An AVI file is analogous to a videotape, and the Visual Basic MCI control is like a VCR. As a matter of fact, the MCI controls resemble the controls of a VCR, sporting buttons to play, rewind, freeze-frame, and stop the AVI file, as shown in Figure 7-4.

An AVI file is actually a collection of individual bitmaps, each making up a single frame of a video animation sequence. These bitmaps are compressed and stored in a single file along with wave audio data. The MCI control can play this file, displaying each frame in rapid succession, while simultaneously playing the synchronized audio track. The result is, on a limited scale, the same as viewing a videotape.

AVI files have some advantages over the technique described in the previous section, where each frame of the animation was stored as a separate .BMP file. The primary advantage comes from the frame compression used when building an animation sequence. This can create files that are significantly smaller than a comparable collection of separate bitmaps. Also, AVI files contain a built-in audio track, so the files can contain such things as synchronized dialog. And AVI files are easier to manage, because they pack all this information into a single package.

Of course, no one would accuse AVI files of being petite. On the contrary, even a modest video clip can eat several megabytes of disk space. Even so, a real-time video clip can add a touch of realism that's impossible to get anywhere else.

Let's build a project that displays a video clip sequence. For comparison, I'll make this project somewhat similar to the bitmap animation project presented in the previous section. Like that project, you'll overlay a sprite on the video sequence. As you'll see, AVI files have their own unique set of trade-offs.

This new project will require Microsoft Video for Windows to be installed on your computer.

First, create a new project called AVI_ANIM.MAK. Add the Visual Basic MCI control, MCI.VBX, and the Common Dialog control, CMDIALOG.VBX, to the project.

Next, add a new form, AVI_ANIM.FRM, to the project. Add the controls described in Table 7-2 to the form.

FIGURE 7-4

The Visual Basic MCI control

TABLE 7-2

Objects and properties of the AVI_ANIM.FRM form

Object	Property	Setting
Form	FormName	frmAVIShow
	BackColor	&H00C0C0C0&
	Caption	"AVI Video Animation"
Label	Name	Label1
	BackStyle	0 'Transparent
	Caption	"Slower"
Label	Name	Label2
	Alignment	1 'Right Justify
	BackStyle	0 'Transparent
	Caption	"Faster"
Label	Name	lblAveFrames
	Alignment	2 'Center
	BackStyle	0 'Transparent
PictureBox	Name	picAVIScreen
	BackColor	&H00FFFFFF&
	ScaleMode	3 'Pixel
MMControl	Name	MMControl1
	UpdateInterval	0
	Visible	0 'False
CommonDialog	Name	CMDialog1
CommandButton	Name	btnStart
	Caption	"&Start"
PictureBox	Name	picSprite
	AutoRedraw	-1 'True
	AutoSize	-1 'True
	BorderStyle	0 'None
	ClipControls	0 'False
	Picture	(set at design time in Properties window)

continued on next page

continued from previous page

Object	Property	Setting
	ScaleMode	3 'Pixel
	Visible	0 'False
PictureBox	Name	picMask
	AutoRedraw	-1 'True
	AutoSize	-1 'True
	BorderStyle	0 'None
	ClipControls	0 'False
	Picture	(set at design time in Properties window)
	ScaleMode	3 'Pixel
	Visible	0 'False
HScrollBar	Name	hscrSpeed
	LargeChange	5
	Max	1
	Min	200
	Value	20
CheckBox	Name	chkTargeting
	BackColor	&H00C0C0C0&
	Caption	"Targeting On"

You'll also want to add a small menu to the form to make it easier to select an AVI file to display. Using the Visual Basic Menu Designer, add a menu, as described in Table 7-3.

TABLE 7-3

The AVI_ANIM.FRM form's menu

Caption	Name
&File	mnuFile
----&Open	mnuFileOpen
----E&xit	mnuFileExit

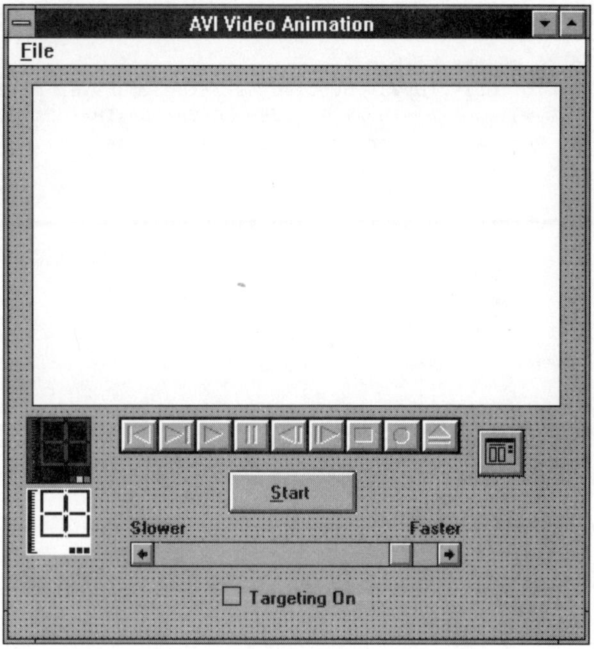

FIGURE 7-5

The AVI_ANIM.FRM form at design time

At design time, the form should look similar to the one shown in Figure 7-5. The PictureBox control, picAVIScreen, will be where the video sequence is displayed. Normally, the MCI control will create its own separate window to display the AVI video clip. For most games, this would probably not be desirable; it would be better if you could control exactly where the clip is displayed. Luckily, it is a simple matter to redirect the video into a PictureBox control, which you can position anywhere you want on the form.

Now you can start adding Visual Basic source code. First, you'll need to declare several constants, variables, and Windows API functions used throughout the project. Add the following Declarations section to the form.

```
Option Explicit
'---------------------------------------------------
' AVI_ANIM.FRM
'---------------------------------------------------

' Constants used in Windows API Call
Const SRCCOPY = &HCC0020
Const SRCAND = &H8800C6
```

continued on next page

continued from previous page

```
Const SRCPAINT = &HEE0086

' Windows API call used to render bitmaps
Declare Function BitBlt Lib "GDI" (ByVal hDestDC As Integer, ByVal DestX As Integer,
ByVal DestY As Integer, ByVal DestWidth As Integer, ByVal DestHeight As Integer, ByVal
hSrcDC As Integer, ByVal SrcX As Integer, ByVal SrcY As Integer, ByVal RasterOp As
Long) As Integer

' The x-y coordinates at which to draw the "targeting" sprite.
Dim DrawX As Integer
Dim DrawY As Integer

' Store the last frame of the AVI file.
Dim LastFrameNum As Integer
```

To make the program more aesthetically pleasing, arrange some of the controls when the form is first displayed. The best place to do this is in the form's Load event. Add the following event to AVI_ANIM.FRM.

```
Sub Form_Load ()
'--------------------------------------------------
' Arrange some of the controls on the form.
'--------------------------------------------------

    ' Set the AVI viewing screen to its maximum size.
    ResetScreenSize

    ' Position the Average Frames label.
    lblAveFrames.Move MMControl1.Left, MMControl1.Top, MMControl1.Width
End Sub
```

The Load event calls ResetScreenSize, a subroutine that adjusts the picAVIScreen control to its largest allowable size on the form. The picAVIScreen PictureBox is where you'll display the video clip. Add this subroutine, as shown below.

```
Sub ResetScreenSize ()
'__________________________________________________
' Adjust the AVI viewing screen (a PictureBox
' control) to its maximum allowable size.
'__________________________________________________
Dim margin As Integer

    margin = 10 * Screen.TwipsPerPixelY
    picAVIScreen.Move margin, margin, Me.ScaleWidth - (margin * 2), MMControl1.Top - (margin * 2)

End Sub
```

Now, add the event routine that's called when the player selects the Open command from the file menu. Add the following Click event to the mnuFileOpen menu object.

```
Sub mnuFileOpen_Click ()
'-----------------------------------------------------
' Retrieve a media file name and attempt to load
' it into the MCI control.
'-----------------------------------------------------
Dim OK As Integer
Dim FileExt As String
Dim AFileName As String

    OK = False
    GetNewFileName AFileName

    ' Extract the file's extension
    If Len(AFileName) > 4 Then FileExt = Right$(AFileName, 4)

    ' Based on the extension, load the media file
    Select Case FileExt
        Case ".AVI"
            'ResetScreenSize
            OK = SetupAVI(AFileName, MMControl1, picAVIScreen)
            Me.Caption = "AVI Animation - [" & LCase$(MMControl1.FileName) & "]"
    End Select

End Sub
```

This event calls the GetNewFileName subroutine, whose purpose is to display the Common Dialog control. This lets the player select an AVI file. Add the GetNewFileName routine, as shown below.

```
Sub GetNewFileName (AFile As String)
'-----------------------------------------------------
' Use the Common File Dialog to retrieve a file name.
'-----------------------------------------------------
Dim Canceled As Integer

    Canceled = False
    On Error GoTo GetNewFileName_Error

    ' Set up the Common File Dialog
    CMDialog1.Filter = "AVI Video Files|*.avi"
    CMDialog1.DialogTitle = "Select AVI Video File"
    CMDialog1.CancelError = True

    ' Open the Common File Dialog
    CMDialog1.Action = 1

    If Not Canceled Then
        AFile = CMDialog1.FileName
    Else
        AFile = ""
    End If
```

continued on next page

continued from previous page

```
Exit Sub
GetNewFileName_Error:
    Canceled = True
    Resume Next
End Sub
```

If the player selects a file with an .AVI extension, the mnuFileOpen Click event calls the SetupAVI function. This function sets up the MMControl1 MCI control so that it can display the selected AVI file. This is done by setting several of MMControl1's properties, most notably its FileName and DeviceType properties, as shown in Listing 7-4.

Listing 7-4 The SetupAVI function

```
Function SetupAVI (ByVal AFileName As String, MMControl1 As MMControl, picAVIScreen As
PictureBox) As Integer
'--------------------------------------------------
' Attempt to load an Audio-Video Interleave (AVI)
' file into a picture box (picAVIScreen) for
' display.
'--------------------------------------------------

    On Error GoTo SetupAVI_Error
    SetupAVI = False

    ' Load the file into the MCI control.
    MMControl1.Command = "Close"
    If MMControl1.FileName <> AFileName Then
        MMControl1.Notify = False
        MMControl1.Wait = True
        MMControl1.Shareable = False
        MMControl1.DeviceType = "AVIVideo"
        MMControl1.FileName = AFileName
    End If

    ' Display the picture control.
    picAVIScreen.Visible = True

    ' This causes the file to be displayed in the picture
    ' box, instead of the default popup window.
    MMControl1.hWndDisplay = picAVIScreen.hWnd

    ' Open the MCI AVI device.
    MMControl1.Command = "Open"
    MMControl1.Command = "Step"

    ' Position the picAVIScreen control for the new AVI file.
    SetAVIDimensions
    MMControl1.Refresh

    SetupAVI = True
```

```
Exit Function
SetupAVI_Error:
    Exit Function
End Function
```

In the SetupAVI function, redirect the AVI file to the PictureBox control. The MCI control has a property, hWndDisplay, that can be used to provide the control with the window handle of an existing window. The MCI control will use this window to display the video, instead of creating a new window. Simply assign the hWnd property of the PictureBox, picAVIScreen, to MMControl's hWndDisplay property, and the AVI file is funneled into picAVIScreen.

The width and height of an AVI video clip varies, and you've made the "movie screen" control, picAVIScreen, rather large. It would be nice if you could adjust the size of this PictureBox to match the size of the clip exactly. You can perform a little Visual Basic trickery to do just that. In the SetupAVI function above, issue the MCI Open and Step commands. These commands prepare the AVI file for viewing. In fact, the Step command actually displays the first frame of the video in the picAVIScreen control. After the Step command, call the SetAVIDimensions subroutine. Add this routine, as shown in Listing 7-5.

Listing 7-5 The SetAVIDimensions routine

```
Sub SetAVIDimensions ()
'-----------------------------------------------
' Readjust the AVI viewing screen PictureBox to the
' actual dimensions of the AVI file.
'-----------------------------------------------
Dim x As Integer
Dim y As Integer
Dim AColor As Long

    ' Look for the first nonwhite pixel in the y direction.
    For y = (picAVIScreen.ScaleHeight) - 2 To 0 Step -1
        AColor = picAVIScreen.Point(1, y)
        If AColor <> RGB(255, 255, 255) Then Exit For
    Next

    ' Look for the first nonwhite pixel in the x direction.
    For x = (picAVIScreen.ScaleWidth) - 2 To 0 Step -1
        AColor = picAVIScreen.Point(x, 1)
        If AColor <> RGB(255, 255, 255) Then Exit For
    Next

    ' Readjust the picture box.
    picAVIScreen.Width = x * Screen.TwipsPerPixelX
    picAVIScreen.Height = y * Screen.TwipsPerPixelY

    ' Center the picture box.
    picAVIScreen.Left = (Me.ScaleWidth - picAVIScreen.Width) / 2
```

continued on next page

continued from previous page

```
    picAVIScreen.Top = (MMControl1.Top - picAVIScreen.Height) / 2

    ' Calculate the new center position of the targeting sprite.
    DrawX = (picAVIScreen.ScaleWidth - picMask.ScaleWidth) / 2
    DrawY = (picAVIScreen.ScaleHeight - picMask.ScaleHeight) / 2

    ' Save the last frame number of this AVI video clip.
    LastFrameNum = MMControl1.Length
End Sub
```

The PictureBox control has a special method, called Point, that returns the color of a pixel at any X-Y location inside the PictureBox. Before loading the AVI file, the PictureBox's background was entirely white. To find the actual size of the AVI video clip, traverse the left edge of the PictureBox (from the bottom) for the first nonwhite pixel. This gives the Y coordinate for the bottom of the video clip. Do the same thing along the top edge of the PictureBox, working from the far right edge toward the left. Then simply resize the PictureBox and center it on the form. Use the new dimensions of the PictureBox to determine the centered X-Y coordinates to display the targeting sprite. Also use the MCI control's Length property to determine the number of frames in the video sequence. You'll need this when you're looping the animation so that you know when you've reached the end of the video clip.

The MCI control provides buttons (Play, Rewind, etc.) that let the user manipulate the video clip. In the case of a game, you will probably want to control these functions inside the program. For that reason, I made the MCI control invisible and added a Start/Stop button that will toggle the video clip on and off.

You're also presented with another problem. You want to display a sprite on top of each animation frame. One way to do this would be to use the MCI control's StatusUpdate event. This event works much like the Timer control; at regular intervals, the MCI control automatically calls the StatusUpdate event. You could set the interval to a very small value and then render the sprite each time StatusUpdate is triggered. Although this technique works, it causes the sprite to flicker. This flicker is created because several frames may be displayed between calls to StatusUpdate.

Another technique, and the one employed here, is to step through each frame of the video under program control. This can be done with a simple Do loop that repeatedly calls the MCI control's Step command. Do this when the Start/Stop button is pressed. Add the Click event in Listing 7-6 to the btnStart control.

Listing 7-6 The btnStart_Click subroutine

```
Sub btnStart_Click ()
'-------------------------------------------------
' When the Start/Stop button is pushed, we run the
' animation sequence. Rather than use the MCI Play
' command, we use the MCI Step command to move
' frame-by-frame through the video clip.
'-------------------------------------------------
```

```
Static Running As Integer
Static FrameNum As Integer
Static StartTime As Single
Static TotalFrames As Long
Dim AveFrames As Single
Dim rc As Integer

    ' Exit if they haven't chosen an AVI file.
    If MMControl1.FileName = "" Then Exit Sub

    ' Toggle the animation on and off
    Running = Not Running

    ' Set the button caption to reflect what state
    ' we're in.
    If Running Then
        btnStart.Caption = "&Stop"
        StartTime = Timer
        TotalFrames = 0
    Else
        btnStart.Caption = "&Start"
        AveFrames = TotalFrames / (Timer - StartTime)
        lblAveFrames = "Average Frames: " & Format$(AveFrames, "#0.0") & " per second"
    End If

    ' Display the video clip, frame by frame.
    Do While Running
        ' When we get to the end of the animation, we go back to
        ' the beginning and start over, creating a continuous loop.
        If FrameNum >= (LastFrameNum - 1) Then MMControl1.Command = "Prev"

        ' Keep Track of the current frame number so we know
        ' when we reach the end.
        FrameNum = (FrameNum + 1) Mod LastFrameNum
        MMControl1.Command = "Step"

        ' Only display the targeting sprite if chkTargeting
        ' is checked.
        If chkTargeting = 1 Then
            ' Draw the Mask onto the background
            rc = BitBlt(picAVIScreen.hDC, DrawX, DrawY, picMask.ScaleWidth,
                picMask.ScaleHeight, picMask.hDC, 0, 0, SRCAND)
            ' Draw the Sprite onto the backgorund
            rc = BitBlt(picAVIScreen.hDC, DrawX, DrawY, picSprite.ScaleWidth,
                picSprite.ScaleHeight, picSprite.hDC, 0, 0, SRCPAINT)
        End If

        ' Add a delay specified by the value of the Speed scroll bar.
        Delay hscrSpeed
        TotalFrames = TotalFrames + 1
    Loop

End Sub
```

Much of this event routine is structured like the btnStart Click event in the earlier bitmap animation project. Most of the work is performed in the Do While Running loop. Simply step through each frame of animation by setting the MCI control's Command property to Step. Track the current frame number, and when you reach the end of the video sequence, "rewind" the clip to the beginning by setting the MCI control's Command property to Prev. This provides the same continuous loop effect that was achieved in the bitmap animation project.

The major downside to displaying the animation frame by frame, rather than using the MCI control's Play command to do it automatically, is that you lose any audio track that accompanies the clip. Also, the Play command uses the timing built into the AVI file, whereas you'll have to create your own timing.

Like before, you want to control the speed of the animation, so you'll again need a subroutine that can delay each subsequent frame by a specified amount of time. Add the following Delay subroutine to the form.

```
Sub Delay (ByVal ms As Single)
'-----------------------------------------------------------
' Delay the program for a specified number of milliseconds.
'-----------------------------------------------------------
Dim StartTimer As Single

    StartTimer = Timer
    Do
        DoEvents
    Loop While (Timer - StartTimer) < (ms / 1000)

End Sub
```

Now all that remains is to clean things up when the user exits the program. First, provide a way to terminate the program from the Exit command of the File menu. Add the following Click event to the mnuFileExit object.

```
Sub mnuFileExit_Click ()
'---------------------------------------------------
' Exit the program by unloading the form.
'---------------------------------------------------

    Unload Me
End Sub
```

This routine unloads the form when triggered. Add the following Unload event to the form to do the actual work.

```
Sub Form_Unload (Cancel As Integer)
'---------------------------------------------------
' End the program when the form is unloaded.
'---------------------------------------------------
```

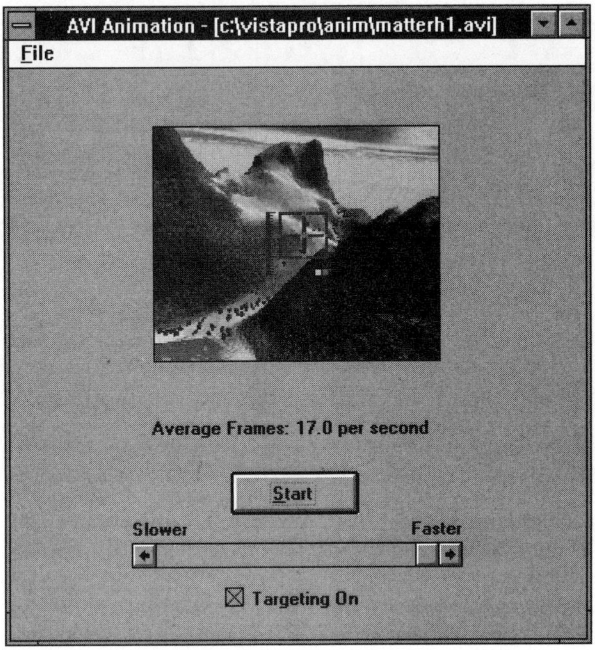

FIGURE 7-6

The AVI Video Animation program at runtime

```
    ' Make sure any AVI file is closed before we
    ' exit.
    MMControl1.Command = "CLOSE"

    End
End Sub
```

This event routine ensures that the MCI control is properly closed, then terminates the program. Now you're ready to run the program. At runtime, you can use the Open command of the File menu to select an .AVI file. I've supplied a couple on the CD. My personal favorite is a fly-by of the Matterhorn. Like the Alps fly-by I used in the bitmap animation example, this file was created using VistaPro, then converted to the AVI format. Figure 7-6 shows what the program looks like at runtime.

There are several things to note about the Video Animation program. First, even though the targeting sprite is displayed after each video frame, there is still a slight flicker to the sprite. But notice how much faster this program displays the animation when compared to its predecessor. This is because the MCI control is handling the display of each frame into the PictureBox each time the MCI Next command is called, and it does this very fast. In general, you will see a fourfold improvement in the average frame rate when using this technique.

Selecting an Animation Method

This chapter shows two distinct methods for displaying animation. Other animation file formats are available. Autodesk Animator files, which generally have an .FLI or .FLC extension, can also be displayed in Visual Basic using the third-party VBPLAY custom control. Whereas AVI files store each frame of the animation sequence in a compressed format, .FLI files take advantage of the nature of animation sequences to achieve compression in another way. If you compare two adjacent frames in an animation sequence, you'll notice that there isn't a lot of difference between the frames. The Autodesk .FLI format takes advantage of this by storing the initial frame and a collection of data that describes the differences between each frame. When an .FLI file is created, each frame is compared to its predecessor and only the differences are stored in the file. When you play back an .FLI file, the first frame is displayed, then the second frame is "created" by applying the difference data to the first frame. Each subsequent frame is constructed in a like manner.

When you look at these technologies, you may be tempted to think that they're rather crude and limited. In a way, you're right. Most video clips are short, small, grainy, and eat up a lot of disk space. But these shortcomings will be quickly surmounted by improvements in hardware. Processor and video speeds improve every month, and hard disk and other storage media capacities increase. The core technology exists today; by learning it now, you'll be ready for tomorrow's possibilites.

In the next chapter, we'll look at techniques for creating terrain and background bitmaps for games and take an in-depth look at Virtual Reality Lab's VistaPro program.

8

Creating Backgrounds and Terrain

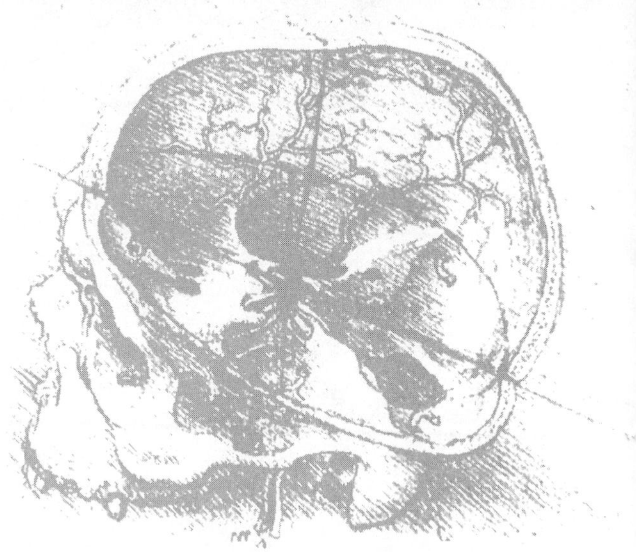

8

Creating Backgrounds and Terrain

Good game designers successfully blend a number of different elements. Sound, motion, color, and responsiveness all contribute to an enjoyable experience for the game player.

Like a good movie, a good game needs to be set in a compelling location. *Gone With the Wind* was set in the turbulent period before and after America's Civil War; the *Star Wars* trilogy was set against the backdrop of a fictitious but dazzlingly well-realized galaxy. Each of these movies has a compelling plot independent of the background. On one level, the *Star Wars* trilogy is the story of a young man from a backwater town who longs for adventure and becomes involved in a struggle against a powerful oppressor, embodied by Darth Vader. The cruel irony that Vader is Luke Skywalker's father creates another level of conflict.

But if you reread my description above, you'll find nothing that forces or even compels this storyline to be set in a galaxy far, far away. The same themes would be valid set against the milieu of the Civil War. The themes are universal; the futuristic background adds a point of reference.

You can look at the backgrounds of games in the same way. Almost all games involve some form of struggle, whether it's blasting your way out of a World War II German castle with a machine gun or fighting medieval wizards with spells and broadswords. Programmers create virtual worlds with games to provide a point of reference for the player. To create those worlds, programmers need a variety of tools. This chapter will look at tools and techniques for creating realistic and compelling backgrounds for your games.

First, we'll look at a technique for building large, seamless backgrounds from a collection of bitmap "tiles." This method is employed by numerous commercial games to create huge, scrolling backgrounds.

We'll also look at a program, VistaPro, that lets you design and render photorealistic three-dimensional worlds. With VistaPro you can create terrain maps, background landscapes, and even three-dimensional fly-bys of real and imagined worlds.

Creating Backgrounds with Tiles

One method for creating backgrounds is to use *tiles*. Tiles are bitmaps that can be joined together at their edges to form a seamless, larger picture. This larger picture becomes the background for the game. Many modern video games use some variation of tiling to avoid creating huge bitmaps. A well-designed set of tiles can be joined in myriad ways to create a large virtual playing field.

The size and number of individual tiles will vary based on the needs of a game. Let's build a small project that uses half a dozen small tiles to build an underground maze. First, design the tiles. To do this, any simple bitmap editor, such as Windows Paintbrush, will work fine. Most of the tiles will represent sections of a tunnel, but you'll also want at least one tile that looks like a solid section of rock with no tunnel sections passing through it. Let's create this bitmap first. Using a bitmap editor, create a 45 pixel by 45 pixel .BMP file that looks similar to Figure 8-1. Save this picture as TILE1.BMP.

Look at the left and right edges of this bitmap. Notice that the "mortar joints" on each side match. The same is true of the top and bottom edges. This is so that when two of these bitmaps are placed alongside each other, the effect is a single, seamless picture. This is the most important point to remember with tiling: Design all the tiles so they can be connected to form a seamless whole.

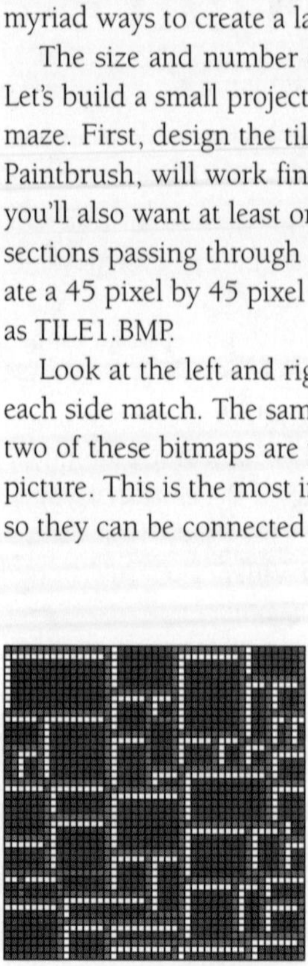

FIGURE 8-1

The first tile bitmap, showing just solid rock

FIGURE 8-2

Tiles TILE2.BMP through TILE6.BMP

Now that you have the first tile, you can build several more based on it. Make five copies of TILE1.BMP and name them TILE2.BMP through TILE6.BMP. Use the bitmap editor to cut tunnels through these bitmaps as shown in Figure 8-2. As with the original tile, be careful that the edges of each bitmap match the edges of other bitmaps.

Now let's build a program that can use these tiles to build a background. Create a new project called TILES.MAK. Add a new module to this project called TILES.BAS. You'll need to create a data type to store an X-Y coordinate, and this can only be created in a module, not a form. Add this code to TILES.BAS.

```
Option Explicit
'---------------------------------------------------
' TILES.BAS
'---------------------------------------------------

' data type used to store an x-y coordinate.
Type tPoint
    X As Integer
    Y As Integer
End Type
```

Next, create a new form called TILES.FRM. This form will contain the controls described in Table 8-1. A large square Shape control will serve as a background. Several smaller squares will be used to position six Image controls, one for each base tile. These base tiles will be used as templates to create the tiled background.

TABLE 8-1

Objects and properties of the TILES.FRM form

Object	Property	Setting
Form	FormName	Form1
	BackColor	&H00C0C0C0&
	Caption	"Bitmap Tiling Example"
Shape	Name	shpBox
	BackColor	&H0080FF80&
	BackStyle	1 'Opaque

continued on next page

continued from previous page

Object	Property	Setting
Shape	Name	shpHolder
	BackColor	&H0080FF80&
	BackStyle	1 'Opaque
	Index	0
Image	Name	imgTileA
	Index	0
	Picture	(set at design time in Properties window)
Shape	Name	shpHolder
	BackColor	&H0080FF80&
	BackStyle	1 'Opaque
	Index	1
Shape	Name	shpHolder
	BackColor	&H0080FF80&
	BackStyle	1 'Opaque
	Index	2
Shape	Name	shpHolder
	BackColor	&H0080FF80&
	BackStyle	1 'Opaque
	Index	3
Image	Name	imgTileA
	Index	1
	Picture	(set at design time in Properties window)
Image	Name	imgTileA
	Index	2
	Picture	(set at design time in Properties window)
Image	Name	imgTileA
	Index	3

Object	Property	Setting
	Picture	(set at design time in Properties window)
Image	Name	imgTileA
	Index	4
	Picture	(set at design time in Properties window)
Image	Name	imgTileA
	Index	5
	Picture	(set at design time in Properties window)
Shape	Name	shpHolder
	BackColor	&H0080FF80&
	BackStyle	1 'Opaque
	Index	4
Shape	Name	shpHolder
	BackColor	&H0080FF80&
	BackStyle	1 'Opaque
	Index	5
Label	Name	Label1
	Alignment	2 'Center
	BackStyle	0 'Transparent
	Caption	"Drag the tiles above onto the background to form connecting tunnels. To remove a tile, double-click over it."
	ForeColor	&H00008000&

At design time, set the Picture property of each imgTile control to one of the .BMP files you created earlier. Then add the following code to the Declarations section of the form.

```
Option Explicit
'-----------------------------------------------------
' TILES.FRM
'-----------------------------------------------------

' There's one base tile for each tile picture.
Const LAST_BASE_TILE = 5

' Boolean indicating if we're currently dragging
' an object.
Dim Dragging As Integer

' Used while dragging an object.
Dim Ofs As tPoint

' The index of the next image to be created in
' the imgTile control array.
Dim NextImage As Integer
```

This section declares the variables and constants you'll use throughout the form. The user will be dragging the imgTile Image controls onto the large shpBox background control. When the tile is dropped, the program actually creates a duplicate of the dragged tile by creating another imgTile control with the Visual Basic Load routine. The original tile is put back in its holding square to be used again. The user can only drag the base imgTile controls, not the ones created to place on the background. Because all tiles are part of a single control array, use the constant LAST_BASE_TILE to distinguish draggable controls.

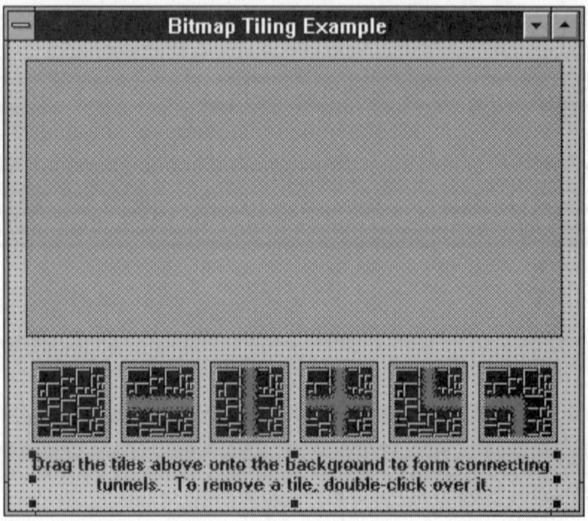

FIGURE 8-3

The TILES.FRM form at design time

Next, add a Load event to the form, as shown below.

```
Sub Form_Load ()
'-------------------------------------------------
' Initialize the next image counter, used to
' load tile controls on the fly.
'-------------------------------------------------

    NextImage = LAST_BASE_TILE + 1
End Sub
```

This routine sets the form-level NextImage variable. This variable indicates the next control array index to create when a tile is dropped on the background.

Much of the rest of the program deals with dragging and dropping the tiles. Dragging and dropping is essentially a three-step process: First, the user holds down the mouse button over the control he or she wants to move; second, the user moves the mouse pointer to the destination location; finally, the user releases the mouse button. These three steps are handled by three Visual Basic events: MouseDown, MouseMove, and MouseUp. You'll need to create these three events for the imgTile controls. First, the MouseDown event:

```
Sub imgTileA_MouseDown (Index As Integer, Button As Integer, Shift As Integer, X As Single, Y As
Single)
'-------------------------------------------------
' If the mouse is held down over an object, prepare
' to drag that object.
'-------------------------------------------------

    If Index > LAST_BASE_TILE Then Exit Sub

    Dragging = True
    Ofs.X = X
    Ofs.Y = Y
End Sub
```

Here, you simply set a Boolean that indicates that you've started to drag an object and you save the initial position of the mouse pointer. Why do you need to set a Boolean to indicate that you've started a drag operation? This becomes apparent when you look at the MouseMove event.

```
Sub imgTileA_MouseMove (Index As Integer, Button As Integer, Shift As Integer, X As Single, Y As
Single)
'-------------------------------------------------
' Drag an object if the mouse is clicked and
' dragged over it.
'-------------------------------------------------

    If Index > LAST_BASE_TILE Then Exit Sub
```

continued on next page

continued from previous page

```
    If Dragging Then
        imgTileA(Index).Move imgTileA(Index).Left + (X - Ofs.X), imgTileA(Index).Top + (Y -
Ofs.Y)
    End If

End Sub
```

In this event, you actually move the tile as the user moves the mouse. However, this event is called any time the mouse moves over an object, regardless of whether the mouse button has been pressed while over the object. Had you not checked, using the Boolean dragging, that a valid drag operation had begun, then any time the mouse swept over a control, the control would be dragged along for the ride!

Now you can add the final step in the drag operation as shown in Listing 8-1, the MouseUp event.

Listing 8-1 imgTileA_MouseUp subroutine

```
Sub imgTileA_MouseUp (Index As Integer, Button As Integer, Shift As Integer, X As Single, Y As
Single)
'--------------------------------------------------
' End the drag process and create and position
' the new tile.
'--------------------------------------------------
Dim Center As tPoint

    If Index > LAST_BASE_TILE Then Exit Sub

    Dragging = False

    ' Calculate the center coordinates for the tile.
    CenterXY imgTileA(Index), Center

    ' If the user has placed the tile inside the background,
    ' then create a new tile control and place it on the
    ' background.
    If InsideControl(shpBox, Center) Then
        ' Create a new image control to drop at this location
        Load imgTileA(NextImage)
        imgTileA(NextImage).Picture = imgTileA(Index).Picture

        ' Adjust the control's position so that it "jumps"
        ' to the nearest tile boundary.
        imgTileA(NextImage).Left = shpBox.Left + (imgTileA(Index).Width * (Center.X \
imgTileA(Index).Width))
        imgTileA(NextImage).Top = shpBox.Top + (imgTileA(Index).Height * (Center.Y \
imgTileA(Index).Height))

        imgTileA(NextImage).Visible = True

        ' Make sure the tile is on top of the background,
```

```
        ' not hiding underneath it!
        imgTileA(NextImage).ZOrder 0

        NextImage = NextImage + 1
    End If

    ' Move the base tile back to its holding position.
    imgTileA(Index).Left = shpHolder(Index).Left + 60
    imgTileA(Index).Top = shpHolder(Index).Top + 60
End Sub
```

If you wanted simply to leave the tile where the user dropped it, you could set the Boolean dragging to False and exit the subroutine. But you want to arrange the tiles so that they fit seamlessly at the edges. You could require that the user drop them into precisely the right location, but that would hardly be friendly. Instead, look at the center coordinates of the tile and bump it into the closest position on the background that makes a perfect fit. First, though, you need to determine the tile's center position, using the following short subroutine.

```
Sub CenterXY (Ctrl As Control, APoint As tPoint)
'----------------------------------------------------
' Find the center coordinates for this control.
'----------------------------------------------------

    APoint.X = (Ctrl.Width / 2) + Ctrl.Left
    APoint.Y = (Ctrl.Height / 2) + Ctrl.Top
End Sub
```

Once you know the center point of the tile, check to make sure it's actually inside the shpBox background control, using another short function that returns a value of True if a point is within the boundaries of a control.

```
Function InsideControl (Ctrl As Control, APoint As tPoint)
'----------------------------------------------------
' Is the point Apoint inside Control Ctrl?
'----------------------------------------------------

    InsideControl = False

    If (APoint.X >= Ctrl.Left) And (APoint.X <= (Ctrl.Left + Ctrl.Width)) Then
        If (APoint.Y >= Ctrl.Top) And (APoint.Y <= (Ctrl.Top + Ctrl.Height)) Then
            InsideControl = True
        End If
    End If
End Function
```

If the center point of the tile is outside the background area, simply put the tile back in its holding box at the bottom of the form. But if it is inside the background area, create a new duplicate tile and place it at the correct spot on the background. The original tile is put back in its holding box to be used again.

Notice that in all three of the Mouse events, you've checked if the Tile control's Index value was greater than the LAST_BASE_TILE constant. If it is, you immediately exit the event routine. This is to prevent the user from dragging one of the tiles that has already been placed on the background.

You could stop here, but you should add the ability for the user to remove a tile if he or she doesn't like its current position. Let the user do this when double-clicking over a tile.

```
Sub imgTileA_DblClick (Index As Integer)
'------------------------------------------------------
' Double-clicking on a placed tile makes it
' disappear. We do this by simply unloading
' the control.
'------------------------------------------------------

    ' Don't unload a base tile!
    If Index > LAST_BASE_TILE Then
        Unload imgTileA(Index)
    End If
End Sub
```

Unlike the other Mouse events, here you check to make sure the Tile control's index is greater than the LAST_BASE_TILE constant. This is to prevent the user from accidentally deleting a base tile.

Now save the project and run the program. Try dragging some of the tiles onto the background area. The tiles should interlock to create the appearance of a solid background bitmap, as shown in Figure 8-4.

You can combine this tiling technique with other bitmap manipulation methods. For example, you could dynamically build a background by using the BitBlt function (covered in depth in Chapter 3) to copy a collection of tiles into an off-screen PictureBox control, then use the techniques described in Chapter 3 to display the picture as a smooth scrolling background.

Creating Virtual Worlds with VistaPro

For many games, you'll want to render realistic three-dimensional terrain. If you're not an artist or you don't have a library of digitized landscapes at your disposal, you may have a problem on your hands. Luckily, tools on the market not only can provide you

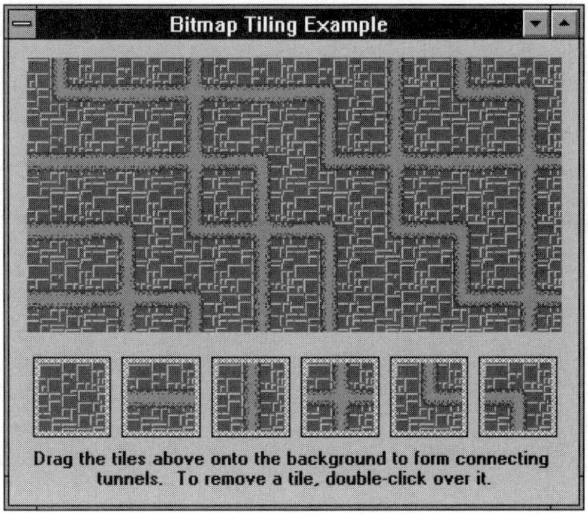

FIGURE 8-4

The tile background project at runtime

with the terrain and landscape snapshots you need, but can give you complete control over virtual worlds.

Imagine being able to travel to the Alps, set up a camera, and take snapshots of the countryside. Don't like the camera angle? Just move 500 feet straight up. Don't like the weather? Add a few clouds. While you're at it, move the sun. Not happy with the terrain? Bop on over to the Matterhorn. How about Mount Saint Helens? The surface of Venus?

This may sound absurd, but a program called VistaPro, from Virtual Reality Laboratories, Inc., lets you do all this and more. The program lets you view three-dimensional terrain maps of dozens of geographical locations.

When you run VistaPro, you are presented with a window split into two sections, as shown in Figure 8-5. The left side provides an overhead, two-dimensional view of a geographical location, in this case, Mount Saint Helens. The right side of the window contains controls that let you interact with the terrain.

Think of VistaPro as a computerized landscape painter. First, tell it where you want it to paint. Next, tell it where to set the camera and in which direction to point it. Then you can specify a staggering number of options. You can add trees, lakes, or rivers; change the density of clouds; even change the seasons of the year. You can turn deserts into gardens or day into night.

Figure 8-6 gives you an idea of the possibilities. This is a picture of the equatorial region of Venus. With VistaPro, I've added a lake, river, trees, grass, and clouds. VistaPro lets you save your creations in Windows bitmap, Targa, and PCX formats.

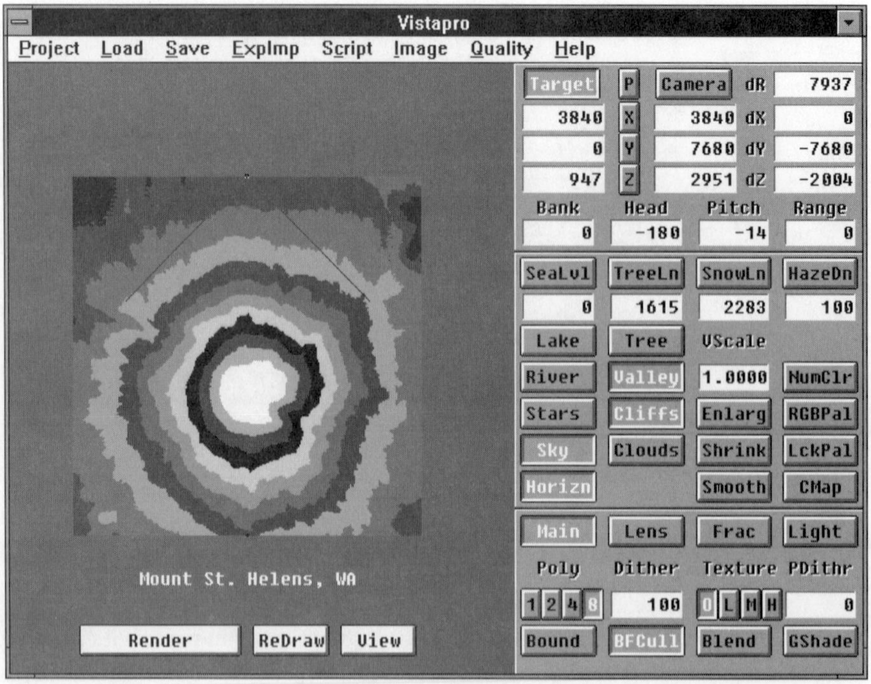

FIGURE 8-5

The VistaPro main window

FIGURE 8-6

Venus terraformed courtesy of VistaPro

FIGURE 8-7

A panoramic view created with VistaPro

Using Wide Camera Angles to Create Scrollable Vistas

VistaPro gives you control of image dimensions and camera angles. This is especially useful when you need to create a wide, continuous landscape. You can use scrolling techniques to display a section of the landscape as if a camera were panning left and right.

One way to create such a landscape is to select the Custom Size option and specify a wide, short bitmap size. Another technique is to use VistaPro's Starboard and Port lens options. Normally, VistaPro renders the view directly in front of the camera. If you set the Port lens option, VistaPro will instead render the view to the left of the camera. Likewise, the Starboard lens option shows the view to the camera's right. You can take the three images rendered, port, forward, and starboard, and join them together with a bitmap editor to create a single panoramic view. An example of this is shown in Figure 8-7.

Creating Terrain Maps with VistaPro

Many games require an aerial view of an area, such as a battlefield or forest. Once you know how to manipulate VistaPro's virtual camera, you can easily create the images.

For overhead shots, you need to set the camera at a fairly high elevation and then point it virtually straight down at the ground. First, move the camera over the area you want to view. Next, set the camera's Z parameter, its elevation, several hundred feet over its current value. This has the effect of raising the camera up off the ground. Next, change the target's location by clicking VistaPro's Target button and then clicking on the map area of the VistaPro window. You'll want to click directly over the camera position. This will have the effect of pointing the camera straight down toward the ground. Through trial and error, you can find a camera elevation that gives you the desired terrain map. Figure 8-8 shows an example of a terrain bitmap created using this technique.

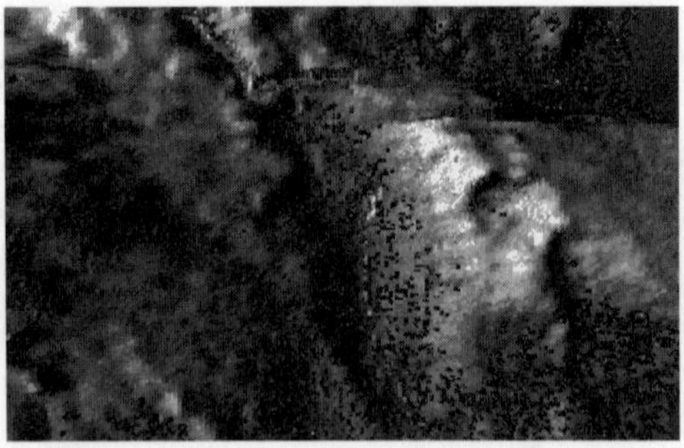

FIGURE 8-8

A terrain map created with VistaPro

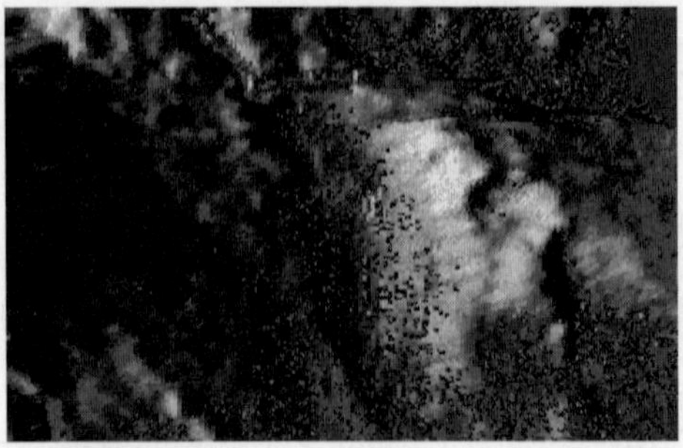

FIGURE 8-9

A terrain map with the sun's declination set at 25 Degrees

Because you're viewing the terrain from directly overhead, the resulting images may lose some of the feeling of depth that more conventional camera angles provide. To create a more enhanced feeling of depth, you can change the declination of the sun to an angle closer to the horizon. This creates shadows on the terrain similar to those found near sunrise or sunset. Figure 8-9 shows the same terrain as Figure 8-8, but with a declination of 25 degrees instead of 45 degrees.

Creating Movies with VistaPro

VistaPro lets you create and run scripts. VistaPro scripts are text files that contain sequences of camera angle coordinates. When you run a script file, VistaPro will generate a separate image "snapshot" for each camera angle in the script file. Script files let you create three-dimensional landscape fly-bys that can be saved as a collection of separate bitmap files or a single VistaPro Animation (.VAN) file. VistaPro includes a separate program to view .VAN files. Another utility program can convert a collection of bitmap files into Microsoft's Audio Video Interleave (.AVI) file format.

For more information about programming animation files, see Chapter 7.

Sources for Bitmaps

Good sources for bitmaps are electronic bulletin boards and online services. The CompuServe information service, with over 2.5 million subscribers, has a wealth of forums through which you can find a wide range of graphics, photographs, and digital movies. Much of this material is copyrighted, but a large amount of material is available without restriction. Finding this material may require some digging and exploration, but the results are worth it.

One of my favorite forums is the Space Flight Forum, which features hundreds of videos, audio clips, and .GIF format photographs and artist renderings, many courtesy of NASA. One advantage of this forum is that most materials in its libraries are copyright free. One example of the type of material that can be found in the Compuserve Space Flight Forum is shown in Figure 8-10. This is an artist's beautiful conception of an earth-orbiting space station, courtesy of NASA.

FIGURE 8-10

A NASA artist's rendering of an earth-orbit space station

You can use combinations of all the techniques described in this chapter—tiling, three-dimensional landscapes, and photographs and paintings—to create your game backgrounds. Most bitmap editors allow you to cut irregular areas of one bitmap and composite the image into a second image. Using this technique, you can combine elements from a variety of sources to create stunning and convincing alternate worlds.

Next, we'll look at an oft-neglected aspect of bitmap manipulation: palettes.

9

Working with Color Palettes

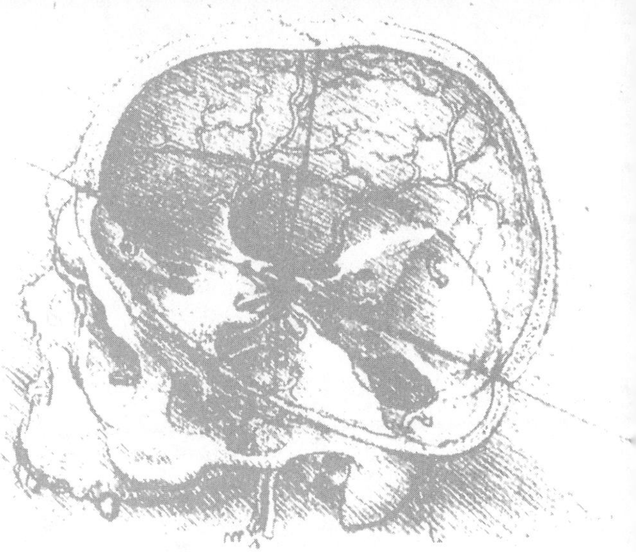

9

Working with Color Palettes

Anyone who has used Microsoft Windows for any length of time is aware of Windows video drivers. These video drivers talk to the computer's graphics adapter (also called a video board) and define what the user sees on his or her video screen. These days, the most popular graphics adapters are VGA-compatible, although some people may still use EGA-compatible video adapters.

One of the capabilities defined by the video driver is the number of simultaneous colors that can be displayed. The colors that can be displayed are often referred to as the color *palette*. For example, the standard Windows VGA video driver supports the display of 16 simultaneous colors. This is not a very wide range, but is more than sufficient for many applications that don't need to display realistic or colorful images.

Unfortunately, colorful and realistic graphics are exactly what people want in many games, which explains the rise of video adapters that display a wider range of colors. The most common of these is the Windows 256-color video driver. Most video adapter vendors now provide these drivers.

A Color-Mixing Example

In Windows, colors are stored in a 32-bit long integer value. This is equivalent to the *Long* data type in Visual Basic. Color information is stored in the lower 3 bytes of this long integer, with each byte associated with the quantity of red, green, or blue found in the color. For example, green is represented as the value &H0000FF00& (in hexadecimal). The FF in this value indicates that the green byte is at full intensity; all the other bytes are zero, so you get a pure green color. To create purple, which is a combination of red and blue, use a value of &H00FF00FF&.

Of course, the value of each color byte need not be FF (which is 255 in decimal). Values below 255 create darker and lighter shades of each color. To get a better idea of how the 3 color bytes interact, let's build a simple color-mixing program in Visual Basic. First create a new project called PALETTE.MAK. Create a single form, called PALETTE.FRM, in the project. This new form will have the objects and properties described in Table 9-1, and the form at design time should look similar to Figure 9-1.

TABLE 9-1

The objects and properties of the PALETTE.FRM form

Object	Property	Setting
Form	FormName	frmColorMixer
	BackColor	&H00C0C0C0&
	Caption	"Color Mixer"
Shape	Name	rgbMixed
	BackColor	&H00FFFFFF&
	FillColor	&H000000FF&
	FillStyle	0 'Solid
	Shape	3 'Circle
Shape	Name	rgbColor
	BackColor	&H00FFFFFF&
	FillColor	&H000000FF&
	FillStyle	0 'Solid
	Index	0
	Shape	3 'Circle
Shape	Name	rgbColor
	BackColor	&H00FFFFFF&
	FillColor	&H000000FF&
	FillStyle	0 'Solid
	Index	1
	Shape	3 'Circle

Object	Property	Setting
Shape	Name	rgbColor
	BackColor	&H00FFFFFF&
	FillColor	&H000000FF&
	FillStyle	0 'Solid
	Index	2
	Shape	3 'Circle
Label	Name	lblColor
	Alignment	2 'Center
	BackStyle	0 'Transparent
	Caption	"&&H00"
	Index	0
Label	Name	lblColor
	Alignment	2 'Center
	BackStyle	0 'Transparent
	Caption	"&&H00"
	Index	1
	Left	3900
Label	Name	lblColor
	Alignment	2 'Center
	BackStyle	0 'Transparent
	Caption	"&&H00"
	Index	2
Label	Name	lblMixed
	Alignment	2 'Center
	BackStyle	0 'Transparent
	Caption	"&&H000000&&"
VScrollBar	Name	rgbScroll
	Index	0
	LargeChange	5
	Max	255

continued on next page

continued from previous page

Object	Property	Setting
VScrollBar	Name	rgbScroll
	Index	1
	LargeChange	5
	Max	255
VScrollBar	Name	rgbScroll
	Index	2
	LargeChange	5
	Max	255

The form consists of a large circle Shape control, where the mixed color will be seen, and a three-circle Shape control array. Each of these three smaller circles will show the red, green, or blue component of the color being mixed. The colors are changed by moving one of the three Vertical Scroller controls, which are also each an element of a control array. Finally, the individual color values are displayed in hexadecimal in three labels (again a control array), and the mixed color value is displayed in another Label control.

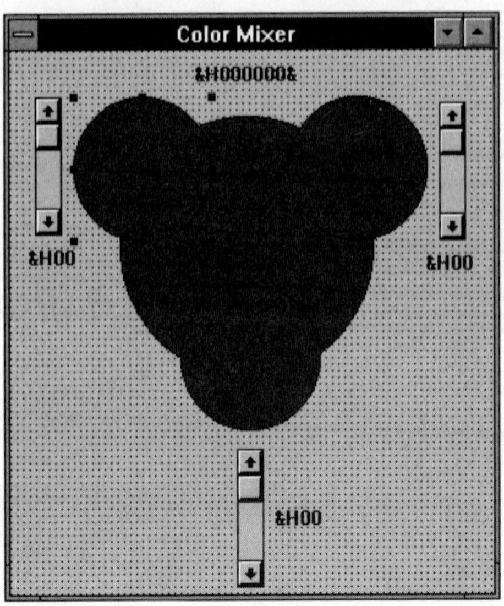

FIGURE 9-1

PALETTE.FRM at design time

> Programming Tip: I used control arrays because they greatly simplified the code. Each of the three scrollers changes the color of its corresponding Shape control, but I only needed to write code for a single scroller Change event. Control arrays can decrease the amount of code you need to write and make it easier to modify that code later. If I hadn't created the scrollers as a control array, I would have been forced to code three separate but almost identical Change events.

The code to make the Color Mixer work is quite simple, as shown in Listing 9-1. First, add a few constants to the form's Declarations section. These three constants will give a name to the three control array indexes.

Listing 9-1 PALETTE.FRM

```
Option Explicit
'------------------------------------------------------------------
' PALETTE.FRM - Color Mixer example.
'------------------------------------------------------------------

Const RED_INDEX = 0
Const GREEN_INDEX = 1
Const BLUE_INDEX = 2
```

Next, add a few lines of code to the form's Load event to set the initial color values. Note that you don't set the color values by assigning a value to a Shape control's FillColor property directly. Instead, the Load event sets a value for each of the three Scroller controls. This causes Visual Basic to fire a Change event for each scroller. As you'll see, the scroller Change event is where all the real work gets done. But first, add the following Load event to the PALETTE.FRM form.

```
Sub Form_Load ()
'------------------------------------------------------------------
' Set the initial values for red, green, and blue.
'------------------------------------------------------------------

    rgbScroll(RED_INDEX) = &H80&
    rgbScroll(GREEN_INDEX) = &H80&
    rgbScroll(BLUE_INDEX) = &H80&
End Sub
```

Now add the Change event for the scrollers. Because they're set up as a control array called rgbScroll, only one event needs to be added.

```
Sub rgbScroll_Change (Index As Integer)
'-------------------------------------------------------------------
' Every time one of the scrollers moves, the associated color is
' changed, but also the mixed color (the large circle) is changed
' to show the result of mixing the three colors together.
'-------------------------------------------------------------------

    ' Change the associated individual color.
    Select Case Index
        Case RED_INDEX:
            rgbColor(Index).FillColor = rgbScroll(Index).Value
        Case GREEN_INDEX:
            rgbColor(Index).FillColor = rgbScroll(Index).Value * &H100&
        Case BLUE_INDEX:
            rgbColor(Index).FillColor = rgbScroll(Index).Value * &H10000
    End Select

    ' Change the mixed color
    rgbMixed.FillColor = rgbColor(2).FillColor + rgbColor(1).FillColor + rgbColor(0).FillColor

    ' Change the values in the labels.
    lblColor(Index) = "&&H" & Format$(Hex$(rgbScroll(Index).Value), "00")
    lblMixed = "&&H" & Format$(Hex$(CLng(rgbMixed.FillColor)), "00000000") & "&&"
End Sub
```

The Change event receives an Index parameter that lets the event know which scroller was clicked. This Index value corresponds to one of three constants: RED_INDEX, GREEN_INDEX, or BLUE_INDEX. The first thing to do is to change the color in the associated small circle. Do this with a simple Select-Case statement. The only difference in handling each color is an adjustment of the color byte value so it is in the proper position. As I mentioned before, a color is stored in the last 3 bytes of a long integer. Each color (red, green, or blue) occupies a single byte. Red, represented as &HFF& in hexadecimal, is the low-order byte and requires no adjustment. Green, which is the next byte over to the left, must be "bit-shifted" into the correct position. Remember that green is represented as the hexadecimal value &HFF00&. Many languages have a bit-shifting operator to handle problems like this, but Visual Basic doesn't. Luckily, shifting a byte to the left can also be done through simple multiplication. Simply multiply the green value from the scroller by 256 decimal, which is &H100& in hex. Likewise, the blue byte, which is the next byte over, can be bit-shifted by multiplying it by &H10000&.

Back in the Change event, after the individual color has been adjusted, you need to create the mixed color. Just add the three colors together and assign the value to rgbMixed's FillColor property. Finally, reflect the new color values in the associated labels.

That's all there is to the example. Now let's run it. This example is intended to show some of the limitations of the 256-color video driver, so you should switch to a

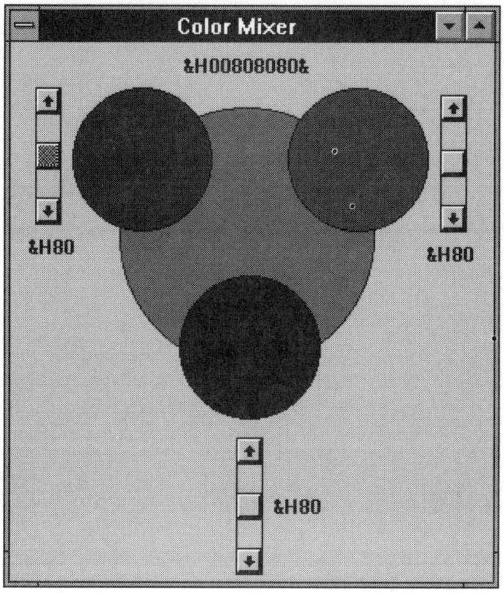

FIGURE 9-2

The color-mixing example at runtime

driver before running the example. At runtime, the program will look like Figure 9-2. Here you see the three individual colors and how they contribute to the mixed color in the center. Experiment by moving each of the scrollers and seeing its effect on the individual and mixed colors.

Problems with 256-Color Palettes

You should notice one thing when playing with the color-mixing example. If you're using a video driver capable of 256 colors or less, not all of the color values show up as true colors. Instead, most colors show up as dithered colors, that is, colors made up of patterns of pixels of two or more colors. A little simple arithmetic will explain why this is so.

Because Windows stores colors in the lower 3 bytes of a long integer, there can be up to &HFFFFFF& + 1 color values (the +1 is to include the zero value). This means &H1000000&, or 16,777,216, color values are possible. A 256-color video driver can't possibly display all those colors—or can it?

The answer is yes and no. Yes, a 256-color video driver can display any of those colors, but it can only display a selection of 256 of them at any one time. This leads to advantages and disadvantages when displaying pictures.

Let's look at an example. Say you digitize a photograph of the sky and convert it to a 256-color bitmap (.BMP) file. Most image-processing applications will create a palette based on the colors in a particular picture. In this example, the sky bitmap's palette would likely contain 256 shades of mostly blue and white, the dominant colors of the sky.

Now let's digitize a second picture, this time a close-up of some red roses. The rose's bitmap palette will look much different, mostly reds, perhaps some greens for the leaves, and some darker colors, approaching black, for shadows and such.

On one level, having custom palettes for each of these pictures is a good thing. Each picture, displayed by itself on the screen, can be seen with a wide range of colors appropriate for that image. The problem arises when you want to display the two pictures simultaneously. Each image has its own 256-color palette, and the two palettes contain quite different colors. What happens now?

The Language of Palettes

First, let me introduce some terminology. Up to now, I've been referring to palettes, but there is really more than one type of palette. The palette that is stored with the bitmap in its .BMP file is called a *logical palette*. Windows maintains a separate palette, called the *system palette,* that defines the colors that can actually be displayed on the screen at any particular time. The system palette (when a 256-color driver is in use) contains 256 color entries. Twenty of these colors, called *static colors,* are always set aside by the system. Sixteen of the 20 static colors are standard VGA colors, while the remaining four are picked to create a good blend with the other colors. This leaves 236 colors available for displaying bitmaps.

The problem is that you have two 256-color bitmaps with radically different logical palettes. Windows assigns one bitmap as the *foreground palette*. This bitmap will get first choice of the 236 available slots in the system palette. After all its colors have been assigned (a 256-color bitmap doesn't necessarily use all 256 slots in its logical palette), then any other bitmaps, which are designated *background palettes,* will have some of their colors assigned to the system palette.

This behavior can create a truly nasty problem called *palette shifting*. As new bitmaps are displayed, the system palette may be rearranged to accommodate them, and this can cause the colors in other bitmaps to change. The result is usually quite jarring, as each of the bitmaps on the screen "flashes" before being reset to the new system palette.

Visual Basic provides some control over palettes by allowing you to select which bitmap (displayed in a form, PictureBox, or Image control), will have the foreground palette. The choice of which control gets the foreground palette is based upon the *z-order* of the controls in contention. Z-order is a term that describes how controls overlap. A control at the top of the z-order will appear on top of other controls. Visual Basic lets you change the z-order of a control using the Zorder method. Passing a value of 0 to a control's Zorder method brings it to the front of the z-order,

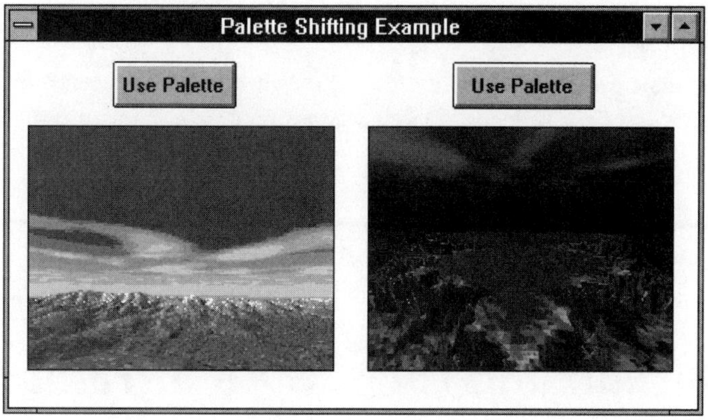

FIGURE 9-3
The Palette Shifting Example program

and also causes it to be used as the foreground palette. Passing a 1 to Zorder sends the control to the back of the z-order.

To see palette shifting in action, I've included a Visual Basic program, called PALETTE2.MAK, on the CD. This program, shown in Figure 9-3, is very simple. Two bitmaps are displayed within two PictureBox controls, side by side on a form. Command buttons sit over each of the pictures. When the user presses the left Command button, the program issues the following Visual Basic command:

```
Picture1.Zorder 0
```

This forces that PictureBox control to the front of the z-order, and also forces its palette into the foreground. When this happens, there is a noticeable and disturbing palette flashing on the screen (assuming you're using a 256-color Windows video driver). Likewise, pressing the right button forces its corresponding PictureBox to the foreground, with an accompanying palette shift.

Limitations of Visual Basic for Palette Handling

Although Visual Basic's ability to select the foreground and background palettes when displaying multiple bitmaps is useful, it isn't sufficient when designing a game that must display several overlapping bitmaps. It doesn't solve the problem of palette shifting.

For games, you need to avoid the palette-shifting problem completely by ensuring that all 256-color bitmaps use the same logical palette. But this isn't as easy as it seems. Luckily, Microsoft has some unsupported tools that can help.

What Are Microsoft's Unsupported Tools?

On its Developer's Network CD, Microsoft provides a wealth of information about Microsoft development tools, as well as numerous example programs. In addition to this, it also provides several so-called unsupported tools. These tools were developed by Microsoft and are distributed as-is. Subscribers are free to use them, but Microsoft provides no support for them.

Nevertheless, most of these tools are quite useful and complete. Let's look at two tools, designed to work in tandem, which can help with some palette problems.

BitEdit and PalEdit: An Introduction

BitEdit is essentially a bitmap editor. Its real strength is revealed when it is used with PalEdit to manipulate the palettes of multiple bitmaps. Figure 9-4 shows two instances of BitEdit and two instances of PalEdit running at the same time. Each instance displays a separate bitmap, each with a markedly different palette.

BitEdit and PalEdit can perform numerous transformations on an image, but for now concentrate on these tools' palette manipulation abilities. BitEdit and PalEdit truly work in tandem. Usually you'll start BitEdit first, and load a bitmap using the

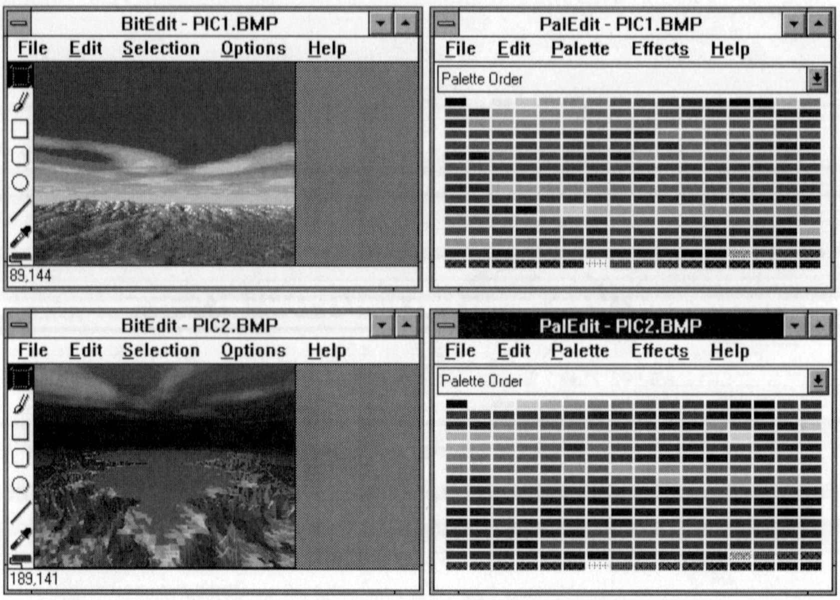

FIGURE 9-4

The BitEdit and PalEdit programs

Open command from the File menu. Once the bitmap is loaded, you can start PalEdit by selecting Show Palette from BitEdit's Options menu. This will start up an instance of PalEdit, with the open bitmap's palette displayed. There is now a link between BitEdit and PalEdit; change the palette in PalEdit, and the image displayed in BitEdit changes as well. Likewise, changes made in BitEdit can affect the palette displayed in PalEdit.

One particularly useful function of these tools is the identification of unused palette entries. These are colors in the palette that are never used in the bitmap. In other words, no pixel in the bitmap has that particular color. By using the Select Unused Colors command from the PalEdit Edit menu, you can select, or highlight, each unused color (selected palette entries are identified in PalEdit with a red border). Once selected, these entries can be removed by using the Delete command from the Edit menu.

Another useful feature of PalEdit is its ability to create an *identity palette* for a bitmap. Many tools used to create and process 256-color images do not bother to include the 20 static colors in the color palettes they create. Because Windows always reserves these 20 colors in the system palette, it's possible that 20 of the bitmap's colors may be displaced. Selecting the Make Identity Palette command from PalEdit's Palette menu will add these 20 entries to the image's logical palette.

Using a Common Palette with BitEdit and PalEdit

Let's look at two techniques for creating a common palette for two bitmaps. Assume that you have two copies of BitEdit running, each with a copy of PalEdit displaying its palette entries. It may be useful to look at Figure 9-4 for reference.

The first method will be the simplest, but also the least desirable. Simply copy the entire palette from one picture and paste it into the other. To do this, pick the Select All command from the Edit menu of one of the instances, then select the Copy command from the same menu. Now move to the Edit menu of BitEdit for the *other* image, and select the Paste Palette command. The new palette will be displayed in this image's copy of PalEdit and the bitmap itself will be altered.

This technique works best when you have one image with a wide range of colors and another image with relatively few colors. BitEdit tries to match the pasted colors as closely as possible to the original palette entries being replaced. For example, it will try to replace a medium blue in the original picture with a similar shade of blue from the pasted palette. Of course, if the new palette has no blues, the result may be less than pleasing. The wider the range of colors in the pasted palette, the better the result.

The second method for creating a common palette requires more work. First, remove all the unused colors from the palettes of both images. In many cases, you may find that only one-half to two-thirds of an image's palette entries are actually used. Next, look at the resulting reduced palettes and determine if they both, when combined, add up to more than 236 entries. If they do, then you'll need to remove some more colors. Doing this may require a little trial and error, but PalEdit provides a feature that can help here too.

First, look at the palette of an image. See if you can find several colors that appear almost identical. If you can, then click on one of these colors to select it. Next, pick the Select Similar Colors command from PalEdit's Edit menu. This will display a small dialog box asking for the number of similar colors to select. Pick a number close to the number of similar colors you noted. PalEdit will now highlight that many palette entries that are similar to the color you originally selected. Now, unselect one of these entries and use the Delete command to remove the others from the palette. If the resulting image, as displayed in BitEdit, has been too degraded by the loss of these colors, use the Undo command to reset the palette, adding back the deleted colors. Repeat this process with both images until you've reduced the palettes to a combined number of no more than 236 entries.

Next, pick one of the image's palettes using the Select All command, followed by the Copy command, both from the PalEdit Edit menu. Switch to the PalEdit of the other image and select Paste from its Edit menu. The resulting palette will be a combination of both palettes. This palette should still have at least 20 entries free. Select Make Identity Palette from the Palette menu to add the 20 static system colors to the palette. Now this image has a combined palette. Select all its palette entries with PalEdit's Select All command, then switch to the other image's BitEdit program and use the Paste command to apply the combined palette to it as well.

This may seem like a rather convoluted method for combining palettes, but it does provide a great degree of control. The big problem with this method is that it doesn't scale up well when working with more than two images. For this case, let's look at another Microsoft tool.

Creating an Average Palette for Multiple Bitmaps Using VidEdit

VidEdit is a tool that comes with Microsoft's Video for Windows (VFW) Developer's Kit. This kit is available to subscribers to the Microsoft Development Platform. To use this tool, you must have the Video for Windows runtime DLLs installed on your system. These also come with the Development Platform.

VidEdit was designed to edit Audio Video Interleave (.AVI) files, the native video format used by VFW. You might wonder what good a video-editing tool would be for manipulating bitmap palettes. But if you think of video as nothing more than a fast-moving sequence of bitmaps, you begin to realize that video sequences may have palette-shifting problems too.

Figure 9-5 shows the VidEdit program. In addition to letting you edit existing .AVI files, VidEdit also lets you build video sequences from a collection of bitmaps. Using the Insert command from VidEdit's File menu, you can add images in a variety of formats, including TrueVision, .TGA, AutoCad Plot files, encapsulated PostScript, and Windows Device Independent Bitmaps (which include .BMP files).

How does this help create a common palette for several images? Well, say you have five bitmaps for which you want to create a common palette. All you need to do is load them as frames into VidEdit, using the Insert command. Next, select the Create Palette command from the Video menu. This displays the dialog box shown in Figure 9-6. Leave the Create From option set to the default value, All Frames, because you want to create a single palette for all five video frames. You do want to change the Colors in Created Palette option to 236 (the default is 256) to leave room for static system colors. VidEdit will now create a common palette for all the images. Depending on the variety of palette entries in the original images, some of the frames may suffer some degradation, but in practice, I've found this to be a quick and reliable way to create common palettes.

FIGURE 9-5

Microsoft's VidEdit program

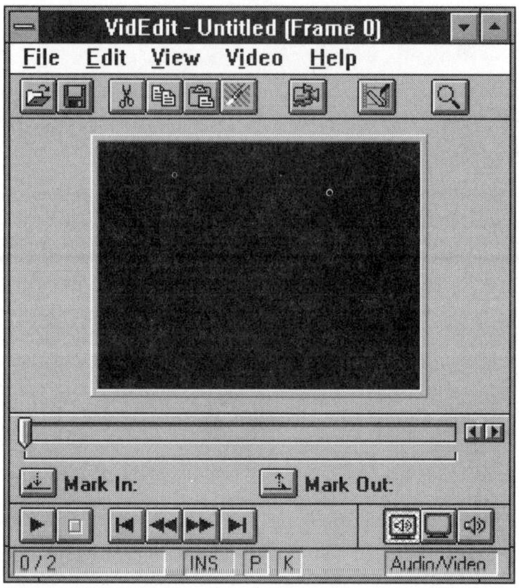

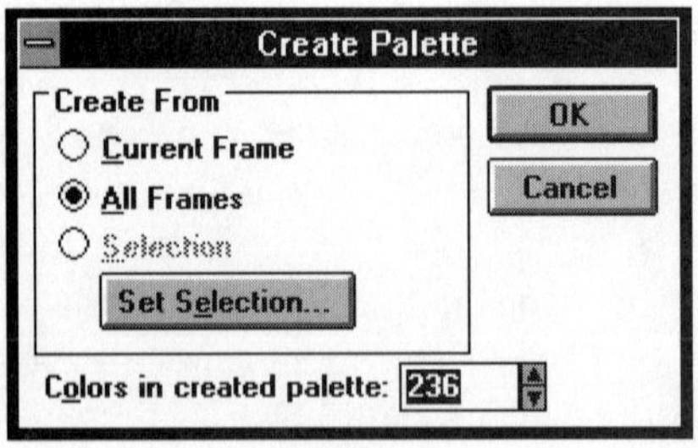

FIGURE 9-6
VidEdit's Create Palette dialog box

Now save the individual frames using the Extract command from VidEdit's File menu. Each frame you extract will be saved with its new palette.

I should mention one caveat in using VidEdit to create palettes. If your bitmaps have varying dimensions, always load the largest bitmap first. If subsequent frames are larger than the first frame, VidEdit will crop them to the starting frame's dimensions, and you may loose a chunk of the larger bitmap. This is not a bug in VidEdit, you're using VidEdit to perform a task for which it wasn't specifically designed, so you must play by its rules.

We've discussed a multitude of techniques in the preceding chapters. Now it's time to put that knowledge to work. The next section dissects seven games in a wide variety of categories, from arcade action to sports to adventure.

Part III

The Gallery

Horizont
Aequator
Ekliptik
Aequinoctiums
Solstitius Kreis
West
M
I
H
E
F
G
C
B
A
a
b

10

Action Arcade Games: Space Hunt

10

Action Arcade Games: Space Hunt

This game is a traditional shoot-em-up set in space. The player is in deep space, flying a small fighter. Enemy ships attack constantly, and the player has to destroy as many enemy ships as possible before the player's shields run out. This game combines many of the techniques described in Part II: a smooth-scrolling bitmapped space scene, sprites and sprite animation, and a layered sound track using the WaveMix library. In addition to these, I've added a new trick: displaying the space scene through the windows of an irregularly shaped cockpit. First, let's see how the game is played.

Playing Space Hunt

Figure 10-1 shows the Space Hunt game. The player is a fighter pilot, looking out of the cockpit of the spaceship. A radar scope shows the locations of enemy ships. A set of directional controls at the bottom center of the screen lets the player move the ship. When enemy ships appear, the player can shoot at them with the ship's lasers. A speed control at the bottom left of the screen adjusts the ship's speed.

All game functions are controlled by the mouse. The directional and speed controls work simply by moving the mouse pointer over them; no mouse click is required. The

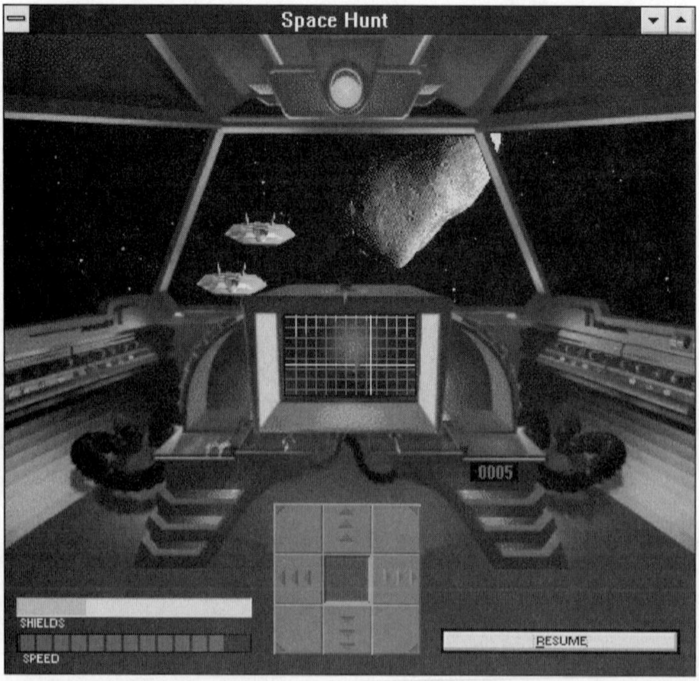

FIGURE 10-1

The Space Hunt game in action

only time a mouse click is required is when the player fires the lasers or wants to pause, resume, or start a game.

Game play begins when the player presses the Start button at the lower-right side of the form. Stars appear outside the ship, and enemy ships appear as red blips on the radar scope. The player's ship appears on the radar scope as a moving white crosshair.

Moving the mouse over one of the eight directional controls moves the ship in that direction. The ship's speed can be adjusted by moving the mouse over the speed control. The more red blocks that appear in the speed control, the faster the ship moves.

When an enemy ship is in view, move the mouse to the window area, and the mouse pointer will change to a gun sight. Clicking the left mouse button fires the lasers. The port and starboard lasers can be seen converging on the targeted area. If the player scores a hit on an enemy ship, the lasers appear red. A miss appears as a green laser shot.

Three direct hits are required to destroy an enemy ship. The mission is to destroy as many of them as possible (the game displays a count of the ships destroyed) before the player's shields are exhausted.

Building a Set of Reusable Game Routines

A lot of games have many basic elements in common. Within a specific genre of games, this is even more true. Any card game needs bitmap images of 52 playing cards. If you're building your second card game, there's no reason to design a new deck of cards; just reuse the ones from your first card game.

Action arcade games likewise have common elements. Usually, an arcade game displays multiple moving sprites on some type of playing field. In many cases the playing field is scrollable; the player sees only some portion of it at any time. Given these similarities between games, it makes sense to build Visual Basic code that can be reused with little or no modification and to store that code separate from the program code that is specific to a particular game. The reusable code then becomes a toolbox from which to grab routines as needed.

That's what I did when I designed Space Hunt. I built a toolbox of routines that would help me create the game at hand, but with an eye toward keeping it general enough that I could build other action games with it.

This toolbox became the Visual Basic module GAMETOOL.BAS. I'll present this module first, before I discuss the Space Hunt-specific code. You need to understand how the tools work first. Before you start, you'll need to create a new Visual Basic project, called SPACEHNT.MAK.

Next, create a new module, GAMETOOL.BAS. The first thing you need to do is declare all the global and module-level variables, constants, and Windows API functions used in this module. Add the following code in Listing 10-1 to the module:

Listing 10-1 GAMETOOL.BAS

```
Option Explicit
'------------------------------------------------------------
' GAMETOOL.BAS
'
' This module contains numerous general-purpose game routines.
' These routines can be used for constructing other games that
' rely on sprite animation, wave audio, etc.
'------------------------------------------------------------

' Used in Sprite Data Type
Type tArea
    hDC As Integer
    Width As Integer
    Height As Integer
End Type

' Sprite data type
```

continued on next page

continued from previous page

```
Type tSprite
    hDC As Integer
    X As Integer
    Y As Integer
    Width As Integer
    Height As Integer

    Xdir As Integer
    Ydir As Integer

    MaxSpeed As Integer
    hSprite As Integer
    Init As Integer

    BG As tArea
    Save As tArea
    Mask As tArea
    Work As tArea
End Type

Global BG_NewX As Integer, BG_NewY As Integer

' Type required when calling GetCursorPos
Type POINTAPI
    X As Integer
    Y As Integer
End Type

' Windows API call that returns the absolute position of the
' mouse pointer.
Declare Sub GetCursorPos Lib "USER" (lpPoint As POINTAPI)

' Functions and constants used to play sounds.
Declare Function sndPlaySound Lib "MMSystem" (ByVal lpsound As String, ByVal flag As Integer) As
Integer
Declare Function sndKillSound Lib "MMSystem" Alias "sndPlaySound" (ByVal lpszNull As Long, ByVal
flags As Integer) As Integer

Global Const SND_SYNC = &H0        ' Return when sound ends (the default)
Global Const SND_ASYNC = &H1       ' Return as soon as sound starts
Global Const SND_NODEFAULT = &H2   ' Don't play default sound if not found
Global Const SND_MEMORY = &H4      ' lpszSoundName -> memory image of file
Global Const SND_LOOP = &H8        ' Loop continuously; needs SND_ASYNC
Global Const SND_NOSTOP = &H10     ' Don't interrupt sound to play new one

' Global string used by NoiseGet() and NoisePlay() to play .WAV files in memory
Global SoundBuffer As String

Global Const WHITE = &HFFFFFF
Global Const BLACK = &H0&
```

```
' Constants used in Windows API Calls
Global Const SRCCOPY = &HCC0020
Global Const SRCAND = &H8800C6
Global Const SRCPAINT = &HEE0086

' Some useful graphics-oriented Windows API calls
Declare Function ExtFloodFill Lib "GDI" (ByVal hDC As Integer, ByVal X As Integer, ByVal Y As
Integer, ByVal crColor As Long, ByVal wFillType As Integer) As Integer
Declare Function GetPixel Lib "GDI" (ByVal hDC As Integer, ByVal X As Integer, ByVal Y As
Integer) As Long
Declare Function SetPixel Lib "GDI" (ByVal hDC As Integer, ByVal X As Integer, ByVal Y As
Integer, ByVal crColor As Long) As Long
Declare Function BitBlt Lib "GDI" (ByVal hDestDC As Integer, ByVal DestX As Integer, ByVal DestY
As Integer, ByVal DestWidth As Integer, ByVal DestHeight As Integer, ByVal hSrcDC As Integer,
ByVal SrcX As Integer, ByVal SrcY As Integer, ByVal RasterOp As Long) As Integer
```

The user-defined data type, tSprite, is an important structure that is used heavily elsewhere in this module. The tSprite type contains information about the "state" of a sprite: information such as the device contexts of the sprite and mask images, its current location, the background bitmap associated with it, and its current speed and direction. Not every game may need to use all these fields, but they're there when needed.

The first routine in GAMETOOL.BAS is BGMove. I wanted a routine that could help me smooth scroll a section of a large bitmap within a "viewport" PictureBox control (for more information on smooth scrolling, see Chapter 3). BGMove can handle smooth scrolling in four directions: up, down, left, and right. Of course, you can also use it to scroll in only two directions (horizontally or vertically). You tell it at what X-Y offset in the source bitmap to start, and BGMove will copy that section of the source bitmap into the destination PictureBox. If the X-Y starting point is too far to the right or bottom of the original bitmap, the BGMove routine will take a section from either the left or top to fill in the destination bitmap. For the resulting image to look right, you have to design your bitmap such that the edges wrap around to the opposite sides so that they appear to form a continuous, never-ending bitmap. A star field bitmap, such as the one used in Space Hunt, is well suited because a star field is a black background randomly scattered with stars and other small celestial objects. Add the BGMove routine as shown in Listing 10-2.

Listing 10-2 The BGMove subroutine

```
Sub BGMove (picBG As PictureBox, picOriginal As PictureBox, ByVal IncX As Integer, ByVal IncY As
Integer)
'-----------------------------------------------------------
' Display a new section of a large background bitmap inside
' a smaller "viewport" PictureBox; the new area is
' relative to the previous region by the offset values IncX
' and IncY.
```

continued on next page

continued from previous page

```
'
' The picOriginal bitmap should be constructed so that the
' edges wrap around so that if a chunk of the right side
' is joined with a chunk of the left side, the resulting
' picture appears continuous.  The same should be true
' of the upper and lower quarters.
'-----------------------------------------------------------
Dim rc As Integer
Dim DivideHoriz As Integer, DivideVert As Integer


    ' Calculate the new starting offset (upper left corner)
    ' to be displayed in picBG.
    BG_NewX = BG_NewX + IncX
    If BG_NewX > picOriginal.ScaleWidth Then
        BG_NewX = BG_NewX - picOriginal.ScaleWidth
    ElseIf BG_NewX < 0 Then
        BG_NewX = BG_NewX + picOriginal.ScaleWidth
    End If
    BG_NewY = BG_NewY + IncY
    If BG_NewY > picOriginal.ScaleHeight Then
        BG_NewY = BG_NewY - picOriginal.ScaleHeight
    ElseIf BG_NewY < 0 Then
        BG_NewY = BG_NewY + picOriginal.ScaleHeight
    End If

    ' Initially assume we won't have to construct the
    ' viewport from pieces of picOriginal
    DivideHoriz = False
    DivideVert = False

    ' Determine if picBG must be built from pieces of picOriginal.
    If (BG_NewX + picBG.ScaleWidth) > picOriginal.ScaleWidth Then DivideVert = True
    If (BG_NewY + picBG.ScaleHeight) > picOriginal.ScaleHeight Then DivideHoriz = True

    ' Construct the background (picBG) from one or more
    ' pieces of the large picOriginal bitmap.
    If Not (DivideVert Or DivideHoriz) Then
        ' Build picBG from a single area of picOriginal.
        rc = BitBlt(picBG.hDC, 0, 0, picBG.ScaleWidth, picBG.ScaleHeight, picOriginal.hDC,
            BG_NewX, BG_NewY, SRCCOPY)

    ElseIf DivideVert And (Not DivideHoriz) Then
        ' Left side (quad 1)
        rc = BitBlt(picBG.hDC, 0, 0, picOriginal.ScaleWidth - BG_NewX, picBG.ScaleHeight,
            picOriginal.hDC, BG_NewX, BG_NewY, SRCCOPY)
        ' Right side (quad 2)
        rc = BitBlt(picBG.hDC, picOriginal.ScaleWidth - BG_NewX, 0, picBG.ScaleWidth -
            (picOriginal.ScaleWidth - BG_NewX), picBG.ScaleHeight, picOriginal.hDC, 0, BG_NewY,
            SRCCOPY)
```

```
    ElseIf (Not DivideVert) And DivideHoriz Then
        ' Top side (quad 1)
        rc = BitBlt(picBG.hDC, 0, 0, picBG.ScaleWidth, picOriginal.ScaleHeight - BG_NewY,
             picOriginal.hDC, BG_NewX, BG_NewY, SRCCOPY)
        ' Bottom side (quad 3)
        rc = BitBlt(picBG.hDC, 0, picOriginal.ScaleHeight - BG_NewY, picBG.ScaleWidth,
             picBG.ScaleHeight - (picOriginal.ScaleHeight - BG_NewY), picOriginal.hDC, BG_NewX,
             0, SRCCOPY)

    ElseIf DivideVert And DivideHoriz Then
        ' Quad 1
        rc = BitBlt(picBG.hDC, 0, 0, picOriginal.ScaleWidth - BG_NewX, picOriginal.ScaleHeight -
             BG_NewY, picOriginal.hDC, BG_NewX, BG_NewY, SRCCOPY)
        ' Quad 2
        rc = BitBlt(picBG.hDC, picOriginal.ScaleWidth - BG_NewX, 0, picBG.ScaleWidth -
             (picOriginal.ScaleWidth - BG_NewX), picOriginal.ScaleHeight - BG_NewY,
             picOriginal.hDC, 0, BG_NewY, SRCCOPY)
        ' Quad 3
        rc = BitBlt(picBG.hDC, picOriginal.ScaleWidth - BG_NewX, picOriginal.ScaleHeight -
             BG_NewY, picBG.ScaleWidth - (picOriginal.ScaleWidth - BG_NewX), picBG.ScaleHeight -
             (picOriginal.ScaleHeight - BG_NewY), picOriginal.hDC, 0, 0, SRCCOPY)
        ' Quad 4
        rc = BitBlt(picBG.hDC, 0, picOriginal.ScaleHeight - BG_NewY, picOriginal.ScaleWidth -
             BG_NewX, picBG.ScaleHeight - (picOriginal.ScaleHeight - BG_NewY), picOriginal.hDC,
             BG_NewX, 0, SRCCOPY)
    End If
End Sub
```

The next routine, MouseIn, is used to check if the mouse pointer is currently inside the boundaries of a specified control on a form. You might wonder why I don't just use the control's MouseMove event for this purpose. Unfortunately, if the mouse is not in motion over the top of a control, no MouseMove events are generated. I wanted a function that would tell me absolutely, if at this time, the mouse is over this control.

Unfortunately, there is no built-in method for figuring this out. I ended up using a Windows API call, GetCursorPos, which returns the mouse's absolute screen coordinates in pixels. I then calculated the absolute screen coordinates of the control on the form, comparing this to the coordinates returned by GetCursorPos. The result is exactly what I wanted, a function that returns a True value when the mouse is inside a control. Add the MouseIn function to GAMETOOL.BAS as shown in Listing 10-3.

Listing 10-3 The MouseIn function

```
Function MouseIn (AForm As Form, ACntl As Control)
'-----------------------------------------------------------
' Determine if the mouse pointer is inside a control.  This
' can be more reliable than the Visual Basic MouseMove event,
' which is only fired when the mouse is actually in motion
' over a control.
'-----------------------------------------------------------
```

continued on next page

continued from previous page

```
Const PIXEL = 3

Dim rect As POINTAPI
Dim SaveFormMode As Integer
Dim SaveCntlMode As Integer
Dim XOffset As Integer
Dim YOffset As Integer
Dim BW As Integer
Dim TitleHeight As Integer
Dim PixX As Integer, PixY As Integer

    On Error Resume Next
    MouseIn = False

    ' Use the Windows API call to get the screen
    ' coordinates of the mouse pointer.
    GetCursorPos rect

    ' Save the current scale modes for the form
    ' and control.
    SaveFormMode = AForm.ScaleMode
    SaveCntlMode = ACntl.ScaleMode

    ' Set the scale modes to Pixel.
    AForm.ScaleMode = PIXEL
    ACntl.ScaleMode = PIXEL

    PixX = Screen.TwipsPerPixelX
    PixY = Screen.TwipsPerPixelY

    ' Calculate the border width and Title Bar height.
    BW = ((AForm.Width / PixX) - AForm.ScaleWidth) \ 2
    TitleHeight = (AForm.Height / PixY) - AForm.ScaleHeight - (BW * 2)

    ' Calculate the true screen offset of the control.
    XOffset = (AForm.Left / PixX) + BW + ACntl.Left
    YOffset = (AForm.Top / PixY) + BW + TitleHeight + ACntl.Top

    ' Determine if mouse pointer is inside control.
    If (rect.X > XOffset) And (rect.X < (XOffset + ACntl.Width)) Then
        If (rect.Y > YOffset) And (rect.Y < (YOffset + ACntl.Height)) Then
            MouseIn = True
        End If
    End If

    ' Reset the original scale modes.
    AForm.ScaleMode = SaveFormMode
    ACntl.ScaleMode = SaveCntlMode
End Function
```

The next two routines, NoiseGet and NoisePlay, are simple routines that can store a wave audio (.WAV) file in memory (in a Visual Basic string), and later play the wave file back. These techniques are covered in more detail in Chapter 6. Add these two routines to GAMETOOL.BAS, as shown in Listing 10-4.

Listing 10-4 NoiseGet and NoisePlay functions

```
Function NoiseGet (ByVal FileName, ASoundBuffer As String) As Integer
'---------------------------------------------------------------
' Load a sound file into the global string variable
' SoundBuffer.  This must be called before NoisePlay
'---------------------------------------------------------------
Dim buffer As String
Dim f As Integer

    On Error GoTo NoiseGet_Error

    buffer = Space$(1024)
    ASoundBuffer = ""
    f = FreeFile
    Open FileName For Binary As f
    Do While Not EOF(f)
        Get #f, , buffer     ' Load in 1K chunks
        ASoundBuffer = ASoundBuffer & buffer
    Loop
    Close f
    ASoundBuffer = Trim$(ASoundBuffer)
    NoiseGet = True
Exit Function

NoiseGet_Error:
    NoiseGet = False
    SoundBuffer = ""
    Exit Function
End Function

Sub NoisePlay (ASoundBuffer As String)
'---------------------------------------------------------------
' Plays a sound previously loaded into memory with function
' NoiseGet().
'---------------------------------------------------------------
Dim r As Integer  ' asynchronously

    If ASoundBuffer = "" Then Exit Sub
    r = sndPlaySound(ASoundBuffer, SND_ASYNC Or SND_MEMORY)

End Sub
```

The remaining routines in GAMETOOL.BAS are sprite related. This set of routines initializes, draws, and moves sprites. I designed these routines so that a sprite could store as much information about itself as possible in a tSprite data type. This simplifies the data that is passed to these subroutines. By putting this information into a user-defined data type, you are taking the first step toward object-oriented programming: data encapsulation.

The first sprite routine is SpriteInit. This routine creates a sprite "object" by initializing much of the data stored in the tSprite data structure. Enter the SpriteInit subroutine, as shown in Listing 10-5.

Listing 10-5 The SpriteInit subroutine

```
Sub SpriteInit (ASprite As tSprite, AForm As Form, picImage As PictureBox, picImageMask As
PictureBox, picBG As PictureBox, MaxSpeed As Integer)
'------------------------------------------------------------
' Initialize a sprite structure.  This MUST be done before
' attempting to use a sprite.
'------------------------------------------------------------
Static NumSprites As Integer

    ' Assign a unique sprite handle to this sprite
    NumSprites = NumSprites + 1
    ASprite.hSprite = NumSprites

    ' Initialize the sprite image.
    Load AForm.picSpriteImage(NumSprites)
    AForm.picSpriteImage(NumSprites).Left = AForm.picSpriteImage(0).Left
    AForm.picSpriteImage(NumSprites).Top = AForm.picSpriteImage(0).Top + (NumSprites * 1500)
    AForm.picSpriteImage(NumSprites).Width = picImage.Width
    AForm.picSpriteImage(NumSprites).Height = picImage.Height
    AForm.picSpriteImage(NumSprites).Picture = picImage.Picture

    ' Initialize the sprite's mask image.
    Load AForm.picSpriteMask(NumSprites)
    AForm.picSpriteMask(NumSprites).Left = AForm.picSpriteMask(0).Left
    AForm.picSpriteMask(NumSprites).Top = AForm.picSpriteMask(0).Top + (NumSprites * 1500)
    AForm.picSpriteMask(NumSprites).Width = picImage.Width
    AForm.picSpriteMask(NumSprites).Height = picImage.Height
    AForm.picSpriteMask(NumSprites).Picture = picImageMask.Picture

    AForm.picSpriteImage(NumSprites).Visible = True
    AForm.picSpriteMask(NumSprites).Visible = True

    ' Initialize the sprite's save area.
    Load AForm.picSpriteSave(NumSprites)
    AForm.picSpriteSave(NumSprites).Left = AForm.picSpriteSave(0).Left
    AForm.picSpriteSave(NumSprites).Top = AForm.picSpriteSave(0) + (NumSprites * 1500)
    AForm.picSpriteSave(NumSprites).Width = picImage.Width + MaxSpeed
    AForm.picSpriteSave(NumSprites).Height = picImage.Height + MaxSpeed

    ' Set the sprite's maximum allowable speed.
    ASprite.MaxSpeed = MaxSpeed

    ' Initialize the sprite data structure.
```

```
    ASprite.hDC = AForm.picSpriteImage(NumSprites).hDC
    ASprite.X = 0
    ASprite.Y = 0
    ASprite.Width = AForm.picSpriteImage(NumSprites).Width
    ASprite.Height = AForm.picSpriteImage(NumSprites).Height

    ASprite.Mask.hDC = AForm.picSpriteMask(NumSprites).hDC
    ASprite.Mask.Width = AForm.picSpriteMask(NumSprites).Width
    ASprite.Mask.Height = AForm.picSpriteMask(NumSprites).Height

    ASprite.BG.hDC = picBG.hDC
    ASprite.BG.Width = picBG.ScaleWidth
    ASprite.BG.Height = picBG.ScaleHeight

    AForm.picSpriteSave(NumSprites).Width = AForm.picSpriteMask(NumSprites).Width
    AForm.picSpriteSave(NumSprites).Height = AForm.picSpriteMask(NumSprites).Height
    ASprite.Save.hDC = AForm.picSpriteSave(NumSprites).hDC
    ASprite.Save.Width = AForm.picSpriteSave(NumSprites).Width
    ASprite.Save.Height = AForm.picSpriteSave(NumSprites).Height

    ASprite.Work.hDC = AForm.picSpriteWork.hDC
    ASprite.Work.Width = AForm.picSpriteWork.Width
    ASprite.Work.Height = AForm.picSpriteWork.Height

    ' This sprite is now ready to be used.
    ASprite.Init = True
End Sub
```

As you'll recall from Chapter 3, sprites are created by using the Windows API BitBlt function to copy a sprite mask, followed by a sprite image, onto a background bitmap. The BitBlt function requires two device contexts: one for the source bitmap (in this case either a sprite or mask image) and another for the destination bitmaps (the background).

The SpriteInit routine is passed a bunch of parameters. But the good news is that you only need to call this routine once, at the beginning of the game. Here is an explanation of each parameter required by SpriteInit:

- ASprite—a variable of type tSprite that will store all the information about the state of the sprite; this variable will be passed to other sprite routines.
- AForm—the Visual Basic form on which the sprite will be rendered.
- picImage—a PictureBox control. The image in this control, through its device context, will be used to draw the sprite image onto a background.
- picImageMask—a PictureBox control that, like picImage, is used to render the sprite image.
- picBG—the background bitmap onto which the sprite will be drawn.

- MaxSpeed—the maximum number of pixels that the sprite will travel in a single move. This is required because some sprite-moving methods require a "save area" bitmap that is larger than the actual sprite by MaxSpeed amount. See Chapter 3 for more information about this technique.

The SpriteDraw routine renders the actual sprite image, as defined in a tSprite variable, onto the background. Add this routine to the GAMETOOL.BAS module as shown below.

```
Sub SpriteDraw (AForm As Form, ASprite As tSprite, X As Integer, Y As Integer)
'-----------------------------------------------------------
' Draw the sprite defined in the structure tSprite at the
' x-y locations specified.
'-----------------------------------------------------------
Dim retcode As Integer
Dim DrawX As Integer
Dim DrawY As Integer

    ' If the sprite hasn't been initialized, don't attempt
    ' to draw it.
    If Not ASprite.Init Then Exit Sub

    ' Save the sprite's new location
    ASprite.X = X
    ASprite.Y = Y

    ' Determine the location to draw the sprite.
    DrawX = ASprite.X - BG_NewX
    If DrawX < -ASprite.Width Then DrawX = DrawX + AForm.picBGoriginal.Width
    DrawY = ASprite.Y - BG_NewY
    If DrawY < -ASprite.Height Then DrawY = DrawY + AForm.picBGoriginal.Height

    ' Draw the Mask onto the background
    retcode = BitBlt(ASprite.BG.hDC, DrawX, DrawY, ASprite.Mask.Width,
            ASprite.Mask.Height, ASprite.Mask.hDC, 0, 0, SRCAND)
    ' Draw the Sprite onto the background
    retcode = BitBlt(ASprite.BG.hDC, DrawX, DrawY, ASprite.Width, ASprite.Height,
            ASprite.hDC, 0, 0, SRCPAINT)
End Sub
```

The SpriteDraw routine requires only four parameters: the form onto which the sprite will be rendered, the sprite object, and the X-Y coordinates where it is to be drawn. The sprite already "knows" what mask and sprite images to use and what background bitmap to render to, because all this information was established in SpriteInit.

With most games, a sprite will move in small increments around the background. In the Space Hunt game, enemy spaceship sprites fly through a background star field bitmap. These ships move in fairly small increments, no more than 6 pixels at a time relative to their previous position. To make it easier to move a sprite some distance relative to its current position, I added a SpriteMove routine. This routine is very simple; two parameters tell it how far in the X and Y directions a sprite will move; the routine adds these values to the sprite's current X and Y coordinates and passes these values to the SpriteDraw routine. Add the SpriteMove routine to GAMETOOL.BAS, as shown below.

```
Sub SpriteMove (AForm As Form, S As tSprite, ByVal dx As Integer, ByVal dy As Integer)
'------------------------------------------------------------
' Move the sprite to the location specified by the given
' offset.  This routine does NOT remove the previous
' sprite image.  This routine should be used in games
' where the viewing area (background and sprites) is
' generated anew for each frame of the game.
'------------------------------------------------------------

    SpriteDraw AForm, S, S.X + dx, S.Y + dy

End Sub
```

Finally, I created a routine that can create a sprite image and a mask image from a single bitmap. This routine, Sprite_MakeFromBMP, "scans" a bitmap pixel by pixel. As it scans, it looks for pixels that match a transparent color passed to it. It changes this color to black on the sprite image and white on the mask image. Likewise, any non-transparent color is left untouched on the sprite image and set to black on the mask image.

The result is a sprite and a mask image created from a single bitmap. This saves you the hassle of building a separate mask for each sprite. When drawing the sprite, simply set aside one color as a transparent color and draw the sprite as usual, ensuring that any background area is drawn in that color. The trade-off for this routine is that it takes a few seconds to scan the bitmap and create the sprite and mask images. Add the Sprite_MakeFromBMP routine to the GAMETOOL.BAS module, as shown in Listing 10-6.

Listing 10-6 The Sprite_MakeFromBMP subroutine

```
Sub Sprite_MakeFromBMP (AForm As Form, SpriteNumber As Integer, TransparentColor As Long)
'------------------------------------------------------------
' This routine can create a sprite and its mask from a
' PictureBox control.  This routine requires that PictureBox
' control arrays exist on the form with the following names:
'
' picSpriteImage - used to create the sprite and mask,
```

continued on next page

continued from previous page

```
    '                   this control becomes the sprite.
    ' picSpriteMask -   this control contains the sprite mask
    '                   created from picSpriteImage.
    '
    ' The picSpriteImage bitmap should be designed with one color
    ' designated as the transparent color (where the game's
    ' background will show through).
    '-----------------------------------------------------------
    Dim OldScaleMode As Integer
    Dim X As Integer, Y As Integer
    Dim color As Long
    Dim rc As Long
    Dim BG As Long, FG As Long

        FG = BLACK
        BG = WHITE

        ' Save the original scale mode and then reset to pixels.
        OldScaleMode = AForm.picSpriteImage(SpriteNumber).ScaleMode
        AForm.picSpriteImage(SpriteNumber).ScaleMode = 3 ' Pixel

        ' Construct the mask and sprite images pixel by pixel.
        For Y = 0 To AForm.picSpriteImage(SpriteNumber).ScaleHeight - 1
            For X = 0 To AForm.picSpriteImage(SpriteNumber).ScaleWidth - 1
                color = GetPixel(AForm.picSpriteImage(SpriteNumber).hDC, X, Y)
                If color = TransparentColor Then
                    rc = setpixel(AForm.picSpriteImage(SpriteNumber).hDC, X, Y, FG)
                    rc = setpixel(AForm.picSpriteMask(SpriteNumber).hDC, X, Y, BG)
                Else
                    rc = setpixel(AForm.picSpriteMask(SpriteNumber).hDC, X, Y, FG)
                End If
            Next
        Next

        ' Restore the original scale mode.
        AForm.picSpriteImage(SpriteNumber).ScaleMode = OldScaleMode
    End Sub
```

Adding the Sound Track

This game uses Microsoft's WaveMix Dynamic Link Library (.DLL), a collection of routines that allows you to build a layered sound track for a game by using a collection of wave audio (.WAV) files. The DLL is covered in depth in Chapter 6. In that chapter, you developed a Visual Basic module called WAVEMIX.BAS as part of a WaveMix project. The WAVEMIX.BAS module simplified the use of the WaveMix DLL. Because the routines in that module were designed to be reusable, simply add the WAVEMIX.BAS module from the example in Chapter 6 to the SPACEHNT.MAK project.

The Space Hunt Form

Before you begin building the Space Hunt game form, you'll need to add another small Visual Basic module. Visual Basic 3.0 doesn't allow you to put user-defined type definitions within a form, so you'll have to create a little module, called SPACEHNT.BAS. Add the following code to this module's Declarations section.

```
Option Explicit
'------------------------------------------------------------
' This little module declares the data type used to keep track
' of the current state of each enemy ship.
'------------------------------------------------------------

Type tShip
    Visible As Integer
    Hits As Integer
    MaxHits As Integer
    AliveTime As Long

    Sprite As tSprite
End Type
```

This user-defined type stores some data for each of the enemy spaceships: how many hits are required to destroy it, how many frames it has been alive, whether it is currently visible, and how may hits it has received so far.

Also, you'll need to add a custom control file, THREED.VBX, to the project. This control contains a three-dimensional panel and a three-dimensional button control that will be used on the form.

Now you're ready to build the Space Hunt main form. One caveat before you begin: There are a lot of controls on this form, and the arrangement of many of them is important. Many of these controls are not seen by the game player. Controls like the large star field bitmap used to create the scene through the windows of the cockpit are stashed "off-stage" to the right or below the area of the form the player actually sees. Because of this, I recommend that you build this form in at least 800x600 resolution. Anything smaller and you probably won't be able to fit everything in. This caveat applies only when building the game; the finished game can easily be played on a standard VGA 640x480 screen.

At design time, the form will look like Figure 10-2. As I said before, there are a lot of controls on this form.

Add a new form to the SPACEHNT.MAK project. Name the form SPACEHNT.FRM. The objects and properties for this form are shown in Table 10-1.

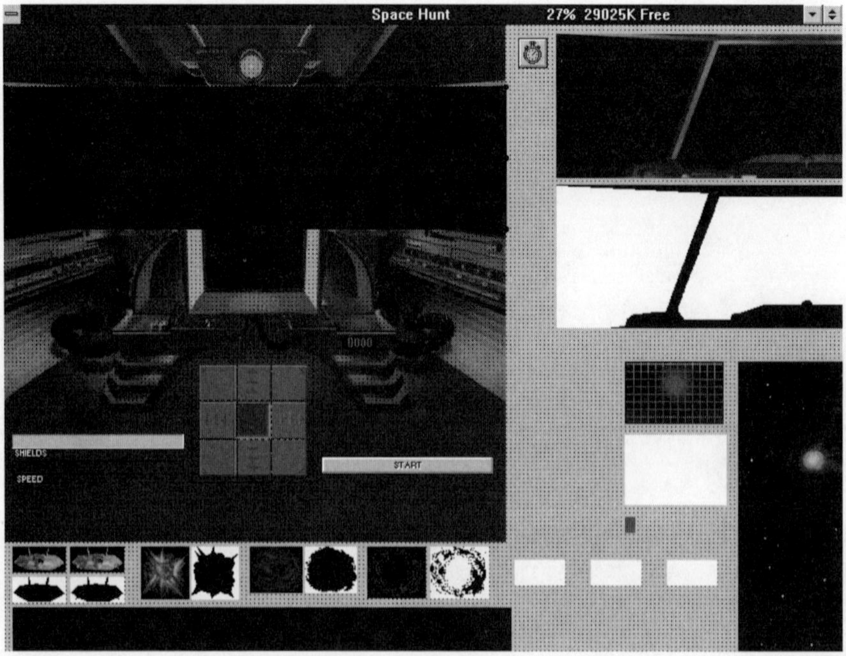

FIGURE 10-2

The Space Hunt game at design time

TABLE 10-1

Objects and properties of the SPACEHNT.FRM form

Object	Property	Setting
Form	FormName	frmToolTest
	AutoRedraw	-1 'True
	BackColor	&H00808080&
	BorderStyle	1 'Fixed Single
	Caption	"Space Hunt"
	Picture	(set at design time to COCKPIT2.BMP)
	ScaleMode	3 'Pixel
Image	Name	Image1
	Height	1530
	Left	2820

Object	Property	Setting
	Picture	(set at design time to CONTROL.BMP)
	Top	4740
	Width	1530
Image	Name	imgLeft
	Height	555
	Left	2700
	MousePointer	2 'Cross
	Top	5220
	Width	675
Image	Name	imgRight
	Height	555
	Left	3840
	MousePointer	2 'Cross
	Top	5220
	Width	615
Image	Name	imgUp
	Height	615
	Left	3360
	MousePointer	2 'Cross
	Top	4620
	Width	495
Image	Name	imgDown
	Height	615
	Left	3360
	MousePointer	2 'Cross
	Top	5760
	Width	495
Image	Name	imgUpLeft

continued on next page

continued from previous page

Object	Property	Setting
	Height	615
	Left	2700
	MousePointer	2 'Cross
	Top	4620
	Width	675
Image	Name	imgDownLeft
	Height	615
	Left	2700
	MousePointer	2 'Cross
	Top	5760
	Width	675
Image	Name	imgUpRight
	Height	615
	Left	3840
	MousePointer	2 'Cross
	Top	4620
	Width	615
Image	Name	imgDownRight
	Height	615
	Left	3840
	MousePointer	2 'Cross
	Top	5760
	Width	615
Label	Name	Label1
	BackStyle	0 'Transparent
	Caption	"SPEED"
	FontBold	0 'False
	FontName	"Small Fonts"
	FontSize	6

Object	Property	Setting
	ForeColor	&H00FFFFFF&
	Height	195
	Left	180
	Top	6240
	Width	1755
Label	Name	Label2
	BackStyle	0 'Transparent
	Caption	"SHIELDS"
	FontBold	0 'False
	FontName	"Small Fonts"
	FontSize	6
	ForeColor	&H00FFFFFF&
	Height	165
	Left	120
	Top	5880
	Width	585
Label	Name	lblDestroyed
	Alignment	1 'Right Justify
	BackColor	&H00000000&
	Caption	"0000"
	FontName	"MS Serif"
	ForeColor	&H000000FF&
	Height	195
	Left	4860
	Top	4320
	Width	495
PictureBox	Name	picBackground
	BackColor	&H00000000&
	BorderStyle	0 'None

continued on next page

continued from previous page

Object	Property	Setting
	DragIcon	(set at design time in Properties window)
	Height	1995
	Left	0
	ScaleMode	3 'Pixel
	Top	855
	Width	7215
PictureBox	Name	picSpriteWork
	AutoRedraw	-1 'True
	BorderStyle	0 'None
	Height	975
	Left	8880
	ScaleMode	3 'Pixel
	Top	5700
	Width	1455
PictureBox	Name	picShip
	AutoRedraw	-1 'True
	AutoSize	-1 'True
	BorderStyle	0 'None
	Height	360
	Left	120
	Picture	(set at design time to SHIP_1.BMP)
	ScaleMode	3 'Pixel
	Top	7260
	Width	780
PictureBox	Name	picBGoriginal
	AutoRedraw	-1 'True
	Height	9015
	Left	10500

Object	Property	Setting
	Picture	(set at design time to BACKDROP.BMP)
	ScaleMode	3 'Pixel
	Top	4680
	Width	12015
PictureBox	Name	picSpriteImage
	AutoRedraw	-1 'True
	AutoSize	-1 'True
	BorderStyle	0 'None
	Height	360
	Index	0
	Left	7320
	ScaleMode	3 'Pixel
	Top	7440
	Width	720
PictureBox	Name	picSpriteMask
	AutoRedraw	-1 'True
	AutoSize	-1 'True
	BorderStyle	0 'None
	Height	360
	Index	0
	Left	8400
	ScaleMode	3 'Pixel
	Top	7440
	Width	720
PictureBox	Name	picSpriteSave
	AutoRedraw	-1 'True
	AutoSize	-1 'True
	BorderStyle	0 'None
	Height	360

continued on next page

continued from previous page

Object	Property	Setting
	Index	0
	Left	9480
	ScaleMode	3 'Pixel
	Top	7440
	Width	720
PictureBox	Name	picBoom1
	AutoRedraw	-1 'True
	AutoSize	-1 'True
	BorderStyle	0 'None
	Height	735
	Index	0
	Left	1980
	Picture	(set at design time to BOOM1.BMP)
	Top	7260
	Width	690
PictureBox	Name	picWorkBG
	AutoRedraw	-1 'True
	BackColor	&H00400000&
	DragIcon	(set at design time in Properties window)
	Height	3255
	Left	120
	ScaleMode	3 'Pixel
	Top	8100
	Width	7155
PictureBox	Name	picScope
	BackColor	&H00000000&
	Height	840
	Left	2925

Object	Property	Setting
	ScaleMode	3 'Pixel
	Top	2820
	Width	1380
PictureBox	Name	picScopeWork
	AutoRedraw	-1 'True
	AutoSize	-1 'True
	BackColor	&H00000000&
	Height	870
	Left	8880
	Picture	(set at design time to SCOPE.BMP)
	ScaleMode	3 'Pixel
	Top	4680
	Width	1410
PictureBox	Name	picSpeed
	BackColor	&H00000080&
	Height	195
	Left	120
	MousePointer	2 'Cross
	Top	6060
	Width	2475
PictureBox	Name	imgBlock
	AutoRedraw	-1 'True
	AutoSize	-1 'True
	BorderStyle	0 'None
	Height	225
	Left	8880
	Picture	(set at design time to BLOCK.BMP)
	Top	6840

continued on next page

continued from previous page

Object	Property	Setting
	Width	150
SSPanel	Name	panShields
	Alignment	1 'Left Justify - MIDDLE
	BackColor	&H00C0C0C0&
	BevelOuter	1 'Inset
	BorderWidth	1
	FloodColor	&H0000C000&
	FloodShowPct	0 'False
	FloodType	1 'Left To Right
	Font3D	3 'Inset w/light shading
	FontName	"Small Fonts"
	FontSize	3
	ForeColor	&H00FF0000&
	Height	195
	Left	120
	Top	5700
	Width	2475
PictureBox	Name	picBoom1
	AutoRedraw	-1 'True
	AutoSize	-1 'True
	BorderStyle	0 'None
	Height	645
	Index	1
	Left	3540
	Picture	(set at design time to BOOM2.BMP)
	Top	7260
	Width	750
PictureBox	Name	picBoom1

Object	Property	Setting
	AutoRedraw	-1 'True
	AutoSize	-1 'True
	BorderStyle	0 'None
	Height	720
	Index	2
	Left	5220
	Picture	(set at design time to BOOM3.BMP)
	Top	7260
	Width	840
PictureBox	Name	picShipFiring
	AutoRedraw	-1 'True
	AutoSize	-1 'True
	BorderStyle	0 'None
	Height	360
	Left	960
	Picture	(set at design time to SHIP_2.BMP)
	ScaleMode	3 'Pixel
	Top	7260
	Width	780
Timer	Name	Timer1
	Enabled	0 'False
	Interval	2
	Left	7380
	Top	180
SSCommand	Name	btnStart
	Caption	"START"
	Font3D	3 'Inset w/light shading
	FontBold	0 'False

continued on next page

continued from previous page

Object	Property	Setting
	FontName	"Small Fonts"
	FontSize	6
	Height	255
	Left	4560
	RoundedCorners	0 'False
	Top	6000
	Width	2475
PictureBox	Name	picPitSprite
	AutoRedraw	-1 'True
	AutoSize	-1 'True
	BorderStyle	0 'None
	Height	2010
	Left	7920
	Picture	(set at design time to PIT_SPR.BMP)
	Top	120
	Width	7200
PictureBox	Name	picPitMask
	AutoRedraw	-1 'True
	AutoSize	-1 'True
	BorderStyle	0 'None
	Height	1995
	Left	7920
	Picture	(set at design time to PIT_MASK.BMP)
	Top	2220
	Width	7215
PictureBox	Name	picShip_m
	AutoRedraw	-1 'True
	AutoSize	-1 'True

Object	Property	Setting
	BorderStyle	0 'None
	Height	360
	Left	120
	Picture	(set at design time to SHIP_1M.BMP)
	ScaleMode	3 'Pixel
	Top	7680
	Width	780
PictureBox	Name	picShipFiring_m
	AutoRedraw	-1 'True
	AutoSize	-1 'True
	BorderStyle	0 'None
	Height	360
	Left	960
	Picture	(set at design time to SHIP_2M.BMP)
	ScaleMode	3 'Pixel
	Top	7680
	Width	780
PictureBox	Name	picBoom1_m
	AutoRedraw	-1 'True
	AutoSize	-1 'True
	BorderStyle	0 'None
	Height	735
	Index	0
	Left	2700
	Picture	(set at design time to BOOM1M.BMP)
	Top	7260
	Width	690

continued on next page

continued from previous page

Object	Property	Setting
PictureBox	Name	picBoom1_m
	AutoRedraw	-1 'True
	AutoSize	-1 'True
	BorderStyle	0 'None
	Height	645
	Index	1
	Left	4320
	Picture	(set at design time to BOOM2M.BMP)
	Top	7260
	Width	750
PictureBox	Name	picBoom1_m
	AutoRedraw	-1 'True
	AutoSize	-1 'True
	BorderStyle	0 'None
	Height	720
	Index	2
	Left	6120
	Picture	(set at design time to BOOM3M.BMP)
	Top	7260
	Width	840

The Picture property of the form and many of the PictureBox controls are set at design time. The most obvious of these is the bitmap used as a background for the form. It shows a forward view of the inside of the player's cockpit (see Figure 10-3). Other controls are placed on top of this bitmap.

Probably the most important control that sits on the cockpit background is the picBackground PictureBox control. This control covers the width of the cockpit and its window areas. It displays a composited image of the star field, enemy ships, laser fire, and the cockpit window frame. I'll show how this compositing is accomplished later.

FIGURE 10-3

The cockpit bitmap

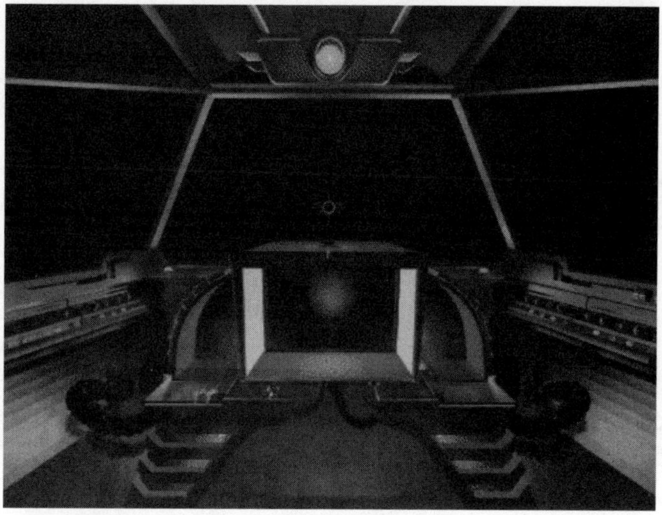

Another PictureBox, picScope, sits directly below the picBackground control, centered inside the central radar scope area. This shows the player's position relative to the enemy ships, letting the player set an intercept course.

Making It All Work

Now it's time to start adding the program code that will make all these controls work. Begin with the SPACEHNT.FRM form's Load event, as that's the first routine called when the game begins. Add the Load subroutine, as shown below.

```
Sub Form_Load ()
'------------------------------------------------------------
' Set up the form when it's first loaded.
'------------------------------------------------------------

    ' Hide the scope and background PictureBoxes.
    picBackground.Visible = False
    picScope.Visible = False

    ' Copy the cockpit "sprite" image into the background PictureBox.
    picBackground.Picture = picPitSprite.Picture

    ' Center the form on the screen.
    Me.Move (Screen.Width - Me.Width) / 2, (Screen.Height - Me.Height) / 2
End Sub
```

The Load routine hides the background and scope PictureBox controls (the player doesn't need to see them until the game starts), copies a picture of the cockpit into the background PictureBox, and centers the form on the player's screen.

I copied the cockpit image onto the picBackground control so that there would be a smooth transition when the game starts. The picBackground control is made visible in the StartGame routine (you'll see it in a moment) a few moments before the first frame is displayed inside picBackground. Without a cockpit window image already in the picBackground control, there would be a brief moment when the picBackground control would appear as a big, ugly, empty, black rectangle—not something you want.

To start the game, the player presses the Start button. This btnStart 3D Button control has a single Click event. Enter it as shown below.

```
Sub btnStart_Click ()
'-------------------------------------------------------------
' Pressing the Start button will either start, pause, or
' resume the game.
'-------------------------------------------------------------
Static Paused As Integer
Dim rc As Long

    ' If the game is currently paused, then resume it.
    If Paused Then
        Paused = False
        btnStart.Caption = "&PAUSE"
        rc = WaveMixActivate(hWaveMix, True)
        Timer1.Enabled = True
    ' If the game is in progress then pause it.
    ElseIf Timer1.Enabled Then
        Paused = True
        btnStart.Caption = "&RESUME"
        rc = WaveMixActivate(hWaveMix, False)
        Timer1.Enabled = False
    ' Otherwise, no game is in progress, so start one.
    Else
        btnStart.Caption = "&PAUSE"
        StartGame
    End If
End Sub
```

The btnStart button actually serves three distinct functions based on what state the game is in. When the program is first loaded, the button starts a new game. If a game is in progress, the button serves as a Pause button, temporarily suspending game play. And if the game is paused, the button acts as a Resume button, continuing the game play from the point when the player paused.

Pausing and resuming a game are simple processes. The game play is controlled from within a Timer control's Timer event. To pause a game, simply disable the Timer control by setting its Enable property to False. The game can then be resumed by resetting the Timer's Enable property to True. The WaveMix DLL, which runs independently of the Timer control (for the background music), must also be suspended and reactivated with calls to its WaveMixActivate function. And, of course, the caption on the button must be changed to reflect whatever its current purpose is.

Setting up and starting a game is handled in a separate subroutine, StartGame, which is called from the btnStart Click event. Add the StartGame subroutine to the SPACEHNT.FRM form, as shown in Listing 10-7.

Listing 10-7 The StartGame subroutine

```
Sub StartGame ()
'------------------------------------------------------------
' Initialize everything and start the game.
'------------------------------------------------------------
Dim rc As Integer
Dim i As Integer
Static NotFirstTime As Integer

    Me.Show
    SetupSounds

    ' Initialize the shields (a 3D Panel control)
    panShields.FloodPercent = 100
    panShields.FloodColor = GREEN

    ' Initial Ship speed (in pixels).
    ScrollSpeed = 5
    picSpeed_Paint
    picSpeed_MouseMove 1, 0, picSpeed.ScaleWidth / 2, 5

    ' Sprites only need to be initialized the first time
    ' the game is played.
    If Not NotFirstTime Then
        For i = 1 To NUM_ENEMY_SHIPS
            SpriteInit Ship(i).Sprite, Me, picShip, picShip_m, picWorkBG, 50
            Ship(i).Visible = 0
            Ship(i).MaxHits = 3
        Next

        SpriteInit ShipFiringSprite, Me, picShipFiring, picShipFiring_m, picWorkBG, 50

        SpriteInit ExplosionSprite(0), Me, picBoom1(0), picBoom1_m(0), picWorkBG, 50
        SpriteInit ExplosionSprite(1), Me, picBoom1(1), picBoom1_m(1), picWorkBG, 50
        SpriteInit ExplosionSprite(2), Me, picBoom1(2), picBoom1_m(2), picWorkBG, 50

        NotFirstTime = True
    End If
```

continued on next page

continued from previous page

```
    ' Start the background music.
    WAVMIX_PlayChannel WAV_Music, True

    ' Draw the enemy ships in their initial positions.
    For i = 1 To NUM_ENEMY_SHIPS
        SpriteDraw Me, Ship(i).Sprite, 50 * i, picBackground.ScaleHeight / i
    Next

    ' Show the background and the scope.
    picBackground.Visible = True
    picScope.Visible = True

    ' Enabling the timer sets the game in motion (see the Timer1.Timer event).
    Timer1.Enabled = True

End Sub
```

The StartGame routine sets up the WaveMix sounds needed for the game (more on this in a moment) and initializes the sprites, sets the player's starting speed, cues up the background music, and then enables the game's Timer control.

To set up the WaveMix sounds, the StartGame routine calls another routine, SetupSounds. Add this routine, as shown below.

```
Sub SetupSounds ()
'-----------------------------------------------------------------
' Load the audio files used by the WaveMix routines for
' layered sound effects.
'-----------------------------------------------------------------
Dim rc As Integer

    ' If the command line contains the word "quiet" then run
    ' with no sound.
    If LCase$(Command$) = "quiet" Then WAVMIX_Quiet = True

    rc = WAVMIX_InitMixer()
    WAV_Music = WAVMIX_AddFile(App.Path & "\MUSIC1.WAV")
    WAV_Turn = WAVMIX_AddFile(App.Path & "\TURN.WAV")
    WAV_LaserHit = WAVMIX_AddFile(App.Path & "\EXPLODE2.WAV")
    WAV_LaserMiss = WAVMIX_AddFile(App.Path & "\LASER1.WAV")
    WAV_ShieldHit = WAVMIX_AddFile(App.Path & "\EXPLODE3.WAV")
    WAV_Alert = WAVMIX_AddFile(App.Path & "\ALERT2.WAV")
End Sub
```

This routine initializes the WaveMix DLL, then calls the WAVEMIX.BAS routine, WAVMIX_AddFile, for each sound effect track the game will use. WAVMIX_AddFile loads each wave audio file from disk and stores it in memory. There are six wave audio tracks in this game. The first is the background music, which is set to loop continuously for the duration of the game. When the player changes the ship's direction, a short sound is played while the course change is made. Two laser fire sound effects, one with a short explosion afterward, are heard when the player clicks the mouse over the picBackground area. An explosion sound is heard when an enemy ship scores a hit on the player's ship. Finally, when the shields are reduced to a critical level, an alarm begins to sound and loops until the game is over. All these sounds, thanks to the WaveMix DLL, can be heard as a single layered sound track.

It's All in the Timing

As with most Visual Basic arcade games, the action in Space Hunt sprouts from a Timer event. There's a lot going on in this event, so I've tried to break some of it into separate subroutines when possible. But because there is a performance trade-off when calling subroutines, I've left a considerable amount of code inside the Timer event itself. Add the following Timer event (Listing 10-8) to the Timer1 control on the SPACEHNT.FRM form.

Listing 10-8 The Timer1_Timer subroutine

```
Sub Timer1_Timer ()
'-------------------------------------------------------------
' This routine is the heart of this game.  It's a trifle
' monolithic, but that is in large part by design.  By
' reducing the number of subroutines called from here, we
' can improve the game performance somewhat.
'
' Each pass through this routine, the game display is
' updated.  This includes the graphics the player sees through
' the view screen, the radar scope, the shield indicator,
' and the "Enemy Destroyed" label.
'-------------------------------------------------------------
Const SHIP_INVIS_TIME = 60
Const ENEMY_SPEED = 6
Const ALERT_LEVEL = 27

Dim rc As Long
Dim GotOne As Integer
Dim ShipNum As Integer
Dim EnemyFireVal As Integer
Dim FireX As Integer
Dim FireY As Integer

Static AlertOn As Integer

    ' Update the background (starfield) based on the
    ' current speed and direction of the player's ship.
    UpdateBackground

    GotOne = False

    ' Clear the scope and show the player's location.
```

continued on next page

continued from previous page

```
ClearScope
ShowYouOnScope

For ShipNum = 1 To NUM_ENEMY_SHIPS
    ' Enemy ships are made invisible when they are destroyed
    ' by setting their Visible field to a positive non-zero
    ' number.  This number is reduced, each pass through
    ' the timer event until, when it reaches zero, the ships
    ' are back in the action again.
    If Ship(ShipNum).Visible = 0 Then

        ' Move this enemy ship (with a bit of randomness thrown in).
        ShipMove Ship(ShipNum).Sprite, Rnd * ENEMY_SPEED, Rnd * ENEMY_SPEED, 0

        ' Show the enemy ship on the radar scope.
        ShowShipOnScope Ship(ShipNum)

        ' See if it's time for this enemy ship to fire.
        Ship(ShipNum).AliveTime = Ship(ShipNum).AliveTime + 1
        EnemyFireVal = (Ship(ShipNum).AliveTime Mod (30 + (ShipNum * 5)))

        ' This enemy ship is shooting at the player.
        If EnemyFireVal = 0 Then

            SpriteDraw Me, ShipFiringSprite, Ship(ShipNum).Sprite.X, Ship(ShipNum).Sprite.Y
            WAVMIX_PlayChannel WAV_ShieldHit, False

            ' Register a hit on the player's shields
            If panShields.FloodPercent > 10 Then
                panShields.FloodPercent = panShields.FloodPercent - 10
                If panShields.FloodPercent < ALERT_LEVEL Then
                    panShields.FloodColor = RED

                    ' Captain! We can't take much more of this!
                    If Not AlertOn Then
                        WAVMIX_PlayChannel WAV_Alert, True
                        AlertOn = True
                    End If
                End If
            Else
                ' GAME OVER...
                EndGame
                AlertOn = False
                Exit Sub
            End If
        ElseIf (EnemyFireVal >= 1) And (EnemyFireVal <= 3) Then
            SpriteDraw Me, ShipFiringSprite, Ship(ShipNum).Sprite.X, Ship(ShipNum).Sprite.Y
        End If

        ' If we fired our lasers, then register any hits on this
        ' enemy ship.
        If LaserFired Then
```

```
            If (Abs(Ship(ShipNum).Sprite.X - (MouseX - 16)) < (Ship(ShipNum).Sprite.Width \
            2)) And (Abs(Ship(ShipNum).Sprite.Y - (MouseY - 16)) <
            (Ship(ShipNum).Sprite.Height \ 2)) Then
                WAVMIX_PlayChannel WAV_LaserHit, False

                Ship(ShipNum).Hits = Ship(ShipNum).Hits + 1
                GotOne = True
                If Ship(ShipNum).Hits >= Ship(ShipNum).MaxHits Then
                    Ship(ShipNum).Visible = SHIP_INVIS_TIME
                End If
            End If
        End If
    Else
        ' Draw Explosions
        If Ship(ShipNum).Visible = SHIP_INVIS_TIME - 1 Then
            SpriteDraw Me, ExplosionSprite(0), Ship(ShipNum).Sprite.X, Ship(ShipNum).Sprite.Y
            ShipsDestroyed = ShipsDestroyed + 1
            lblDestroyed = Format$(ShipsDestroyed, "0000") & " "
        ElseIf Ship(ShipNum).Visible = SHIP_INVIS_TIME - 2 Then
            SpriteDraw Me, ExplosionSprite(1), Ship(ShipNum).Sprite.X, Ship(ShipNum).Sprite.Y
        ElseIf Ship(ShipNum).Visible = SHIP_INVIS_TIME - 3 Then
            SpriteDraw Me, ExplosionSprite(2), Ship(ShipNum).Sprite.X, Ship(ShipNum).Sprite.Y
        End If

        ' Bump down the amount of time before this ship reappears.
        Ship(ShipNum).Visible = Ship(ShipNum).Visible - 1
        Ship(ShipNum).Hits = 0
        Ship(ShipNum).AliveTime = 0
    End If
Next

' Draw the laser effects.
If LaserFired Then
    If Not GotOne Then
        WAVMIX_PlayChannel WAV_LaserMiss, False
        picWorkBG.ForeColor = GREEN
    Else
        picWorkBG.ForeColor = RED
    End If
    FireX = MouseX - BG_NewX
    FireY = MouseY - BG_NewY
    If FireX < 0 Then FireX = FireX + picBGOriginal.Width
    If FireY < 0 Then FireY = FireY + picBGOriginal.Height
    rc = MoveTo(picWorkBG.hDC, 0, picWorkBG.Height)
    rc = LineTo(picWorkBG.hDC, FireX, FireY)
    rc = MoveTo(picWorkBG.hDC, picWorkBG.ScaleWidth, picWorkBG.ScaleHeight)
    rc = LineTo(picWorkBG.hDC, FireX, FireY)
End If

' Draw the cockpit mask into the work area.
rc = BitBlt(picWorkBG.hDC, 0, 0, picPitMask.Width, picPitMask.Height, picPitMask.hDC, 0, 0,
    SRCAND)
```

continued on next page

continued from previous page

```
    rc = BitBlt(picWorkBG.hDC, 0, 0, picPitMask.Width, picPitMask.Height, picPitSprite.hDC, 0, 0,
        SRCPAINT)

    ' Draw the whole thing back onto the screen.
    rc = BitBlt(picBackground.hDC, 0, 0, picBackground.Width, picBackground.Height,
        picWorkBG.hDC, 0, 0, SRCCOPY)

    LaserFired = False
End Sub
```

A game like Space Hunt is like an interactive animated movie. In this case, most of the action is viewed from inside the picBackground control, where the player can see the enemy ships and the picScope control, which the player can use to zero in on those ships when they're outside visual range. Given this analogy, each time the Timer event is called, you must create a new animation frame. That's a good way to get a handle on all the things going on in this event.

First, the Timer event calls the UpdateBackground subroutine. This routine checks to see if the mouse pointer is inside one of the ship's directional controls. The ship is steered when the player moves the mouse inside one of eight controls, which are actually just Image controls. There's one control for each of the eight compass points. Add the UpdateBackground routine, as shown in Listing 10-9.

Listing 10-9 The UpdateBackground subroutine

```
Sub UpdateBackground ()
'--------------------------------------------------------------
' The first step in building a new view is to copy the
' next section of the original background onto the working
' background picture box.
'--------------------------------------------------------------
Static LastXdir As Integer
Static LastYdir As Integer

    ' Move the background image in one of eight possible directions based
    ' on which "hotspot" the mouse pointer is over.
    If MouseIn(Me, imgRight) Then
        BGMove picWorkBG, picBGOriginal, ScrollSpeed, 0
        LastXdir = 1
        LastYdir = 0
        WAVMIX_PlayChannel WAV_Turn, False
    ElseIf MouseIn(Me, imgLeft) Then
        BGMove picWorkBG, picBGOriginal, -ScrollSpeed, 0
        LastXdir = -1
        LastYdir = 0
        WAVMIX_PlayChannel WAV_Turn, False
    ElseIf MouseIn(Me, imgUp) Then
        BGMove picWorkBG, picBGOriginal, 0, -ScrollSpeed
        LastXdir = 0
        LastYdir = -1
```

```
            WAVMIX_PlayChannel WAV_Turn, False
        ElseIf MouseIn(Me, imgDown) Then
            BGMove picWorkBG, picBGOriginal, 0, ScrollSpeed
            LastXdir = 0
            LastYdir = 1
            WAVMIX_PlayChannel WAV_Turn, False
        ElseIf MouseIn(Me, imgUpLeft) Then
            BGMove picWorkBG, picBGOriginal, -ScrollSpeed, -ScrollSpeed
            LastXdir = -1
            LastYdir = -1
            WAVMIX_PlayChannel WAV_Turn, False
        ElseIf MouseIn(Me, imgDownLeft) Then
            BGMove picWorkBG, picBGOriginal, -ScrollSpeed, ScrollSpeed
            LastXdir = -1
            LastYdir = 1
            WAVMIX_PlayChannel WAV_Turn, False
        ElseIf MouseIn(Me, imgUpRight) Then
            BGMove picWorkBG, picBGOriginal, ScrollSpeed, -ScrollSpeed
            LastXdir = 1
            LastYdir = -1
            WAVMIX_PlayChannel WAV_Turn, False
        ElseIf MouseIn(Me, imgDownRight) Then
            BGMove picWorkBG, picBGOriginal, ScrollSpeed, ScrollSpeed
            LastXdir = 1
            LastYdir = 1
            WAVMIX_PlayChannel WAV_Turn, False
        Else
            ' If we're not over any directional control, just keep
            ' moving (slowly) on our current heading.
            BGMove picWorkBG, picBGOriginal, LastXdir * 2, LastYdir * 2
        End If

End Sub
```

The UpdateBackground routine uses the general purpose MouseIn routine to see if the mouse pointer is inside one of the directional controls and adjusts the ship's direction accordingly. Using the new ship position, it copies a section of the star field bitmap from the picBGOriginal PictureBox control into the picWorkBG PictureBox. As its name implies, picWorkBG is a work area where the background image is created. Each frame is first built in layers in the picWorkBG control; first the star field background, then the enemy ships, then the laser fire, and finally the cockpit window area. All this work takes place "off stage."

When the frame is complete, it's copied into the picBackground control for the player to see. By building the frame in this way, you avoid image flicker.

The Timer event next calls two subroutines, ClearScope and ShowYouOnScope. The names are fairly descriptive. ClearScope wipes out the current contents of the scope (whatever was there from the previous frame) and ShowYouOnScope draws vertical and horizontal crosshairs on the scope, indicating the player's current location in space. Add both these routines, as shown below.

```
Sub ClearScope ()
'-------------------------------------------------------------
' Clear the tracking radar scope.
'-------------------------------------------------------------
Dim retcode As Integer

    ' Clear the scope screen
    retcode = BitBlt(picScope.hDC, 0, 0, picScope.Width, picScope.Height,
picScopeWork.hDC, 0, 0, SRCCOPY)

End Sub

Sub ShowYouOnScope ()
'-------------------------------------------------------------
' Show the location of the player's ship as a sliding
' crosshair on the radar scope
'-------------------------------------------------------------
Dim X As Integer
Dim Y As Integer
Dim retcode As Long

    X = picScope.ScaleWidth * ((BG_NewX + (picBackground.ScaleWidth / 2)) /
        picBGOriginal.ScaleWidth)
    Y = picScope.ScaleHeight * ((BG_NewY + (picBackground.ScaleHeight / 2)) /
        picBGOriginal.ScaleHeight)
    If X > picScope.ScaleWidth Then X = X - picScope.ScaleWidth
    If Y > picScope.ScaleHeight Then Y = Y - picScope.ScaleHeight

    picScope.ForeColor = WHITE

    ' Draw the crosshairs the width and height of the scope.
    retcode = MoveTo(picScope.hDC, X, 0)
    retcode = LineTo(picScope.hDC, X, picScope.ScaleHeight)
    retcode = MoveTo(picScope.hDC, 0, Y)
    retcode = LineTo(picScope.hDC, picScope.ScaleWidth, Y)
End Sub
```

Back to the Timer event. The maximum number of enemy ships displayed at one time is determined by the NUM_ENEMY_SHIPS constant, which is currently set to 3 (you could modify the value to add more ships). The Timer event loops through the Ship array, checking to see if a ship has been hit, is in the process of exploding, is ready to fire its guns, and so on.

The logic works like this: There are three enemy ships, and each one must be hit by three direct laser hits before it is destroyed. The catch is, the enemy ship sprite is rendered invisible for a certain number of game frames, specified by the constant SHIP_INVIS_TIME. Each subsequent frame, the "destroyed" ship waits, and its Visible field is decreased by one. When the Visible field is reduced to zero, the ship once again becomes visible and reenters the game. By reducing the value of SHIP_INVIS_TIME, you can make destroyed ships reappear faster.

The enemy ships do not shoot at the player in each frame. If they did, the game would be very short. Instead, each ship fires when the Boolean EnemyFireVal is True. This value becomes True after a certain preset number of frames have passed since the last time the enemy ship fired.

Each time an enemy ship fires, the player's shields are reduced (the enemy ships have *extremely* good targeting computers). If the shields drop below a preset percentage, specified by the constant ALERT_LEVEL, the shields indicator turns from green to red, and an alarm begins to sound. The shields indicator is a 3D Panel control.

I said earlier that when an enemy ship is hit by three direct laser hits, it is destroyed (or rendered invisible, if you will). This is *almost* true. Before it actually disappears, the enemy ship appears to explode. This is done using a bit of sprite animation, and occurs over the course of three frames. The game contains three explosion sprites, which are displayed to achieve the effect of an exploding ship.

The player uses the mouse pointer to aim the ship's lasers and presses the mouse button to fire. To add to the visual effects, two lines are drawn from the lower corners of the picBackground area to the mouse pointer location.

One problem I had to overcome was how to make the space action appear outside the cockpit windows, which are irregular (i.e., not rectangular) shapes. As you'll recall, the BitBlt function only copies rectangular areas. The solution was to turn a rectangular area of the cockpit bitmap into a large sprite. The cockpit sprite and mask images are stored in two PictureBoxes, picPitSprite and picPitMask, shown in Figure 10-4. The last thing I did in the Timer event before copying the frame to the screen was to lay these bitmaps over the image, creating the illusion that the action is happening outside the cockpit windows.

FIGURE 10-4

The cockpit image (top) and mask used to overlay the space scene (bottom)

To show an enemy ship's location on the radar scope, the ShowShipOnScope subroutine is called for each visible enemy ship. Add this routine to SPACEHNT.FRM, as shown below.

```
Sub ShowShipOnScope (AShip As tShip)
'-------------------------------------------------------------
' Show an enemy ship on the radar scope.
'-------------------------------------------------------------
Dim X As Integer
Dim Y As Integer
Dim retcode As Long

    X = picScope.ScaleWidth * (AShip.Sprite.X / picBGOriginal.ScaleWidth)
    Y = picScope.ScaleHeight * (AShip.Sprite.Y / picBGOriginal.ScaleHeight)

    ' Show enemy ships as red.
    picScope.ForeColor = RED
    retcode = ellipse(picScope.hDC, X, Y, X + 2, Y + 2)
    retcode = ellipse(picScope.hDC, X, Y, X + 3, Y + 3)
End Sub
```

The enemy ship is rendered on the scope as a tiny red circle. This is drawn using the Windows API function ellipse.

The radar scope shows the location of enemy ships, but in this game, space is hardly infinite. In fact, space is limited to the confines of the 800x600 pixel star field bitmap stored in picBGOriginal. The enemy ships can't travel outside the boundaries of that bitmap. When they reach an edge, they change direction, bouncing off the edges of known space. A good way to think of the radar scope is as a thumbnail sketch of picBGOriginal. In fact, if you watch the scope, you'll see the enemy ships make "course corrections" at the edge of the scope. These course corrections can add some nice randomness to game play, as enemy ships can suddenly change directions when the player is trying to aim.

The ShipMove function is called in the Timer event to draw an enemy ship at its new location. This routine is passed a sprite data type, along with X and Y increments by which the ship is to be moved. These X and Y values are the product of two values: the ENEMY_SPEED constant, which is set to a value of 6, and the result of the Visual Basic Rnd function, which generates a random number. This means that in each frame an enemy ship will move at most 6 pixels. The randomness adds a quirkiness to the movement that makes the ships appear to be evading the player. It also makes them harder to track and hit. Add the ShipMove function, as shown below.

```
Sub ShipMove (Ship As tSprite, X As Integer, Y As Integer, Action As Integer)
'-------------------------------------------------------------
' Move the ship to its specified x-y location.
'-------------------------------------------------------------
Dim NewX As Integer
Dim NewY As Integer

    ' If the ship is not moving (and it won't be the
```

```
    ' first time this routine is called), then set
    ' initial x and y directions.
    If Ship.Xdir = 0 Then Ship.Xdir = 1
    If Ship.Ydir = 0 Then Ship.Ydir = 1

    ' See if a direction change is needed.
    NewX = Ship.X + (Ship.Xdir * X)
    If (NewX > (picBGOriginal.Width - Ship.Width)) Or (NewX < 0) Then
        Ship.Xdir = -Ship.Xdir
    End If

    NewY = Ship.Y + (Ship.Ydir * Y)
    If (NewY > (picBGOriginal.Height - Ship.Height)) Or (NewY < 0) Then
        Ship.Ydir = -Ship.Ydir
    End If

    ' Move the sprite.
    SpriteMove Me, Ship, X * Ship.Xdir, Y * Ship.Ydir
End Sub
```

When a game is over, the Timer event calls the EndGame routine. This routine shuts everything down in preparation for another game. After calling the EndGame routine, the Timer event is exited. Add the EndGame routine, as shown below.

```
Sub EndGame ()
'-------------------------------------------------------------
' Close everything down.
'-------------------------------------------------------------
Dim rc As Long

    ' Shut down the WaveMix .DLL.
    WAVMIX_Close

    ' Turn off the timer.
    Timer1.Enabled = False

    ' Hide the scope picture box.
    picScope.Visible = False

    ' The silly alien taunts you...
    rc = sndPlaySound(App.Path & "\ALIEN.WAV", SND_ASYNC)

    ' Shields are gone.
    panShields.FloodPercent = 0

    ' Ready to start again?
    btnStart.Caption = "&START"
    Me.Refresh

    ' Wait a couple of seconds
    Pause 5

    picBackground.Visible = False
End Sub
```

Notice in EndGame that you call the WAVMIX_Close routine to shut down the WaveMix DLL. Then a few statements later you use the Windows API sndPlaySound function to play a wave file. Why not just use WaveMix? Well, when you load up the wave files, they each eat a chunk of system memory. Because the alien voice wave file is only played at the end of the game and no game play is going on, you can afford the slight delay that may occur when the wave file is loaded from disk.

I wanted a custom mouse gun sight cursor to appear when the player moved the mouse pointer at an enemy ship. Visual Basic 3.0 lets you change a mouse pointer to any of several shapes using the MousePointer property, but it doesn't let you define one of your own design. Visual Basic 4.0 does let you do this, but I wanted this game to work with Visual Basic 3.0 as well. Luckily, a simple trick lets you accomplish the effect of a custom mouse pointer.

> **Programming Tip: When a Visual Basic program initiates a drag event, the mouse pointer is replaced by an icon defined in a control's DragIcon property. By making the picBackground PictureBox control believe that a drag event is occurring, you can cause the DragIcon to appear inside the PictureBox.**

Let's put this trick to work. Add these two events to the picBackground control.

```
Sub picBackground_DragDrop (Source As Control, X As Single, Y As Single)
'------------------------------------------------------------
' Determine where the player fired the laser.
'------------------------------------------------------------

    ' Display the custom cursor by initiating a drag event.
    ' This displays the DragIcon in place of the mouse pointer.
    picBackground.Drag

    ' The player must have clicked the mouse, so fire the
    ' laser when the timer event is called next.
    LaserFired = True

    ' Remember this mouse location.
    MouseX = BG_NewX + X
    If MouseX > picBGOriginal.ScaleWidth Then MouseX = MouseX - picBGOriginal.ScaleWidth
    MouseY = BG_NewY + Y
    If MouseY > picBGOriginal.ScaleHeight Then MouseY = MouseY - picBGOriginal.ScaleHeight
End Sub

Sub picBackground_MouseMove (Button As Integer, Shift As Integer, X As Single, Y As Single)
```

```
'-------------------------------------------------------------
' Draw a custom cursor by starting a drag event.
'-------------------------------------------------------------

    If picBackground.Tag <> "Mouse" Then
        picBackground.Drag
        picBackground.Tag = "Mouse"
    End If
End Sub
```

The DragDrop event actually serves two purposes. It helps display the DragIcon custom cursor (which you set to a cursor image of your own design in the Visual Basic Properties window), and it serves in place of a Click event. Because the DragDrop event is fired when a mouse button is pressed, you can use this as an opportunity to set the LaserFired Boolean and the MouseX and MouseY values. These are used in the Timer event to determine if the player has just fired the lasers.

To force the termination of the drag event when the mouse moves off the picBackground PictureBox, add the following DragOver event to the form itself.

```
Sub Form_DragOver (Source As Control, X As Single, Y As Single, State As Integer)
'-------------------------------------------------------------
' Turn off the custom mouse "gunsite" cursor if user drags
' mouse over the form (off the picBackground control).
'-------------------------------------------------------------

    If Source.Tag = "Mouse" Then
        Source.Drag 0
        Source.Tag = ""
    End If
End Sub
```

I wanted to let the player change the speed of the ship. This should have been simple enough, but I really didn't like any of the conventional controls. I wanted a control that could be manipulated entirely via the mouse. My first thought was to use a Scroll Bar control, and this certainly would have worked. But I wanted something a little more responsive. A Scroll Bar requires that the player hold down the mouse button. Also, to get from the slowest speed to the fastest speed, the Scroll Bar must traverse through all the values in between. In an arcade game, this seemed too slow.

So I decided to build my own control. What I came up with was a control whose value can be changed by simply moving the mouse over it. Move the mouse near the control's center, and the speed shifts to 50 percent. Sweep the mouse over the right side of the control, and the speed increases to 100 percent.

Did I build this new control in C++ as a VBX custom control? Not at all. I built it in Visual Basic using two PictureBox controls. The control is shown in Figure 10-5. It's a PictureBox, picSpeed, with a dark red background. Into this PictureBox I copied the image from a smaller PictureBox, picBlock, which has a bright red background. The

FIGURE 10-5

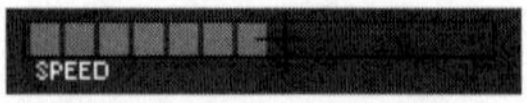

The custom speed control

number of block images copied into picSpeed depends on the position of the mouse when it moves over picSpeed. Add this MouseMove event for the picSpeed control.

```
Sub picSpeed_MouseMove (Button As Integer, Shift As Integer, X As Single, Y As Single)
'-------------------------------------------------------------
' Create our own custom Speed control in a PictureBox.
' Similar to a Scroller control, this control is set
' when the user sweeps the mouse over it.  No mouse clicking
' is required.
'-------------------------------------------------------------
Static PrevNumBlocks As Integer

Dim i As Integer
Dim NumBlocks As Integer

    ' How many blocks should we display?
    NumBlocks = X \ (picBlock.ScaleWidth + 2)

    ' If it's the same number as last time, exit.
    If PrevNumBlocks = NumBlocks Then Exit Sub

    ' Otherwise, redraw the control...
    picSpeed.Picture = LoadPicture()

    For i = 1 To TotalBlocks
        If i <= NumBlocks Then
            picBlockVisible i
        End If
    Next

    PrevNumBlocks = NumBlocks
    ScrollSpeed = NumBlocks
End Sub
```

This routine draws as many small blocks inside picSpeed as will fit to the left of the mouse pointer. It positions the blocks evenly by calling the subroutine picBlockVisible. This routine uses the BitBlt Windows API function to copy an image of the picBlock at a specified position. Add the picBlockVisible routine to the SPACEHNT.FRM form, as shown below.

```
Sub picBlockVisible (i As Integer)
'-------------------------------------------------------
' This routine makes one of the little blocks in the Speed
' Control invisible.
'-------------------------------------------------------
Dim ATop As Integer
Dim ALeft As Integer
Dim rc As Integer

    ATop = (picSpeed.ScaleHeight - picBlock.ScaleHeight) \ 2
    ALeft = ((i - 1) * (picBlock.ScaleWidth + 2)) + 2
    rc = BitBlt(picSpeed.hDC, ALeft, ATop, picBlock.Width, picBlock.Height, picBlock.hDC, 0, 0,
         SRCCOPY)
End Sub
```

You also need to add a Paint event to the picSpeed control so that you can redraw the picBlock images if the form is obscured by another form or has been minimized. Add the following Paint event for the picSpeed PictureBox control.

```
Sub picSpeed_Paint ()
'-------------------------------------------------------------
' Redraw the custom Speed control.
'-------------------------------------------------------------
Const PIXEL = 3
Dim i As Integer

    picSpeed.ScaleMode = PIXEL
    picBlock.ScaleMode = PIXEL
    If TotalBlocks = 0 Then
        TotalBlocks = (picSpeed.ScaleWidth / (picBlock.ScaleWidth + 2))
        For i = 1 To TotalBlocks
            picBlockVisible i
        Next
    End If

End Sub
```

Speaking of minimizing, what happens when the player decides to minimize the game? If you did nothing, the game would continue to play on its own, quickly defeating the player. This hardly seems fair, so I added some code to the form's Resize event to suspend the game when the player minimizes the form and then automatically resume it when the form is restored to normal. Add this Resize event to the form, as shown below.

```
Sub Form_Resize ()
'-------------------------------------------------------------
' Pause the game when the form is minimized, then resume
' it when it is redisplayed.
'-------------------------------------------------------------
```

continued on next page

continued from previous page

```
Const MINIMIZED = 1
Static Paused As Integer
Dim rc As Long

    If Paused Then
        Paused = False
        rc = WaveMixActivate(hWaveMix, True)
        Timer1.Enabled = True
    End If

    If (WindowState = MINIMIZED) And (Timer1.Enabled) Then
        rc = WaveMixActivate(hWaveMix, False)
        Timer1.Enabled = False
        Paused = True
    End If
End Sub
```

Now the game is almost finished. You need to add a small Pause routine that delays processing for a few seconds. You want to do this sometimes to achieve a desired timing. For example, at the end of the game there is a brief pause, during which the enemy ships continue to appear outside the window before the scene turns to black. Add the Pause routine, as shown below.

```
Sub Pause (Seconds As Single)
'------------------------------------------------------------
' Delay for a specified number of seconds.
'------------------------------------------------------------
Dim Start As Single

    Start = Timer
    Do While (Timer - Start) < Seconds
        DoEvents
    Loop
End Sub
```

Finally, to ensure everything gets cleaned up properly when the player exits the game, add the following Unload event to the form.

```
Sub Form_Unload (Cancel As Integer)
'------------------------------------------------------------
' Make sure to shut down the WaveMix .DLL properly to ensure
' that any memory it has allocated is freed correctly.
'------------------------------------------------------------

    WAVMIX_Close
End Sub
```

The only clean up you need to worry about is the WaveMix DLL, so a simple call to WAVMIX_Close to free up all the audio resources is all that's needed.

Now the game is complete. Make sure that the SPACEHNT form is resized at design time to show only the cockpit area. Now you're ready to play the game. Good hunting!

Suggested Enhancements

A game like Space Hunt lends itself well to enhancements. As I built it, I started thinking of numerous ways to improve it. You'll probably think of a few yourself, but in the meantime, here are my suggestions.

- More enemy ship designs—it would be fun to see a variety of enemy ship designs, each with their own unique behaviors.
- Some friendly ships—these would be ships you don't want to hit. They might show up on the radar scope as a different color, or perhaps the player would have to identify friend or foe by sight.
- Shield replenishment—the way it works now, the shields go in one direction, down. It would make the game more interesting if the shields would gradually be restored.
- Limit the player's laser fire—currently, the player can fire the lasers with wild abandon—unlike the shields, these weapons seem inexhaustible. If the lasers could only fire ten times before being depleted, then the player would have to improve accuracy to survive.
- Better sprite animation—explosions are now just three frames long; five or six frames would be much more impressive. Likewise, when the enemy ships fire, only one sprite shows the gunfire. This could be animated with several sprites over multiple frames to create a more realistic effect.

I'll continue the space theme in the next chapter, when we tackle a lunar lander simulation.

11

Simulations: Lunar Lander

11

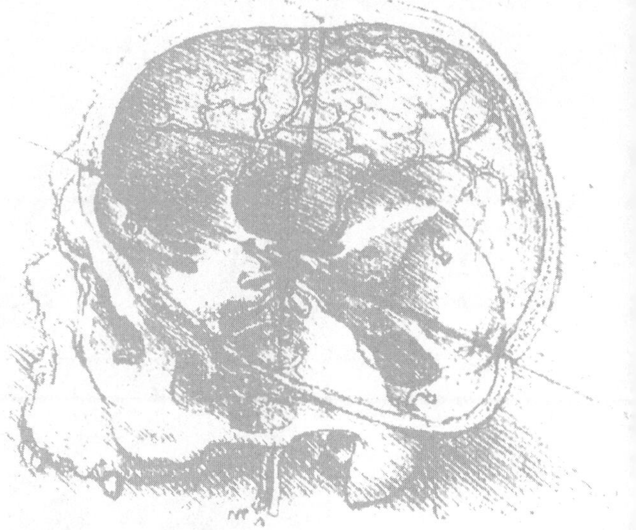

Simulations: Lunar Lander

Simulations are programs that attempt to mimic the behavior of an object or group of objects. These objects may be things that exist in the real world, such as airplanes or automobiles. Many times, however, simulations imitate things that don't yet exist in the real world.

Lunar Lander lets the player simulate landing a futuristic landing craft on the surface of the moon. This game helps illustrate the basic points involved in creating a simulation.

The Lunar Lander Game

The simulation presented here imitates a fictitious lunar lander as it descends toward the surface of the moon. The player represents the pilot; he or she uses thruster controls to guide the ship to a safe landing on a landing pad.

The game, shown in Figure 11-1, is equipped with three thruster buttons to control the lander's descent. The effects of gravity and inertia are simulated. Gravity causes the ship to accelerate as it descends, unless the player compensates by applying the vertical thruster. The goal of the simulation is to land the craft squarely on the landing pad at a very slow velocity, with as much fuel remaining as possible. Each

FIGURE 11-1

The Lunar Lander game

time the thrusters are used, the fuel gauge shows fuel depletion. When the fuel is gone, none of the thrusters will function, and the lander will begin to descend like a stone.

Unlike many games that provide the player with a numeric score at game's end, Lunar Lander gives the player a rank and some feedback, criticism, or praise based on the quality of the landing.

Building Your Own Lunar Lander

The first step in creating any Visual Basic program is to create a new project. As with any project, create a separate subdirectory on your hard drive for this one, perhaps called \LANDER. Name the project file LANDER.MAK.

Before building the game's main form, you need to declare some data types, Windows API functions, and support subroutines used in the game. Create a new Visual Basic module called LANDER.BAS. Add to this module the Declarations section shown in Listing 11-1.

Listing 11-1 The LANDER.BAS Declaration section

```
Option Explicit
'--------------------------------------------------------
' LANDER.BAS
'--------------------------------------------------------

' Data type that stores information about the
' state of the lander.
Type tLander
    xPos As Integer
    yPos As Integer
    xSpeed As Single
    ySpeed As Single
    FuelAmount As Integer
End Type

' Data type to store x-y coordinates.
Type tPosition
    x As Integer
    y As Integer
End Type

' ScaleMode property constant
Global Const PIXELS = 3

' Constants used in BitBlt Windows API Call
Global Const SRCCOPY = &HCC0020
Global Const SRCAND = &H8800C6
Global Const SRCPAINT = &HEE0086

' Windows API call used to copy bitmaps
Declare Function BitBlt Lib "GDI" (ByVal hDestDC As Integer, ByVal DestX
As Integer, ByVal DestY As Integer, ByVal DestWidth As Integer, ByVal
DestHeight As Integer, ByVal hSrcDC As Integer, ByVal SrcX As Integer,
ByVal SrcY As Integer, ByVal RasterOp As Long) As Integer

' Functions and constants used to play sounds.
Global Const SND_SYNC = &H0          ' Return when sound ends (the default)
Global Const SND_ASYNC = &H1         ' Return as soon as sound starts
Global Const SND_NODEFAULT = &H2     ' Don't play default sound if not found
Global Const SND_MEMORY = &H4        ' lpszSoundName -> memory image of file
Global Const SND_LOOP = &H8          ' Loop continuously; needs SND_ASYNC
Global Const SND_NOSTOP = &H10       ' Don't interrupt sound to play new one

Declare Function sndPlaySound Lib "MMSystem" (ByVal lpsound As String,
ByVal flag As Integer) As Integer
Declare Function sndKillSound Lib "MMSystem" Alias "sndPlaySound" (ByVal
lpszNull As Long, ByVal flags As Integer) As Integer
```

The tLander data type will be used to store information about the current state of the lander: its position, speed, and how much fuel it has left. I could have stored this information in several separate variables, but data types are a good way to keep information about an object, in this case the lunar lander, tied together in a well-organized package.

Most of the remaining declarations either define Windows API functions or define constants required by API calls. This program uses the essential Windows BitBlt call to draw the landscape and lunar lander. The program also uses the sndPlaySound API function to handle playing sound effects. The two sound effects used most often are heard when the vertical and horizontal thrusters are fired.

As you'll recall from Chapter 6, the sndPlaySound function plays wave audio (.WAV) files on computers equipped with either a sound card or a PC speaker driver. Usually, sndPlaySound is used to play these files directly from disk. This may not be desirable in a game, as the disk access required to load the .WAV files may interrupt the game. To avoid this, Lunar Lander uses two short routines. Add the routines shown in Listing 11-2 to LANDER.BAS.

Listing 11-2 The NoiseGet and NoisePlay functions

```
Function NoiseGet (ByVal FileName, ASoundBuffer As String) As Integer
'--------------------------------------------------------------
' Load a sound file into the global string variable
' SoundBuffer. This must be called before NoisePlay
'--------------------------------------------------------------
Dim buffer As String
Dim f As Integer

    On Error GoTo NoiseGet_Error

    buffer = Space$(1024)
    ASoundBuffer = ""
    f = FreeFile
    Open FileName For Binary As f
    Do While Not EOF(f)
        Get #f, , buffer      ' Load in 1K chunks
        ASoundBuffer = ASoundBuffer & buffer
    Loop
    Close f
    ASoundBuffer = Trim$(ASoundBuffer)

Exit Function

NoiseGet_Error:
    NoiseGet = False
    ASoundBuffer = ""
    Exit Function
End Function
```

```
Sub NoisePlay (ASoundBuffer As String)
'------------------------------------------------------------
' Plays a sound previously loaded into memory with function
' NoiseGet().
'------------------------------------------------------------
Dim r As Integer  ' asynchronously

    If ASoundBuffer = "" Then Exit Sub
    r = sndPlaySound(ASoundBuffer, SND_ASYNC Or SND_MEMORY)

End Sub
```

The first routine, NoiseGet, reads a .WAV file from disk and stores it in a Visual Basic string variable. This routine is called when the game is first started to load the necessary sound effects into memory.

In addition to playing .WAV files from disk, the sndPlaySound function can also play wave audio files that have been stored in memory. This is precisely what the NoisePlay subroutine does. Normally, the first parameter passed to sndPlaySound represents a .WAV file name. But when the special SND_MEMORY constant is specified, the first parameter actually refers to a buffer in memory where the contents of a wave audio file are stored. Because of the limitations on the length of Visual Basic strings, this technique only works for relatively short .WAV files, but is more than sufficient for the current needs.

Building the Lunar Lander Form

Now let's build the Visual Basic form where the game will be played. Add a new form called LANDER.FRM to the LANDER.MAK project.

The player sees a large viewing screen with a small horizontal scope below it. To the right of the viewing screen are three thruster button controls; a start/pause button; text labels that indicate the lander's speed, altitude, and distance from target; and a text window that provides help and feedback. But there are other controls that the player never sees. Most of these are PictureBox controls used to hold sprites and sprite masks, the large background landscape, and a working area where the scene the player eventually sees is created. At design time, the form looks like Figure 11-2.

The form shown in Figure 11-2 is resized after it is created so that the sprite, landscape, and other "off-stage" controls can't be seen. To keep the user from resizing the form and thus revealing these images, I made the form's border nonresizable (by changing the BorderStyle property to Single Line) and disabled the form's maximize button.

To create this form, add the controls listed in Table 11-1 to the form. Situating the controls on the form will be easiest if your Windows video driver is at least capable of 800x600 pixel resolution. Although the finished game is playable at standard VGA 640x480 resolution, the hidden controls are easier to place on the form at design time if your screen has a higher resolution.

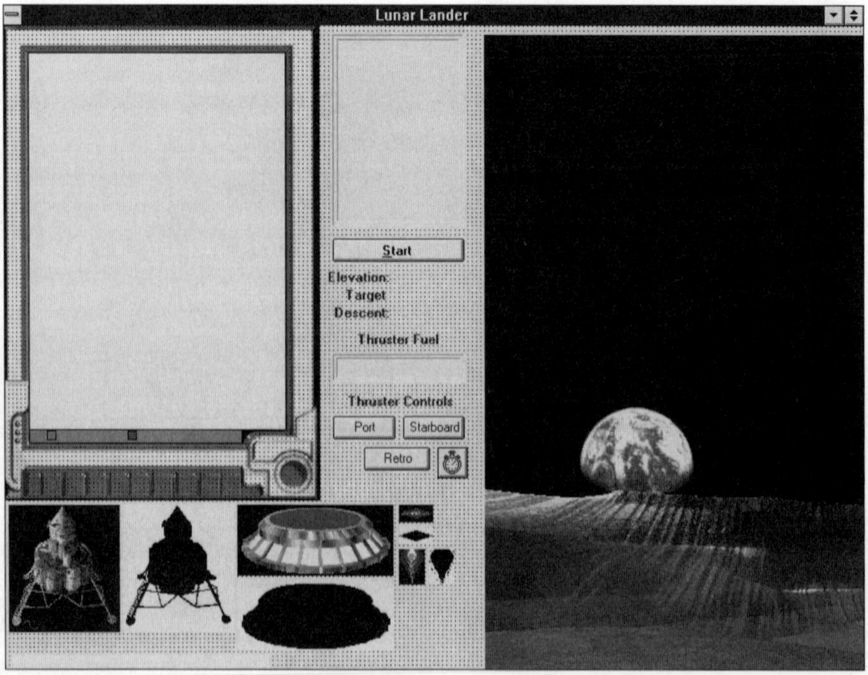

FIGURE 11-2

The LANDER.FRM form at design time

TABLE 11-1

Objects and properties of the LANDER.FRM form

Object	Property	Setting
Form	FormName	frmLander
	BackColor	&H00C0C0C0&
	BorderStyle	1 'Fixed Single
	Caption	"Lunar Lander"
	FillColor	&H0000C000&
	Height	6810
	Left	750
	Picture	(set at design time in Properties window)
	Top	795
	Width	6750

Object	Property	Setting
Label	Name	Label1
	Alignment	2 'Center
	BackStyle	0 'Transparent
	Caption	"Thruster Fuel"
	ForeColor	&H00FF0000&
	Height	195
	Left	4920
	Top	4140
	Width	1215
Label	Name	Label2
	Alignment	2 'Center
	BackStyle	0 'Transparent
	Caption	"Thruster Controls"
	ForeColor	&H00FF0000&
	Height	195
	Left	4680
	Top	4980
	Width	1755
Label	Name	Label3
	Alignment	1 'Right Justify
	BackStyle	0 'Transparent
	Caption	"Elevation:"
	ForeColor	&H00FF0000&
	Height	195
	Left	4500
	Top	3300
	Width	915
Label	Name	Label4
	Alignment	1 'Right Justify

continued on next page

continued from previous page

Object	Property	Setting
	BackStyle	0 'Transparent
	Caption	"Target Loc:"
	ForeColor	&H00FF0000&
	Height	195
	Left	4560
	Top	3540
	Width	855
Label	Name	lblTargetLoc
	Alignment	1 'Right Justify
	BackStyle	0 'Transparent
	ForeColor	&H000000FF&
	Height	195
	Left	5400
	Top	3540
	Width	1035
Label	Name	lblElevation
	Alignment	1 'Right Justify
	BackStyle	0 'Transparent
	ForeColor	&H000000FF&
	Height	195
	Left	5460
	Top	3300
	Width	975
Label	Name	lblDescent
	Alignment	1 'Right Justify
	BackStyle	0 'Transparent
	ForeColor	&H000000FF&
	Height	195
	Left	5400
	Top	3780
	Width	1035

Object	Property	Setting
Label	Name	Label6
	Alignment	1 'Right Justify
	BackStyle	0 'Transparent
	Caption	"Descent:"
	ForeColor	&H00FF0000&
	Height	195
	Left	4560
	Top	3780
	Width	855
SSCommand	Name	btnLeft
	Caption	"Port"
	Font3D	3 'Inset w/light shading
	FontBold	0 'False
	Height	315
	Left	4620
	Top	5280
	Width	855
SSCommand	Name	btnRight
	Caption	"Starboard"
	Font3D	3 'Inset w/light shading
	FontBold	0 'False
	Height	315
	Left	5580
	Top	5280
	Width	855
SSCommand	Name	btnUp
	Caption	"Retro"
	Font3D	3 'Inset w/light shading
	FontBold	0 'False
	Height	315
	Left	5040

continued on next page

continued from previous page

Object	Property	Setting
	Top	5700
	Width	915
SSPanel	Name	panFuel
	BackColor	&H00C0C0C0&
	BevelInner	1 'Inset
	BevelOuter	1 'Inset
	BorderWidth	2
	Caption	"SSPanel1"
	FloodColor	&H000000FF&
	FloodShowPct	0 'False
	FloodType	1 'Left To Right
	Font3D	3 'Inset w/light shading
	ForeColor	&H00FF0000&
	Height	375
	Left	4620
	Top	4440
	Width	1815
SSPanel	Name	panInfo
	Alignment	0 'Left Justify - TOP
	BackColor	&H00C0C0C0&
	BevelInner	1 'Inset
	BevelOuter	1 'Inset
	Font3D	0 'None
	FontBold	0 'False
	FontName	"Arial"
	ForeColor	&H00FF0000&
	Height	2595
	Left	4620
	Top	120
	Width	1815

Object	Property	Setting
PictureBox	Name	picViewer
	Height	5115
	Left	360
	Top	360
	Width	3615
PictureBox	Name	picBG
	AutoRedraw	-1 'True
	AutoSize	-1 'True
	BorderStyle	0 'None
	Height	10500
	Left	6720
	Picture	(set at design time in Properties window)
	Top	120
	Width	9600
PictureBox	Name	picLander_s
	AutoRedraw	-1 'True
	AutoSize	-1 'True
	BorderStyle	0 'None
	Height	1725
	Left	60
	Picture	(set at design time in Properties window)
	Top	6480
	Width	1575
PictureBox	Name	picLander_m
	AutoRedraw	-1 'True
	AutoSize	-1 'True
	BorderStyle	0 'None
	Height	1725
	Left	1680

continued on next page

continued from previous page

Object	Property	Setting
	Picture	(set at design time in Properties window)
	Top	6480
	Width	1575
PictureBox	Name	picPad_s
	AutoRedraw	-1 'True
	AutoSize	-1 'True
	BorderStyle	0 'None
	Height	960
	Left	3300
	Picture	(set at design time in Properties window)
	Top	6480
	Width	2145
PictureBox	Name	picPad_m
	AutoRedraw	-1 'True
	AutoSize	-1 'True
	BorderStyle	0 'None
	Height	960
	Left	3300
	Picture	(set at design time in Properties window)
	Top	7500
	Width	2145
CommandButton	Name	btnStart
	Caption	"&Start"
	Height	315
	Left	4620
	Top	2880
	Width	1815

Object	Property	Setting
Timer	Name	Timer1
	Enabled	0 'False
	Interval	55
	Left	6060
	Top	5700
PictureBox	Name	picWork
	AutoRedraw	-1 'True
	BorderStyle	0 'None
	Height	5115
	Left	120
	Top	8520
	Width	3615
PictureBox	Name	picScanner
	BackColor	&H00808080&
	Height	195
	Left	360
	Top	5460
	Width	3015
PictureBox	Name	picThrustH_s
	AutoRedraw	-1 'True
	AutoSize	-1 'True
	BorderStyle	0 'None
	Height	240
	Left	5520
	Picture	(set at design time in Properties window)
	Top	6480
	Width	480
PictureBox	Name	picThrustH_m

continued on next page

continued from previous page

Object	Property	Setting
	AutoRedraw	-1 'True
	AutoSize	-1 'True
	BorderStyle	0 'None
	Height	240
	Left	5520
	Picture	(set at design time in Properties window)
	Top	6780
	Width	480
PictureBox	Name	picThrustV_s
	AutoRedraw	-1 'True
	AutoSize	-1 'True
	BorderStyle	0 'None
	Height	480
	Left	5520
	Picture	(set at design time in Properties window)
	Top	7080
	Width	360
PictureBox	Name	picThrustV_m
	AutoRedraw	-1 'True
	AutoSize	-1 'True
	BorderStyle	0 'None
	Height	480
	Left	5940
	Picture	(set at design time in Properties window)
	Top	7080
	Width	360

In addition to the objects above, you'll need to add two more controls. The Shape controls listed in Table 11-2 are placed *inside* the picScanner PictureBox control. To do this, first select the picScanner control by clicking the mouse on it once, so that the control's resizing "handles" appear around its edge. Then simply select the Shape control from the Visual Basic Toolbox and place it on the picScanner control. To make sure the Shape control is actually inside the picScanner control, try to drag the Shape control outside the borders of picScanner. If you can't move it outside of picScanner, then it's been placed correctly.

TABLE 11-2

The Shape controls placed inside picScanner

Object	Property	Setting
Shape	Name	shpLander
	FillColor	&H0000C000&
	FillStyle	0 'Solid
	Height	135
	Left	240
	Top	0
	Width	135
Shape	Name	shpPad
	FillColor	&H000000FF&
	FillStyle	0 'Solid
	Height	135
	Left	1380
	Top	0
	Width	135

Creating Your Own World

How do you create a realistic lunar landscape? I used VistaPro, a program designed to create computer-generated realistic landscapes. VistaPro is covered in detail in Chapter 8. VistaPro created the basic landscape, then I pasted an actual image of the earth from a scanned photograph and composited it over the horizon. The result is the landscape shown in Figure 11-3.

FIGURE 11-3

The lunar landscape

Making It All Work

Now let's begin to add the Visual Basic code to the Lunar Lander form. First, add the declarations used by other routines within the form. These are placed in the LANDER.FRM form's Declarations section, as shown in Listing 11-3.

Listing 11-3 LANDER.FRM Declarations section

```
Option Explicit
'-------------------------------------------------------------
' LANDER.FRM
'-------------------------------------------------------------

' Color constant.
```

```
Const BLACK = 0

' Game state constants
Const GAME_OVER = 0
Const GAME_RUNNING = 1
Const GAME_PAUSED = 2

' Information about the lander
Dim mLander As tLander

' Location of the landing pad.
Dim mPad As tPosition

' Location of upper-left corner of visible
' background relative to the large background
' bitmap.
Dim mBG As tPosition

' Current state of each thruster.
Dim mLeftThrusterOn As Integer
Dim mRightThrusterOn As Integer
Dim mBottomThrusterOn As Integer

' Buffers that hold the Wave Audio for the
' thruster sounds
Dim mSndThrust1 As String
Dim mSndThrust2 As String

' Game state (eg., Paused, Running...)
Dim mCurrentState As Integer

' Used to keep lander positioned in center of screen.
Dim mCentered As tPosition
```

Most of the variables declared in Listing 11-3 help track different objects and their states as the game progresses. The mLander variable, of type tLander, tracks the lander's speed, position, and fuel. The mPad variable stores the X-Y coordinates of the landing pad. The mCurrentState variable indicates whether the game is currently running, stopped, or paused.

Now add a Load event to the form. This event is triggered once when the program is first started, so it provides a good place to initialize variables you'll use throughout the game. For example, PictureBox controls have a ScaleMode property that determines the units of measurement used when drawing objects inside them. By default, Visual Basic uses units called twips, but the Windows API function BitBlt uses pixels. So in the Load event, set the ScaleModes of all the PictureBoxes to pixels. The Load event is also the ideal place to load the thruster sound effect .WAV files into memory.

Add the Load event to the LANDER.FRM form as shown in Listing 11-4.

Listing 11-4 The Load event

```
Sub Form_Load ()
'------------------------------------------------------------
' Prepare the form.
'------------------------------------------------------------
Dim AppPath As String
Dim rc As Integer

    ' Initialize the random number generator.
    Randomize

    ' Center the form on the screen.
    Me.Move (Screen.Width - Me.Width) / 2, (Screen.Height - Me.Height) / 2

    picViewer.BackColor = BLACK

    ' Make sure all bitmaps are set to pixel scale modes.
    ' This is what BitBlt expects.
    picBG.ScaleMode = PIXELS
    picViewer.ScaleMode = PIXELS
    picLander_s.ScaleMode = PIXELS
    picLander_m.ScaleMode = PIXELS
    picPad_s.ScaleMode = PIXELS
    picPad_m.ScaleMode = PIXELS
    picThrustH_s.ScaleMode = PIXELS
    picThrustH_m.ScaleMode = PIXELS
    picThrustV_s.ScaleMode = PIXELS
    picThrustV_m.ScaleMode = PIXELS

    ' Load Sound Effects
    AppPath = App.Path
    If Right$(AppPath, 1) <> "\" Then AppPath = AppPath & "\"
    rc = NoiseGet(AppPath & "THRUSTR1.WAV", mSndThrust1)
    rc = NoiseGet(AppPath & "THRUSTR2.WAV", mSndThrust2)

    ' Display game information.
    GameInfo

    ' Calculate the center of the Viewer.
    mCentered.x = (picViewer.ScaleWidth - picLander_s.ScaleWidth) \ 2
    mCentered.y = (picViewer.ScaleHeight - picLander_s.ScaleHeight) \ 2
End Sub
```

The Load event calls one subroutine, GameInfo, that initializes some text displayed in a 3D Panel control. Add the GameInfo routine, as shown below.

```
Sub GameInfo ()
'------------------------------------------------------------
' Display brief playing instructions.
'------------------------------------------------------------
```

```
    panInfo.Caption = "Use the thruster controls to bring your "
    panInfo.Caption = panInfo.Caption & "Lander to a soft landing on the Target "
    panInfo.Caption = panInfo.Caption & "Pad. The scope at the bottom of the view "
    panInfo.Caption = panInfo.Caption & "screen shows your position relative to the pad."
End Sub
```

To start the game, the player presses the btnStart Command Button control. This button serves three purposes: it starts a new game or, while a game is in progress, it pauses or resumes the game. Add the Click event in Listing 11-5 for the btnStart control on the LANDER.FRM form.

Listing 11-5 The btnStart_Click subroutine

```
Sub btnStart_Click ()
'------------------------------------------------------------
' Start, pause, or resume the game.
'------------------------------------------------------------

    ' Check the current game state.
    Select Case mCurrentState
        ' Start a new game.
        Case GAME_OVER:
            mLander.yPos = 5         ' Position the lander
            Position_Pad             ' Position the landing pad.

            ' Set initial speed, position, and fuel
            ' for the lander.
            mLander.xSpeed = 0
            mLander.ySpeed = 1
            mLander.xPos = mCentered.x
            mLander.yPos = 5
            mLander.FuelAmount = 100

            ' ViewPort shows the far upper-left corner
            ' of the landscape.
            mBG.x = 0
            mBG.y = 0

            mCurrentState = GAME_RUNNING
            EnableThrusterControls True
            btnStart.Caption = "&Pause"
            GameInfo

            ' Start generating Timer events.
            Timer1.Enabled = True

        ' Pause the game.
        Case GAME_RUNNING:
            Timer1.Enabled = False
            EnableThrusterControls False
```

continued on next page

continued from previous page

```
            btnStart.Caption = "&Resume"
            mCurrentState = GAME_PAUSED

        ' Resume a paused game.
        Case GAME_PAUSED:
            Timer1.Enabled = True
            EnableThrusterControls True
            btnStart.Caption = "&Pause"
            mCurrentState = GAME_RUNNING
    End Select
End Sub
```

This event routine uses a Visual Basic Select-Case statement to look at the value of the mCurrentState variable and act based on the current state of the game. For example, if the value of mCurrentState is equal to the constant GAME_OVER, then you need to set up and begin a new game, as well as change the game state to GAME_RUNNING.

Note that the Click event above calls a routine called EnableThrusterControls. This routine does exactly what its name implies, either enabling or disabling the thruster buttons based on the True or False value passed to it. Add the EnableThrusterControls routine, as shown below.

```
Sub EnableThrusterControls (ABoolean As Integer)
'-------------------------------------------------------------
' Enable or disable the thruster buttons based on true/false
' value, ABoolean.
'-------------------------------------------------------------

    btnLeft.Enabled = ABoolean
    btnRight.Enabled = ABoolean
    btnUp.Enabled = ABoolean
End Sub
```

Another routine called in btnStart's Click event is Position_Pad. When a new game is started, the program picks a random spot on the lunar landscape and places the landing pad there. This varies the difficulty level from game to game, as the player has no idea where the destination is until the game begins. The landing pad's position is stored in the mPad variable as a pair of X-Y coordinates. Add the Position_Pad routine, as shown below.

```
Sub Position_Pad ()
'-------------------------------------------------------------
' Randomly place the landing pad on the background.
'-------------------------------------------------------------

    mPad.x = (picBG.ScaleWidth - picPad_s.ScaleWidth) * Rnd
    mPad.y = picBG.ScaleHeight - picPad_m.ScaleHeight

End Sub
```

The game begins when the Timer control is enabled. The Timer control generates Timer events during which you update the progress of the game. The ship's position is adjusted to account for gravity, inertia, and thrusters. The on-screen indicators, such as speed and elevation, are updated. To see how this is accomplished, add a Timer event to the Timer1 control, as shown in Listing 11-6 to the LANDER.FRM form.

Listing 11-6 Timer event

```
Sub Timer1_Timer ()
'-------------------------------------------------------------
' The Timer event handles most of the game action.
'-------------------------------------------------------------
Dim DistanceToTarget As Integer
Dim Elevation As Integer

    ' Adjust the fuel gauge.
    Adjust_Fuel

    ' Increase ship speed (due to gravity).
    Apply_Gravity

    ' Horizontal Inertia
    Apply_Inertia

    ' Calculate the ship's next y position.
    Calculate_Lander_Y

    ' Have we hit the ground?
    Have_We_Landed Elevation, DistanceToTarget

    ' Update the status indicators on the screen.
    Update_Status Elevation, DistanceToTarget

    ' Calculate the ship's next x position.
    Calculate_Lander_X

    ' Adjust the background to keep the ship in the center of the screen.
    Adjust_Background

    ' Draw the Background into the work area PictureBox.
    Draw_Background

    ' Draw the Lander's thrusters onto the background, if they're on.
    Draw_Thrusters

    ' Copy the Lander into the work area bitmap.
    Draw_Lander

    ' Copy everything into viewer.
```

continued on next page

continued from previous page

```
    Update_Viewer

    ' Update the scanner at the bottom of the Viewer.
    Update_Scanner
End Sub
```

Notice that the Timer event is a collection of calls to other subroutines. In fact, there's not a line of Visual Basic code in the Timer event, save for subroutine calls and two variable declarations. By breaking this event into separate subroutines, the actual flow of events becomes more understandable. There is a trade-off involved, however. A slight overhead is involved in calling subroutines that can slow processing by a small amount. Because you want the Timer event to happen very quickly, you have to be careful when doing things that might slow it down. In this particular case, the effect of the subroutines is not particularly noticeable, and is offset by the improved readability of the source code.

What do all these subroutines do? Let's take them from the top, so that you can see how a single Timer event moves the game forward.

First, add the Adjust_Fuel subroutine, as shown below.

```
Sub Adjust_Fuel ()
'-------------------------------------------------------------
' Adjust the fuel gauge.
'-------------------------------------------------------------

    If mLander.FuelAmount > 0 Then
        panFuel.FloodPercent = mLander.FuelAmount
    Else
        panFuel.FloodPercent = 0
    End If
End Sub
```

This routine updates the fuel gauge, which is actually a 3D Panel control used as a percentage meter. As you'll see shortly, the fuel is decreased each time the thrusters are used.

Next, the program needs to adjust the ship's downward velocity to simulate the effects of gravity. Add the Apply_Gravity subroutine to LANDER.FRM, as shown below.

```
Sub Apply_Gravity ()
'-------------------------------------------------------------
' Increase ship speed (due to gravity).
'-------------------------------------------------------------

    If mLander.ySpeed > 0 Then
        mLander.ySpeed = mLander.ySpeed * 1.05
    Else
        mLander.ySpeed = mLander.ySpeed + .09
    End If
End Sub
```

The Apply_Gravity routine looks at the lander's current vertical (up and down) speed and adjusts it to simulate gravity. There's nothing magic about the values I used; they're based more on trial and error than anything else. When the lander is descending, the downward velocity is increased by 5 percent on each pass through the Timer event. I wanted to make it more difficult for the ship to ascend, so when the lander begins to move upward (its ySpeed becoming negative), I added .09 to its downward speed to compensate for the upward movement.

Next, add the Apply_Inertia routine. This routine simulates resistance when the horizontal thrusters are used. Add the routine, as shown below.

```
Sub Apply_Inertia ()
'--------------------------------------------------------------
' Horizontal Inertia
'--------------------------------------------------------------

    If mLander.xSpeed > 0 Then
        mLander.xSpeed = mLander.xSpeed - .02
    ElseIf mLander.xSpeed < 0 Then
        mLander.xSpeed = mLander.xSpeed + .02
    End If
End Sub
```

This routine decreases the horizontal velocity to slow down sideways motion. This lets the lander appear to slow down after the port or starboard thrusters have been used.

Next, the program determines new Y coordinate, or rather the distance from the ground. Add the Calculate_Lander_Y routine to the form, as shown below.

```
Sub Calculate_Lander_Y ()
'--------------------------------------------------------------
' Calculate the Lander's next Y Position.
'--------------------------------------------------------------
Dim prevYPos As Integer

    prevYPos = mLander.yPos

    ' Calculate the ship's next y position.
    mLander.yPos = mLander.yPos + mLander.ySpeed

    ' Make sure the ship can't just sit still...
    If prevYPos = mLander.yPos Then
        If mLander.ySpeed < 0 Then
            mLander.yPos = mLander.yPos - 1
        Else
            mLander.yPos = mLander.yPos + 1
        End If
    End If
End Sub
```

Now that you know how far off the ground the ship is, you need to know if the ship has actually landed (or crashed, as the case may be). The Have_We_Landed subroutine serves this purpose, as shown below.

```
Sub Have_We_Landed (Elevation As Integer, DistanceToTarget As Integer)
'-------------------------------------------------------------
' Check to see if the lander has hit the ground yet.
'-------------------------------------------------------------
Dim GroundYPos As Integer

    ' Have we hit the ground?
    GroundYPos = (picBG.ScaleHeight) - (picPad_s.ScaleHeight \ 2)
    Elevation = GroundYPos - (mLander.yPos + picLander_s.ScaleHeight) + 20
    DistanceToTarget = (mPad.x + (picPad_s.ScaleWidth \ 2)) - (mLander.xPos +
                       (picLander_s.ScaleWidth \ 2))

    If (mLander.yPos + picLander_s.ScaleHeight - 20) >= GroundYPos Then
        EnableThrusterControls False
        btnStart.Caption = "&Start"
        mCurrentState = GAME_OVER
        Timer1.Enabled = False
        ShowGameRating mLander.ySpeed, DistanceToTarget, mLander.FuelAmount
    End If
End Sub
```

Notice that the routine above calculates two values that will be used later in the Timer event: elevation and distance to target. This routine looks at the lander's distance from the ground. If the ship has landed, the routine ends the game by disabling the game timer and displaying the player's game rating. This is handled in the ShowGameRating subroutine. Add this routine to the LANDER.FRM form, as shown in Listing 11-7.

Listing 11-7 The ShowGameRating subroutine

```
Sub ShowGameRating (ByVal Speed As Single, ByVal Distance As Integer, Fuel As Integer)
'-------------------------------------------------------------
' When the game is over, rate the player based on amount of
' fuel remaining, distance from the pad, and how softly
' the player touched down.
'-------------------------------------------------------------
Dim Rating As Integer
Dim rc As Integer
Dim Info As String
Dim CRLF As String
Dim Direction As String

    CRLF = Chr$(13) & Chr$(10)

    Info = "Rank: "

    ' Calculate a numeric rating based on speed, distance
```

```
' from target, and remaining fuel.
Rating = Abs(Speed) + Abs(Distance \ 10) + (10 - (Fuel \ 10))

' Really bad ratings get a "bad" landing noise.
If Rating < 20 Then
    rc = sndPlaySound(App.Path & "\LAND_OK.WAV", SND_ASYNC)
Else
    rc = sndPlaySound(App.Path & "\LAND_BAD.WAV", SND_ASYNC)
End If

' Assign a "rank" to the player.
If Rating < 5 Then
    Info = Info & "Captain"
ElseIf Rating < 10 Then
    Info = Info & "Commander"
ElseIf Rating < 15 Then
    Info = Info & "Lieutenant"
ElseIf Rating < 20 Then
    Info = Info & "Ensign"
ElseIf Rating < 25 Then
    Info = Info & "Freighter Pilot"
ElseIf Rating < 30 Then
    Info = Info & "Rookie"
Else
    Info = Info & "Kamikaze"
End If

' Give helpful advice and encouragement to the player.
If Speed < 2 Then
    Info = Info & CRLF & CRLF & "That was a very soft landing. "
ElseIf Speed < 3.5 Then
    Info = Info & CRLF & CRLF & "That landing was a bit bumpy. "
ElseIf Speed < 6 Then
    Info = Info & CRLF & CRLF & "Not a bad landing, but keep practicing. "
ElseIf Speed < 10 Then
    Info = Info & CRLF & CRLF & "Too fast!  Your landing caused minor structural damage to
          the ship. "
ElseIf Speed < 20 Then
    Info = Info & CRLF & CRLF & "Ouch!  This lander has major damage. "
Else
    Info = Info & CRLF & CRLF & "Nice work, loser. You just totaled another lander. "
End If

If Distance > 0 Then
    Direction = "right"
ElseIf Distance < 0 Then
    Direction = "left"
End If
Distance = Abs(Distance)

' Give still more encouragement and advice to the player.
If Distance < 7 Then
```

continued on next page

continued from previous page

```
            Info = Info & CRLF & CRLF & "Your accuracy is amazing. "
        ElseIf Distance < 24 Then
            Info = Info & CRLF & CRLF & "Your accuracy is pretty good. "
        ElseIf Distance < 90 Then
            Info = Info & CRLF & CRLF & "The target pad is a little to your " & Direction & ". "
        ElseIf Distance < 200 Then
            Info = Info & CRLF & CRLF & "Have the base doctor fit you with a new pair of glasses. "
        Else
            Info = Info & CRLF & CRLF & "Where the heck were you going?  The target is way over to
                your " & Direction & ". "
        End If

        panInfo = Info
    End Sub
```

Rather than simply showing some numeric score to the player, this routine gives the user a ranking, such as Ensign or Freighter Pilot, as well as helpful and occasionally snide suggestions based on the player's performance. The ranking is determined by a completely arbitrary calculation based on the player's final speed, distance from target, and remaining fuel. The ranking rewards accurate, soft landings that use little fuel.

The "helpful" comments are based on the final speed of the lander and the distance from the target. As you can see in the subroutine, comments range from glowing praise to derision.

Back in the Timer event, assuming that the player has not yet landed, the program updates the form's status indicators. Add the Update_Status routine, as shown below.

```
Sub Update_Status (Elevation As Integer, DistanceToTarget As Integer)
'-----------------------------------------------------------
' Update the status indicators on the screen.
'-----------------------------------------------------------

    lblDescent = Format$(mLander.ySpeed, "00.00") & " mps"
    If Elevation > 0 Then
        lblElevation = Format$(Elevation) & " m"
    Else
        lblElevation = "0 m"
    End If
    If DistanceToTarget > 0 Then
        lblTargetLoc = Format$(Abs(DistanceToTarget)) & " m Stbd"
    ElseIf DistanceToTarget < 0 Then
        lblTargetLoc = Format$(Abs(DistanceToTarget)) & " m Port"
    Else
        lblTargetLoc = "Directly Below"
    End If
End Sub
```

Next, the Timer event calculates the lander's new X position, using the simple Calculate_Lander_X routine shown below. This routine simply moves the lander's X position based on its current speed.

```
Sub Calculate_Lander_X ()
'------------------------------------------------------------
' Calculate the ship's next x position.
'------------------------------------------------------------

    mLander.xPos = mLander.xPos + mLander.xSpeed
End Sub
```

Now the program has all the information required to update the screen. If possible, you want the lander to stay within the center of the view screen, so add the following Adjust_Background routine, which attempts to keep the lander centered. The only time the lander cannot be centered is when it moves near or beyond the edges of the lunar landscape bitmap. In those cases, adjust the background as much as possible.

```
Sub Adjust_Background ()
'------------------------------------------------------------
' Adjust the background to keep the ship in the center of the screen.
'------------------------------------------------------------

    If (mLander.xPos > mCentered.x) And (mLander.xPos < (picBG.ScaleWidth -
    picLander_s.ScaleWidth - mCentered.x)) Then
        mBG.x = mLander.xPos - mCentered.x
    End If

    If (mLander.yPos > mCentered.y) And (mLander.yPos < (picBG.ScaleHeight -
    picLander_s.ScaleHeight - mCentered.y)) Then
        mBG.y = mLander.yPos - mCentered.y
    End If
End Sub
```

Now begins the work of compositing the frame image that the player will see. First, copy an area of the landscape into the work area PictureBox.

```
Sub Draw_Background ()
'------------------------------------------------------------
' Draw the Background into the work area PictureBox.
'------------------------------------------------------------
Dim rc As Integer

    ' Copy a section of the landscape bitmap into the work area.
    rc = BitBlt(picWork.hDC, 0, 0, picViewer.ScaleWidth, picViewer.ScaleHeight,
        picBG.hDC, mBG.x, mBG.y, SRCCOPY)
    ' Overlay the Landing Pad onto the background.
    SpriteBlt picWork, picPad_s, picPad_m, mPad.x - mBG.x, mPad.y - mBG.y
End Sub
```

The Draw_Background routine above uses a simple BitBlt call to copy the landscape, then calls a routine called SpriteBlt to overlay the landing pad image on the background. The SpriteBlt routine simplifies drawing a sprite onto another bitmap.

SpriteBlt takes five parameters, the destination PictureBox, the sprite PictureBox, the mask PictureBox, and the destination X-Y coordinates. You'll be using the SpriteBit routine again, so add it to the LANDER.FRM form as shown below.

```
Sub SpriteBlt (Dest As PictureBox, Sprite As PictureBox, Mask As PictureBox, Dx As Integer,
Dy As Integer)
'------------------------------------------------------------
' Draw a sprite onto background Dest at x-y locations Dx
' and Dy, using Mask and Sprite.
'------------------------------------------------------------
Dim rc As Integer

    rc = BitBlt(Dest.hDC, Dx, Dy, Mask.ScaleWidth, Mask.ScaleHeight, Mask.hDC, 0, 0, SRCAND)
    rc = BitBlt(Dest.hDC, Dx, Dy, Sprite.ScaleWidth, Sprite.ScaleHeight, Sprite.hDC, 0, 0,
         SRCPAINT)
End Sub
```

Next, the program needs to draw the thruster sprites onto the working area PictureBox. Add the Draw_Thrusters routine, as shown below.

```
Sub Draw_Thrusters ()
'------------------------------------------------------------
' Draw the lander's thrusters onto the background, if they're on.
'------------------------------------------------------------

    If Timer1.Enabled Then
        ' Horizontal Left Thrusters
        If mLeftThrusterOn Then
            SpriteBlt picWork, picThrustH_s, picThrustH_m, mLander.xPos - mBG.x + 5,
            mLander.yPos - mBG.y + 40
            mLeftThrusterOn = False
        End If

        ' Horizontal Right Thrusters
        If mRightThrusterOn Then
            SpriteBlt picWork, picThrustH_s, picThrustH_m, (mLander.xPos - mBG.x) +
            (picLander_s.ScaleWidth - picThrustH_m.ScaleWidth) - 5, mLander.yPos -
            mBG.y + 40
            mRightThrusterOn = False
        End If

        ' Bottom Thruster
        If mBottomThrusterOn Then
            SpriteBlt picWork, picThrustV_s, picThrustV_m, mLander.xPos - mBG.x +
            ((picLander_s.ScaleWidth - picThrustV_s.ScaleWidth) / 2), mLander.yPos -
            mBG.y + (picLander_s.ScaleHeight - picThrustV_s.ScaleHeight)
            mBottomThrusterOn = False
        End If
    End If
End Sub
```

There are three thrusters, so the program checks if each is on and then draws the corresponding thruster sprite using the SpriteBlt routine. Why did you draw the thrusters before the lander? By placing the lander sprite on top of the thruster images, the thrusters appear to be behind the lander. Let's draw the lander sprite. Add Draw_Lander, as shown below.

```
Sub Draw_Lander ()
'----------------------------------------------------------
' Copy the Lander into the work area bitmap.
'----------------------------------------------------------

    SpriteBlt picWork, picLander_s, picLander_m, mLander.xPos - mBG.x, mLander.yPos - mBG.y
End Sub
```

Now that the entire view screen image is composed in the work area PictureBox, copy it to the screen with the Update_Viewer routine, shown below. This routine consists of a single, fast BitBlt, that copies the contents of picWork into the picViewer PictureBox.

```
Sub Update_Viewer ()
'----------------------------------------------------------
' Copy everything into viewer.
'----------------------------------------------------------
Dim rc As Integer

    rc = BitBlt(picViewer.hDC, 0, 0, picViewer.ScaleWidth, picViewer.ScaleHeight,
         picWork.hDC, 0, 0, SRCCOPY)
End Sub
```

The last routine in the Timer event is Update_Scanner. The scanner is a small PictureBox that sits directly below the picViewer view screen PictureBox. The scanner shows the lander's position relative to the landing pad. The player uses the scanner to position the lander until the landing pad comes into view in the picViewer control. The program needs to update the lander's position in the scanner each time the ship moves.

```
Sub Update_Scanner ()
'----------------------------------------------------------
' Update the scanner at the bottom of the view screen.
'----------------------------------------------------------

    shpLander.Left = ((mLander.xPos + (picLander_s.ScaleWidth \ 2)) / picBG.ScaleWidth)
                     * picScanner.ScaleWidth
    shpPad.Left = ((mPad.x + (picPad_s.ScaleWidth \ 2)) / picBG.ScaleWidth) *
                  picScanner.ScaleWidth
End Sub
```

Now that you've added all the subroutines needed to run the Timer event, it's time to move on to the thruster controls. These are actually three 3D command buttons, one for each thruster. First, let's look at the horizontal thruster buttons, btnLeft and btnRight. Add a Click event for each button, as shown below.

```
Sub btnLeft_Click ()
'----------------------------------------------------------------
' Fire left (port) thruster.
'----------------------------------------------------------------

    ' No fuel, no thrust.
    If mLander.FuelAmount <= 0 Then Exit Sub

    NoisePlay mSndThrust2
    mLeftThrusterOn = True

    ' Increase speed in x direction.
    mLander.xSpeed = mLander.xSpeed + .4

    ' Decrease fuel.
    mLander.FuelAmount = mLander.FuelAmount - 1
End Sub

Sub btnRight_Click ()
'----------------------------------------------------------------
' Fire right (starboard) thruster.
'----------------------------------------------------------------

    ' Uh Oh! No fuel left...
    If mLander.FuelAmount <= 0 Then Exit Sub

    NoisePlay mSndThrust2
    mRightThrusterOn = True

    ' Increase speed in the -x direction.
    mLander.xSpeed = mLander.xSpeed - .4

    ' Decrease fuel.
    mLander.FuelAmount = mLander.FuelAmount - 1
End Sub
```

These routines first check if there is any fuel remaining. No fuel, then no thrust. In this case, the routines are quickly exited. Otherwise, the NoisePlay routine is called to play the thruster's wave audio file, which was loaded into memory when the form was loaded. Then the Boolean mLeftThrusterOn or mRightThrusterOn is set to True. This lets the Timer event know that the thruster's sprite image needs to be drawn when the next Timer event is triggered. Next, the lander's XSpeed is adjusted to simulate the effect of the thruster, and the lander's FuelAmount is reduced.

The vertical thruster, controlled by the btnUp button, handles things in a similar way. Add its Click event, as shown below.

```
Sub btnUp_Click ()
'-------------------------------------------------------------
' Fire the bottom thruster.
'-------------------------------------------------------------

    ' No fuel, no thrust.
    If mLander.FuelAmount <= 0 Then Exit Sub

    NoisePlay mSndThrust1
    mBottomThrusterOn = True

    ' Adjust vertical speed.
    If mLander.ySpeed > .8 Then
        mLander.ySpeed = mLander.ySpeed * .75
    Else
        mLander.ySpeed = mLander.ySpeed - .9
    End If

    ' Decrease fuel
    mLander.FuelAmount = mLander.FuelAmount - 2
End Sub
```

Note that the vertical thrusters use twice as much fuel as the horizontal thrusters. Also, the YSpeed adjustments are slightly different if the ship is ascending or descending. The values were selected because they provided a more realistic feel to the simulation.

With the addition of the thruster controls, the game is now complete. Save the project and then give it a try!

Enhancements and Improvements

As with any program, there is always room for customization and improvement. I'm sure you'll think of your own ideas, but here are some you might consider.

- Add more and better feedback to the player when the game is over.
- Add some additional sprites showing the lander in various states of damage. These can be shown when the lander hits the ground too quickly.
- Revamp the sound effects by using the WaveMix DLL to add a layered sound track.

We'll come back down to earth in the next chapter, where we'll build a golf game that can be customized by the player using nothing but a simple text editor and a bitmap editor.

12

Sport Games: Golf

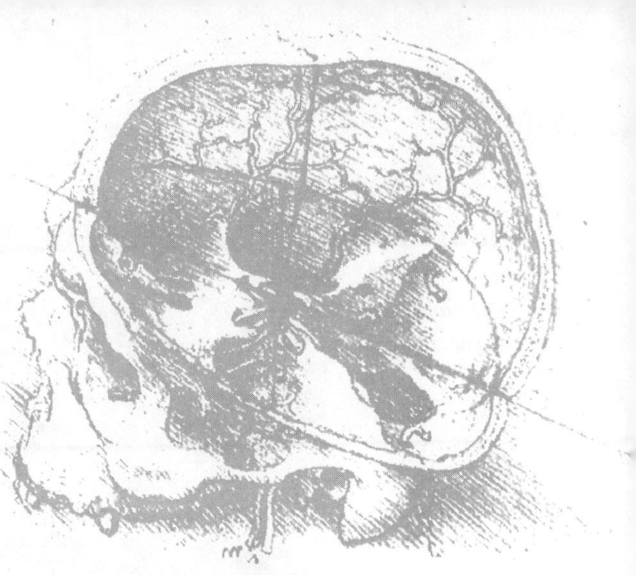

12

Sports Games: Golf

Almost since the beginning of computer games, sports simulations have been one of the most popular genres. They're natural: The player is usually already familiar with how the game is played. In this chapter, we'll build a complete golf simulation. And just to make things more interesting, we'll make it possible for the players to create their own golf courses.

How the Game Is Played

The game of Golf, shown in Figure 12-1, provides an overhead view of each golf hole. These holes are simply bitmaps created with a bitmap editor such as Windows Paintbrush. To start a new game, the player presses the New Game button, and the first hole is displayed. Label controls on the right side of the form display scoring and other information during the game.

The player hits the ball by double-clicking the mouse pointer behind the ball. The ball moves in a straight line away from the mouse pointer. The player must avoid obstacles such as trees, sand traps, and water hazards. The program detects these objects by their color; I'll discuss this more in the next section.

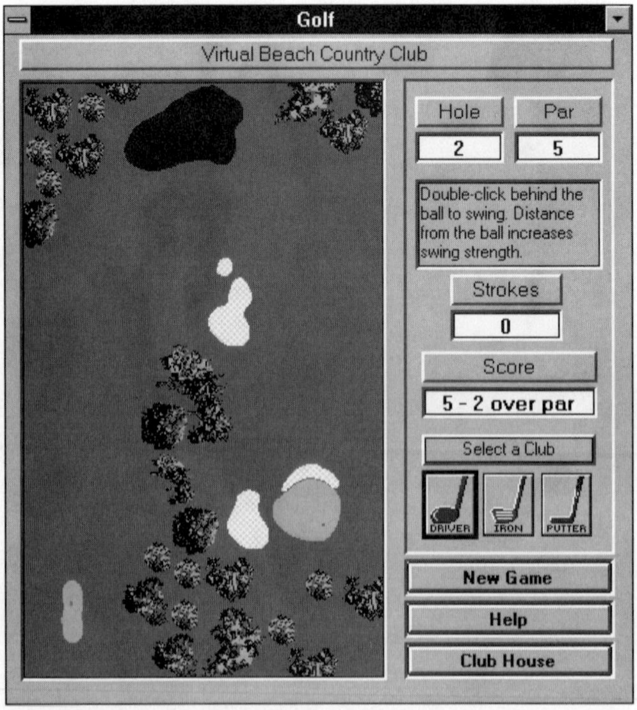

FIGURE 12-1

The Golf game at runtime

A hole is completed when the player successfully lands the ball (shown as a tiny purple block) into the hole (displayed as a small red circle). New holes are displayed until the course is completed.

Letting the Player Customize a Game

I wanted to create a game that could easily be customized by the player. I wanted to make it as simple as possible to create a new golf course with no programming changes. To do this, I needed to make some design decisions. The most important of these decisions is that each hole of the golf course would be displayed as a single 250x400 pixel bitmap. This bitmap would provide an aerial view of the hole. To make things easy, I assigned specific colors for specific objects: white and yellow for sand traps, blue for water, black and brown for trees. In this way, the player needs only to follow the color rules to create a proper bitmap for a new hole. The program uses the colors in the bitmap to determine, for example, if the ball has landed in a sand trap.

Just creating bitmaps was not quite enough. The player has to have some way to tell the program the order in which to display each hole, as well as information on the par for the hole (for nongolfers, par is the number of strokes the player should need to get the ball into a particular hole). To handle this, I decided to use a simple text file. The program looks for this file, called GAMEINFO.TXT, in the same directory as the Golf executable (.EXE) file. A sample GAMEINFO.TXT file is shown below.

```
COURSE: Virtual Beach Country Club

NEW HOLE
FILE: FAIRWY01.BMP
TEE: 127,351
PAR: 3

NEW HOLE
FILE: FAIRWY03.BMP
TEE: 33,343
PAR: 4
```

The sample file above describes the fictional Virtual Beach Country Club golf course, a small course consisting of only two holes.

The format of this file is very simple; most information is in the form:

```
<keyword>: <value>
```

For example, the Course keyword indicates the name that will appear in a large banner label at the top of the form. Each new hole is indicated by a text line stating "NEW HOLE" followed by keyword lines defining information about the hole.

The first keyword, File, indicates the name of the bitmap file that should be displayed for this particular hole. The Tee keyword provides X-Y coordinates for where the ball should initially be placed. This was one of the few things I could not build into the bitmap itself. It may have been possible to designate some color as the tee color, and then scan the bitmap to find its location, but this would have been time consuming. Instead, I decided to let the player tell the program where he or she wants the tee placed. The X-Y coordinates are easy to obtain by loading the bitmap into Windows Paintbrush (or some other bitmap editor) and using the Cursor Position command from Paintbrush's View menu. Finally, the Par keyword indicates the number of strokes it should take to finish the hole. This is used during scoring to provide a more realistic "under par" or "over par" score.

Building Golf

We'll start building Golf by creating a new project, aptly named GOLF.MAK. Create a new subdirectory for the Golf project to make it easier to keep track of its associated files.

Create a new Basic module called GOLF.BAS. This module will contain some global constants and Windows API function declarations, as well as a few general purpose routines that can be reused later in other projects.

Add the constants and API functions in Listing 12-1 to the Declarations section of GOLF.BAS.

Listing 12-1 GOLF.BAS constants

```
Option Explicit
'-------------------------------------------------------------
' Global constants, data types, and function calls used by
' the GOLF.MAK project.
'-------------------------------------------------------------

' ScaleMode constants
Global Const TWIPS = 1
Global Const PIXELS = 3

' MsgBox constants
Global Const MB_OK = 0                      ' OK button
Global Const MB_ICONSTOP = 16               ' Critical message
Global Const MB_ICONQUESTION = 32           ' Warning query
Global Const MB_ICONEXCLAMATION = 48        ' Warning message
Global Const MB_ICONINFORMATION = 64        ' Information message

' RGB color constants
Global Const BLUE = &HFF0000
Global Const DK_BLUE = &H800000
Global Const WHITE = &HFFFFFF
Global Const RED = &HFF&
Global Const BLACK = &H0&
Global Const CYAN = &HFFFF00
Global Const DK_CYAN = &H808000
Global Const YELLOW = &HFFFF&
Global Const BROWN = &H8080&
Global Const GREEN = &HFF00&
Global Const DK_GREEN = &H8000&
Global Const MAGENTA = &HFF00FF

' Data type defining an x-y coordinate.
Type tLocation
    X As Integer
    Y As Integer
End Type

' Data type defining information related to
' a particular golf hole.
Type tHole
```

```
    FileName As String * 12
    Tee As tLocation
    Par As Integer
    Tips As String
End Type

' The location of the program.
Global AppPath As String

' Constants for 3D Borders
Global Const BORDER_INSET = 0
Global Const BORDER_RAISED = 1

' Functions and constants used to play sounds.
Global Const SND_SYNC = &H0          ' Return when sound ends (the default)
Global Const SND_ASYNC = &H1         ' Return as soon as sound starts
Declare Function sndPlaySound Lib "MMSystem" (ByVal lpsound As String, ByVal FLAG As
Integer) As Integer

' Function that returns the color at a particular
' x-y location.
Declare Function GetPixel Lib "GDI" (ByVal hDC As Integer, ByVal X As Integer, ByVal Y
As Integer) As Long

' Constant and function used to quickly copy bitmaps.
Global Const SRCCOPY = &HCC0020
Declare Function BitBlt Lib "GDI" (ByVal hDestDC As Integer, ByVal X As Integer, ByVal
Y As Integer, ByVal NWidth As Integer, ByVal nHeight As Integer, ByVal hSrcDC As
Integer, ByVal XSrc As Integer, ByVal YSrc As Integer, ByVal dwRop As Long) As Integer
```

Because much of the game logic depends on the colors in each hole's bitmap, it shouldn't be a surprise that much of the section above is concerned with colors. In particular, notice the simple but very important GetPixel function. This function returns the color of a pixel at a particular X-Y location. GetPixel will be used to figure out if the ball has hit a tree or landed in a sand trap or water hazard.

Next, add the subroutine CenterForm to GOLF.BAS. This routine will center any form on the screen.

```
Sub CenterForm (AForm As Form)
'-------------------------------------------------------------
' Center a form on the screen.
'-------------------------------------------------------------

    AForm.Move (Screen.Width - AForm.Width) \ 2, (Screen.Height - AForm.Height) \ 2
End Sub
```

The GetDistance function returns the distance between two X-Y coordinates. This is used to determine how far a ball has gone. Add this function, as shown below.

```
Function GetDistance (Ax As Integer, Ay As Integer, Bx As Integer, By As Integer) As Single
'-----------------------------------------------------------
' Return the straight-line distance between two x-y points.
'-----------------------------------------------------------

    GetDistance = Abs(Sqr((Ax - Bx) ^ 2 + (Ay - By) ^ 2))
End Function
```

The subroutine Make3D draws a three-dimensional border around a control. It can be used to create either a raised or an inset appearance, with varying border widths. Add it to the module, as shown in Listing 12-2.

Listing 12-2 Make3D subroutine

```
Sub Make3D (AForm As Form, ctl As Control, ByVal BorderStyle As Integer, ByVal
BorderWidth As Integer)
'----------------------------------------------------------------------
' Wrap a 3D effect around a control on a form.
'----------------------------------------------------------------------
' Color Constants
Const DARK_GRAY = &H808080
Const WHITE = &HFFFFFF
Const BLACK = &H0

Dim RightSide As Single
Dim BW As Integer
Dim LeftTopColor As Long, RightBottomColor As Long
Dim i As Integer
Dim SaveMode As Integer

    If Not ctl.Visible Then Exit Sub

    SaveMode = AForm.ScaleMode
    AForm.ScaleMode = PIXELS

    Select Case BorderStyle
        Case 0: ' Inset
            LeftTopColor = DARK_GRAY
            RightBottomColor = WHITE
        Case 1: ' Raised
            LeftTopColor = WHITE
            RightBottomColor = DARK_GRAY
    End Select

    ' Set the top shading line.
    For BW = 1 To BorderWidth
        ' Top
        AForm.CurrentX = ctl.Left - BW
```

```
        AForm.CurrentY = ctl.Top - BW
        AForm.Line -(ctl.Left + ctl.Width + (BW - 1), ctl.Top - BW), LeftTopColor ↵
                ' Right
        AForm.Line -(ctl.Left + ctl.Width + (BW - 1), ctl.Top + ctl.Height + ↵
                (BW - 1)), RightBottomColor
        ' Bottom
        AForm.Line -(ctl.Left - BW, ctl.Top + ctl.Height + (BW - 1)), RightBottomColor ↵
                ' Left
        AForm.Line -(ctl.Left - BW, ctl.Top - BW), LeftTopColor
    Next

    AForm.ScaleMode = SaveMode
End Sub
```

The next routine uses Make3D to draw three-dimensional borders around certain controls automatically. This routine, called Paint3D, uses the Visual Basic Controls collection. The collection is a list of all the controls on a form. The Paint3D routine inspects the Tag property of each control, looking for the strings "/3d_inset/" or "/3d_raised/". If either string is found within a Tag, then that control is given the appropriate three-dimensional border. The beauty of this approach is that it requires no further programming to add new 3D controls to a form; only setting their Tag property is required. Add Paint3D, as shown below.

```
Sub Paint3D (AForm As Form)
'-------------------------------------------------------------------------
' Put a 3D border around any control tagged "/3D_INSET/" or "/3D_RAISED/."
'-------------------------------------------------------------------------
Dim i As Integer

    For i = 0 To AForm.Controls.Count - 1
        If UCase$(AForm.Controls(i).Tag) = "/3D_RAISED/" Then
            Make3D AForm, AForm.Controls(i), BORDER_RAISED, 2
        ElseIf UCase$(AForm.Controls(i).Tag) = "/3D_INSET/" Then
            Make3D AForm, AForm.Controls(i), BORDER_INSET, 2
        End If
    Next
End Sub
```

Occasionally during the game you'll need to introduce short delays. This is necessary to add a sense of realism. For example, when the ball is in flight, a slight delay is added as the ball's trajectory is drawn. This makes the ball appear to be moving at a realistic speed. Add the Pause routine to the GOLF.BAS module. Pause uses the Timer function to implement a simple delay loop. Pause will cause a subroutine to wait for a specified number of seconds or fractions of seconds. The delay loop doesn't prevent other Windows events from taking place, but will delay the execution of any subroutine where it is used.

```
Sub Pause (Seconds As Single)
'------------------------------------------------------------
' Wait for a specified number of seconds.
'------------------------------------------------------------
Dim EndTime As Single

    EndTime = Timer + Seconds
    While Timer < EndTime
        DoEvents
    Wend
End Sub
```

Finally, add the PopField function to the form. This is a string-handling function that can be useful when parsing lines of text. PopField breaks a string apart based on the location of a field separator string. Usually this string is a single character, like a space or a comma, but the function will allow any string for a field separator. The function returns a string containing everything in the original string up to (but not including) the field separator. The function also chops the original string so that it begins at the first character beyond the field separator.

The PopField function is used in the game to interpret a text file, GAMEINFO.TXT, that contains information needed to set up each hole in the golf course. See Listing 12-3.

Listing 12-3 PopField function

```
Function PopField (AStr As String, ByVal FS As String) As String
'------------------------------------------------------------
' Returns a substring of AStr. If FS is in AStr, PopField
' returns the beginning of AStr, up to (but not including)
' FS. AStr is also chopped so that it begins at the first
' character beyond FS.
'
' If FS is not in AStr, PopField returns the contents of AStr
' and sets AStr to a null string ("").
'
' PopField is usually used to parse a text file or text line.
'------------------------------------------------------------
Dim pos As Integer

    ' Look for the field separator.
    pos = InStr(AStr, FS)

    ' Found the field separator.
    If pos > 1 Then
        PopField = Left$(AStr, pos - 1)
        AStr = Mid$(AStr, pos + 1)

    ' Field separator is at beginning of AStr.
```

```
    ElseIf pos = 1 Then
        PopField = ""
        If Len(AStr) > 1 Then
            AStr = Mid$(AStr, pos + 1)
        Else
            AStr = ""
        End If

    ' Field separator not in AStr.
    Else
        PopField = AStr
        AStr = ""
    End If
End Function
```

Adding the Main Form to Golf

Now let's add the main form to the Golf game. At design time, the form should look like Figure 12-2. After placing all the controls on the form, resize the form to its run-time size (as shown in Figure 12-1). First add a new form, GOLF.FRM, to the GOLF.MAK project.

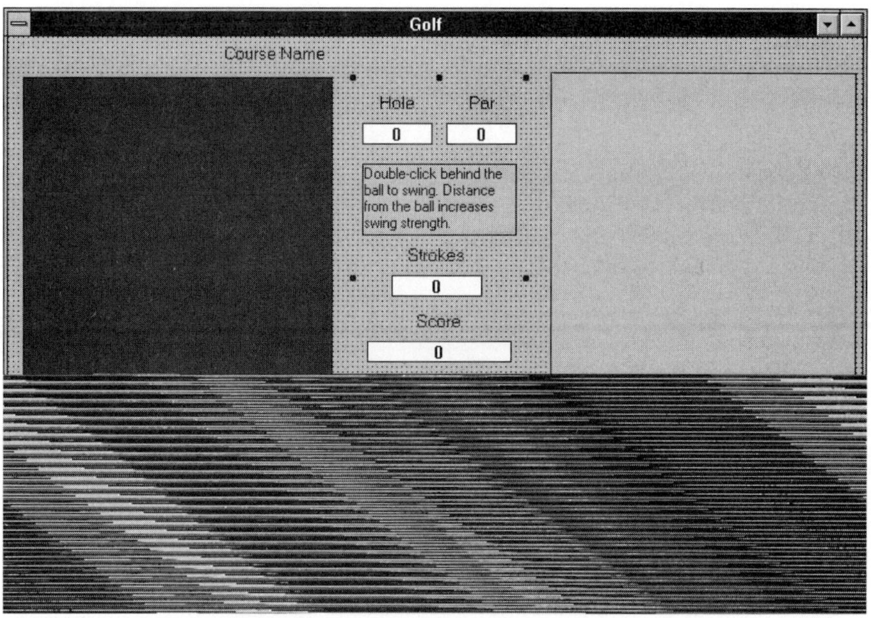

FIGURE 12-2

The GOLF.FRM form at design time

Add the objects in Table 12-1 to the GOLF.FRM form at design time.

TABLE 12-1

Objects and properties of the GOLF.FRM form

Object	Property	Setting
Form	FormName	Form1
	AutoRedraw	-1 'True
	BackColor	&H00C0C0C0&
	BorderStyle	1 'Fixed Single
	Caption	"Golf"
	MaxButton	0 'False
Label	Name	lblFrame1
	BackStyle	0 'Transparent
	ForeColor	&H00C0C0C0&
	Height	4755
	Left	4200
	Tag	"/3d_inset/"
	Top	480
	Width	2115
Shape	Name	Shape1
	BorderColor	&H000000FF&
	BorderWidth	4
	Height	660
	Left	4380
	Top	4440
	Width	540
Label	Name	Label1
	Alignment	2 'Center
	BackStyle	0 'Transparent
	Caption	"Hole"
	FontBold	0 'False
	FontSize	9.75
	ForeColor	&H00800000&

Object	Property	Setting
	Tag	"/3d_raised/"
Label	Name	Label3
	Alignment	2 'Center
	BackStyle	0 'Transparent
	Caption	"Par"
	FontBold	0 'False
	FontSize	9.75
	ForeColor	&H00800000&
	Tag	"/3d_raised/"
Label	Name	Label4
	Alignment	2 'Center
	BackStyle	0 'Transparent
	Caption	"Strokes"
	FontBold	0 'False
	FontSize	9.75
	ForeColor	&H00800000&
	Tag	"/3d_raised/"
Label	Name	lblHole
	Alignment	2 'Center
	BackColor	&H0080FFFF&
	BorderStyle	1 'Fixed Single
	Caption	"0"
	FontSize	9.75
	ForeColor	&H00FF0000&
	Tag	"/3d_inset/"
Label	Name	lblStrokes
	Alignment	2 'Center
	BackColor	&H0080FFFF&
	FontSize	9.75

continued on next page

continued from previous page

Object	Property	Setting
	BorderStyle	1 'Fixed Single
	Caption	"0"
	ForeColor	&H00FF0000&
	Tag	"/3d_inset/"
Label	Name	lblPar
	Alignment	2 'Center
	BackColor	&H0080FFFF&
	BorderStyle	1 'Fixed Single
	Caption	"0"
	FontSize	9.75
	ForeColor	&H00FF0000&
	Tag	"/3d_inset/"
Label	Name	lblScore
	Alignment	2 'Center
	BackColor	&H0080FFFF&
	BorderStyle	1 'Fixed Single
	Caption	"0"
	FontSize	9.75
	ForeColor	&H00FF0000&
	Tag	"/3d_inset/"
Label	Name	Label6
	Alignment	2 'Center
	BackStyle	0 'Transparent
	Caption	"Score"
	FontBold	0 'False
	FontSize	9.75
	ForeColor	&H00800000&
	Tag	"/3d_raised/"
Image	Name	imgClub

Object	Property	Setting
	BorderStyle	1 'Fixed Single
	Index	0
	Picture	(set at design time in Properties window)
Image	Name	imgClub
	BorderStyle	1 'Fixed Single
	Index	1
	Picture	(set at design time in Properties window)
Image	Name	imgClub
	BorderStyle	1 'Fixed Single
	Index	2
	Picture	(set at design time in Properties window)
Label	Name	Label5
	Alignment	2 'Center
	BackStyle	0 'Transparent
	BorderStyle	1 'Fixed Single
	Caption	"Select a Club"
	FontBold	0 'False
	ForeColor	&H00800000&
	Tag	"/3d_raised/"
Label	Name	lblInfo
	BackColor	&H00C0C0C0&
	BorderStyle	1 'Fixed Single
	Caption	"Double-click behind the ball to swing. Distance from the ball increases swing strength."
	FontBold	0 'False

continued on next page

continued from previous page

Object	Property	Setting
	ForeColor	&H00800000&
	Tag	"/3d_inset/"
Label	Name	lblCourseName
	Alignment	2 'Center
	BackStyle	0 'Transparent
	Caption	"Course Name"
	FontBold	0 'False
	FontSize	9.75
	ForeColor	&H00800000&
	Tag	"/3d_raised/"
PictureBox	Name	picBG
	AutoRedraw	-1 'True
	AutoSize	-1 'True
	BackColor	&H00008000&
	FillStyle	0 'Solid
	Height	6030
	Left	180
	MousePointer	2 'Cross
	ScaleMode	3 'Pixel
	Tag	"/3d_inset/"
	Top	480
	Width	3780
CommandButton	Name	btnQuit
	Caption	"Club House"
	Tag	"/3d_inset/"
CommandButton	Name	btnNewGame
	Caption	"New Game"
	Tag	"/3d_inset/"

Object	Property	Setting
PictureBox	Name	picReference
	AutoRedraw	-1 'True
	AutoSize	-1 'True
	BackColor	&H00C0C0C0&
	FillStyle	0 'Solid
	MousePointer	2 'Cross
	ScaleMode	3 'Pixel
	Tag	"/3d_inset/"
CommandButton	Name	btnHelp
	Caption	"Help"
	Tag	"/3d_inset/"

Both PictureBox controls, picBG and picReference, should be exactly the same dimensions, 250 pixels x 400 pixels. This is the size of a golf course hole bitmap. Although they will automatically resize when a bitmap is loaded (because their AutoSize property is set to True), it's a good idea to size them properly at design time. This avoids any visible resizing when the form is first displayed.

Programming Tip: Design your program code to avoid, or at least reduce, the amount of on-screen resizing of forms and controls. In programming, as in other areas, first impressions are important. When forms or controls appear, then suddenly shift or flicker, the result can be confusing and distracting to the player.

Several variables and constants need to be declared for use by the form. Add them to the GOLF.FRM form's Declarations section, as shown in Listing 12-4.

Listing 12-4 Declaring variables and constants in GOLF.FRM

```
Option Explicit
'-------------------------------------------------------------
' Constants and module-level variables used in GOLF.FRM
'-------------------------------------------------------------

' Valid game states.
Const GAME_OVER = 0
Const GAME_IN_PROGRESS = 1

' Available clubs (we travel light).
Const CLUB_DRIVER = 0
Const CLUB_IRON = 1
Const CLUB_PUTTER = 2

' The ball's coordinates.
Dim mBall As tLocation

Dim mMouse As tLocation
Dim mDelta As tLocation

' An array of structures defining individual
' holes in the course.
Dim mHole(1 To 18) As tHole

' The actual number of holes in the
' current course.
Dim mNumHoles As Integer

' The available clubs.
Dim mClubFactor(0 To 2)  As Integer
Dim mClubNumber As Integer

Dim mGameState As Integer

' The total par for the course so far;
' used for displaying score.
Dim mTotalPar As Integer
```

Most of the variables and constants in Listing 12-4 are used to track the state of the game: what club is being used, how many holes are in this golf course, the total par, and so forth.

Let's begin adding subroutines to the form. A good place to begin is the form's Load event, as this is executed first when the program is started. Add the Load event to the form, as shown below.

```
Sub Form_Load ()
'-------------------------------------------------------------
' Read the game data and set up the first game.
'-------------------------------------------------------------
```

```
    Randomize
    AppPath = App.Path
    If Right$(AppPath, 1) <> "\" Then AppPath = AppPath & "\"

    ReadGameData
    InitClubs

    Me.Show
    CenterForm Me
    Paint Me
    Pause 1

    btnNewGame_Click
End Sub
```

The Load event calls several subroutines. First it calls ReadGameData, a subroutine used to load information about the golf course. To make Golf easy to customize, the definition of the golf course is stored in a simple text file, GAMEINFO.TXT. This file must be loaded when the program begins. Most of the information from this file is stored in the mHole array that was defined in GOLF.FRM's Declarations section. Add ReadGameData to the form, as shown in Listing 12-5.

Listing 12-5 ReadGameData subroutine

```
Sub ReadGameData ()
'----------------------------------------------------------
' Read the GAMEINFO.TXT file, and build the data structures
' that define the holes.
'----------------------------------------------------------
Dim fnum As Integer
Dim ALine As String
Dim HoleNum As Integer
Dim DefaultTee As tLocation
Dim DefaultPar As Integer
Dim ID As String

    On Error Resume Next

    DefaultTee.x = picBG.ScaleWidth \ 2
    DefaultTee.y = picBG.ScaleHeight - 50
    DefaultPar = 5

    fnum = FreeFile
    Open AppPath & "GAMEINFO.TXT" For Input As fnum
    If Err > 0 Then
        MsgBox "Couldn't find the game definition file.", MB_OK Or
        MB_ICONEXCLAMATION, "Golf"
        Unload Me
    End If
```

continued on next page

continued from previous page

```
    HoleNum = 0
    While Not EOF(fnum)
        Line Input #fnum, ALine
        ALine = Trim$(ALine)
        If UCase$(ALine) = "NEW HOLE" Then
            HoleNum = HoleNum + 1
        Else
            ID = Trim$(UCase$(PopField(ALine, ":")))
            Select Case ID
                Case "COURSE":
                    lblCourseName = Trim$(ALine)
                Case "FILE":
                    mHole(HoleNum).FileName = Trim$(ALine)
                Case "TEE":
                    mHole(HoleNum).Tee.x = CInt(PopField(ALine, ","))
                    If Err > 0 Then mHole(HoleNum).Tee.x = DefaultTee.x
                    mHole(HoleNum).Tee.y = CInt(ALine)
                    If Err > 0 Then mHole(HoleNum).Tee.y = DefaultTee.y
                Case "PAR"
                    mHole(HoleNum).Par = CInt(ALine)
                    If Err > 0 Then mHole(HoleNum).Par = DefaultPar
            End Select
        End If

    Wend

    Close fnum
    mNumHoles = HoleNum

    On Error GoTo 0
End Sub
```

Another routine called from GOLF.FRM's Load event is InitClubs. This short routine defines the three available golf clubs and their relative strengths. What this means during game play is that a driver will move the ball farther than an iron will when used with the same force. Likewise, an iron will move the ball farther than a putter.

```
Sub InitClubs ()
'------------------------------------------------------------
' Set the club factor array. This determines the distance
' that the ball will go when hit with a particular type of
' club.
'------------------------------------------------------------

    mClubFactor(CLUB_DRIVER) = 8
    mClubFactor(CLUB_IRON) = 3
    mClubFactor(CLUB_PUTTER) = 1
End Sub
```

The last routine called in GOLF.FRM's Load event is the New Game button's Click event. This simulates the player pressing the button, so when the program is started, a new game is ready to be played. Add the following Click event for the btnNewGame Command Button control.

```
Sub btnNewGame_Click ()
'----------------------------------------------------------------
' Reset everything for a new game.
'----------------------------------------------------------------

    mGameState = GAME_IN_PROGRESS
    mTotalPar = 0
    lblScore = "0 - Par"

    SetupHole 1
End Sub
```

First, the Click event sets the mGameState variable to GAME_IN_PROGRESS. This is necessary to avoid letting the player hit the ball after a game is completed. The Click event also calls the SetupHole subroutine. This routine is called at the beginning of each new hole. SetupHole handles displaying the bitmap for the new hole and placing the ball on the hole's tee. The parameter passed to SetupHole is the hole number. This number also corresponds to an index in the mHole array, which contains all the required information about the hole (see Listing 12-6).

Listing 12-6 SetupHole subroutine

```
Sub SetupHole (ByVal HoleNum As Integer)
'----------------------------------------------------------------
' Set up a new hole: draw the background, reset labels, and
' place the ball on the tee.
'----------------------------------------------------------------
Dim x As Integer
Dim BltLeft As Integer
Dim rc As Integer

    On Error Resume Next
    picReference.Picture = LoadPicture(AppPath & mHole(HoleNum).FileName)
    If Err > 0 Then
        MsgBox "Couldn't find bitmap for Hole " & Format$(HoleNum) & "!", MB_OK Or MB_ICONSTOP, ↵
                "Golf"
        End
    End If

    ' Slide the background in from the right, with sound effects.
    rc = sndPlaySound(AppPath & "SLIDE.WAV", SND_ASYNC)
    picBG.AutoRedraw = False
```

continued on next page

continued from previous page

```
    For x = 2 To picBG.ScaleWidth
        BltLeft = picBG.ScaleWidth - x
        rc = BitBlt(picBG.hDC, BltLeft, 0, x, picBG.ScaleHeight, picReference.hDC, 0, 0, SRCCOPY)
        Pause .001
    Next
    picBG.AutoRedraw = True
    picBG.Picture = picReference.Picture

    ' Initialize variables for this hole.
    lblHole = HoleNum
    lblPar = mHole(lblHole).Par
    mBall.x = mHole(lblHole).Tee.x
    mBall.y = mHole(lblHole).Tee.y
    lblStrokes = 0

    DrawBall

    ' The default club will be a driver.
    imgClub_Click CLUB_DRIVER

End Sub
```

Notice the For loop in the SetupHole routine shown above. This loop is used to create an interesting visual effect. Each new hole appears to slide into place from the right side of the picBG PictureBox. An accompanying sound (courtesy of a .WAV file) adds to the effect. This special effect is unnecessary to game play, but little touches like this add to the player's overall enjoyment of the game.

The player selects one of three golf clubs by clicking a picture of the desired club on the GOLF.FRM form. The selected club is indicated by a red border. The three club pictures are displayed in an array of three Image controls, and the red highlighting border is handled by a simple Shape control. When the player clicks on one of the three images, the Image control array's Click event is triggered. Add this Click event, as shown below.

```
Sub imgClub_Click (Index As Integer)
'------------------------------------------------------------
' Select a new club.
'------------------------------------------------------------

    Shape1.Move imgClub(Index).Left, imgClub(Index).Top
    mClubNumber = Index
End Sub
```

This simple routine moves the Shape control so that it surrounds the selected Image control. It also sets the mClubNumber variable so that the rest of the program will know which club the player is now using.

The SetupHole routine also calls a routine called DrawBall. This routine does exactly what you would expect: It draws the golf ball at its current position on the picBG bitmap. Add this routine, as shown below.

```
Sub DrawBall ()
'------------------------------------------------------------
' Redraw the ball at its current x-y position.
'------------------------------------------------------------

    picBG.Cls

    picBG.DrawWidth = 2
    picBG.PSet (mBall.x, mBall.y), MAGENTA
    picBG.DrawWidth = 1

End Sub
```

The player "hits" the ball by double-clicking on the picBG PictureBox. The player double-clicks behind the ball, and the ball moves along a straight line formed by the mouse's X-Y coordinates and the ball's original location. The farther the mouse pointer is from the ball's original location, the farther the ball will go.

Most of the game action is handled within the picBG PictureBox's DblClick event. There is one problem that you must overcome first, however. The DblClick event does not pass the X-Y location of the mouse pointer, which you need to know to calculate the ball's trajectory. The MouseMove event does provide this information, so you need only add the following event to the picBG PictureBox control.

```
Sub picBG_MouseMove (Button As Integer, Shift As Integer, x As Single, y
As Single)
'------------------------------------------------------------
' Keep track of the mouse's position.
'------------------------------------------------------------

    mMouse.x = x
    mMouse.y = y
End Sub
```

This routine stores the mouse's last X-Y position in the module level variable, mMouse. This variable will then be available within picBG's DblClick event.

As I mentioned earlier, much of the action takes place within the DblClick event. First, add the event, as shown in Listing 12-7, to the picBG PictureBox control.

Listing 12-7 The picBG_DblClick subroutine

```
Sub picBG_DblClick ()
'------------------------------------------------------------
' Hit the ball. This is where most of the action happens.
'------------------------------------------------------------
Dim rc As Integer
Dim slope As Single
Dim Dist As Single
Dim MaxDist As Single
Dim direct As tLocation
```

continued on next page

continued from previous page

```
Dim i As Integer
Dim xf As Single, yf As Single
Dim OK As Integer

Dim BG_Color As Long
Dim Location As String

Dim PauseFactor As Single

Dim InTree As Integer
Dim InSandTrap As Integer

Dim Temp As tLocation
Dim MoveDir As Integer

Dim WaveFileName As String

    ' Can't hit the ball if you're not playing a game.
    If mGameState = GAME_OVER Then Exit Sub

    InTree = False

    lblInfo = "Double-click behind the ball to swing. "
    lblInfo = lblInfo & "Distance from the ball increases swing strength."

    mDelta.x = mBall.x - mMouse.x
    If mDelta.x = 0 Then mDelta.x = 1
    mDelta.y = mBall.y - mMouse.y

    MaxDist = Sqr(mDelta.x ^ 2 + mDelta.y ^ 2) * mClubFactor(mClubNumber)

    ' If this is the player's first shot, they're on the tee, so
    ' they can hit a bit farther.
    If lblStrokes > 0 Then
        If MaxDist > (picBG.ScaleHeight / 3) Then MaxDist = picBG.ScaleHeight / 3
    End If

    ' Bump up strokes
    lblStrokes = lblStrokes + 1

    ' What color is the ball over?
    BG_Color = GetPixel(picReference.hDC, mBall.x, mBall.y)

    ' Are we in a tree?
    If (BG_Color = BLACK) Or (BG_Color = BROWN) Then
        InTree = True
        MaxDist = 2 * mClubFactor(mClubNumber)
    End If

    ' In a sand trap...
    If (BG_Color = WHITE) Or (BG_Color = YELLOW) Then
```

```
        ' If they want to make any progress, they'd better
        ' use the iron.
        If mClubNumber = CLUB_IRON Then
            MaxDist = MaxDist * .75
        Else
            MaxDist = 2
        End If
    End If

    slope = Abs(mDelta.y / mDelta.x)

    If mDelta.x > 0 Then
        direct.x = 1
    ElseIf mDelta.x < 0 Then
        direct.x = -1
    Else
        direct.x = 0
    End If

    If mDelta.y > 0 Then
        direct.y = 1
    ElseIf mDelta.y < 0 Then
        direct.y = -1
    Else
        direct.y = 0
    End If

    xf = mBall.x
    yf = mBall.y

    OK = True
    i = 0
    picBG.CurrentX = mBall.x
    picBG.CurrentY = mBall.y

    ' Pick the appropriate sound for the club used.
    Select Case mClubNumber
        Case CLUB_DRIVER: WaveFileName = "SWING1.WAV"
        Case CLUB_IRON: WaveFileName = "SWING2.WAV"
        Case CLUB_PUTTER: WaveFileName = "SWING3.WAV"
    End Select

    rc = sndPlaySound(AppPath & WaveFileName, SND_ASYNC)
    Pause .25

    PauseFactor = .001 * Abs(mDelta.y * 1.85)

    ' Draw the ball as it moves, showing its trajectory.
    While OK
        i = i + 1
        xf = xf + direct.x
```

continued on next page

continued from previous page

```
        yf = yf + (slope * direct.y)

        Dist = Sqr(CInt(mBall.x - xf) ^ 2 + CInt(mBall.y - yf) ^ 2)
        If Dist >= MaxDist Then OK = False
        picBG.Line -(CInt(xf), CInt(yf)), QBColor(4)
        Pause PauseFactor
        BG_Color = GetPixel(picReference.hDC, CInt(xf), CInt(yf))

        ' Yikes! Out of Bounds!
        If OutOfBounds(CInt(xf), CInt(yf)) Then
            lblStrokes = lblStrokes + 2

            If CInt(Rnd * 2) = 1 Then
                lblInfo = "Your ball went out of bounds (and hit the club house). Two
                          stroke penalty."
                rc = sndPlaySound(AppPath & "OUTOBND1.WAV", SND_ASYNC)
            Else
                lblInfo = "Your ball went out of bounds (and hit a by-stander). Two
                          stroke penalty."
                rc = sndPlaySound(AppPath & "OUTOBND2.WAV", SND_ASYNC)
            End If

            DrawBall
            Exit Sub
        End If

        ' Oops! Hit a Tree!
        If (BG_Color = BLACK) And (Not InTree) Then
            rc = sndPlaySound(AppPath & "TREEHIT.WAV", SND_ASYNC)
            OK = False
        End If

        ' In the Hole!
        If InHole(CInt(xf), CInt(yf)) Then
            rc = sndPlaySound(AppPath & "INHOLE.WAV", SND_SYNC)

            ' Scoring...
            lblScore = CInt(Left(lblScore, InStr(lblScore, " ") - 1)) + lblStrokes
            mTotalPar = mTotalPar + lblPar
            If lblScore > mTotalPar Then
                lblScore = Format$(lblScore) & " - " & Format$(lblScore - mTotalPar) &
                          " over par"
            ElseIf lblScore < mTotalPar Then
                lblScore = Format$(lblScore) & " - " & Format$(mTotalPar - lblScore) &
                          " under par"
            Else
                lblScore = Format$(lblScore) & " - Par"
            End If
```

```
            If lblHole = mNumHoles Then
                mGameState = GAME_OVER
                rc = sndPlaySound(AppPath & "APPLAUS2.WAV", SND_ASYNC)
                Exit Sub
            Else
                SetupHole lblHole + 1
                Exit Sub
            End If
        End If


    Wend
    mBall.x = CInt(xf)
    mBall.y = CInt(yf)

    ' Where is the ball?
    BG_Color = GetPixel(picReference.hDC, mBall.x, mBall.y)
    Location = GetLocationByColor(BG_Color)

    ' Did it land in the water?
    If Location = "WATER" Then
        Temp.x = mBall.x
        Temp.y = mBall.y
        lblInfo = "One stroke penalty for going in the water hazard."
        lblStrokes = lblStrokes + 1

        rc = sndPlaySound(AppPath & "SPLASH.WAV", SND_ASYNC)
        If mBall.x > (picBG.ScaleWidth / 2) Then
            MoveDir = -5
        Else
            MoveDir = 5
        End If
        While ((BG_Color = BLUE) Or (BG_Color = DK_BLUE) Or (BG_Color = DK_CYAN))
            Temp.x = Temp.x + MoveDir
            picBG.Line -(Temp.x, Temp.y), YELLOW
            Pause .25

            BG_Color = GetPixel(picReference.hDC, Temp.x, Temp.y)
        Wend
        mBall.x = Temp.x

    ' Did it land in a sand trap?
    ElseIf Location = "SANDTRAP" Then
        lblInfo = "You're in a bunker."
        rc = sndPlaySound(AppPath & "BUNKER2.WAV", SND_ASYNC)
    End If

    DrawBall

End Sub
```

Before examining the routine above, let's review some of the assumptions and constraints of the game. On an abstract level, the ball cannot be hit over trees, but it can go over water hazards and sand traps. At a programmatic level, these objects are determined by their color on the bitmap. For example, if the ball stops on a pixel that is blue, then the program assumes it has landed in the water. Likewise, other colors denote sand traps, or trees, or the hole itself.

The picBG_DblClick event starts by determining how far the ball should travel given the club used and how hard the ball was hit. This distance is saved in the MaxDist variable.

Next, the routine checks the color of the bitmap at the ball's current location. If the ball is in a sand trap or tree, the MaxDist variable is adjusted. It should be harder to hit a ball out of a tree or sand trap.

The routine does some calculations to move the ball along the correct trajectory, then begins a loop that will draw the path of the ball. As the ball is moved, its location is checked to ensure that it does not go out of bounds (off the bitmap). If it does, the ball is returned to its original position. The function OutOfBounds is used to determine if the ball is still on the bitmap. Add this routine to GOLF.FRM, as shown below.

```
Function OutOfBounds (x As Integer, y As Integer) As Integer
'-------------------------------------------------------------
' Returns True if the x-y coordinate is outside the bitmap.
'-------------------------------------------------------------
Dim BoundsMargin As Integer

    BoundsMargin = 4

    OutOfBounds = False
    If (x < BoundsMargin) Or (x > picBG.ScaleWidth - BoundsMargin) Or (y < BoundsMargin) Or (y >
    picBG.ScaleHeight - BoundsMargin) Then
        OutOfBounds = True
    End If

End Function
```

Notice that the ball is considered out of bounds if it's within 4 pixels of the bitmap's edge. This is to ensure that the player can always "get behind" the ball to hit it. If you allow the ball to move all the way, to the left edge of the bitmap, for example, the player will never be able to move the mouse cursor to the left of the ball. The ball would be stuck at the edge of the bitmap. The BoundsMargin variable avoids this problem.

Back to picBG's DblClick event. As the ball is moving, check to see if the ball has collided with a tree. Determine this by checking the bitmap color under the ball. Black is the color reserved for trees, and this color will cause the ball to stop. If the ball was already in a tree when it was hit, don't stop the ball. If you did, the player would only be able to get out of the tree by moving 1 pixel to a stroke, and this wouldn't be very realistic.

The last possibility to be concerned about is the most important: Did the ball go in the hole? This check is handled by its own function, called InHole. Add this function, as shown below.

```
Function InHole (x As Integer, y As Integer) As Integer
'------------------------------------------------------------
' Return True if this x-y location is in the hole, false
' otherwise.
'------------------------------------------------------------
Dim DC As Integer
    DC = picReference.hDC

    If GetPixel(DC, x, y) = RED Or GetPixel(DC, x + 1, y) = RED Then
        InHole = True
    ElseIf GetPixel(DC, x, y - 1) = RED Or GetPixel(DC, x + 1, y - 1) = RED Then
        InHole = True
    ElseIf GetPixel(DC, x, y + 1) = RED Or GetPixel(DC, x + 1, y + 1) = RED Then
        InHole = True
    Else
        InHole = False
    End If
End Function
```

The hole is designated on the bitmap by a tiny red circle. It's the only object on the bitmap allowed to be red, so if the ball is over a red area, it must be in the hole.

Checking if the ball is in the hole is not the last thing to worry about. When the ball comes to rest, you must check if it landed in the water or a sand trap. If the ball landed in a sand trap you only need to make the appropriate sound effect, but if it landed in water, you need to take some additional action.

Because the player is not equipped with diving gear, the program must remove the ball from the water and place it at the edge of a water hazard. To make this effect more amusing, draw a line from the point the ball entered the water to its eventual position at the water's edge.

To determine if the ball landed in sand or water, add the GetLocationByColor function to GOLF.FRM.

```
Function GetLocationByColor (AColor As Long) As String
'------------------------------------------------------------
' Given a color, return a string indicating what that color
' corresponds to.
'------------------------------------------------------------
Dim i As Integer

    Select Case AColor
```

continued on next page

continued from previous page

```
        Case RED: GetLocationByColor = "HOLE"
        Case BLUE, DK_BLUE, DK_CYAN: GetLocationByColor = "WATER"
        Case WHITE, YELLOW: GetLocationByColor = "SANDTRAP"
        Case Else
            GetLocationByColor = ""
    End Select
End Function
```

To provide an easy way to quit the game, the program displays a "Club House" button. This button, called btnQuit, exits the program. Add its Click event, as shown below.

```
Sub btnQuit_Click ()
'---------------------------------------------------------------
' Exit the program.
'---------------------------------------------------------------

    Unload Me
End Sub
```

Finally, this form has one other button, labeled Help. Pressing this button displays an About box form, with information on how to play and customize the game. This button, btnHelp, has the following Click event.

```
Sub btnHelp_Click ()
'---------------------------------------------------------------
' Display the help screen.
'---------------------------------------------------------------
Const SHOW_MODAL = 1

    frmAboutGolf.Show SHOW_MODAL
End Sub
```

Adding the About Box Form to Golf

Golf's About form provides some simple information about how to play and customize the game. The information is stored in simple text files created using Windows Notepad. At runtime, the About form, shown in Figure 12-3, is displayed when the user presses the Help button on Golf's main form.

To create this About form, first add a new form called ABOUT.FRM to the GOLF.MAK project. This form should have the objects and properties described in Table 12-2.

FIGURE 12-3

The About form at runtime

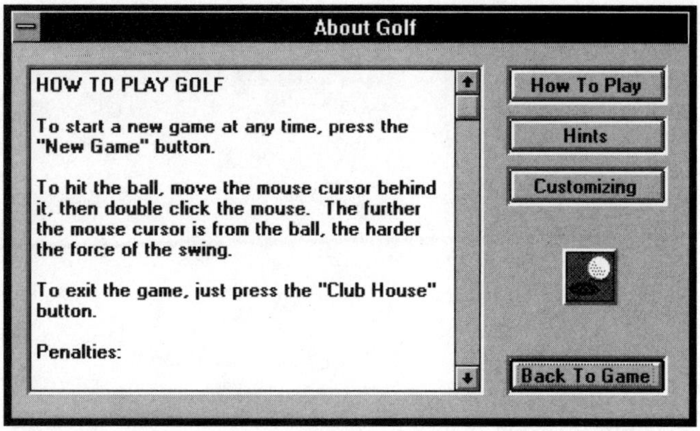

TABLE 12-2

Objects and properties for the ABOUT.FRM form

Object	Property	Setting
Form	FormName	frmAboutGolf
	BackColor	&H00C0C0C0&
	BorderStyle	3 'Fixed Double
	Caption	"About Golf"
	Height	3975
	Left	1380
	MaxButton	0 'False
	MinButton	0 'False
	Top	1530
	Width	6735
Image	Name	Image1
	Picture	(set at design time in Properties window)
	Tag	"/3d_raised/"
TextBox	Name	txtHelp
	MultiLine	-1 'True
	ScrollBars	2 'Vertical

continued from previous page

Object	Property	Setting
	Tag	"/3d_inset/"
CommandButton	Name	btnCancel
	Caption	"Back To Game"
	Tag	"/3d_inset/"
CommandButton	Name	btnHowToPlay
	Caption	"How To Play"
	Tag	"/3d_inset/"
CommandButton	Name	btnCustomizing
	Caption	"Customizing"
	Tag	"/3d_inset/"
CommandButton	Name	btnHints
	Caption	"Hints"
	Tag	"/3d_inset/"

Even though the purpose of the About form is simple, it contains a few useful and interesting tricks. Start by adding the following code to ABOUT.FRM's Declarations section.

```
Option Explicit
'-------------------------------------------------------------
' Constants and function used in ABOUT.FRM.
'-------------------------------------------------------------

Const WM_USER = &H400
Const EM_SETREADONLY = (WM_USER + 31)
Declare Function SendMessage Lib "User" (ByVal hWnd As Integer, ByVal
wMsg As Integer, ByVal wParam As Integer, ByVal lParam As Any) As Long
```

The constants and API declaration above are used to make a standard Visual Basic TextBox control read-only. I wanted a scrollable multiline text box in which to display help information, but I didn't want the player to be able to change the text that was displayed. While setting a TextBox control's Enabled property to False prevents editing, it also disables scrolling. Fortunately, the Windows API provides a simple solution. Using the SendMessage API call, tell the TextBox not to allow editing. Add the following Load event to the ABOUT.FRM form.

```
Sub Form_Load ()
'-------------------------------------------------------------
' When the form is loaded, make the text box read-only, and
' display the How-To help information.
'-------------------------------------------------------------
Dim rc As Long

    CenterForm Me

    ' Set the text box to read-only mode:
    rc = SendMessage(txtHelp.hWnd, EM_SETREADONLY, True, 0&)

    btnHowToPlay_Click
End Sub
```

The SendMessage call passes the EM_SETREADONLY message to the window handle of the TextBox control, txtHelp. Now the TextBox cannot be edited, but its text can be scrolled, and you can change the text from within the program using its Text property.

The Load event also calls the btnHowToPlay Command Button's Click event. Add this event, as shown below.

```
Sub btnHowToPlay_Click ()
'-------------------------------------------------------------
' Display the How-To help information.
'-------------------------------------------------------------

    DisplayHelp "HOWTO.TXT"
End Sub
```

The Click event calls the DisplayHelp routine, which reads the contents of a short text file, HOWTO.TXT, and displays it in the txtHelp TextBox control. Add the DisplayHelp routine, as shown below.

```
Sub DisplayHelp (AFile As String)
'-------------------------------------------------------------
' Display a particular help file in the control txtHelp.
'-------------------------------------------------------------

    txtHelp = ReadFile(AppPath & AFile)
End Sub
```

The routine above simply calls another function, ReadFile, which handles the actual reading of the file. Let's add the ReadFile function.

```
Function ReadFile (ByVal Filename As String) As String
'-------------------------------------------------------------
' Read an entire file into a text string.
'-------------------------------------------------------------
Dim fnum As Integer
```

continued on next page

continued from previous page

```
Dim AStr As String

    fnum = FreeFile
    Open Filename For Binary As fnum

    AStr = String$(LOF(fnum), " ")
    Get #fnum, , AStr

    Close fnum
    ReadFile = AStr
End Function
```

You may find the ReadFile function useful in other applications. It's great when you need to read in small (less than about 12K bytes) text files quickly. It uses the Visual Basic Get command to read the text file in one big chunk. This chunk is then returned to the calling function.

Like HOWTO.TXT, the other help information is also stored in files and loaded when the appropriate button is pushed. Add Click events for each of these buttons as shown below.

```
Sub btnHints_Click ()
'-------------------------------------------------------------
' Display the Hints help information.
'-------------------------------------------------------------

    DisplayHelp "HINTS.TXT"
End Sub

Sub btnCustomizing_Click ()
'-------------------------------------------------------------
' Display the Customization help information.
'-------------------------------------------------------------

    DisplayHelp "CUSTOMIZ.TXT"
End Sub
```

To give the About form a three-dimensional appearance consistent with the main Golf form, it calls the Paint3D routine. It calls it from within ABOUT.FRM's Paint event. Add the Paint Event, as shown below.

```
Sub Form_Paint ()
'---------------------------------------------------------------------------
' Put a 3D border around any control tagged "/3D_INSET/" or "/3D_RAISED/."
'---------------------------------------------------------------------------

    Paint3D Me
End Sub
```

Finally, the btnCancel Command button, labeled "Back to Game," gets rid of the About form and returns the player to the main Golf form. Add the btnCancel Click event, as shown below.

```
Sub btnCancel_Click ()
'-------------------------------------------------------------
' Exit this form.
'-------------------------------------------------------------

    Unload Me
End Sub
```

Running Golf

Now the game is complete. The game also requires several .WAV audio files, the GAMEINFO.TXT file to describe the golf course, and bitmaps for each hole. These are all included on the accompanying CD. All these files should be in the same directory, along with the executable of Golf. With these files in place, you should have no trouble running the game.

Suggestions and Enhancements

Golf was a lot of fun to write, but as usual, I can always see room for improvement. Here are some of my suggestions for changes and improvements.

- Add a wider selection of clubs. Right now the player can choose from only three. In particular, the game really needs a pitching wedge for sand traps.
- Add more realism to the game. It would be nice if the ball could hook or slice, or even arc based on wind direction. Likewise, when on the green, it would be nice to add some subtlety to the putting.
- To make it easier to spot the ball, add a blinking highlight box over the ball for a few seconds after it lands. This could easily be done with a Shape control.

These are my suggestions; you may have some radically different ideas on where to go with this game. Next we'll take a look at war games, and build a battlefield simulation based on the American Civil War.

13

Strategy Games: Raytraced Reversi for Windows

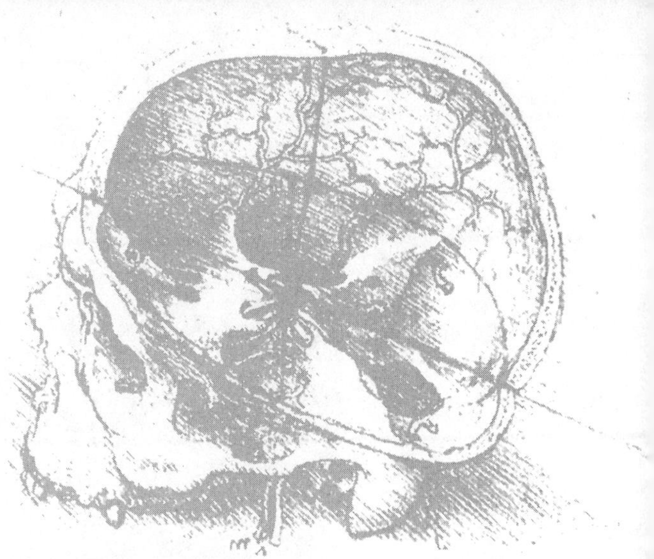

13

Strategy Games: Raytraced Reversi for Windows

Strategy games propose a unique challenge in that the programmer needs to create a viable computer opponent to play against the player. In addition, because they are fairly common (Reversi was included in Windows 3.0), any successful strategy board game must set itself apart from all the other games out there. For this Reversi game, I've created some exceptional three-dimensional board pieces using the popular freeware utility POV-Ray. I also included some quality sound effects. These elements take advantage of Windows' multimedia capabilities and make the game more interesting than the "run of the mill" board game. As a quick refresher, the rules for playing Reversi are summarized below.

Playing Reversi

Reversi is played on a standard grid, similar to a checkerboard. The size of the grid isn't important, although the number of rows and columns should be an even number, so that the starting game position is in the exact center of the board. The game

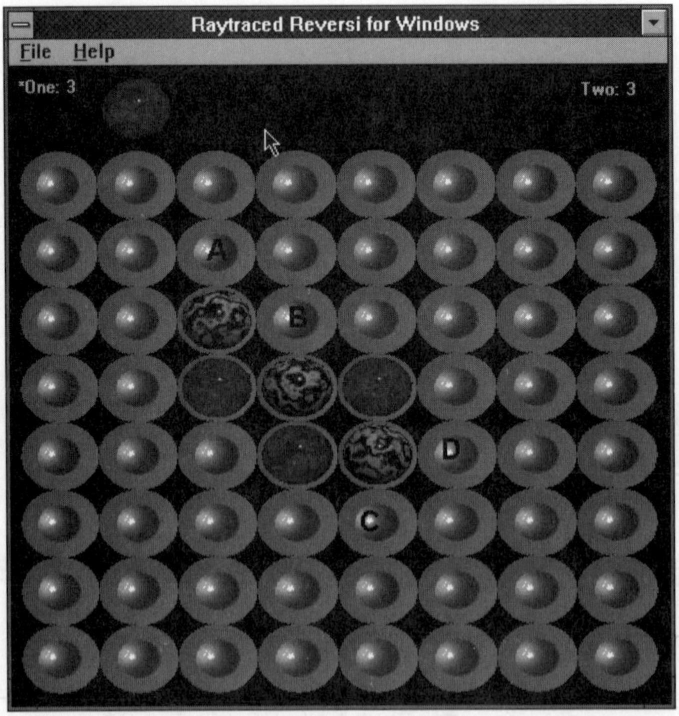

FIGURE 13-1

Placing a piece in Reversi

begins with four pieces in the center of the board, two pieces to each player. A player moves by placing a piece on any square where he or she can "trap" one or more of the opponent's pieces, as shown in Figure 13-1. A piece (or pieces) is trapped if it lies between the new piece and one of the existing pieces in a horizontal, vertical, or diagonal line. Trapping can happen in multiple directions in a single turn. All trapped pieces convert to the player who trapped the piece. In the situation in Figure 13-1, a player could place a piece in any one of four spots to capture an opponent piece: A) capturing down, B) capturing right, C) capturing up, D) capturing left. A player must pass a turn if there are no valid moves. The game ends when the board is filled. The player with the most pieces on the board is the winner.

Creating the Graphics

For common games such as this one, the piece creation and other artwork separate the good games from the mediocre. To this end, you'll create two extra pieces and let the player choose which piece he or she wishes to use. You'll also leave the game open-ended in design, so that new pieces can be added simply by copying the appropriate files into the game directory. The creation of additional pieces fosters new marketing opportunities, as well. For example, if the new game is going to be marketed as a shareware game, additional pieces can be used as an incentive for users to register the game. Or, if the game is a commercial product, you can introduce "piece packs" for the game to be sold as an add-on product. You'll create the pieces for Reversi using the Persistence of Vision ray tracer (known as POV-Ray), which produces beautifully shaded photorealistic pictures from a simple program-like script.

Using POV-Ray

POV-Ray uses scene description files as input. A scene description file is a text file that describes a camera location, the location of light sources, and all the objects in a scene. Objects consist of geometric primitives such as spheres, cubes, cones, and planes. Each object can be given a texture or color. There are many built-in textures and colors to choose from, and you can create your own. Once a complete scene description file is created, you run the POV-Ray executable, using the scene description file as a command line. POV-Ray reads the file and coverts it into a Targa graphic file that depicts the scene described.

This chapter is not intended to be a complete description of all the abilities of POV-Ray. POV-Ray comes with extensive documentation, as well as numerous sample images; if you don't already know how to use POV-Ray, you can learn fairly quickly. There are also several excellent Waite Group books detailing the use of POV-Ray, including *Ray Tracing Creations*. The best part about POV-Ray is that it's 100 percent FREE! (That's one way to keep software production costs down!) POV-Ray can be found in the Graphics Developer's Forum on CompuServe.

Creating the Pieces

Rotating spheres were chosen for the Reversi pieces mainly because shaded spheres give the illusion of depth better than any other geometric object. The POV-Ray scene description file for one of the game pieces, PEARTH, is shown in Listing 13-1.

Listing 13-1 Pearth.POV

```
#include "colors.inc"        //POV include files
#include "textures.inc"
#include "shapes.inc"

camera {                     //Camera location.
   location  <0.129, -6.063, 0.000>
   direction <0.0,     0.0,  2.4880>
```

continued on next page

continued from previous page

```
   sky        <0.0,     0.0,  1.0>
   up         <0.0,     0.0,  1.0>
   right      <1.3333,  0.0,  0.0>
   look_at    <0.000, 0.000, 0.000>
}

light_source { <3, -18, 10.316> color rgb <1.000, 1.000, 1.000>}

#declare MyAgate =                 //blue to white texture
 texture {
 pigment
  {agate
   color_map
    {[0.0, 0.3   color blue 0.9 color blue 0.8]
     [0.3, 1.001 color blue 0.8 color rgb<1,1,1>]
    }
  }
 finish { Phong_Shiny }
}

object {
  sphere {<0,0,0>,1}
  texture { MyAgate scale .5 }
  rotate <0,clock*5,-clock*5>
}
```

This scene file creates a single sphere with a turbulent blue and white pattern on it, shown in Figure 13-2. I created this texture on a trial-and-error basis. I rendered the sphere many times, changing single elements of the texture until I liked the final result. The other example pieces were created in a similar way. In each case, the scene file in Listing 13-1 was used as the starting point, and only the texture was changed.

Notice the line rotate <0,clock*5,-clock*5> at the end of the description of the sphere. This line animates the object. POV-Ray supports a "clock parameter," which

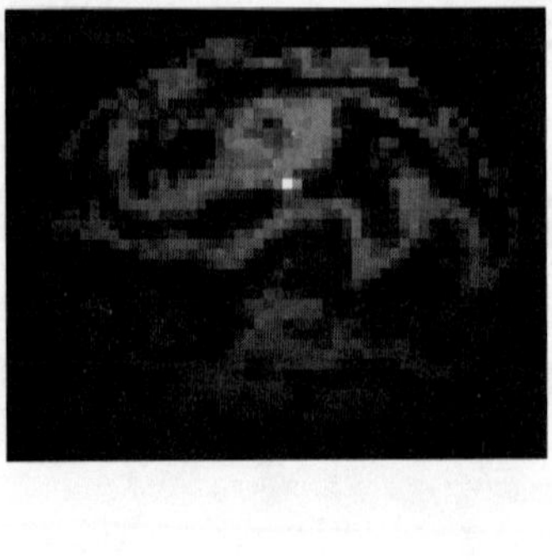

FIGURE 13-2

PEARTH01.BMP: The blue and white sphere created by PEARTH.POV

allows you to pass a value that can be used anywhere in the scene description file. To use this parameter, add the switch +Knn to the POV-Ray command line, where nn is the number you wish to substitute as the clock value. The following sample command line demonstrates a render of PEARTH.POV, passing in a clock parameter of 4 (the +K04 at the end of the line is the clock parameter).

```
POV-Ray -ipearth.pov -o.\tga\pearth09.tga +x +q9 +linclude +b32 +v -p +K04
```

To get the sphere to rotate smoothly, choose some number of frames to render, and divide 360 by that number to calculate the number of degrees of rotation between successive frames. The Reversi spheres have 72 frames, so the number of degrees of change between each frame is (360 / 72) = 5 degrees. Therefore, to render each frame, pass in the values 0,1,2,.....71 as the clock parameter, and then multiply the clock value by 5 to get the desired angle of rotation. You can also rotate the sphere along two axes (in the example object, the Y and Z axes), or change the direction of rotation by adding the minus sign to the (clock * 5) calculation. The important thing is to always use the clock * 5 calculation for a single axis, because if this number is changed, the angle difference between the last and first frames will not be the correct value, and the animation between these two frames will not be smooth.

The batch file RENDRALL.BAT demonstrates how each frame is rendered. There are 72 calls to POV-Ray in the batch file, one for each frame. The only two elements that change from line to line are the clock parameter and the name of the output file. The batch file looks as follows.

```
POV-Ray -ipearth.pov -o.\tga\pearth01.tga +w160 +h100 +x +q9  +linclude +b32 +v -p +K00
POV-Ray -ipearth.pov -o.\tga\pearth02.tga +w160 +h100 +x +q9  +linclude +b32 +v -p +K01
POV-Ray -ipearth.pov -o.\tga\pearth03.tga +w160 +h100 +x +q9  +linclude +b32 +v -p +K02
POV-Ray -ipearth.pov -o.\tga\pearth04.tga +w160 +h100 +x +q9  +linclude +b32 +v -p +K03
.
.
POV-Ray -ipearth.pov -o.\tga\pearth72.tga +w160 +h100 +x +q9  +linclude +b32 +v -p +K71
```

Graphic Conversion

The next thing to do is take the 72 individual images created by POV-Ray and convert them to a single bitmap. This saves on the number of Windows resources the game will need. The alternative would be to use 72 picture box controls for each piece! It is a fairly straightforward process to tile all of the individual bitmaps into a single image, as shown in Figure 13-3.

Image Alchemy

Image Alchemy, by Handmade Software, is a DOS command line utility that provides all of the image conversion and palette manipulation abilities recommended to create

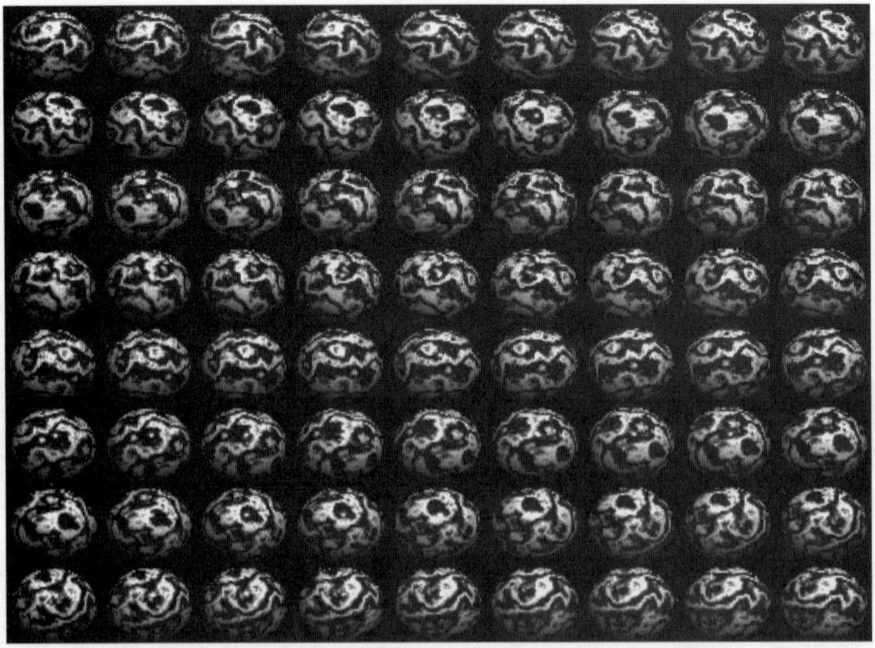

FIGURE 13-3

PEARTH.BMP: The 72 frames used to animate a Reversi piece, converted to a single bitmap

the game graphics. The output images from POV-Ray are 16 million color Targa images, which are converted into 256-color Windows bitmaps. The following Image Alchemy command accomplishes this.

```
alchemy \Pov-Ray\tga\pearth*.tga -w -x72 -y45 -f winpal.bmp
```

Note that the size of each image is also changed to 72x45 pixels. The *eventual* frame size will be 56x45, but because that aspect ratio is different than the original image size, converting directly to that size would result in "squashed" images. A 72x45 pixel picture has the same aspect ratio as the original image.

Using ANIMBLD: Concatenating the Bitmaps

The final step is to concatenate, or combine, all of the individual bitmaps together into one large bitmap. A Visual Basic utility program called ANIMBLD (animation builder) will accomplish this. The source code to this program is included in the ANIMBLD directory on the CD included with this book.

ANIMBLD is meant to be a programmer's utility; it does not have fancy help files, about boxes, title screens, etc. Its purpose is to take all the individually numbered

BMP files in a directory and copy them in numeric order into a final bitmap. A simple user's guide follows.

Once ANIMBLD starts, type the name of the directory into the top text control marked File, as well as the name of the first file of the animation sequence, *without the numbered suffix*. For example, if the files are named C:\ALCHEMY\PEARTHnn.BMP, type C:\ALCHEMY\PEARTH into the text box. Once ANIMBLD finds the file named C:\ALCHEMY\PEARTH01.BMP, it will load it into two picture controls: one that shows the image at normal size and one that shows the image at a blown-up size (hard-coded to be three times normal size).

The four controls labeled Top, Left, Width, and Height are used for bitmap clipping. Recall that all of the BMP files are 72x45 pixels, and you want them to be 56x45 pixels. This means you must remove 16 pixels from the width of each individual frame. To accomplish this, type an 8 in the control marked Left and a 56 in the control marked Width. You can also use the mouse on the blown-up image to drag a rectangle around the area.

On the right side of the form, two spin buttons marked Rows and Columns specify the number of horizontal and vertical frames in the final image. As you click on these spin buttons, you will notice the final destination picture box resize.

To start the actual build, click the button marked GO!. ANIMBLD will loop through the specified directory, taking each file with the pattern input into the File control and BitBlt it into the proper place in the destination bitmap. When the build is done, click on the Save button, and the final image will be saved to disk. ANIMBLD will use the file name entered in the File control as the final file name, with a .BMP extension. You now have a finished piece!

Creating Board Tiles

The same basic steps are involved in creating the individual board tiles, except that animation isn't needed for them as it was for the pieces. The board tile is designed in POV-Ray, rendered, then converted using Image Alchemy to a bitmap of the desired size. To differentiate between piece graphics and board graphics in Reversi, all the piece graphics begin with the letter "P" and all the board graphics begin with a "B". The code in Reversi automatically loads all bitmaps with the correct letter into list boxes used for choosing which piece and board graphics should be used in the games. Three sample board graphics were created using a basic disk shape.

Listing 13-2 shows a sample POV-Ray script for one of the board tiles.

Listing 13-2 Bjade.POV, creates one of the board tile graphics

```
#include "colors.inc"
#include "textures.inc"
#include "shapes.inc"
```

continued on next page

continued from previous page

```
camera {
  location  <0.114, 0.000, 25.000>
  direction <0.0,    0.0,  2.8106>
  sky       <0.0,    0.0,  1.0>
  up        <0.0,    0.0,  1.0>
  right     <1.3333, 0.0,  0.0>
  look_at   <0.000, 0.000, 0.000>
}

light_source { <8, 24, 44> color White }


#declare base = cylinder {
  <0,0,1>, <0,0,0>, 1
  scale <4.000000, 4.000000, 1.410552>
}

#declare spcut = object {
  sphere {<0,0,0>,1}
  scale <2.855976, 2.855976, 2.855976>
  translate <0.000000, 0.000000, 3.192279>
}

difference {
  object { base }
  object { spcut }
  texture { Jade scale 2 }
}
```

Writing the Program

Now that you have all the graphics you need for the Reversi game, it's time to get down to the code writing. I'll break the game into broad concepts; each concept will be highlighted and explained with some actual code:

- Loading and drawing the playing board
- Loading the pieces and creating masks
- Animating a piece across the board
- Creating the computer opponent: rudimentary artificial intelligence
- Keeping score
- Creating a slick opening animation sequence
- Adding sound

Loading and Drawing the Playing Board

The board for this Reversi game is going to be 8 tiles wide by 8 tiles high. Global integer arrays bLeft%() and bTop%() will hold the upper-left coordinates of each board location. The subroutine shown in Listing 13-3 initializes these arrays.

Listing 13-3 SetupCoords procedure

```
Sub SetupCoords ()

'-----------------------------------------
'sets up bLeft% and bTop% coordinate arrays
'-----------------------------------------
'Width and height of the board tiles.  A few pixels
'are added to leave a small space between tiles
Const gTWid% = 57
Const gTHgt% = 47

'loop vars
Dim i%, j%
'top left coordinate of first tile
Dim tSpot%, lSpot%

    gBoardSize% = 8      'dim globals
    ReDim Board(gBoardSize% - 1, gBoardSize% - 1)
    ReDim bLeft%(gBoardSize% - 1, gBoardSize% - 1)
    ReDim bTop%(gBoardSize% - 1, gBoardSize% - 1)

    tSpot% = 56
    lSpot% = 5

'fill Left and top global arrays
    For i = 0 To gBoardSize% - 1
        bLeft%(0, i) = lSpot%
        bTop%(0, i) = tSpot% + (i * gTHgt%)
        bLeft%(i, 0) = lSpot% + (i * gTWid%)
        bTop%(i, 0) = tSpot%
    Next

    For i = 1 To gBoardSize% - 1
    For j = 1 To gBoardSize% - 1
        bLeft%(i, j) = bLeft%(i - 1, j) + gTWid%
        bTop%(i, j) = bTop%(i, j - 1) + gTHgt%
    Next
    Next
End Sub
```

Now that the board coordinates are defined, you can call the procedure LoadBoard, shown in Listing 13-4. This procedure gets the board tile file name from the INI file using the Windows API call GetPrivateProfileString. Then it loads this bitmap into the appropriate picture box, makes a mask for it, and draws each of the tiles on the screen using the transparent put operation (AND the mask, OR the bitmap).

Listing 13-4 LoadBoard procedure

```
Sub LoadBoard ()

'----------------------------------------
'load the board bitmap and draw the board
'----------------------------------------
Dim r%, i%, j%
Dim BrdFile$          'name of board bitmap

    Screen.MousePointer = 11

    'get .BMP filename from ini
    gBoardName$ = Space(128)
    r% = GetPrivateProfileString(gOptString$, "BoardName",
        "XXX", gBoardName$, Len(gBoardName$), gIniFile$)
    If Left$(gBoardName$, 3) = "XXX" Then
        MsgBox "Error: BoardName entry not found in .INI"
        End
    Else
        gBoardName$ = Stripnul$(gBoardName$)
        If UCase$(Right$(gBoardName$, 4)) <> ".BMP" Then gBoardName$ = gBoardName$ + ".BMP"
    End If

    'load file: abort if does not exist
    BrdFile$ = gAppPath$ + Dir$(gAppPath$ + gBoardName$)
    If Len(BrdFile$) > 0 Then
        RRev.BPiecePic(0).Picture = LoadPicture(BrdFile$)
        RRev.BPiecePic(1).Width = RRev.BPiecePic(0).Width
        RRev.BPiecePic(1).Height = RRev.BPiecePic(0).Height
        Call MakeMask(RRev.BPiecePic(1), RRev.BPiecePic(0).Picture)
    Else
        MsgBox "Error: " + BrdFile$ + " not found "
        End
    End If

    RRev.BoardPic.Picture = LoadPicture(BrdFile$)
    r% = BitBlt(RRev.BoardPic.hDC, 0, 0, RRev.BPiecePic(0).ScaleWidth,
        RRev.BPiecePic(0).ScaleHeight, RRev.BPiecePic(0).hDC, 0, 0, BLACKNESS)

    For i = 0 To gBoardSize% - 1
        For j = 0 To gBoardSize% - 1
            r% = BitBlt(RRev.BoardPic.hDC, bLeft%(i, j), bTop%(i, j),
                RRev.BPiecePic(1).ScaleWidth, RRev.BPiecePic(1).ScaleHeight,
                RRev.BPiecePic(1).hDC, 0, 0, SRCAND)
```

```
        r% = BitBlt(RRev.BoardPic.hDC, bLeft%(i, j), bTop%(i, j),
            RRev.BPiecePic(0).ScaleWidth, RRev.BPiecePic(0).ScaleHeight,
            RRev.BPiecePic(0).hDC, 0, 0, SRCPAINT)
      Next
    Next

    Screen.MousePointer = 0

End Sub
```

A Visual Basic LoadPicture command is used not only on the board tile source picture box, but also on the main picture box (BoardPic); the same area is then BitBltted over using the BLACKNESS operation to cover up the picture. (About halfway through the program code a comment reads "palette align board.") This gets the palette of BoardPic to be the same palette used by the board and piece graphics. If you BitBlt into picture box BoardPic without setting its Picture property in this way, BoardPic's palette will not be the same as the board and piece picture boxes, and the output will not look right. This extra LoadPicture resolves this problem.

Loading the Pieces and Creating Masks

The process of loading pieces is almost identical to the process of loading the board tile. For each piece, read the name of the bitmap out of the INI file, load the bitmap into a picture box control using LoadPicture, and make a mask. In addition, set global integer variables Pheight% and Pwidth% to be the height and width of each frame of each piece. The functions that accomplish this are LoadPieces, which handles the reading of the INI file, and LoadClip, which does the LoadPicture and the call to MakeMask. The routines are separate because LoadClip is called by itself if the user decides to change the pieces midgame. Listing 13-5 features the LoadClip subroutine.

Listing 13-5 LoadClip subroutine

```
Sub LoadClip (PNum%, pc As Control)

'-------------------------------------------------------
'loads a piece into proper picture box and makes its mask
'-------------------------------------------------------
Dim FName$

    FName$ = UCase$(gAppPath$ & Piece$(PNum%))
    If Right(FName$, 4) <> ".BMP" Then
        FName$ = FName$ + ".BMP"
    End If
    If Len(Dir$(FName$)) > 0 Then
        pc.Picture = LoadPicture(FName$)
```

continued on next page

continued from previous page

```
        PWidth%(PNum%) = RRev.Picclip(PNum%).Width / 9
        PHeight%(PNum%) = RRev.Picclip(PNum%).Height / 8

        RRev.MaskClip(PNum%).Height = RRev.Picclip(PNum%).Height
        RRev.MaskClip(PNum%).Width = RRev.Picclip(PNum%).Width
        Call MakeMask(RRev.MaskClip(PNum%), RRev.Picclip(PNum%).Picture)

    Else
        MsgBox "Error: " + FName$ + " not found"
        End
    End If

End Sub
```

Animating a Piece Across the Board

When the user clicks on a valid empty square to place a piece, the piece flies across the board from a random starting spot and lands on the square the user picked. In addition to the simple moving of the piece across the board, you'll also change the frame of the piece as it moves, giving the appearance that the piece is spinning into its proper position.

The basic steps to accomplish this are as follows (see Listing 13-6). First, determine a random starting point on an edge of the board. Next, divide the number of pixels between the start and end points, in both the X and Y directions, by the number of frames you wish to use in the animation sequence. This determines how many pixels to move the piece between frames. Now start a loop, one iteration for each frame to be drawn. In this loop, save the background image in a holding place (picture box OldPic) so it can be restored later (you only need to save the point that's about to be drawn over, not the entire board). Then calculate X and Y coordinates for the current frame, based on the X,Y offset values computed above. Finally, place the desired piece on the board using a call to pTransparentBlt. In the next iteration of the loop, the background picture saved in OldPic is restored, then the process is repeated once for each frame.

Listing 13-6 AnimPutPiece procedure

```
Sub AnimPutPiece (clr%, Toi%, Toj%)

'-----------------------------------------------------------------
'animates a piece from a random edge of the board to its place
'clr%: piece to draw (HUMAN/PUTER)
'Toi%,Toj%: coordinates to place piece
'-----------------------------------------------------------------
'work variables
Dim i%, j%, lp%, r%
```

```
'from/to animation coordinates
Dim xfrom%, yfrom%, xto%, yto%

'number of frames
Dim Divisions%

'loop frames forward or (1) backward (-1)
Dim inc%

'current frame
Dim idx%

'pixels to move between each frame
Dim iinc!, jinc!

'current pixel location
Dim ifloat!, jfloat!

'replace old screen flag: set after 1st frame
Dim LocalBegun%

    'set up background picture
    RRev.OldPic.Width = PWidth%(clr% - 1)
    RRev.OldPic.Height = PHeight%(clr% - 1)

    'choose random start position
    i = (Rnd * 1000) Mod 4
    Select Case i
    Case 0  'left
        xfrom% = 0
        yfrom% = Rnd * RRev.BoardPic.ScaleHeight
    Case 1  'right
        xfrom% = RRev.BoardPic.ScaleWidth
        yfrom% = Rnd * RRev.BoardPic.ScaleHeight
    Case 2  'up
        xfrom% = Rnd * RRev.BoardPic.ScaleWidth
        yfrom% = 0
    Case 3  'down
        xfrom% = Rnd * RRev.BoardPic.ScaleWidth
        yfrom% = RRev.BoardPic.ScaleHeight
    End Select

    'destination location
    xto% = bLeft%(Toi%, Toj%) + PLEFT
    yto% = bTop%(Toi%, Toj%) + PTOP

    'determine number of frames from global
    Divisions% = 22 - gDivisions%

    'randomly cycle forward through animation or backward
    If (Rnd * 100) Mod 2 Then
```

continued on next page

continued from previous page

```
        inc% = -1
    Else
        inc% = 1
    End If
    idx% = Int(Rnd * 72)

    'increment between frames in x,y directions
    'use floats for less rounding errors
    iinc! = (xto% - xfrom%) / Divisions%
    jinc! = (yto% - yfrom%) / Divisions%
    ifloat! = xfrom%: jfloat! = yfrom%

    'special case: animation turned off
    If Not gAnimOn% Then
        Divisions% = 1
        ifloat! = xto% - iinc!
        jfloat! = yto% - jinc!
    End If
    RRev.OldPic.Cls

    'start main loop
    For lp% = 0 To Divisions% - 1

        'next frame (forward or backward)
        idx% = (idx% + inc%) Mod 72
        If idx% < 0 Then idx% = idx% + 72

        'replace background if not first iteration
        If LocalBegun% Then
            r% = BitBlt(RRev.BoardPic.hDC, i, j, RRev.OldPic.Width,
                RRev.OldPic.Height, RRev.OldPic.hDC, 0, 0, SRCCOPY)
        End If

        LocalBegun% = True

        'increment current location
        ifloat! = ifloat! + iinc!
        jfloat! = jfloat! + jinc!

        'round current pixels to integers
        i = Int(ifloat! + .5): j = Int(jfloat! + .5)

        'save background
        r% = BitBlt(RRev.OldPic.hDC, 0, 0, RRev.OldPic.Width,
            RRev.OldPic.Height, RRev.BoardPic.hDC, i, j, SRCCOPY)

       'place the piece
       Call pTransparentBlt(clr% - 1, i, j, idx%)

        RRev.BoardPic.Refresh
    Next
```

```
    'one last frame in exact location
    idx% = (idx% + inc%) Mod 72
    If idx% < 0 Then idx% = idx% + 72

    i = bLeft%(Toi%, Toj%) + PLEFT
    j = bTop%(Toi%, Toj%) + PTOP
    Call pTransparentBlt(clr% - 1, i, j, idx%)
    Board(Toi%, Toj%) = clr%

    'increment the score by one
    Call IncScore(clr%, 1)
end Sub
```

Creating the Computer Opponent: Rudimentary Artificial Intelligence

To many people, creating a computer opponent is the most difficult task to complete in game design. This section provides a basic methodology for simple board games that will work in many situations. The hardest part of an artificial intelligence routine is to assign a numeric value to a given board configuration: a value that describes how "good" the board configuration is to one of the players. Once this is accomplished, the program can simply loop through all possible moves, and choose the move with the best value.

In the case of the Reversi game, the number of opponent's pieces captured by a given move can be used for the board's "value" for that move. Capturing five pieces in one turn is better than capturing only one, because it leaves the player with more pieces at the end of the turn. Having the most pieces at the end of the game is the final goal, so having the maximum pieces at the end of each turn would help accomplish that goal.

However, this methodology is simplistic. Suppose, for example, that only two moves exist at a given time. The first move allows the computer to take four pieces, the second move allows the computer to capture only two pieces. Using the logic described above, the former move would be the logical choice. Suppose further, however, that after the computer captures the four pieces, the opponent can immediately capture a new piece *and* those original four pieces again, which means the computer has lost all of those pieces! (This type of board configuration is quite common in Reversi, by the way). It makes no sense then to make the first move, if the opponent can capture all of the pieces back on his or her next turn.

The concept of making a move based on what the opponent can do after that move is called *move look ahead*. The goal is to build into the game a way for the computer to move look ahead. To make the algorithm even more complete, one could look *two* moves ahead, past the opponent's next move to the move *after* the next one, and so on. The number of possible board configurations increases exponentially with every turn you wish to look ahead.

There are entire texts devoted to the subject of game artificial intelligence and look-ahead algorithms. The following describes a simple one-level look-ahead algorithm, where the computer looks at the opponent's next two moves. The computer will "think" in accordance with this general algorithm.

1. Find the three best moves (the three that result in the most captures).
2. Pretend to make each of these moves.
3. After making each move, find the best move the opponent can make.
4. Choose the move that results in the least amount of captures by the opponent on the next move.

Note that because there are several separate elements to this algorithm, you can easily shut off individual elements to make a weaker computer player. This provides an easy method to allow for different difficulty levels in the game. The highest difficulty level would use all the steps of the algorithm, and the lowest level might only try to take as many pieces as possible on every turn, with no look-ahead. (Other methods of adding difficulty are covered in Chapter 2.)

SpotValue is the function that returns a numeric value that represents how "good" a move would be, based on how many of the opponent's pieces would be captured by moving there. Additional weighing is given to edge and corner moves. Listing 13-7 describes how to provide artificial intelligence.

Listing 13-7 SpotValue function

```
Function SpotValue% (ByVal x, ByVal y, PColor%)

'-----------------------------------------------
'calculates how "good" given move is, based on how
'many pieces the piece could take by moving here
'-----------------------------------------------

Dim i%, j%              'work variables
Dim origx%, origy%      'original spot
Dim Done%, Found%       'loop terminators
Dim num%                'number opponents in 1 direction
Dim TotalScore%         'holding place for final result

origx = x
origy = y

'try all directions around the piece.  Set Done% if empty location found, or if off edge
'of board.  Set Found% if another one of PColor pieces found.  Use num% to sum
'opponent pieces in between
```

```
For i = -1 To 1
For j = -1 To 1
    If i = 0 And j = 0 Then
        'if both 0, no direction, skip
    Else
        num% = 0
        x = origx: y = origy
        Done% = False: Found% = False

        Do While Not Done And Not Found%
            If (y + j) < 0 Or (x + i) < 0 Or (x + i) = gBoardSize% Or (y + j) = gBoardSize%
            Then Done = True
            Else
                Select Case Board%(x + i, y + j)
                Case 0              'empty spot, done looking this direction
                    Done = True
                Case PColor%        'found a piece of my color at end
                    Found% = True
                Case Else           'must be enemy piece, increment counter and keep going
                    num% = num% + 1
                    x = x + i
                    y = y + j
                End Select
            End If
        Loop
        If Found% Then                  'inc score only if my piece found at end
            TotalScore% = TotalScore% + num%
        End If
    End If
Next
Next

If TotalScore% > 0 Then         'increase score of edges and corners
    If origx = 0 Or origx = gBoardSize% - 1 Then TotalScore% = TotalScore% + 3
    If origy = 0 Or origy = gBoardSize% - 1 Then TotalScore% = TotalScore% + 3
End If

SpotValue% = TotalScore%

End Function
```

If a move exists, Subroutine TryEdges makes the best move on the corners and edges of the board. It does this by calling function SpotValue for all empty edge and corner board locations to get each move's "strength," and maximizing this value to get the best possible move. Corners are tried first; the computer will always move a corner piece if it is available. If a corner is not available, then all edges are tried, and the best edge move is made if one exists. Variable Moved% is set to True if a move is made and returned to the calling program. (See Listing 13-8.)

Listing 13-8 TryEdges subroutine

```
Sub TryEdges (Moved%)

'----------------------------------------------------------------
'Make a move on the edge/corner of the board, if one exists
'----------------------------------------------------------------

Dim i%, j%, r%                'work variables
Dim MaxScore%                 'best spot found value
Dim maxx%, maxy%              'best spot found coords
Dim st%                       'current board value

' try four corners first
i = 0: j = 0: GoSub TryThisOne
i = 0: j = gBoardSize% - 1: GoSub TryThisOne
j = 0: i = gBoardSize% - 1: GoSub TryThisOne
j = gBoardSize% - 1: i = gBoardSize% - 1: GoSub TryThisOne


MaxScore% = 0
For i = 2 To gBoardSize% - 2

      If Board%(0, i) = 0 Then                         'try left edge
          st% = SpotValue(0, i, PUTER)
          If st% > MaxScore% Then
              MaxScore% = st%
              maxx = 0
              maxy = i
          End If
      End If

      If Board%(gBoardSize% - 1, i) = 0 Then       'try right edge
          st% = SpotValue(gBoardSize% - 1, i, PUTER)
          If st% > MaxScore% Then
              MaxScore% = st%
              maxx = gBoardSize% - 1
              maxy = i
          End If
      End If

      If Board%(i, 0) = 0 Then                         'try top edge
          st% = SpotValue(i, 0, PUTER)
          If st% > MaxScore% Then
              MaxScore% = st%
              maxx = i
              maxy = 0
          End If
      End If
```

```
        If Board%(i, gBoardSize% - 1) = 0 Then      'try bottom edge
            st% = SpotValue(i, gBoardSize% - 1, PUTER)
            If st% > MaxScore% Then
                MaxScore% = st%
                maxx = i
                maxy = gBoardSize% - 1
            End If
        End If

Next

If MaxScore% > 0 Then                     'found a move: make it
    gComputerCanMove% = True
    r% = MoveAndChange(maxx%, maxy%, PUTER, True)
    Moved% = True
End If
Exit Sub

'*****************************************

TryThisOne:

If Board%(i, j) = 0 Then
    st% = SpotValue(i, j, PUTER)        'found a move, make it and leave
    If st% > 0 Then
        r% = MoveAndChange(i, j, PUTER, True)
        gComputerCanMove% = True
        Moved% = True
        Exit Sub
    End If
End If
Return
End Sub
```

Subroutine MoveTakeMore (Listing 13-9) is the main artificial intelligence routine of the computer opponent. It first finds the three best moves available on the board. For each of these three moves, it also finds the best move the opponent could make should the computer move there. Finally, it chooses the move that *minimizes* the opponent's best move. (Another routine, MoveTakeLess, is also used by the computer. It is almost identical to MoveTakeMore, but it finds the three *worst* legal moves the computer could make, and then chooses the move that would minimize the captures in the opponent's next turn. The program uses this algorithm for the first two-thirds of the game on higher difficulty levels.) Making the *worst* possible move seems counterintuitive, but the purpose is to minimize countercaptures by the opponent. If the computer takes a long row of pieces, but that row is bordered by an opponent's piece on one end, the opponent can take all the pieces back on the next turn.

Listing 13-9 MoveTakeMore subroutine

```
Sub MoveTakeMore ()

'________________________________
'maximize and make best move
'________________________________

Dim i, j, z%, r%, x%, y%                'work variables
Dim st%                                 'value of current spot
Dim NumPoss%                            'number possible moves
Dim MinVal%, MinMove%                   'minimum value

ReDim MyPossibles%(3, 3)            '(val, x,y)
ReDim HisPossibles%(3, 4)           '(val, x,y,<ptr to MyPossibles> )
ReDim TBoard%(gBoardSize%, gBoardSize%)

For z = 1 To 3
    MyPossibles%(z, 1) = -1
    HisPossibles%(z, 1) = -1
Next

For i = 0 To gBoardSize% - 1
    For j = 0 To gBoardSize% - 1
        TBoard%(i, j) = Board%(i, j)
        If Board%(i, j) = 0 Then
            st% = SpotValue%(i, j, PUTER)        'get three Max moves
            If st% > 0 Then
                NumPoss% = NumPoss% + 1
                gComputerCanMove% = True
            End If
            For z = 1 To 3
                If st% > MyPossibles%(z, 1) Then
                     MyPossibles%(z, 1) = st%
                     MyPossibles%(z, 2) = i
                     MyPossibles%(z, 3) = j
                     Exit For
                End If
            Next
        End If
    Next
Next

'now, for each of the three moves found above, find the BEST possible move the human player
'can make, and save it

For z = 1 To 3

    If MyPossibles(z, 1) > 0 Then                      'Try this Spot
```

```
        r% = MoveAndChange(MyPossibles(z, 2), MyPossibles(z, 3), PUTER, False)
        For i = 0 To gBoardSize% - 1
            For j = 0 To gBoardSize% - 1

                If Board%(i, j) = 0 Then
                    st% = SpotValue%(i, j, HUMAN)        'Maximize his or her best move
                     If st% > HisPossibles%(z, 1) Then
                          HisPossibles%(z, 1) = st%
                          HisPossibles%(z, 2) = i        'not really needed
                          HisPossibles%(z, 3) = j        'not really needed
                          HisPossibles%(z, 4) = z        'points to which MyPos move to make
                     End If
                End If
             Next
         Next

         For x = 0 To gBoardSize% - 1
            For y = 0 To gBoardSize% - 1
                Board%(x, y) = TBoard%(x, y)
            Next
         Next

    End If
Next

'finally, of the three moves, take one that MINIMIZES the human's BEST move

If NumPoss% > 1 Then

    MinVal = 9999
    MinMove = 0
    For i = 1 To 3
     If HisPossibles%(i, 1) < MinVal% And HisPossibles%(i, 1) > -1 Then
            MinVal% = HisPossibles%(i, 1)
            MinMove% = HisPossibles%(i, 4)          'which one of MyPoss
     End If
    Next

    If MinMove% > 0 Then
        r% = MoveAndChange%(MyPossibles(MinMove%, 2), MyPossibles(MinMove%, 3), PUTER, True)
    End If

ElseIf NumPoss% = 1 Then
    r% = MoveAndChange%(MyPossibles(1, 2), MyPossibles(1, 3), PUTER, True)
End If

End Sub
```

Keeping Score

The score in Reversi is simply the number of pieces each player has on the board. This game uses text boxes named ScoreBox(0) and ScoreBox(1) for keeping score. Whenever a piece is laid down on the board or converted to an opponent's piece, routine IncScore, below, is called. The first parameter is the ScoreBox control to update, the second is the amount to update the score by.

```
Sub IncScore (clr%, Amt%)

'-------------------------------
'changes score box score by Amt%
'-------------------------------
Dim oldval%              'original score in box

    oldval% = Val(Mid$(RRev.ScoreBox(clr% - 1).Text, 6))
    RRev.ScoreBox(clr% - 1).Text = Left$(RRev.ScoreBox(clr% - 1).Text, 6) & (oldval% + Amt%)

End Sub
```

In the case of a piece being converted to the opposite color, IncScore is called twice: once to increment the score of the player capturing the piece, and again to decrement the score of the player losing the piece.

```
Call IncScore(PColor%, 1)      'pcolor% is the player capturing
Call IncScore(oppclr%, -1)     'oppclr% is the other player
```

Other score-keeping techniques are covered in Chapter 2.

Creating a Slick Opening Animation Sequence

Routine AnimPutPiece, described above, animates a single piece moving across the board to a final spot. By making a few simple changes, the same routine can serve as a basis for a procedure that simultaneously moves several pieces across the board. These changes are as follows.

- The X and Y origin coordinates, destination coordinates, and current coordinates need to be arrays, not single variables, where each array element represents one of the four objects.
- When saving and replacing the background image behind the pieces, the entire board will be saved and replaced, not just the area around a single piece. On the negative side, this means replacing much more data between frames; however, on the positive side, the background image

doesn't change between frames. Therefore, the background image (the blank board) only needs to be saved once.

With these changes in mind, Listing 13-10 is the OpeningAnimation procedure. An example of the procedure in action is shown in Figure 13-4.

Listing 13-10 OpeningAnimation subroutine

```
Sub OpeningAnimation ()

'-----------------------------------------
'The opening animation sequence.
'4 pieces floating to their initial spots
'-----------------------------------------
Dim r%, i%, j%, lp%, z%    'work variables
Dim Divisions%

ReDim xfrom%(4), yfrom%(4)
ReDim xto%(4), yto%(4)
ReDim inc%(4), idx%(4), clr%(4)
ReDim iinc!(4), jinc!(4)
ReDim ifloat!(4), jfloat!(4)

    'save background
    RRev.BackPic.Height = RRev.BoardPic.Height
    RRev.BackPic.Width = RRev.BoardPic.Width
    r% = BitBlt(RRev.BackPic.hDC, 0, 0, RRev.BoardPic.Width, RRev.BoardPic.Height,
         RRev.BoardPic.hDC, 0, 0, SRCCOPY)

    'set up number of frames from global
    Divisions% = 22 - gDivisions%

    'set four start and end coordinates
    xfrom%(1) = RRev.BoardPic.ScaleWidth
    yfrom%(1) = bTop%(1, 1)
    xto%(1) = bLeft%(3, 3) + PLEFT
    yto%(1) = bTop%(3, 3) + PTOP
    clr%(1) = PUTER

    xfrom%(2) = 0
    yfrom%(2) = 0
    xto%(2) = bLeft%(3, 4) + PLEFT
    yto%(2) = bTop%(3, 4) + PTOP
    clr%(2) = HUMAN

    xfrom%(3) = 0
    yfrom%(3) = RRev.BoardPic.ScaleHeight
    xto%(3) = bLeft%(4, 4) + PLEFT
    yto%(3) = bTop%(4, 4) + PTOP
```

continued on next page

continued from previous page

```
    clr%(3) = PUTER

    xfrom%(4) = RRev.BoardPic.ScaleWidth
    yfrom%(4) = RRev.BoardPic.ScaleHeight
    xto%(4) = bLeft%(4, 3) + PLEFT
    yto%(4) = bTop%(4, 3) + PTOP
    clr%(4) = HUMAN

    For i = 1 To 4
        'random direction for each piece
        If (Rnd * 100) Mod 2 Then
            inc%(i) = -1
        Else
            inc%(i) = 1
        End If
        'random start frame
        idx%(i) = Int(Rnd * 72)

        'pixel increment for each piece, x and y directions
        iinc!(i) = (xto%(i) - xfrom%(i)) / Divisions%
        jinc!(i) = (yto%(i) - yfrom%(i)) / Divisions%
        ifloat!(i) = xfrom%(i): jfloat!(i) = yfrom%(i)

    Next

    'special case: animation not on
    If Not gAnimOn% Then
        Divisions% = 1
        For i = 1 To 4
            ifloat!(i) = xto%(i) - iinc!(i)
            jfloat!(i) = yto%(i) - jinc!(i)
        Next
    End If

    For lp% = 0 To Divisions% - 1

        'restore background
        r% = BitBlt(RRev.BoardPic.hDC, 0, 0, RRev.BoardPic.ScaleWidth,
            RRev.BoardPic.ScaleHeight, RRev.BackPic.hDC, 0, 0, SRCCOPY)

        'place each piece
        For z% = 1 To 4

            idx%(z%) = (idx%(z%) + inc%(z)) Mod 72
            If idx%(z%) < 0 Then idx%(z%) = idx%(z%) + 72

            i = Int(ifloat!(z%) + .5): j = Int(jfloat!(z%) + .5)

            ifloat!(z%) = ifloat!(z%) + iinc!(z%)
            jfloat!(z%) = jfloat!(z%) + jinc!(z%)
```

```
            i = Int(ifloat!(z%) + .5): j = Int(jfloat!(z%) + .5)
            Call pTransparentBlt(clr%(z%) - 1, i, j, idx%(z%))

        Next
        RRev.BoardPic.Refresh
    Next

    'one more restore
    r% = BitBlt(RRev.BoardPic.hDC, 0, 0, RRev.BoardPic.ScaleWidth,
         RRev.BoardPic.ScaleHeight, RRev.BackPic.hDC, 0, 0, SRCCOPY)

    'set the board array and place the final graphic
    Board%(3, 3) = PUTER: Call PutPiece(PUTER, 3, 3, idx%(1))
    Board%(3, 4) = HUMAN: Call PutPiece(HUMAN, 3, 4, idx%(2))
    Board%(4, 4) = PUTER: Call PutPiece(PUTER, 4, 4, idx%(3))
    Board%(4, 3) = HUMAN: Call PutPiece(HUMAN, 4, 3, idx%(4))

End Sub
```

FIGURE 13-4

The opening animation sequence; the four pieces are spinning to their starting spots of the game

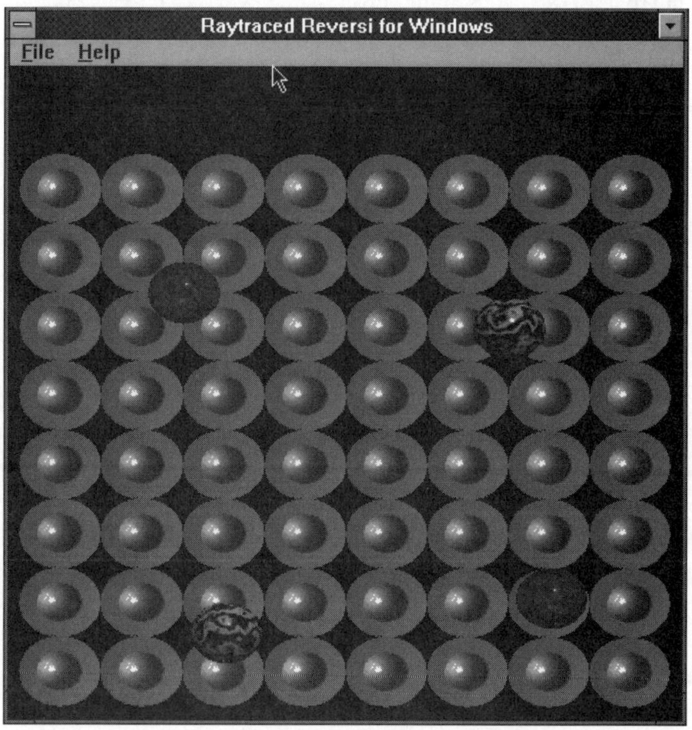

Adding Sound

Chapter 6 covers sound techniques in detail. For the purposes of this game, choose a simple call—the Windows 3.1 routine sndPlaySound. The first parameter passed to this function is the name of a .WAV file, the second is a set of flags that controls how the sound is played.

```
Sub PlayWave (sndname$)

Dim r%
If Len(sndname$) = 0 Then Exit Sub
r% = sndPlaySound(sndname$, SND_ASYNC)

End Sub
```

Below is the calling syntax for the procedure above.

```
Call PlayWave(gAppPath$+"BOING!.WAV")
```

The combination of a reasonably intelligent opponent, along with some spiffy graphics and sounds, should make a classic strategy game like Reversi more interesting than the stock computer board game. Next we'll focus on another specific type of strategy game, the war game, and build a simulation based on the American Civil War.

14

War Games: Blue and Gray

14

War Games: Blue and Gray

The war game is a variation of the more general category of strategy games; war games are strategy games with a historical, or at least pseudo-historical, setting. A strategy game is played using wits rather than hand-eye coordination. The classic strategy war game of western civilization is chess.

In this chapter, you'll learn the basic elements of strategy games: how to build the computer equivalent of a game board, how to place and move pieces around on that board, and how to make the computer program appear to be an intelligent opponent.

Blue and Gray, shown in Figure 14-1, is a war strategy game within the setting of the American Civil War.

How the Game Is Played

In Blue and Gray, the player takes the role of the offense, or blue side, and the computer plays the defense, or gray side. The game takes place on a playing field divided into a 12x12 square game board. Each side has a set number of playing pieces, including cavalry, infantry, and artillery. In addition, the offense has a spy game piece and the defense has a flag piece. The goal of the offense is to capture the defense's flag.

FIGURE 14-1

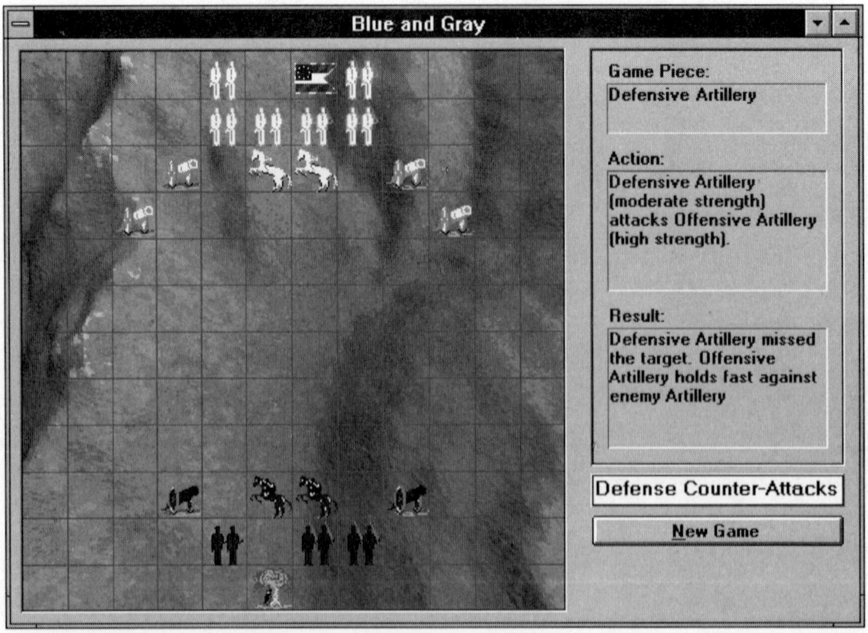

Blue and Gray, a war strategy game

Each side takes turns making a move. A move may be the physical movement of a piece to an adjacent square or an attack on an enemy piece.

With the exception of artillery, a piece must be adjacent to an enemy piece to attack it. An attack is initiated by attempting to move to the enemy's square. If the attacking piece is successful in defeating the enemy piece, it moves to the vanquished piece's square, and the vanquished piece is removed from the game board. Artillery attacks in the same way, but it doesn't have to be adjacent to an enemy piece. Artillery has a limited range, so it becomes ineffective when attacking distant targets.

Each playing piece has a certain strength associated with it. This strength is reduced when a piece is attacked. A piece is defeated (and removed from the game board) when its strength is reduced to zero. To determine the strength of an offensive piece, the player need only move the mouse pointer over it and its strength is displayed in the "Game Piece" area of the game form. Finding out the strength of the defensive pieces is not that easy, but it can be done. The spy game piece can "attack" a defensive piece by attempting to move onto its space. But instead of reducing the strength of the defensive piece, its strength is revealed in the "Result" area of the game form.

To succeed at this game, the player must use strategy to breach the gray side's defenses and capture the flag successfully. The defense has more artillery pieces, which makes a simple frontal assault with infantry and cavalry a dire undertaking. A more creative assault is necessary to win at this game. Now let's see how to build it.

Building Blue and Gray

Create a new project called BLUEGRAY.MAK. In this new project add a new Visual Basic module, called BLUEGRAY.BAS. This module contains the declarations for global constants and variables used throughout the program, as well as an external function declaration for sndPlaySound, the Windows API function for playing wave audio files. This module also contains a Visual Basic subroutine that gives Visual Basic controls a three-dimensional border.

First, add the code in Listing 14-1 to the Declarations section of BLUEGRAY.BAS:

Listing 14-1 BLUEGRAY.BAS Declarations section

```
Option Explicit
'---------------------------------------------------------------------
' global constants, variables and functions used by project.
'---------------------------------------------------------------------

Global Const P_WIDTH = 32         ' Width (in pixels) of playing piece.
Global Const BOARD_DIM = 12       ' Number of playing squares on board.

' ScaleMode constants
Global Const TWIPS = 1
Global Const PIXELS = 3

' RGB color constants
Global Const BLUE = &HFF0000
Global Const RED = &HFF&
Global Const BLACK = &H0&
Global Const YELLOW = &HFFFF&
Global Const GREEN = &HFF00&

' Game States
Global Const GAME_OVER = 0
Global Const SELECT_PIECE = 1
Global Const MOVE_PIECE = 2
Global Const DEFENSE_MOVE = 3

' Maximum number of playing pieces per side.
Global Const MAX_PIECES = 15

' Which side?
Global Const NEITHER = -1
Global Const DEFENSE = 0
Global Const OFFENSE = 1
```

continued on next page

continued from previous page

```
' Game Piece Types
Global Const INFANTRY = 1
Global Const CAVALRY = 2
Global Const ARTILLERY = 3
Global Const SPY = 5
Global Const FLAG = 6

' Strength Constants
Global Const NONE = 0
Global Const LOW = 1
Global Const MODERATE = 2
Global Const HIGH = 3

' Constants for 3D Borders
Global Const BORDER_INSET = 0
Global Const BORDER_RAISED = 1

' Data type that holds the state of a
' single playing piece.
Type tPiece
    side As Integer
    type As Integer
    strength As Integer
    row As Integer
    col As Integer
    ImageEl As Integer
End Type

' The current mouse location in board rows and columns
Global gMouseRow As Integer
Global gMouseCol As Integer

' Array of offensive pieces
Global gOffense(1 To MAX_PIECES)  As tPiece
Global gLastOffense As Integer

' Array of defensive pieces
Global gDefense(1 To MAX_PIECES)  As tPiece
Global gLastDefense As Integer

' Arrays with descriptions of different game properties
' stored as strings
Global gPieceName(1 To 6)  As String
Global gStrengthName(0 To 3) As String
Global gSideName(0 To 1)  As String

' The current game state
Global gGameState As Integer

' The currently selected game piece
Global gCurrentPiece As Integer
```

```
' Functions and constants used to play sounds.
Declare Function sndPlaySound Lib "MMSystem" (ByVal lpsound As String, ByVal FLAG As
Integer) As Integer

Global Const SND_SYNC = &H0         ' Return when sound ends (the default)
Global Const SND_ASYNC = &H1        ' Return as soon as sound starts
```

Particularly noteworthy in this section is the tPiece data type. This data type holds information about each playing piece: which side it's on (offense or defense), what type of piece it is, its strength relative to other pieces, its row and column position on the board, and the icon image associated with it. The two arrays, gOffense and gDefense, contain this information for each side in the game.

Next, add a subroutine that draws a three-dimensional border around any control. Add the code to Make3D to BLUEGRAY.BAS, as shown in Listing 14-2.

Listing 14-2 Make3D subroutine

```
Sub Make3D (AForm As Form, ctl As Control, ByVal BorderStyle As Integer, ByVal
BorderWidth As Integer)
'-----------------------------------------------------------------------
' Wrap a 3D effect around a control on a form.
'-----------------------------------------------------------------------
' Color Constants
Const DARK_GRAY = &H808080
Const WHITE = &HFFFFFF
Const BLACK = &H0

Dim AdjustX As Integer, AdjustY As Integer
Dim RightSide As Single
Dim BW As Integer
Dim LeftTopColor As Long, RightBottomColor As Long
Dim i As Integer
Dim SaveMode As Integer

    If Not ctl.Visible Then Exit Sub

    SaveMode = AForm.ScaleMode
    AForm.ScaleMode = TWIPS

    AdjustX = Screen.TwipsPerPixelX
    AdjustY = Screen.TwipsPerPixelY

    Select Case BorderStyle
        Case 0: ' Inset
            LeftTopColor = DARK_GRAY
            RightBottomColor = WHITE
        Case 1: ' Raised
            LeftTopColor = WHITE
            RightBottomColor = DARK_GRAY
    End Select
```

continued on next page

continued from previous page

```
    ' Set the top shading line.
    For BW = 1 To BorderWidth
        ' Top
        AForm.CurrentX = ctl.Left - (AdjustX * BW)
        AForm.CurrentY = ctl.Top - (AdjustY * BW)
        AForm.Line -(ctl.Left + ctl.Width + (AdjustX * (BW - 1)), ctl.Top - (AdjustY *
        BW)), LeftTopColor
        ' Right
        AForm.Line -(ctl.Left + ctl.Width + (AdjustX * (BW - 1)), ctl.Top + ctl.Height
        + (AdjustY * (BW - 1))), RightBottomColor
        ' Bottom
        AForm.Line -(ctl.Left - (AdjustX * BW), ctl.Top + ctl.Height + (AdjustY * (BW
        - 1))), RightBottomColor
        ' Left
        AForm.Line -(ctl.Left - (AdjustX * BW), ctl.Top - (AdjustY * BW)),
        LeftTopColor
    Next

    AForm.ScaleMode = SaveMode
End Sub
```

The Make3D subroutine accepts four parameters: a form, a control on that form, and a border style and width. A BorderStyle value of 0 draws an inset border around the specified control; a BorderStyle of 1 draws a raised three-dimensional border around it. The BorderWidth parameter tells Make3D how many pixels wide to draw the border. This routine uses the Visual Basic line method to draw a gray and white border on the form itself around the specified control.

Now let's add the main form to the game. Add a new form called BLUEGRAY.FRM to your project. This form will have the objects and properties described in Table 14-1.

TABLE 14-1
Objects and properties of the BLUEGRAY.FRM Form

Object	Property	Setting
Form	FormName	Form1
	BackColor	&H00C0C0C0&
	Caption	"Blue and Gray"
	Height	6435
	Left	900
	ScaleMode	3 'Pixel
	Top	315
	Width	9120

Object	Property	Setting
Label	Name	lbl3DFrame1
	BackStyle	0 'Transparent
	BorderStyle	1 'Fixed Single
	Height	4275
	Left	6180
	Tag	"/3d_inset/"
	Top	120
	Width	2655
Label	Name	Label2
	BackStyle	0 'Transparent
	Caption	"Game Piece:"
	Height	195
	Left	6360
	Top	240
	Width	1815
Label	Name	lblAction
	BackStyle	0 'Transparent
	ForeColor	&H00FF0000&
	Height	1215
	Left	6360
	Tag	"/3d_inset/"
	Top	1380
	Width	2295
Label	Name	Label3
	BackStyle	0 'Transparent
	Caption	"Action:"
	Height	195
	Left	6360
	Top	1140

continued on next page

continued from previous page

Object	Property	Setting
	Width	1215
Label	Name	lblResult
	BackStyle	0 'Transparent
	ForeColor	&H00FF0000&
	Height	1215
	Left	6360
	Tag	"/3d_inset/"
	Top	3000
	Width	2295
Label	Name	Label5
	BackStyle	0 'Transparent
	Caption	"Result:"
	Height	195
	Left	6360
	Top	2760
	Width	1215
Label	Name	lblPrompt
	Alignment	2 'Center
	BackColor	&H0080FFFF&
	BorderStyle	1 'Fixed Single
	Caption	"Game Over"
	FontSize	9.75
	ForeColor	&H00000080&
	Height	315
	Left	6180
	Tag	"/3d_raised/"
	Top	4500
	Width	2655

Object	Property	Setting
PictureBox	Name	picField
	AutoRedraw	-1 'True
	BackColor	&H00808080&
	Height	3195
	Left	120
	Picture	(set at design time in Properties window)
	ScaleMode	3 'Pixel
	Tag	"/3d_inset/"
	Top	120
	Width	4365
CommandButton	Name	btnStart
	Caption	"&New Game"
	Height	315
	Left	6180
	Top	4920
	Width	2655
PictureBox	Name	picInfo
	BackColor	&H00C0C0C0&
	BorderStyle	0 'None
	Height	495
	Left	6360
	Tag	"/3d_inset/"
	Top	480
	Width	2295

Three controls also need to be placed inside the picField PictureBox control on this form. To do this, select the picField control by clicking once on its interior. Then place the controls described in Table 14-2 onto picField's surface. The Shape controls will be used to draw highlighting "boxes" around game pieces. The two Image controls will be used to create a control array of playing piece icons in the Visual Basic program code. Note that the Index property of all these controls is set to 0. Controls are created at design time with their Index property blank; you must set this property to 0 so that these controls can be "cloned" at runtime using the Visual Basic Load function

TABLE 14-2

Objects placed inside the picField control

Object	Property	Setting
Shape	Name	shpHilite
	BackColor	&H00FFFFFF&
	BorderColor	&H000000FF&
	BorderWidth	2
	Height	435
	Index	0
	Left	540
	Top	600
	Visible	0 'False
	Width	495
Shape	Name	shpHilite
	BackColor	&H00FFFFFF&
	BorderColor	&H00FFFFFF&
	BorderWidth	2
	Height	435
	Index	1
	Left	480
	Top	1500
	Visible	0 'False
	Width	495
Image	Name	imgOffense
	Height	480
	Index	0
	Left	1860

Object	Property	Setting
	Picture	(set at design time in Properties window)
	Top	1920
	Visible	0 'False
	Width	480
Image	Name	imgDefense
	Height	480
	Index	0
	Left	2820
	Picture	(set at design time in Properties window)
	Top	1740
	Visible	0 'False
	Width	480

When the form is completed, it should look similar to the one shown in Figure 14-2. As an optional feature, you can also create a bitmap background to simulate terrain and assign it to the picField control's Picture property.

Now you can begin to add the program code to make this game work. Although there are no module-level variables to declare in this game, it's good practice to add the following option in BLUEGRAY.FRM's Declarations section.

```
Option Explicit
'----------------------------------------------------------------------
' CW.FRM
'----------------------------------------------------------------------
```

The Option Explicit statement causes Visual Basic to complain if you fail to declare variables using the Dim statement. This option helps prevent errors that can crop up when you accidentally misspell a variable, such as using a variable called My_Var when you meant to use MyVar. These types of errors can be insidiously difficult to track down.

Now add the Load event in Listing 14-3 to the form. There are quite a number of variables to initialize at the outset, and this is the logical place to handle them.

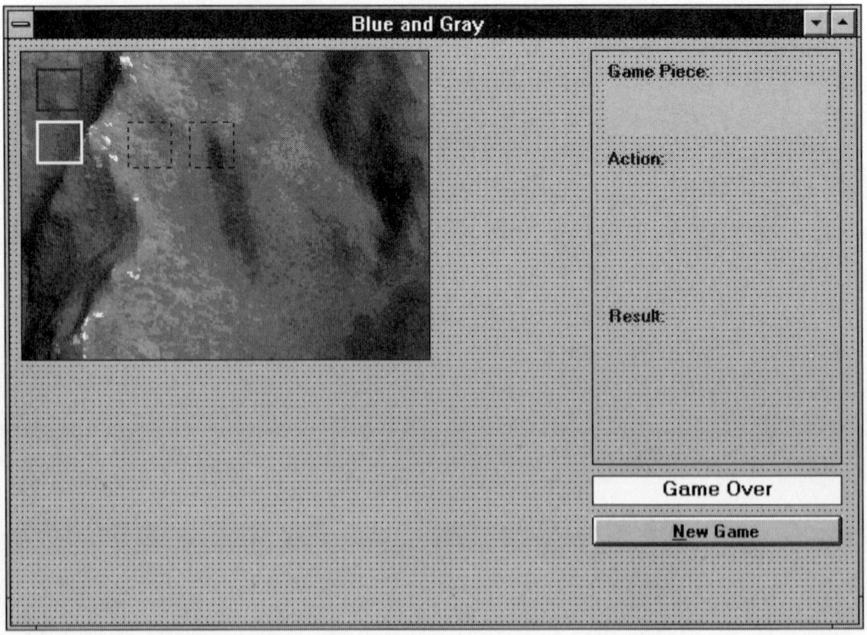

FIGURE 14-2

The Blue and Gray game at design time

Listing 14-3 Load event

```
Sub Form_Load ()
'-----------------------------------------------------------------------
' Set up the playing board and initialize variables used throughout
' the game.
'-----------------------------------------------------------------------
Dim i As Integer
Dim TitleHeight As Integer
Dim BorderWidth As Integer

    Randomize

    ' Calculate the main form's dimensions
    Me.ScaleMode = TWIPS
    BorderWidth = (Me.Width - Me.ScaleWidth)
    TitleHeight = (Me.Height - Me.ScaleHeight - BorderWidth)
    Me.ScaleMode = PIXELS

    picField.Width = BOARD_DIM * P_WIDTH + 1
    picField.Height = picField.Width
```

```
    Me.Height = (picField.Height + (picField.Top * 2)) *
    Screen.TwipsPerPixelY + BorderWidth + TitleHeight

    ' Initialize the highlighting boxes
    shpHilite(0).Width = P_WIDTH + 2
    shpHilite(0).Height = P_WIDTH + 2
    shpHilite(0).ZOrder 0

    shpHilite(1).Width = P_WIDTH + 2
    shpHilite(1).Height = P_WIDTH + 2
    shpHilite(1).ZOrder 0

    ' Center the form on the screen.
    Me.Move (Screen.Width - Me.Width) / 2, (Screen.Height - Me.Height) / 2
    Me.Hide

    ' Set up the playing board.
    For i = 1 To BOARD_DIM - 1
        picField.Line (0, i * P_WIDTH)-(picField.ScaleWidth, i * P_WIDTH),
        RGB(0, 128, 0), BF
        picField.Line (i * P_WIDTH, 0)-(i * P_WIDTH,
        picField.ScaleHeight), RGB(0, 128, 0), BF
    Next

    gLastOffense = 0
    gLastDefense = 0

    ' Piece names used in descriptions.
    gPieceName(INFANTRY) = "Infantry"
    gPieceName(ARTILLERY) = "Artillery"
    gPieceName(CAVALRY) = "Cavalry"
    gPieceName(SPY) = "Spy"
    gPieceName(FLAG) = "Flag"

    ' Strength levels used in descriptions.
    gStrengthName(NONE) = "gone"
    gStrengthName(LOW) = "low"
    gStrengthName(MODERATE) = "moderate"
    gStrengthName(HIGH) = "high"

    ' Names of the sides used in descriptions.
    gSideName(OFFENSE) = "Offensive"
    gSideName(DEFENSE) = "Defensive"

    ' Prepare for the first game.
    btnStart_Click
End Sub
```

Here you set up the dimensions and appearance of the playing field, which is essentially a 12x12 square grid. This is created in a PictureBox control by drawing horizontal and vertical lines to divide the area.

During the course of the game, you need to keep the player informed of the action as it takes place. To help do this, several arrays of strings are set up here, with the names of each side; descriptions of strength, such as high or moderate; and the names of each "piece."

The Load event's last act is to call the btnStart Command Button's Click event. This simulates the player pressing the New Game button on the form, and has the effect of setting up a new game. Add btnStart's Click event, as shown below.

```
Sub btnStart_Click ()
'-----------------------------------------------------------------------
' Start a new game.
'-----------------------------------------------------------------------

    SetupOffense
    SetupDefense
    gGameState = SELECT_PIECE
    lblPrompt = "Select a Piece to Move"
    Me.Show
End Sub
```

This short routine calls to other routines, SetupOffense and SetupDefense, that create and place the playing pieces on the board. The Click event also sets the initial value of the gGameState variable. This important variable helps determine what the player can legally do at any point during the game. For example, a player cannot attack an opponent's piece before selecting one of his or her own to attack with. The game starts in the SELECT_PIECE state, indicating that the only legal action that the player can make is to select one of his or her own pieces.

The player has the role of offensive player and the computer is the defensive player. To set up the offensive pieces, add the following subroutine to the form.

```
Sub SetupOffense ()
'-----------------------------------------------------------------------
' Set up the pieces used by the Offense.
'-----------------------------------------------------------------------
Dim i As Integer

    For i = 1 To gLastOffense
        Unload imgOffense(i)
    Next

    gLastOffense = 1
    InitPiece gLastOffense, OFFENSE, INFANTRY, HIGH, 10, 4

    gLastOffense = gLastOffense + 1
    InitPiece gLastOffense, OFFENSE, CAVALRY, MODERATE, 9, 5

    gLastOffense = gLastOffense + 1
    InitPiece gLastOffense, OFFENSE, ARTILLERY, HIGH, 9, 3
```

```
    gLastOffense = gLastOffense + 1
    InitPiece gLastOffense, OFFENSE, INFANTRY, MODERATE, 10, 6

    gLastOffense = gLastOffense + 1
    InitPiece gLastOffense, OFFENSE, SPY, LOW, 11, 5

    gLastOffense = gLastOffense + 1
    InitPiece gLastOffense, OFFENSE, CAVALRY, HIGH, 9, 6

    gLastOffense = gLastOffense + 1
    InitPiece gLastOffense, OFFENSE, INFANTRY, MODERATE, 10, 7

    gLastOffense = gLastOffense + 1
    InitPiece gLastOffense, OFFENSE, ARTILLERY, MODERATE, 9, 8

End Sub
```

This routine is straightforward because the offensive pieces are always in the same location and have the same strengths. To simplify the creation of pieces, I wrote the InitPiece subroutine. This subroutine, which you will add shortly, also places a piece at a particular row and column on the playing board. For example, the last call to InitPiece in the SetupOffense routine creates a moderately strong artillery piece for the offensive side and places it at row 9, column 8 on the playing board.

Now let's set up the defensive side. Remember, the defense is played by computer, so you'll handle generating the defensive pieces differently from the offense. Add the subroutine in Listing 14-4 to BLUEGRAY.FRM.

Listing 14-4 SetupDefense subroutine

```
Sub SetupDefense ()
'-----------------------------------------------------------------------
' Set up the pieces used by the Defense.
'-----------------------------------------------------------------------
Dim i As Integer
Dim MaxStrength As Integer

    For i = 1 To gLastDefense
        Unload imgDefense(i)
    Next

    gLastDefense = 1

    InitPiece gLastDefense, DEFENSE, FLAG, LOW, 0, 6

    gLastDefense = gLastDefense + 1
    InitPiece gLastDefense, DEFENSE, INFANTRY, NONE, 0, 4
    gLastDefense = gLastDefense + 1
```

continued on next page

continued from previous page

```
    InitPiece gLastDefense, DEFENSE, INFANTRY, NONE, 0, 7
    gLastDefense = gLastDefense + 1
    InitPiece gLastDefense, DEFENSE, INFANTRY, NONE, 1, 4
    gLastDefense = gLastDefense + 1
    InitPiece gLastDefense, DEFENSE, INFANTRY, NONE, 1, 5
    gLastDefense = gLastDefense + 1
    InitPiece gLastDefense, DEFENSE, INFANTRY, NONE, 1, 6
    gLastDefense = gLastDefense + 1
    InitPiece gLastDefense, DEFENSE, INFANTRY, NONE, 1, 7

    gLastDefense = gLastDefense + 1
    InitPiece gLastDefense, DEFENSE, CAVALRY, NONE, 2, 5
    gLastDefense = gLastDefense + 1
    InitPiece gLastDefense, DEFENSE, CAVALRY, NONE, 2, 6

    gLastDefense = gLastDefense + 1
    InitPiece gLastDefense, DEFENSE, ARTILLERY, NONE, 2, 3
    gLastDefense = gLastDefense + 1
    InitPiece gLastDefense, DEFENSE, ARTILLERY, NONE, 2, 8
    gLastDefense = gLastDefense + 1
    InitPiece gLastDefense, DEFENSE, ARTILLERY, NONE, 3, 2
    gLastDefense = gLastDefense + 1
    InitPiece gLastDefense, DEFENSE, ARTILLERY, NONE, 3, 9

    MaxStrength = 24
    For i = 2 To gLastDefense
        gDefense(i).strength = Rnd * 2 + 1
        MaxStrength = MaxStrength - gDefense(i).strength
    Next
    For i = 2 To gLastDefense
        If (MaxStrength > 0) And (gDefense(i).strength < HIGH) Then
            gDefense(i).strength = gDefense(i).strength + 1
            MaxStrength = MaxStrength + 1
        End If
    Next

End Sub
```

Although this routine creates the pieces using the same InitPiece routine as in the SetupOffense subroutine, notice that the pieces are initially given no strength. At the end of the SetupDefense routine, the pieces are assigned random strengths, then these strengths are augmented until a minimum total strength is achieved for the defensive side. This means that for each game, the defensive side has roughly the same overall strength, but how that strength is distributed varies. So an offensive strategy that works for one game may be ineffective in the next, as it would be in real life.

Now you're ready to add the InitPiece routine used in the previous two subroutines. Add the code in Listing 14-5 to the BLUEGRAY.FRM form.

Listing 14-5 InitPiece routine

```
Sub InitPiece (PieceNum As Integer, ASide As Integer, AType As Integer, AStrength As
Integer, ARow As Integer, ACol As Integer)
'---------------------------------------------------------------------
' Initialize a game piece's data structure in preparation for a new
' game.
'---------------------------------------------------------------------
Dim APiece As tPiece
Dim AppPath As String

    APiece.side = ASide
    APiece.type = AType
    APiece.strength = AStrength
    APiece.row = ARow
    APiece.col = ACol

    AppPath = App.Path
    If (Right$(AppPath, 1) <> "\") Then AppPath = AppPath & "\"

    If ASide = OFFENSE Then
        Load imgOffense(PieceNum)
        Select Case AType
            Case INFANTRY:
                imgOffense(PieceNum).Picture = LoadPicture(AppPath & "O_INFTRY.ICO")
            Case CAVALRY:
                imgOffense(PieceNum).Picture = LoadPicture(AppPath & "O_CAVLRY.ICO")
            Case ARTILLERY:
                imgOffense(PieceNum).Picture = LoadPicture(AppPath & "O_ARTLRY.ICO")
            Case SPY:
                imgOffense(PieceNum).Picture = LoadPicture(AppPath & "O_SPY.ICO")
        End Select
        gOffense(PieceNum) = APiece
        DrawIcon imgOffense(PieceNum), ARow, ACol
        imgOffense(PieceNum).Visible = True
    ElseIf ASide = DEFENSE Then
        Load imgDefense(PieceNum)
        Select Case AType
            Case INFANTRY:
                imgDefense(PieceNum).Picture = LoadPicture(AppPath & "D_INFTRY.ICO")
            Case CAVALRY:
                imgDefense(PieceNum).Picture = LoadPicture(AppPath & "D_CAVLRY.ICO")
            Case ARTILLERY:
                imgDefense(PieceNum).Picture = LoadPicture(AppPath & "D_ARTLRY.ICO")
            Case FLAG:
                imgDefense(PieceNum).Picture = LoadPicture(AppPath & "D_FLAG.ICO")
        End Select
        gDefense(PieceNum) = APiece
        DrawIcon imgDefense(PieceNum), ARow, ACol
        imgDefense(PieceNum).Visible = True
    End If
End Sub
```

The InitPiece routine is quite simple, concerned mostly with setting the values in the associated tPiece data structure and loading the correct icon for the particular piece.

The InitPiece subroutine does introduce one new subroutine, called DrawIcon. The playing pieces are displayed on the board as standard 32x32 pixel icons that have been loaded into Image controls. Why handle the pieces this way? Well, icons work like bargain-basement sprites; when they are placed on top of a bitmap, the background can still be seen through the transparent areas of the icon. Because this game doesn't require the constant super-fast movement of images that an arcade game does, Image controls provide a good, easily programmed alternative.

Add the DrawIcon routine, as shown below.

```
Sub DrawIcon (AnImage As Image, r As Integer, c As Integer)
'-------------------------------------------------------------------------
' Move an icon (stored in an image control) to a row/column location.
'-------------------------------------------------------------------------

   AnImage.Move c * P_WIDTH + 2, r * P_WIDTH + 2
End Sub
```

There isn't much to the routine above. It translates a game board row and column location into actual pixel coordinates and places the specified Image control at that location using the Move method. You might wonder why I'd write a subroutine that contains only one line of code. Well, because this subroutine is used throughout the program to move the playing pieces, encapsulating it into a subroutine helps if you decide later to change the way a piece is displayed. Instead of having to find all the appropriate Move methods that you would have strewn through the program, you can simply change the DrawIcon routine.

Now that the pieces are set up, you need to add the code that allows the player to move them. First, though, let's review how the game is played. The player clicks on a piece, which is then highlighted with a red box. The player then has several options: select another piece, in which case the new piece is highlighted; click on an empty square adjacent to the selected piece, indicating that the player wants to move the piece to that location; or if the player is adjacent to an enemy piece, click on that piece, indicating he or she wants to attack that piece. In addition, if the player has selected an artillery piece, he or she may select any enemy piece as a target, though the range of an artillery piece is directly proportional to its current strength.

After the player has taken a turn, as described above, the computer gets a chance to counterattack, but we'll look at that sequence of events later.

From the description above, it should be clear that many of the game actions are initiated through mouse Click events on either the playing board or the playing pieces. For example, the player must first select a piece to move by clicking on it. The selected piece is displayed on the board as an imgOffense Image control, so you'll need to add a Click event for this control; but first, add a MouseMove event for the control.

```
Sub imgOffense_MouseMove (index As Integer, Button As Integer, Shift As Integer, X As
Single, Y As Single)
'------------------------------------------------------------------------
' Give the player information about a piece when the mouse
' is over it.
'------------------------------------------------------------------------

    gMouseRow = gOffense(index).row
    gMouseCol = gOffense(index).col

    picInfo.Cls
    picInfo.ForeColor = BLUE
    picInfo.Print "Offensive "; gPieceName(gOffense(index).type)

    picInfo.Print "Strength is ";
    Select Case gOffense(index).strength
        Case NONE: picInfo.ForeColor = BLACK
        Case LOW: picInfo.ForeColor = RED
        Case MODERATE: picInfo.ForeColor = YELLOW
        Case HIGH: picInfo.ForeColor = GREEN

    End Select
    picInfo.Print UCase$(gStrengthName(gOffense(index).strength))

End Sub
```

Recall that a MouseMove event is fired any time the mouse pointer moves over an object. This event will serve two purposes. First, it sets the gMouseRow and gMouseCol global variables, which track the current position of the mouse on the playing field. Remember that the game views the playing field as a 12x12 game board. The gMouseRow and gMouseCol variables translate the mouse's position from pixels to these game board squares.

The second purpose of imgOffense's MouseMove event is to give the player some information about the game piece the mouse is currently over. This information is in the form of a text description displayed in the picInfo PictureBox control. The name of the piece, which side its on, and its strength are revealed. You may wonder why this information is displayed in a PictureBox control, instead of the more obvious Label control. I wanted to highlight the playing piece's strength using text of a different color—red for low strength, yellow for moderate strength, and green for high strength. This could have been done using separate Label controls and adjusting their ForeColor property, but then I would have had to deal with positioning the labels so they formed a normally spaced sentence. Instead of doing this, I opted for a PictureBox control. Using this control's Print method, you can write text into the PictureBox. Changing the control's ForeColor property changes the color of any text displayed subsequently using the Print method, but doesn't affect any text already printed. And the PictureBox handles the proper sentence spacing.

Now you're ready to add the imgOffense Click event.

```
Sub imgOffense_Click (index As Integer)
'------------------------------------------------------------------------
' If the game is in SELECT_PIECE or MOVE_PIECE state, clicking on an
' offensive piece has the effect of making it the currently selected
' piece.
'------------------------------------------------------------------------

    If (gGameState = SELECT_PIECE) Or (gGameState = MOVE_PIECE) Then
        Highlight 0, gMouseRow, gMouseCol, True
        gCurrentPiece = index
        gGameState = MOVE_PIECE
        lblPrompt = "Move Selected Piece"
    End If
End Sub
```

The guts of this routine are guarded by an If statement that checks the global game state variable, gGameState. This is to ensure that the player doesn't select a game piece at an inopportune time, such as when the computer is in the middle of a counter-attack. The If statement ensures that the game proceeds in an orderly fashion.

Inside the If statement, the actions are quite simple. The highlight routine draws a red square around the selected piece, a global variable is set to track the current piece, the game state variable is changed to indicate that the new state is MOVE_PIECE, and a prompt label is set to help the player understand what the next action should be.

Let's take a look at the Highlight subroutine. Add this subroutine to the project as shown below.

```
Sub Highlight (index As Integer, r As Integer, c As Integer, OnOff As Integer)
'------------------------------------------------------------------------
' Turn on or off the highlight square.
'------------------------------------------------------------------------

    shpHilite(index).Visible = OnOff
    shpHilite(index).Move c * P_WIDTH, r * P_WIDTH
End Sub
```

This routine is used in several places throughout the program. If you recall, when the form was built, two Shape controls were added inside the picField PictureBox control. These shapes were a red and a white square, called shpHilite(0) and shpHilite(1), respectively. These controls are used to highlight a piece or pieces. In the current case, when an offensive piece is selected, the piece is highlighted by displaying the red shpHilite(0) square around the playing piece. The Highlight subroutine displays or erases (by setting the Shape control's Visible property) one of the shpHilite controls at a specified row and column. The Highlight routine is also used later to display the two pieces involved during an attack.

Now that the player has selected a piece to move, let's move the piece. In programming terms, there are only three possiblilities to deal with: the player may click on another one of his or her own pieces, the player may click on an empty square on the game board, or the player may click on an enemy piece. The program has to deal with all three occurrences.

Remember that the game is currently in the MOVE_PIECE state. If the player clicks on another of his or her own pieces, you're covered: The imgOffense control corresponding to that piece will receive a Click event and regard this as a request to select this new piece to move.

If the player clicks on an empty space, this will trigger a Click event for the playing field. But before adding the Click event, let's see what happens when the player moves the mouse pointer over an empty space on the playing field. Add the following picField MouseMove event to the BLUEGRAY.FRM form

```
Sub picField_MouseMove (Button As Integer, Shift As Integer, X As Single, Y As Single)
'------------------------------------------------------------------------
' Set the current board row and column, and clear any information
' displayed in picInfo.
'------------------------------------------------------------------------
Dim r As Integer, c As Integer

    XYtoRC X, Y, gMouseRow, gMouseCol
    picInfo.Cls
End Sub
```

This simple routine translates the mouse's X and Y coordinates into the rows and columns of the game board. It also clears the picInfo PictureBox, which displays information about the game piece currently underneath the mouse pointer. There is no piece at this location, so no information is displayed. Add the XYtoRC routine to the program, as shown below.

```
Sub XYtoRC (ByVal X As Integer, ByVal Y As Integer, r As Integer, c As Integer)
'------------------------------------------------------------------------
' Translate an x-y coordinate into a board row and column.
'------------------------------------------------------------------------

    r = Y \ P_WIDTH
    c = X \ P_WIDTH
End Sub
```

Now let's get back to the player, who wants to move to an empty space on the playing field. Add the following Click event for the picField control.

```
Sub picField_Click ()
'-------------------------------------------------------------------
' If player is in the process of moving a piece, clicking on an empty
' adjacent field will move the piece to that location. This counts
' as a move, so defense will counterattack afterwards.
'-------------------------------------------------------------------
Dim row As Integer
Dim col As Integer

    If gGameState = MOVE_PIECE Then
        gGameState = DEFENSE_MOVE
        row = gOffense(gCurrentPiece).row
        col = gOffense(gCurrentPiece).col

        ' If it's a legal move.
        If ((Abs(row - gMouseRow) <= 1) And (Abs(col - gMouseCol) <= 1)) Then
            Highlight 0, gMouseRow, gMouseCol, False
            MovePiece gOffense(gCurrentPiece), gCurrentPiece, gMouseRow, gMouseCol

            lblAction = "Offense moves " & gPieceName(gOffense(gCurrentPiece).type) & "."
            lblResult = ""
            Pause 1

            ' Execute defensive moves
            DefenseMove
            gGameState = SELECT_PIECE
            lblPrompt = "Select a Piece to Move"
        Else
            gGameState = MOVE_PIECE
            gMouseRow = gOffense(gCurrentPiece).row
            gMouseCol = gOffense(gCurrentPiece).col
        End If
    End If

End Sub
```

First, the Click event makes sure that the game state is MOVE_PIECE, otherwise there's no point in continuing. Next, the Click event checks to see if the move is legal, which means that the piece is adjacent to the empty square. If the move is legal, the Click event turns off the highlighting and moves the piece to its new location. Moving a playing piece is encapsulated in the MovePiece subroutine, shown below.

```
Sub MovePiece (APiece As tPiece, Elem As Integer, row As Integer, col As Integer)
'--------------------------------------------------------------------
' Move a game piece to a specified row and column.
'--------------------------------------------------------------------

    APiece.row = row
    APiece.col = col
    If APiece.side = OFFENSE Then
        DrawIcon imgOffense(Elem), row, col
```

```
    Else
        DrawIcon imgDefense(Elem), row, col
    End If
End Sub
```

The MovePiece routine simply updates the specified playing piece's tPiece data structure with the row and column of its new location, then uses the DrawIcon routine to redisplay the piece's corresponding icon.

Back in the picField Click event, once the player has moved, it's time for the computer to counterattack. This is all handled in the DefenseMove subroutine. We'll look at that a little later. You've seen what happens when the player moves to an empty space. Let's see what happens when a player tries to move onto an enemy-occupied square.

The program knows this happens because the player has clicked the mouse on an imgDefense Image control, one of the defensive pieces. But as with the offensive pieces earlier, let's take a quick look at what happens when the player moves the mouse over an enemy (defensive) piece. Add the following imgDefense MouseMove event to the BLUEGRAY.FRM form.

```
Sub imgDefense_MouseMove (index As Integer, Button As Integer, Shift As Integer, X As
Single, Y As Single)
'----------------------------------------------------------------------
' Display the name of the Defensive piece when the mouse moves over it.
'----------------------------------------------------------------------

    gMouseRow = gDefense(index).row
    gMouseCol = gDefense(index).col

    picInfo.Cls
    picInfo.ForeColor = BLUE
    picInfo.Print "Defensive "; gPieceName(gDefense(index).type)

End Sub
```

This is similar to its counterpart, the imgOffense MouseMove event. The important difference is that the picInfo control displays only the name of the piece; the strength of the enemy piece is not revealed.

Now add the imgDefense Click event as shown in Listing 14-6.

Listing 14-6 The imgDefense_Click event

```
Sub imgDefense_Click (index As Integer)
'---------------------------------------------------------------------
' Clicking on a defensive piece indicates an attack on that piece by
' the player (offense), if the game state is MOVE_PIECE. After the
' offensive move is completed, Defense counterattacks.
'---------------------------------------------------------------------
Dim row As Integer
```

continued on next page

continued from previous page

```
Dim col As Integer
Dim Defeated As Integer
Dim LegalMove As Integer

    If gGameState = MOVE_PIECE Then
        row = gOffense(gCurrentPiece).row
        col = gOffense(gCurrentPiece).col
        ' If it's a legal move.
        LegalMove = ((Abs(row - gMouseRow) <= 1) And (Abs(col - gMouseCol) <= 1))

        If LegalMove Or (gOffense(gCurrentPiece).type = ARTILLERY) Then
            Highlight 0, gMouseRow, gMouseCol, False
            gGameState = SELECT_PIECE
            lblPrompt = "Select a Piece to Move"

            ' Execute offensive moves
            Defeated = Attack(gOffense(gCurrentPiece), gDefense(index))
            If Defeated Then
                imgDefense(index).Visible = False
                If Not (gOffense(gCurrentPiece).type = ARTILLERY) Then
                    MovePiece gOffense(gCurrentPiece), gCurrentPiece, gDefense(index).row,
                    gDefense(index).col
                End If
            End If

            Pause 3

            ' Execute defensive moves
            DefenseMove
            gGameState = SELECT_PIECE
            lblPrompt = "Select a Piece to Move"

        End If
    End If

End Sub
```

In the Click event, first check that you're in the proper game state (MOVE_PIECE), then determine if the move itself is legal. For most pieces, a legal attack must come from an adjacent square. The exception to this rule is the artillery piece, which can attack any piece, although the success of its attack is far from assured.

If the move is a legal attack move, the Attack function is called. This function accepts two tPiece parameters: the piece that is attacking and the piece that is being attacked. Add the Attack function, as shown in Listing 14-7.

Listing 14-7 The Attack function

```
Function Attack (Attacker As tPiece, Defender As tPiece) As Integer
'---------------------------------------------------------------------
' One player attacks another. This routine is used by both sides to
' determine the outcome of an attack by one piece against another.
'---------------------------------------------------------------------
```

```
Dim OldStrength As Integer
Dim Distance As Double
Dim i As Integer
Dim AppPath As String
Dim SoundFile As String
Dim rc As Integer

    AppPath = App.Path
    If Right$(AppPath, 1) <> "\" Then AppPath = AppPath & "\"

    OldStrength = Defender.strength
    Describe Attacker, Defender
    Select Case Attacker.type
        Case INFANTRY:
            Select Case Defender.type
                Case INFANTRY:
                    Defender.strength = Defender.strength - 1
                Case ARTILLERY, CAVALRY:
                    If (Attacker.strength > Defender.strength) Then
                        Defender.strength = Defender.strength - 1
                    End If
            End Select
            SoundFile = "GUNFIRE.WAV"
        Case ARTILLERY:
            Distance = GetDistance(Attacker, Defender)
            If Distance <= (Attacker.strength * 2) Then
                Defender.strength = Defender.strength - 1
            End If
            SoundFile = "CANNON.WAV"
        Case CAVALRY:
            Select Case Defender.type
                Case INFANTRY:
                    Defender.strength = Defender.strength - 2
                Case ARTILLERY, CAVALRY:
                    Defender.strength = Defender.strength - 1
            End Select
            SoundFile = "GALLOP.WAV"
        Case SPY:
            SoundFile = "THUNDER.WAV"
    End Select

    ' Give the spy a chance...
    If Defender.type = SPY Then
        If (Rnd * 15) = 3 Then
            Defender.strength = 0
        End If
    ' The player got the flag!
    ElseIf (Defender.type = FLAG) And (Attacker.type <> SPY) Then
        gGameState = GAME_OVER
        lblPrompt = "Game Over"

    End If
```

continued on next page

continued from previous page

```
    If (SoundFile <> "") Then rc = sndPlaySound(AppPath & SoundFile, SND_ASYNC)

    If Attacker.side = OFFENSE Then
        lblResult.ForeColor = BLUE
    Else
        lblResult.ForeColor = RED
    End If

    ' Describe the results of the attack in the lblResult label.
    lblResult = gSideName(Defender.side) & " "
    lblResult = lblResult & gPieceName(Defender.type)
    If Defender.strength <= 0 Then
        Defender.strength = 0
        Attack = True
        lblResult = lblResult & " defeated."
    ElseIf OldStrength > Defender.strength Then
        Attack = False
        lblResult = lblResult & " sustains casualties."
    Else
        Attack = False
        If Attacker.type = SPY Then
            lblResult = gSideName(Attacker.side) & " Spy observes that enemy "
            lblResult = lblResult & gPieceName(Defender.type) & " strength is "
            lblResult = lblResult & gStrengthName(Defender.strength) & "."
        Else
            If Attacker.type = ARTILLERY Then
                lblResult = gSideName(Attacker.side) &
                            " Artillery missed the target. " & lblResult
            End If
            lblResult = lblResult & " holds fast against enemy " &
                        gPieceName(Attacker.type)
        End If
    End If

    ' Blink the attacker and attacked pieces.
    For i = 1 To 5
        Highlight 1, Defender.row, Defender.col, True
        Highlight 0, Attacker.row, Attacker.col, True
        Pause .25
        Highlight 1, Defender.row, Defender.col, False
        Highlight 0, Attacker.row, Attacker.col, False
        Pause .25
    Next
End Function
```

An attack is resolved by a set of rules based mainly on the types of pieces involved. The attack routine makes liberal use of Select Case statements to perform specific actions based on the types of both the attacker and the defender. Let's look at a particular case: a cavalry piece attacks an infantry piece. Look in the Select Case Attacker.type statement for the Case CAVALRY: entry. Subordinate to the Case

CAVALRY is a Select Case Defender.type statement. Within this statement is a Case INFANTRY: entry. The statement subordinate to this is

```
Defender.strength = Defender.strength - 2
```

This indicates that when a cavalry piece attacks an infantry piece, the infantry piece will lose two strength points. This is how most of the attacks work, with a specific action based on the types of the two pieces. There are some notable exceptions to this rule.

When a spy "attacks," the defending piece does not lose any strength. Rather, the defender's strength is revealed to the player. This can be helpful in determining how to mount an attack. Likewise, a spy can be attacked, but its chances of being defeated are based on the outcome of a randomly generated number.

Attacks by artillery pieces are also handled differently. The distance between the attacking artillery piece and the defending piece is calculated. If the distance is less than twice the artillery's strength value (admittedly an arbitrary value), then the attack is successful and the defender loses a strength point. Otherwise, the attack has no effect. To determine the distance between two pieces, the GetDistance function is used. Add this function, as shown below.

```
Function GetDistance (A As tPiece, B As tPiece) As Double
'----------------------------------------------------------------------
' Calculate the linear distance between two squares.
'----------------------------------------------------------------------

    GetDistance = Sqr((Abs(A.row - B.row) ^ 2) + (Abs(A.col - B.col) ^ 2))
End Function
```

During an attack, you want to let the player know what is transpiring. First, you want to tell the player who is attacking whom. This action is displayed in the lblAction Label control by way of the Describe subroutine, shown in Listing 14-8.

Listing 14-8 Describe subroutine

```
Sub Describe (Attacker As tPiece, Defender As tPiece)
'-----------------------------------------------------------------------
' Describe (in the lblAction label) what action the attacker is taking.
'-----------------------------------------------------------------------
Dim Desc As String
Dim ActionVerb As String

    Desc = ""

    If Attacker.type = SPY Then
        ActionVerb = "spies on"
    Else
        ActionVerb = "attacks"
    End If
```

continued on next page

continued from previous page

```
        Desc = gSideName(Attacker.side)
        Desc = Desc & " " & gPieceName(Attacker.type)
        Desc = Desc & " (" & gStrengthName(Attacker.strength) & " strength) "
        Desc = Desc & ActionVerb & " "
        Desc = Desc & gSideName(Defender.side) & " "
        Desc = Desc & gPieceName(Defender.type) & " ("
        Desc = Desc & gStrengthName(Defender.strength) & " strength). "

        If Attacker.side = OFFENSE Then
           lblAction.ForeColor = BLUE
        Else
           lblAction.ForeColor = RED
        End If

        lblAction = Desc

End Sub
```

Given the attacking and defending pieces, this routine can construct a sentence that describes the action taking place. For example, this routine might generate the sentence "Defensive cavalry attacks offensive infantry" or "Offensive spy spies on defensive artillery."

In the Attack function, you also describe the results of the attack. If the attack caused a reduction in the defender's strength, "Defensive cavalry sustains casualties" might be displayed.

When a defending piece's strength is reduced to zero, the piece is defeated and its image icon is removed from the board. This is done by setting the piece's associated Image control's Visible property to False.

During the attack, the defending and attacking pieces are both highlighted (using the Highlight subroutine). Also, a wave audio (.WAV) file with an appropriate sound effect is played.

The player has human intelligence to develop a strategy, but the computer's defensive moves must all be preprogrammed. After each move by the player, the computer counterattacks. These counterattacks are handled in the DefenseMove subroutine, shown in Listing 14-9.

Listing 14-9 DefenseMove subroutine

```
Sub DefenseMove ()
'-----------------------------------------------------------------------
' Defense Counterattacks. The computer plays defense, so we must
' try to make the computer relatively intelligent.
'-----------------------------------------------------------------------
Dim i As Integer
Dim r As Integer
Dim c As Integer
Dim side As Integer
```

```
Dim element As Integer
Dim Defeated As Integer
Dim WorkingArtillery As Integer
Dim NearestTarget As Integer
Dim NearestDistance As Double
Dim Distance As Double

    element = -1
    gGameState = DEFENSE_MOVE
    lblPrompt = "Defense Counter-Attacks"

    ' Look for enemy adjacent to us.
    For i = 1 To gLastDefense
        r = gDefense(i).row
        c = gDefense(i).col
        If imgDefense(i).Visible Then
            ' N
            If WhatPieceHere(side, element, r - 1, c) = OFFENSE Then
            ' NE
            ElseIf WhatPieceHere(side, element, r - 1, c + 1) = OFFENSE Then
            ' E
            ElseIf WhatPieceHere(side, element, r, c + 1) = OFFENSE Then
            ' SE
            ElseIf WhatPieceHere(side, element, r + 1, c + 1) = OFFENSE Then
            ' S
            ElseIf WhatPieceHere(side, element, r + 1, c) = OFFENSE Then
            ' SW
            ElseIf WhatPieceHere(side, element, r + 1, c - 1) = OFFENSE Then
            ' W
            ElseIf WhatPieceHere(side, element, r - 1, c) = OFFENSE Then
            ' NW
            ElseIf WhatPieceHere(side, element, r - 1, c - 1) = OFFENSE Then
            End If

            If side > 0 Then Exit For
        End If
    Next

    ' If someone is close by, attack him.
    If side > 0 Then
        Defeated = Attack(gDefense(i), gOffense(element))
        If Defeated Then
            imgOffense(element).Visible = False
            If Not (gDefense(i).type = ARTILLERY) Then
                MovePiece gDefense(i), i, gMouseRow, gMouseCol
            End If
        End If
    Else
        ' Look for target to shoot artillery at.
        WorkingArtillery = -1
        For i = 1 To gLastDefense
```

continued on next page

continued from previous page

```
            If gDefense(i).type = ARTILLERY And imgDefense(i).Visible Then
                WorkingArtillery = i
                Exit For
            End If
        Next
        NearestDistance = 100
        If WorkingArtillery > 0 Then
            For i = 1 To gLastOffense
                If imgOffense(i).Visible Then
                    Distance = GetDistance(gDefense(WorkingArtillery), gOffense(i))
                    If Distance < NearestDistance Then
                        NearestDistance = Distance
                        NearestTarget = i
                    End If
                End If
            Next
            Defeated = Attack(gDefense(WorkingArtillery), gOffense(NearestTarget))
            If Defeated Then
                imgOffense(NearestTarget).Visible = False
            End If
        End If
    End If
End Sub
```

Making a computer program intelligent is a virtually impossible task, and certainly one far beyond the scope of this book. Making a program *appear* intelligent is considerably easier, and this is what you are trying to accomplish with the DefenseMove routine.

It is DefenseMove's job to select an attacking piece and a target piece. It does this by first traversing the gDefense array, looking for any visible playing piece with an offensive piece next to it. The thinking here is that the biggest threat to the defense is nearby. The defense will attack the first adjacent enemy piece it finds.

If there are no targets nearby, the defense will look for a target at which to shoot its artillery. In the early stages of the game, this will be the standard counterattack move. Initially, an artillery attack will be ineffective; even a high strength artillery piece is too far away to hit an offensive piece in its initial position. But the DefenseMove routine uses the GetDistance routine to select the target closest to the artillery piece, thus ensuring the better result.

These two strategies, attacking adjacent pieces or firing artillery, make up the entire strategy for the computer's defensive side. As it turns out, these are very effective strategies. The player will find it very difficult in most games to do significant damage by attempting a simple frontal attack. Pieces that move within range of the enemy artillery will be decimated methodically, and the defensive side has twice the artillery pieces of the offense.

The DefenseMove routine calls the same Attack function introduced earlier. The actual attack is handled in exactly the same way, regardless of which side is doing it.

The DefenseMove routine calls a support routine that hasn't been used elsewhere: the WhatPieceHere routine. This simple routine is used when searching for a nearby offensive target. Given a row and column on the board, this routine tells what playing piece, and which side it's on, is at that location. This routine is called once for each of the eight squares around a defensive piece. The first offensive piece found becomes the target of an attack.

Add the WhatPieceHere function, as shown below.

```
Function WhatPieceHere (side As Integer, element As Integer, r As Integer, c As Integer) As
Integer
'---------------------------------------------------------------------
' Determine what piece (if any) is at this row and column.
'---------------------------------------------------------------------
Dim i As Integer

    side = NEITHER

    ' Check Offense
    For i = 1 To gLastOffense
        If (gOffense(i).row = r) And (gOffense(i).col = c) And (imgOffense(i).Visible) Then
            side = OFFENSE
            element = i
            Exit For
        End If
    Next

    ' Check Defense
    For i = 1 To gLastDefense
        If (gDefense(i).row = r) And (gDefense(i).col = c) And (imgDefense(i).Visible) Then
            side = DEFENSE
            element = i
            Exit For
        End If
    Next
    WhatPieceHere = side
End Function
```

The WhatPieceHere function traverses the gOffense and gDefense arrays, looking for one that is visible and at the specified row and column positions. Now all that remains are a couple of support routines. The first, called Pause, is used to delay processing for a few seconds or fractions of a second. Sometimes computers can process things too fast, and you need to introduce a delay. In this case, you display the results of an attack by the player in a Label control, followed immediately by the computer's counterattack and its result. If you did this as quickly as the computer is capable of, the player would not be able to read the results of an attack within the lblResult Label control before its text was replaced with the results of the counterattack. To overcome this problem, introduce a few seconds of pause between the attack and counterattack.

Add the Pause routine, as shown below.

```
Sub Pause (Seconds As Single)
'------------------------------------------------------------------------
' Pause for a specified number of seconds.
'------------------------------------------------------------------------
Dim StartTime As Single

    StartTime = Timer

    Do
        DoEvents
    Loop Until (Timer - StartTime) >= Seconds
End Sub
```

Finally, add a Paint event to the BLUEGRAY.FRM form. This routine handles drawing three-dimensional borders around selective controls, using the Make3D routine introduced earlier in this chapter. Add the Paint routine, as shown below.

```
Sub Form_Paint ()
'------------------------------------------------------------------------
' Put a 3D border around any control tagged "/3D_INSET/" or "/3D_RAISED/."
'------------------------------------------------------------------------
Dim i As Integer

    For i = 0 To Me.Controls.Count - 1
        If UCase$(Me.Controls(i).Tag) = "/3D_RAISED/" Then
            Make3D Me, Me.Controls(i), BORDER_RAISED, 1
        ElseIf UCase$(Me.Controls(i).Tag) = "/3D_INSET/" Then
            Make3D Me, Me.Controls(i), BORDER_INSET, 1
        End If
    Next

End Sub
```

The Paint event shows a trick I've found very useful: using a control's Tag property to hold special information. This routine looks at the Tag property of each control on the form for the string "/3D_INSET/" or "/3D_RAISED/". If either string is found, the control is passed to the Make3D routine, which draws a three-dimensional border around the control.

Improving and Extending Blue and Gray

This game was designed to be easy to extend. In particular, the DefenseMove and Attack routines can easily be extended to increase the complexity of the game, make the game more realistic, and make the computer opponent appear more intelligent.

For example, you might want to add to the DefenseMove routine a strategy where selective pieces, such as cavalry or infantry, would move closer to the flag to protect it. Or you could make attacks more realistic by basing them on the relative strengths of each piece. If a moderate strength infantry piece attacks a high strength infantry piece, it probably would not cause as much damage as two evenly matched infantry pieces would.

The game could also be extended to add whole new types of pieces or different layouts for each side. You could even let the player select the quantity and types of each piece for the offense.

Next, we'll look at one of the oldest categories of computer games, one that predates the age of the personal computer: the adventure game.

15

Adventure Games: VB Adventure

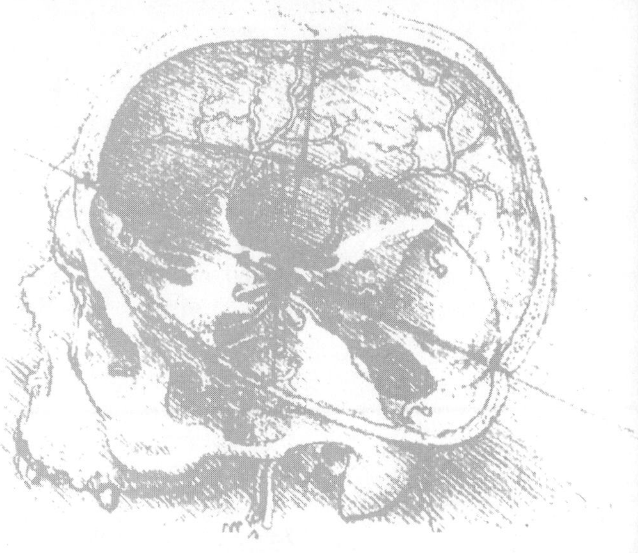

15

Adventure Games: VB Adventure

The game presented here has a noble lineage. Its ancestry dates back to the Massachusetts Institute of Technology (MIT) in the early 1970s, where a programmer named Will Crowther wrote a program designed to let a computer referee a fantasy role-playing game. The program ran on a DEC PDP-10. That program was then modified by Don Woods, who turned it into what we now call a text adventure game. The program was originally called ADVENT (due to the six-character limitation for file names on the TOPS-10 operating system) and later it was known simply as Adventure.

Adventure ran on a text-based terminal. There were no graphics. The player navigated through a world of underground caves by typing simple commands like "go north." Along the way, players encountered monsters and dwarves and, if they didn't get killed, maybe even a little treasure.

Perhaps because of its simplicity, Adventure was incredibly compelling and hugely addictive. The world of Adventure was described only in words; it was up to the players to fill in the rest with their imagination.

Today, computers are everywhere. They can display graphics in over 16 million colors, show movies, and play realistic stereo sound. But the adventure game still survives.

The game presented in this chapter owes much to the original Adventure, while taking full advantage of the abilities of the modern PC. The game includes pictures and sound, but attempts to retain the best qualities of the original. The player is still presented with text describing the situation, but the player's movements and actions are now performed with a mouse.

How to Play VB Adventure

VB Adventure is a game of exploration and danger. The premise of the game, as shown in Figure 15-1, is that the player is separated from his or her tour group and must find it.

Game play is simple. The player sees his or her current location in a bitmap in the upper left of the form. Below the bitmap is a text description. This text may present additional clues, hints, and information.

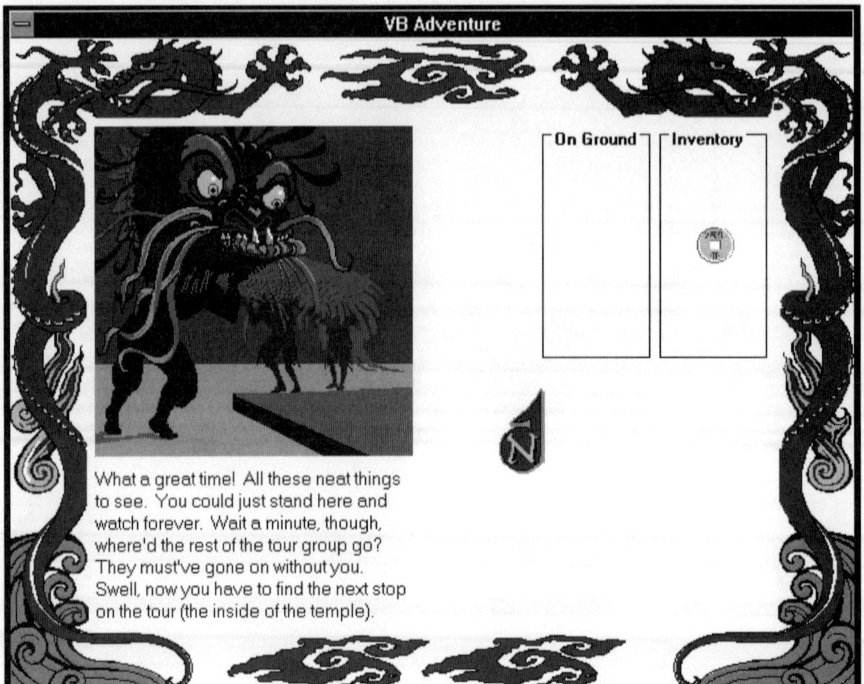

FIGURE 15-1

The VB Adventure game

The player moves by pressing one of the available action buttons. These buttons usually provide compass directions, such as north or east. Only certain buttons are available at any location. For example, in Figure 15-1, the player can only go in a northerly direction.

In the upper-right corner are two frames, one marked "On Ground" and the other marked "Inventory." When the player enters a new location, objects at that location may appear in the On Ground frame. The player can pick up these objects by dragging them to the Inventory frame. Other frames may occasionally appear, letting the player give objects to a person or place objects into or onto other objects.

Those are the rules needed to play the game. Now let's see how the game was constructed.

Building VB Adventure

The world of VB Adventure is described almost entirely in a text file that I'll call a *description file*. The file describes the items and locations (called *rooms*) in the virtual world of VB Adventure.

The text file is divided into three sections: item definitions, command definitions, and room definitions. We'll look at each of these sections in turn. But first, create a new file, using a text editor such as Windows Notepad. Create a new file called ADVEN.DSC and add the following lines to the file.

```
ITEM DEFINITIONS

Item Name: Coin
Picture: COIN.ICO|COINDRAG.ICO

Item Name: Shovel
Picture: SHOVEL.ICO|SHOVDRAG.ICO

Item Name: Incense
Picture: INCENSE.ICO|INCEDRAG.ICO

Item Name: BBQ Pork
Picture: BBQPORK.ICO|BBQPDRAG.ICO
```

The *Item Definitions* section describes the objects that exist in the adventure world. This section also shows the syntax used in the description file. Each section is headed by a section name, in this case ITEM DEFINITIONS. Subsequent nonblank lines follow the basic format:

```
KEYWORD: VALUE
```

In the Item Definitions section, there are two keywords, *Item Name* and *Picture*. The Item Name is a simple description of an object. The Picture indicates the icon files used to display the object. The first icon is shown within the frame boxes, whereas the second icon is displayed when the player drags the object between frames.

The second section of the description file describes different actions the player may take. Add this section, called *Command Definitions,* to ADVEN.DSC, as shown below.

```
COMMAND DEFINITIONS

Action Name: North
Picture: NORTH.BMP
PictureDown: NORTHD.BMP
X: 5520
Y: 3820

Action Name: South
Picture: SOUTH.BMP
PictureDown: SOUTHD.BMP
X: 5520
Y: 5290

Action Name: East
Picture: EAST.BMP
PictureDown: EASTD.BMP
X: 6030
Y: 4780

Action Name: West
Picture: WEST.BMP
PictureDown: WESTD.BMP
X: 4560
Y: 4780

Action Name: Dig
Picture: DIG.BMP
PictureDown: DIGD.BMP
X: 4800
Y: 3820
```

The Command Definitions section defines a series of commands. These commands usually deal with navigation through the various rooms that make up the adventure. A command is described by an *Action Name* keyword, such as West or North or Dig. Each command also has two corresponding bitmaps. These bitmaps are used to create a simulated push button that the player uses to execute the command. The Picture keyword gives the file name of the button bitmap in its up position, while the PictureDown keyword provides the bitmap file name for the button in its down position. The X and Y keywords specify the location of the button on the Visual Basic form.

The final section, *Room Definitions,* describes the rooms that make up the adventure. The description includes objects in the room, audio wave files to be played when the room is entered, and commands that can be used while in the room. ("Room" is a general term used to describe a specific location in the adventure. A room may be a section of a street or a place in the woods or just about anything the adventure creator can describe.)

Add the Room Definitions section to the ADVEN.DSC file, as shown in Listing 15-1.

Listing 15-1 Room Definitions

```
ROOM DEFINITIONS

Room Name: TouristTrap
Description: What a great time!  All these neat things to see.  You could just stand
here and watch forever.  Wait a minute, though, where'd the rest of the tour group go?
They must've gone on without you.  Swell, now you have to find the next stop on the
tour (the inside of the temple).
Command: North|GO Village2
Picture: TOURTRAP.BMP
Sound: FIRECRAK.WAV

Room Name: Village2
Description: You're just entering a small village.  The road goes north and south here.
Command: North|GO Village3
Command: South|GO TouristTrap
Picture: VILLAGE1.BMP

Room Name: Village3
Description: You're on the outskirts of a small village.  The road here goes north,
south, and west.
Command: North|GO VillageDog
Command: South|GO Village2
Command: West|GO Village4
Picture: VILLAGE2.BMP

Room Name: Village4
Description: You're in a side street on the outskirts of a small village.  The road
here goes south and east.
Command: South|GO Restaurant
Command: East|GO Village3
Picture: VILLAGE1.BMP

Room Name: Restaurant
Description: You're in a small restaurant.  The waiter would like to take your order
now.  You can leave to the north.
```

continued on next page

continued from previous page

```
Command: North|GO Village4
Picture: WAITER.BMP
Container: Waiter|Coin|CREATE BBQ Pork|The waiter takes the money, thanks you, and
leaves ... he comes back momentarily with a small plate of barbeque pork.

Room Name: VillageDog
Description: You're in a small village.  There's a nasty, frothing, snarling dog here.
He doesn't seem to like you.
Command: North|GO Village7|DogFood|The dog snarls and bites and generally blocks your
way.
Command: South|GO Village3
Picture: VILLADOG.BMP
Sound: DOG.WAV
Container: Dog|BBQ Pork|SET DogFood|The dog seems to calm down as it munches on the
meat.

Room Name: Village7
Description: You're on a road near the center of a small village.  The road turns here.
It goes south and west.
Command: South|GO VillageDog
Command: West|GO Village8
Picture: VILLAGE2.BMP

Room Name: Village8
Description: You're at a crossroads in the center of a small village.  To the north you
can see an ornate building.  To the west looks like a small farm.  To the south and
east are more villages.
Command: North|GO Temple
Command: South|GO Village9
Command: East|GO Village7
Command: West|GO Field10
Picture: VILLAGE1.BMP

Room Name: Village9
Description: You're on a small side street in the village.  The road turns here.  You
can go north or west.
Command: North|GO Village8
Command: West|GO Village11
Picture: VILLAGE2.BMP

Room Name: Field10
Description: You're in an entrance to a big field.  You can see a farmer here.  He's
working with his back to you.
Command: South|GO Village11
Command: East|GO Village8
Command: West|GO Field13
Command: Dig
Picture: FIELD.BMP
Sound: FIELD.WAV

Room Name: Village11
```

```
Description: You're on a small side street on the west end of the village.  Quite a
ways to the west you can see a farm.  The road here leads north, south, and east.
Command: North|GO Field10
Command: South|GO Village12
Command: East|GO Village9
Picture: VILLAGE1.BMP

Room Name: Village12
Description: This is a dead end street.  You can go north.
Command: North|GO Village11
Picture: VILLAGE2.BMP
Item: Shovel

Room Name: Field13
Description: You're in the middle of a big field.  To the south you can see something
... you can't quite tell what.
Command: South|GO Field14
Command: East|GO Field10
Command: Dig
Picture: FIELD.BMP
Sound: FIELD.WAV

Room Name: Field14
Description: You're in the far end of a big field.  You're next to a small mound of
freshly disturbed dirt.
Command: North|GO Field13
Command: Dig|CREATE Incense|Shovel|The ground is too hard here.  You need some kind of
digging tool.
Picture: FIELD.BMP
Sound: FIELD2.WAV

Room Name: Temple
Description: You're outside a huge ornate temple.  There are people milling around
here.  Right in the middle of the path in front of the entrance is a brazier with
incense burning in it.  You can go north (into the temple) or south (back to the
village).
Command: North|GO InnerTemple|BurnIncense|A priest stops you.  He says there is
something you must do first ... then he walks off.
Command: South|GO Village8
Picture: TEMPLEO.BMP
Sound: GONG.WAV
Container: Brazier|Incense|SET BurnIncense|You feel a sense of peace as the incense
burns with the incense placed there by others ...

Room Name: InnerTemple
Description: You're inside the temple.  You found your tour group!  The End.  You've
done it!
Command: South|GO Temple
Picture: TEMPLEI.BMP
Sound: END.WAV
```

(Please note that some of the keyword statements in the section above span multiple lines. In your file, these statements should all be contained on a single text line.)

To see how rooms are defined, let's look at one room described above, the room named VillageDog. After the Description keyword, you'll see a few sentences. These sentences describe where the player is ("You're in a small village.") and what the situation is ("There's a nasty, frothing, snarling dog here. He doesn't seem to like you.").

Next, there are two lines containing Command keywords. These statements describe the commands available in this room. From the VillageDog room, the player can only move north or south. In fact, the player can only move north under certain circumstances, but I'll explain that in a moment.

Next, there are Picture and Sound keywords, which specify file names of the large bitmap picture of the room and the wave audio file heard when the room is entered. A Sound statement is optional, but you should always supply a Picture statement.

The Container statement describes an object in the room. This object is called a container because it can be given an item. A specific item may evoke a response when placed in a container.

In the VillageDog room, there is one container, called Dog. Look at the Container statement for Dog:

```
Container: Dog|BBQ Pork|SET DogFood|The dog seems to calm down as it
munches on the meat.
```

To the VB Adventure program, this statement says, "There is a dog in this room. If the player puts the item 'BBQ Pork' in the dog container, set an internal flag, 'DogFood,' and display the message 'The dog seems to calm down as it munches on the meat' to the player."

This statement has repercussions for the North command described earlier. That statement reads:

```
Command: North|GO Village7|DogFood|The dog snarls and bites and generally
blocks your way.
```

To the VB Adventure program, this statement says, "When the player issues the North command, jump to the room described in section Village7, but only if the DogFood flag has been set. If the DogFood flag has not been set, then present the message 'The dog snarls and bites and generally blocks your way.' to the player."

These two statements (the North command and the Dog container) set up a requirement that the player feed the dog before the player can proceed north. This provides the puzzle element of the VB Adventure game.

This also shows how navigation through the various rooms is handled. In effect, you create hyperlinks between different rooms. This makes it easy to expand the adventure by adding rooms and linking them to existing ones.

Creating the VB Adventure Main Form

Now that you've seen how the Description File describes the flow of the game, let's construct the game itself. Create a new project called ADVEN.MAK. As always, it's recommended that you create a new subdirectory for this project and place all associated files in that subdirectory.

Create a new form called ADVEN.FRM. Add the objects and properties described in Table 15-1 to this form.

TABLE 15-1

Objects and properties of the ADVEN.FRM form

Object	Property	Setting
Form	FormName	Adven
	AutoRedraw	-1 'True
	BorderStyle	3 'Fixed Double
	Caption	"VB Adventure"
	Height	7455
	Left	1065
	Picture	BACKGRND.BMP
	Top	570
	Width	9660
Label	Name	Desc
	BackStyle	0 'Transparent
	Caption	"Desc"
	FontBold	0 'False
	FontSize	9.75
	Height	1695
	Left	960
	Top	4680
	Width	3615
PictureBox	Name	AreaPicture
	AutoRedraw	-1 'True
	AutoSize	-1 'True

continued on next page

continued from previous page

Object	Property	Setting
	BorderStyle	0 'None
	Height	3600
	Left	960
	Top	960
	Width	3600
PictureBox	Name	Action
	AutoRedraw	-1 'True
	AutoSize	-1 'True
	BorderStyle	0 'None
	Height	495
	Index	0
	Left	5280
	Top	4440
	Visible	0 'False
	Width	855
PictureBox	Name	PictureUp
	AutoRedraw	-1 'True
	AutoSize	-1 'True
	BorderStyle	0 'None
	Height	480
	Index	0
	Left	5280
	Picture	(set at design time in Properties window)
	Top	5040
	Visible	0 'False
	Width	930
PictureBox	Name	PictureDown
	AutoRedraw	-1 'True

Object	Property	Setting
	AutoSize	-1 'True
	BorderStyle	0 'None
	Height	480
	Index	0
	Left	5280
	Picture	(set at design time in Properties window)
	Top	5640
	Visible	0 'False
	Width	930
PictureBox	Name	Item
	AutoRedraw	-1 'True
	AutoSize	-1 'True
	BorderStyle	0 'None
	DragMode	1 'Automatic
	Enabled	0 'False
	Height	375
	Index	0
	Left	5340
	Top	3840
	Visible	0 'False
	Width	375
Frame	Name	Ground
	Caption	"On Ground"
	Height	2535
	Left	6000
	Top	960
	Width	1215
Frame	Name	Inventory

continued on next page

continued from previous page

Object	Property	Setting
	Caption	"Inventory"
	Height	2535
	Left	7320
	Top	960
	Width	1215
Frame	Name	Contain
	Caption	"Frame1"
	Height	1455
	Left	4680
	Top	960
	Visible	0 'False
	Width	1215

At design time, your form should look similar to the one shown in Figure 15-2.

Next, you can begin to write the code for VB Adventure. In the Declarations section of ADVEN.FRM, add the following code.

```
Option Explicit
'----------------------------------------------------------------
' ADVEN.FRM
'----------------------------------------------------------------
Const SM_CXDLGFRAME = 7
Const SM_CYDLGFRAME = 8
Const SM_CYSIZE = 31

Declare Function GetSystemMetrics Lib "User" (ByVal nIndex As Integer) As Integer
```

This code defines a Windows API call and some constants used to call it. The GetSystemMetrics call can be used to retrieve a wide range of information about the dimensions of Windows objects such as title bars and borders. This information is not directly available in Visual Basic. This information is used when initially sizing ADVEN.FRM in its Load event. Add this Load event, as shown below.

```
Sub Form_Load ()
'----------------------------------------------------------------
' Adjust the form's size, and load the game's description file.
'----------------------------------------------------------------

    Width = (636 + 2 * GetSystemMetrics(SM_CXDLGFRAME)) * Screen.TwipsPerPixelX
```

FIGURE 15-2

◉ ◉ ◉ ◉ ◉ ◉

The VB Adventure main form at design time

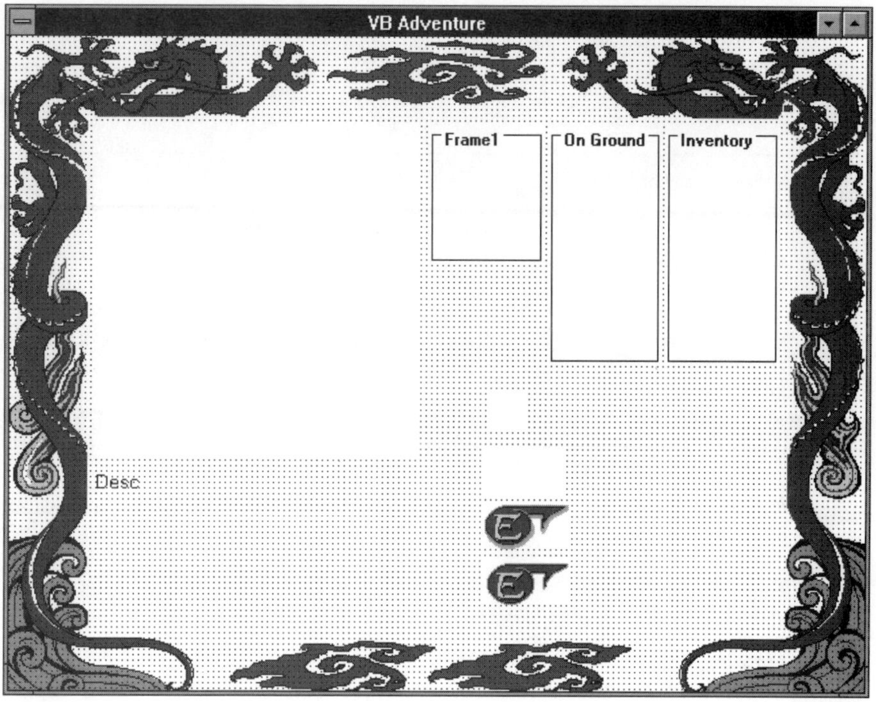


```
    Height = (480 + GetSystemMetrics(SM_CYSIZE) + 2 * GetSystemMetrics(SM_CYDLGFRAME)) *
             Screen.TwipsPerPixelY

    ' load adventure
    AreaLoadFile App.Path & "\ADVEN.DSC"

    ' player starts out with money
    AddInventory "Coin"

    ' go to first room
    AreaChange "TouristTrap"
End Sub
```

The Load event sets the dimensions of the form, then calls a routine to load and parse the description file. Two other routines are called to provide the player with an initial inventory and move to the starting room.

The player performs commands by pressing command buttons. Instead of using boring conventional rectangular command button controls, this game uses custom buttons using the PictureBox control. The Action PictureBox is displayed using an "up" and a "down" bitmap. The player normally sees the "up" bitmap; the "down" bitmap is displayed when the player clicks the mouse down over the Action

PictureBox. Display of the appropriate bitmap is handled in Action's MouseDown and MouseUp events. Add these events, as shown below.

```
Sub Action_MouseDown (Index As Integer, Button As Integer, Shift As Integer, X As
Single, Y As Single)
'------------------------------------------------------------------
' Simulate button click
'------------------------------------------------------------------

    Action(Index).Picture = PictureDown(Index).Picture
End Sub

Sub Action_MouseUp (Index As Integer, Button As Integer, Shift As Integer, X As
Single, Y As Single)
'------------------------------------------------------------------
' Simulate button click
'------------------------------------------------------------------

    Action(Index).Picture = PictureUp(Index).Picture
End Sub
```

Performing the action command itself is handled in the Action PictureBox's Click event. Add this event to the ADVEN.FRM form.

```
Sub Action_Click (Index As Integer)
'------------------------------------------------------------------
' Handles click of action
'------------------------------------------------------------------

    ActionExecute CStr(Action(Index).Tag)
End Sub
```

The Click event calls a subroutine that handles processing the command. The other task the form must perform is processing DragDrop events when items are moved between the Inventory, Ground, and various Container frames. Each frame has a similar DragDrop event. Add these, as shown in Listing 15-2.

Listing 15-2 DragDrop events

```
Sub Contain_DragDrop (Source As Control, X As Single, Y As Single)
'------------------------------------------------------------------
' This event is fired when an object is dropped over a
' container.
'------------------------------------------------------------------

    ' if it's already in inventory, ignore it
    If IsInCurAreaContainer(CStr(Source.Tag)) Then
        Exit Sub
    End If
```

```
    ' add to the inventory
    SetCurAreaContainer CStr(Source.Tag)

    ' if it's in the container, get rid of it
    If IsInInventory(CStr(Source.Tag)) Then
        RemoveInventory CStr(Source.Tag)
    Else
        RemoveCurAreaItem CStr(Source.Tag)
    End If

    ' redraw items
    RedrawAreaItems
End Sub

Sub Ground_DragDrop (Source As Control, X As Single, Y As Single)
'-----------------------------------------------------------------
' This event is fired when an object is dropped over the
' ground frame.
'-----------------------------------------------------------------

    ' ignore if already lying on the ground here
    If IsInCurArea(CStr(Source.Tag)) Then
        Exit Sub
    End If

    ' add to the current area
    AddCurAreaItem CStr(Source.Tag)

    ' if it's in the container, get rid of it
    If IsInCurAreaContainer(CStr(Source.Tag)) Then
        SetCurAreaContainer ""
    Else
        RemoveInventory CStr(Source.Tag)
    End If

    ' redraw items
    RedrawAreaItems
End Sub

Sub Inventory_DragDrop (Source As Control, X As Single, Y As Single)
'-----------------------------------------------------------------
' This event is fired when an object is dropped over the
' inventory frame.
'-----------------------------------------------------------------

    ' if it's already in inventory, ignore it
    If IsInInventory(CStr(Source.Tag)) Then
        Exit Sub
    End If

    ' add to the inventory
```

continued on next page

continued from previous page

```
    AddInventory CStr(Source.Tag)

    ' if it's in the container, get rid of it
    If IsInCurAreaContainer(CStr(Source.Tag)) Then
        SetCurAreaContainer ""
    Else
        RemoveCurAreaItem CStr(Source.Tag)
    End If

    ' redraw items
    RedrawAreaItems
End Sub
```

Finally, the form needs a simple Unload event. This event stops any audio file that the game is currently playing; otherwise the sound would linger after the game has disappeared.

```
Sub Form_Unload (Cancel As Integer)
'--------------------------------------------------------------
' Stop any sound currently playing, then exit.
'--------------------------------------------------------------

    StopSound
End Sub
```

Parsing a World—The VB Adventure Support Routines

Most of the logic of the VB Adventure program is handled in two Visual Basic modules. The largest of these is AREA.BAS. Add this as a new module to the ADVEN.MAK project.

The AREA.BAS module contains the code that parses the game's Description file, as well as handling important actions such as processing commands and jumping between rooms. Begin by adding the code in Listing 15-3 to AREA.BAS's Declarations section.

Listing 15-3 AREA.BAS declarations

```
Option Explicit
'--------------------------------------------------------------
' AREA.BAS
'--------------------------------------------------------------

' API play sound
Declare Function sndPlaySound Lib "MMSYSTEM" (ByVal lpSound As String, ByVal flags As
Integer) As Integer
```

```
Declare Function sndStopSound Lib "MMSystem" Alias "sndPlaySound" (ByVal lpszNull As
Long, ByVal flags As Integer) As Integer

' constants for sndPlaySound
Const SND_SYNC = (0)
Const SND_ASYNC = (1)
Const SND_NODEFAULT = (2)
Const SND_MEMORY = (4)
Const SND_LOOP = (8)
Const SND_NOSTOP = (16)

' structure for screen action desc
Type ScreenAction
    Name As String
    X As Integer
    Y As Integer
    PictureFilename As String
    PictureDownFilename As String
End Type

' structure for items
Type Item
    Name As String
    Description As String
    PictureFilename As String
End Type

' structure for Command
Type Action
    Name As String
    GameFlag As String
    Code As String
    FailText As String
End Type

' structure for container
Type Container
    Name As String
    TriggerItem As String
    HoldingItem As String
    Code As String
    SuccessText As String
End Type

' structure that holds each area
Type Area
    Name As String
    Description As String
    NumActions As Integer
    Actions(1 To 10) As Action
    NumItems As Integer
```

continued on next page

continued from previous page

```
    Items(1 To 10) As String
    PictureFilename As String
    SoundFilename As String
    ItemContainer As Container
End Type

Global NumInventory As Integer          ' number of items on person
Global Inventory(1 To 40) As String     ' items on person

Global Areas(1 To 40) As Area           ' array of areas
Global Screens(1 To 40) As ScreenAction ' array of actions
Global Items(1 To 40) As Item           ' array of items
Global NumItems As Integer              ' number of items in the game
Global NumAreas As Integer              ' number of areas in the game
Global NumScreens As Integer            ' number of btns on screen

Global CurArea As String                ' current area name

Const C_AREA = 1
Const C_ITEM = 2
Const C_SCREEN = 3

' flags that can be set while running to represent
' events that've occurred
Dim NumGameFlags As Integer
Dim GameFlags(1 To 20) As String
```

The ActionExecute routine is called when the player clicks one of the Action buttons. Often the action command jumps the player to another room. Sometimes, however, some criteria must be met before the player can proceed. This routine checks that the criteria have been met and displays an appropriate message if they have not.

```
Sub ActionExecute (ActionName As String)
'-----------------------------------------------------------------
' Execute action from mouse click
'-----------------------------------------------------------------
Dim ActionIdx As Integer      ' index of action
Dim AreaIdx As Integer        ' current area

    ' current index
    AreaIdx = AreaIndex(CurArea)
    ActionIdx = ActionIndex(CurArea, ActionName)

    ' if this action requires that something previous has happened ... '
    If Areas(AreaIdx).Actions(ActionIdx).GameFlag <> "" Then
        ' if the flag isn't set and the player doesn't have
        ' this item ... say message, get out
        If Not IsInInventory(Areas(AreaIdx).Actions(ActionIdx).GameFlag)
        And Not IsGameFlagSet(Areas(AreaIdx).Actions(ActionIdx).GameFlag)
        Then
            MsgBox Areas(AreaIdx).Actions(ActionIdx).FailText
```

```
            Exit Sub
        End If
    End If

    ' execute command
    ActionExecuteLow Areas(AreaIdx).Actions(ActionIdx).Code
End Sub
```

The ActionExecuteLow routine is the low-level procedure that actually performs a given action. This routine parses the string, ActStr, looking for a valid command.

```
Sub ActionExecuteLow (ActStr As String)
'----------------------------------------------------------------
' Performs actual action, no checking, no flags
'----------------------------------------------------------------

    ' check for movement command
    If UCase(Left(ActStr, 3)) = "GO " Then
        ' move to the new area
        AreaChange Trim(Mid(ActStr, 4))
    ElseIf UCase(Left(ActStr, 7)) = "CREATE " Then
        ' add item to local area
        AddCurAreaItem Trim(Mid(ActStr, 8))
    ElseIf UCase(Left(ActStr, 4)) = "SET " Then
        ' add item to local area
        GameFlagSet Trim(Mid(ActStr, 5))
    End If
End Sub
```

As shown above, the game currently recognizes three distinct actions: go, create, and set. Each of these is processed in its own subroutine.

First, the AreaChange routine is called when an attempt is made to move from one room, or area, to another. Information about each room is stored in the Areas array. The AreaChange routine checks if the requirements for the move have been met (such as feeding the angry dog) and presents an appropriate message if they have not. Add the AreaChange routine, as shown in Listing 15-4.

Listing 15-4 AreaChange routine

```
Sub AreaChange (AreaName As String)
'----------------------------------------------------------------
' Handles change of area
'----------------------------------------------------------------
Dim NewIndex     ' index of new area
Dim ScrIndex     ' index for scan of screen actions '

    ' get index of current area
    NewIndex = AreaIndex(AreaName)

    ' save name of area for later
```

continued on next page

continued from previous page

```
    CurArea = Areas(NewIndex).Name

    ' load picture
    Adven.AreaPicture.Picture = LoadPicture(App.Path & "\" &
    Areas(NewIndex).PictureFilename)

    ' show description
    Adven.Desc.Caption = Areas(NewIndex).Description

    For ScrIndex = 1 To NumScreens
        ' show action button if allowed in this area
        Adven.Action(ScrIndex).Visible = (ActionIndex(AreaName,
        Screens(ScrIndex).Name) <> 0)
    Next ScrIndex

    ' if there's a container, show it
    If Areas(NewIndex).ItemContainer.Name <> "" Then
        Adven.Contain.Caption = Areas(NewIndex).ItemContainer.Name
        Adven.Contain.Enabled = True
        Adven.Contain.Visible = True
    Else
        Adven.Contain.Visible = False
        Adven.Contain.Enabled = False
    End If

    ' show items in area
    RedrawAreaItems

    ' stop any sounds that might be playing from previous venue.
    StopSound

    ' play sound, if there is one (non-exclusive)
    If Areas(NewIndex).SoundFilename <> "" Then
        PlaySound Areas(NewIndex).SoundFilename, False
    End If
End Sub
```

Next, the AddCurAreaItem routine is called in response to a Create command. This routine will create an instance of the item specified by the ItemName parameter. This item is placed in the Ground frame of the current room. This item is then available for the player to pick up.

```
Sub AddCurAreaItem (ItemName As String)
'----------------------------------------------------------------
' Add the item to the current area.
'----------------------------------------------------------------
Dim AreaIdx As Integer  ' current area

    ' if we already have it here, get out
    If IsInCurArea(ItemName) Then
        Exit Sub
    End If
```

```
    ' current index
    AreaIdx = AreaIndex(CurArea)

    ' add the item
    Areas(AreaIdx).NumItems = Areas(AreaIdx).NumItems + 1
    Areas(AreaIdx).Items(Areas(AreaIdx).NumItems) = ItemName
    RedrawAreaItems
End Sub
```

Finally, the Set command is implemented in the GameFlagSet routine. This routine adds the flag, specified by the FlagName parameter, to the list of active flags. A flag is active when some specified criterion, such as feeding the angry dog, has been met.

```
Sub GameFlagSet (FlagName As String)
'-----------------------------------------------------------------
' Set the game flag.
'-----------------------------------------------------------------

    ' if this flag hasn't been set before '
    If Not IsGameFlagSet(FlagName) Then
        ' one more game flag
        NumGameFlags = NumGameFlags + 1

        ' add flag to list
        GameFlags(NumGameFlags) = FlagName
    End If
End Sub
```

A complementary function, IsGameFlagSet, is used to check if a flag has previously been set. Flags are stored in an array of strings, GameFlags. This function traverses the array and returns a value of True if the flag is set.

```
Function IsGameFlagSet (FlagName As String) As Integer
'-----------------------------------------------------------------
' Returns True if the flag is set
'-----------------------------------------------------------------
Dim I As Integer

    ' scan for flag
    For I = 1 To NumGameFlags
        ' if it's found ... '
        If UCase(FlagName) = UCase(GameFlags(I)) Then
            ' ... let the caller know '
            IsGameFlagSet = True
            Exit Function
        End If
    Next I

    IsGameFlagSet = False
End Function
```

The AreaIndex routine translates an AreaName string such as "Restaurant" into an index into the Area array. This points out a necessity when describing rooms in the Description File: Make sure all room names are unique.

```
Function AreaIndex (AreaName As String) As Integer
'-----------------------------------------------------------------
' Get index of area based on the name
'-----------------------------------------------------------------
Dim I As Integer     ' index for search

    ' scan the list for the name
    For I = 1 To NumAreas
        If UCase(AreaName) = UCase(Areas(I).Name) Then
            ' if found, return index to calling routine
            AreaIndex = I
            Exit Function
        End If
    Next I

    ' area not found, exit program
    MsgBox AreaName & ": Area not found.  Fatal error."
    End
End Function
```

Similar to AreaIndex, the ActionIndex function returns the array index of an action. If the action, specified by the CommandName parameter, exists for the given area, then its corresponding array index is returned.

```
Function ActionIndex (AreaName As String, CommandName As String)
'-----------------------------------------------------------------
' Returns index of command that's found in area name
'-----------------------------------------------------------------
Dim AreaIdx As Integer       ' index of area
Dim ActionIdx As Integer     ' index of command in area

    ' get index of area
    AreaIdx = AreaIndex(AreaName)

    ' scan for action name
    For ActionIdx = 1 To Areas(AreaIdx).NumActions
        If UCase(CommandName) =
        UCase(Areas(AreaIdx).Actions(ActionIdx).Name) Then
            ActionIndex = ActionIdx
            Exit Function
        End If
    Next ActionIdx

    ' return not found
    ActionIndex = 0
End Function
```

The AreaLoadFile routine parses a given Description file. This routine uses information in the Description file to build internal arrays of items, rooms, and valid commands. All this information is parsed when the program is first loaded. Add the AreaLoadFile routine, as shown in Listing 15-5.

Listing 15-5 AreaLoadFile routine

```
Sub AreaLoadFile (Filename)
'------------------------------------------------------------
' Read and parse a file.
'------------------------------------------------------------
Dim CurClassType As Integer      ' type of current class
Dim CurClassIndex As Integer     ' integer of current class
Dim FileHandle As Integer        ' handle to file
Dim InputLine As String          ' line from disk

    ' get file handle number
    FileHandle = FreeFile

    ' open file
    Open Filename For Input As #FileHandle

    ' load entire file
    Do While Not EOF(FileHandle)
        Dim FieldName As String          ' name of field loaded
        Dim FieldValue As String         ' value of field loaded
        Dim FieldSepOffset As Integer    ' offset of field separator '

        ' read line
        Line Input #FileHandle, InputLine

        ' remove extra spaces
        InputLine = Trim(InputLine)

        ' get offset of field separator
        FieldSepOffset = InStr(InputLine, ":")

        ' if we have data to use
        If (InputLine <> "") And (FieldSepOffset > 0) Then
            ' get the field name and data
            FieldName = Trim(UCase(Left(InputLine, FieldSepOffset - 1)))
            FieldValue = Trim(Mid(InputLine, FieldSepOffset + 1))

            ' if this is the start of a new area
            If FieldName = "ROOM NAME" Then
                ' we have one more area now
                NumAreas = NumAreas + 1

                ' set up local vars for subsequent reads
                CurClassType = C_AREA
```

continued on next page

continued from previous page

```
    CurClassIndex = NumAreas

    ' save name
    Areas(CurClassIndex).Name = FieldValue
ElseIf FieldName = "ACTION NAME" Then
    ' we have one more screen action now
    NumScreens = NumScreens + 1

    ' set up local vars for subsequent reads
    CurClassType = C_SCREEN
    CurClassIndex = NumScreens

    ' save name
    Screens(CurClassIndex).Name = FieldValue

    ' load new bitmap for item
    Load Adven.Action(NumScreens)
    Load Adven.PictureDown(NumScreens)
    Load Adven.PictureUp(NumScreens)
    Adven.Action(NumScreens).Tag = FieldValue
ElseIf FieldName = "ITEM NAME" Then
    ' we have one more item now
    NumItems = NumItems + 1

    ' set up local vars for subsequent reads
    CurClassType = C_ITEM
    CurClassIndex = NumItems

    ' save name
    Items(CurClassIndex).Name = FieldValue
    Load Adven.Item(NumItems)
    Adven.Item(NumItems).Tag = FieldValue
' get data for picture filenames
ElseIf FieldName = "PICTURE" Then
    If CurClassType = C_AREA Then
        Areas(CurClassIndex).PictureFilename = FieldValue
    ElseIf CurClassType = C_ITEM Then
        Dim SepOffset As Integer

        SepOffset = InStr(FieldValue, "|")

        If SepOffset <> 0 Then
            Items(CurClassIndex).PictureFilename = Trim(Left(FieldValue,
            SepOffset - 1))
            Adven.Item(CurClassIndex).Picture = LoadPicture(App.Path & "\"
            & Trim(Left(FieldValue, SepOffset - 1)))
            Adven.Item(CurClassIndex).DragIcon = LoadPicture(App.Path &
            "\" & Trim(Mid(FieldValue, SepOffset + 1)))
        Else
            Items(CurClassIndex).PictureFilename = FieldValue
            Adven.Item(CurClassIndex).Picture = LoadPicture(App.Path & "\"
            & FieldValue)
```

```
                    Adven.Item(CurClassIndex).DragIcon =
                    Adven.Item(CurClassIndex).Picture
                End If
            ElseIf CurClassType = C_SCREEN Then
                Screens(CurClassIndex).PictureFilename = FieldValue
                Adven.Action(CurClassIndex).Picture = LoadPicture(App.Path & "\" &
                FieldValue)
                Adven.PictureUp(CurClassIndex).Picture = LoadPicture(App.Path &
                "\" & FieldValue)
            End If
        ElseIf (FieldName = "PICTUREDOWN") And (CurClassType = C_SCREEN) Then
            Adven.PictureDown(CurClassIndex).Picture = LoadPicture(App.Path & "\"
            & FieldValue)
        ' sound loading
        ElseIf (FieldName = "SOUND") And (CurClassType = C_AREA) Then
            Areas(CurClassIndex).SoundFilename = FieldValue
        ElseIf (FieldName = "X") And (CurClassType = C_SCREEN) Then
            ' save position and set pos of bitmap
            Screens(CurClassIndex).X = Val(FieldValue)
            Adven.Action(CurClassIndex).Left = Val(FieldValue)
        ElseIf (FieldName = "Y") And (CurClassType = C_SCREEN) Then
            ' save position and set pos of bitmap
            Screens(CurClassIndex).Y = Val(FieldValue)
            Adven.Action(CurClassIndex).Top = Val(FieldValue)
        ' check for area command
        ElseIf (FieldName = "COMMAND") And (CurClassType = C_AREA) Then
            ' one more action in this area
            Areas(CurClassIndex).NumActions = Areas(CurClassIndex).NumActions + 1

            ' parse the string into the action
            ActionParse
            Areas(CurClassIndex).Actions(Areas(CurClassIndex).NumActions),
            FieldValue
        ' add item to this area
        ElseIf (FieldName = "ITEM") And (CurClassType = C_AREA) Then
            ' parse the string into the container
            CurArea = Areas(CurClassIndex).Name
            AddCurAreaItem FieldValue
        ' check for area container
        ElseIf (FieldName = "CONTAINER") And (CurClassType = C_AREA) Then
            ' parse the string into the container
            ContainerParse Areas(CurClassIndex).ItemContainer, FieldValue
        ' load area description
        ElseIf (FieldName = "DESCRIPTION") And (CurClassType = C_AREA) Then
            Areas(CurClassIndex).Description = Trim(FieldValue)
        End If
    End If
Loop

' close file
Close #FileHandle
End Sub
```

The AreaLoadFile routine calls two support routines, ActionParse and ContainerParse, that assist it in parsing lines from the Description file and building the necessary data structures. Add these routines, as shown in Listing 15-6.

Listing 15-6 ActionParse and ContainerParse routines

```
Sub ActionParse (NewAction As Action, InputLine As String)
'---------------------------------------------------------------
' Parse string into action
'---------------------------------------------------------------
Dim TempStr         ' temp string for parsing
Dim SepOffset       ' offset of separator
Dim FieldIndex      ' index of field we're extracting

    NewAction.Name = ""
    NewAction.Code = ""
    NewAction.GameFlag = ""
    NewAction.FailText = ""
    FieldIndex = 0

    ' get temp string for parsing
    TempStr = Trim(InputLine)

    ' parse while we still have stuff
    Do While Len(TempStr)
        Dim CurField ' data of current field

        ' separate string
        SepOffset = InStr(TempStr, "|")
        If SepOffset = 0 Then
            ' last item in string
            CurField = TempStr
            TempStr = ""
        Else
            ' get next item in string
            CurField = Trim(Left(TempStr, SepOffset - 1))
            TempStr = Trim(Mid(TempStr, SepOffset + 1))
        End If

        ' put item into structure
        Select Case FieldIndex
            Case 0: NewAction.Name = CurField
            Case 1: NewAction.Code = CurField
            Case 2: NewAction.GameFlag = CurField
            Case 3: NewAction.FailText = CurField
        End Select

        ' more to next field
        FieldIndex = FieldIndex + 1
    Loop
```

```
End Sub

Sub ContainerParse (NewContainer As Container, InputLine As String)
'-----------------------------------------------------------------
' Parse container info out of an input line.
'-----------------------------------------------------------------
Dim TempStr          ' temp string for parsing
Dim SepOffset        ' offset of separator
Dim FieldIndex       ' index of field we're extracting

    NewContainer.Name = ""
    NewContainer.Code = ""
    NewContainer.TriggerItem = ""
    NewContainer.SuccessText = ""
    NewContainer.HoldingItem = ""
    FieldIndex = 0

    ' get temp string for parsing
    TempStr = Trim(InputLine)

    ' parse while we still have stuff
    Do While Len(TempStr)
        Dim CurField ' data of current field

        ' separate string
        SepOffset = InStr(TempStr, "|")
        If SepOffset = 0 Then
            ' last item in string
            CurField = TempStr
            TempStr = ""
        Else
            ' get next item in string
            CurField = Trim(Left(TempStr, SepOffset - 1))
            TempStr = Trim(Mid(TempStr, SepOffset + 1))
        End If

        ' put item into structure
        Select Case FieldIndex
            Case 0: NewContainer.Name = CurField
            Case 1: NewContainer.TriggerItem = CurField
            Case 2: NewContainer.Code = CurField
            Case 3: NewContainer.SuccessText = CurField
        End Select

        ' more to next field
        FieldIndex = FieldIndex + 1
    Loop
End Sub
```

The RedrawAreaItems routine is used throughout the program, whenever it's necessary to redraw items that are visible in the Inventory, Ground, and Container frames. This happens most often when the player moves to a new room or moves an item from one frame to another. It's this routine's job to ensure that the items are arranged in a tidy fashion within their respective frames, as shown in Listing 15-7.

Listing 15-7 RedrawAreaItems routine

```
Sub RedrawAreaItems ()
'-------------------------------------------------------------
' Redraw all items on screen
'-------------------------------------------------------------
Dim I As Integer
Dim GrndCurX As Integer
Dim GrndCurY As Integer
Dim GrndDeltaY As Integer
Dim InvCurX As Integer
Dim InvCurY As Integer
Dim InvDeltaY As Integer
Dim TempOut As Integer

    ' if we're not set up yet, get out
    If CurArea = "" Then
        Exit Sub
    End If

    ' compute inventory positions
    InvCurX = (Adven.Inventory.Width - Adven.Item(0).Width - 4 *
              Screen.TwipsPerPixelX) / 2
    InvCurY = (Adven.Inventory.Height - (GetInventoryCount() * Adven.Item(0).Height))
              / (GetInventoryCount() + 1)
    InvDeltaY = InvCurY + Adven.Item(0).Height
    GrndCurX = (Adven.Ground.Width - Adven.Item(0).Width - 4 * Screen.TwipsPerPixelX)
              / 2
    GrndCurY = (Adven.Ground.Height - (GetRoomItemCount() * Adven.Item(0).Height)) /
              (GetRoomItemCount() + 1)
    GrndDeltaY = GrndCurY + Adven.Item(0).Height

    ' scan items to check for display
    For I = 1 To NumItems
        ' if the item is in the current area
        If IsInCurArea(CStr(Adven.Item(I).Tag)) Then
            ' add it to the list
            TempOut = SetParent(Adven.Item(I).hWnd, Adven.Ground.hWnd)

            Adven.Item(I).Left = GrndCurX
            Adven.Item(I).Top = GrndCurY
            Adven.Item(I).Enabled = True
            Adven.Item(I).Visible = True

            GrndCurY = GrndCurY + GrndDeltaY
```

```
        ' if the item is in inventory
        ElseIf IsInInventory(CStr(Adven.Item(I).Tag)) Then
            ' add it to the inventory list
            TempOut = SetParent(Adven.Item(I).hWnd, Adven.Inventory.hWnd)

            Adven.Item(I).Left = InvCurX
            Adven.Item(I).Top = InvCurY
            Adven.Item(I).Enabled = True
            Adven.Item(I).Visible = True

            InvCurY = InvCurY + InvDeltaY
        ' if it's in the container
        ElseIf IsInCurAreaContainer(CStr(Adven.Item(I).Tag)) Then
            ' show it in the container
            TempOut = SetParent(Adven.Item(I).hWnd, Adven.Contain.hWnd)

            Adven.Item(I).Left = (Adven.Contain.Width - Adven.Item(I).Width) / 2
            Adven.Item(I).Top = (Adven.Contain.Height - Adven.Item(I).Height) / 2
            Adven.Item(I).Enabled = True
            Adven.Item(I).Visible = True
        Else
            ' otherwise, don't show it
            Adven.Item(I).Enabled = False
            Adven.Item(I).Visible = False
        End If
    Next I

    DoEvents
End Sub
```

The RedrawAreaItems routine uses the function GetRoomItemCount to determine how many items are in the current room. Add this routine, as shown below.

```
Function GetRoomItemCount () As Integer
'----------------------------------------------------------------
' Return the number of items in the current area
'----------------------------------------------------------------
Dim AreaIdx As Integer ' current area

    ' current index
    AreaIdx = AreaIndex(CurArea)

    ' return count
    GetRoomItemCount = Areas(AreaIdx).NumItems
End Function
```

Another support routine used widely in VB Adventure is the IsInCurAreaContainer function. This function returns True if a specified item is inside the container in the current room. Add this function, as shown below.

```
Function IsInCurAreaContainer (ItemName As String) As Integer
'----------------------------------------------------------------
' Returns true if item is in the current area's container
'----------------------------------------------------------------
Dim AreaIdx As Integer ' current area

    ' current index
    AreaIdx = AreaIndex(CurArea)

    ' check for the item
    IsInCurAreaContainer = (UCase(Areas(AreaIdx).ItemContainer.HoldingItem) = UCase(ItemName))
End Function
```

A related function is IsInCurArea. This function returns True if a given item is on the ground in the current room. This routine traverses the current area's Items array, looking for an entry that matches the ItemName parameter.

```
Function IsInCurArea (ItemName As String) As Integer
'----------------------------------------------------------------
' Returns true if the item is in the current room
'----------------------------------------------------------------
Dim I As Integer
Dim AreaIdx As Integer ' current area

    ' current index
    AreaIdx = AreaIndex(CurArea)

    ' scan room items
    For I = 1 To Areas(AreaIdx).NumItems
        If UCase(ItemName) = UCase(Areas(AreaIdx).Items(I)) Then
            ' found it!
            IsInCurArea = True
            Exit Function
        End If
    Next I

    ' didn't find it
    IsInCurArea = False
End Function
```

When the player picks an object off the ground in a room, the item must be removed from that area's Items array. This job is handled by the RemoveCurAreaItem routine.

```
Sub RemoveCurAreaItem (ItemName As String)
'----------------------------------------------------------------
' Remove item from current area
'----------------------------------------------------------------
Dim I As Integer
Dim J As Integer
Dim AreaIdx As Integer ' current area
```

```
    ' current index
    AreaIdx = AreaIndex(CurArea)

    J = 0

    ' scan inventory and remove item
    For I = 1 To Areas(AreaIdx).NumItems
        If UCase(Areas(AreaIdx).Items(I)) <> UCase(ItemName) Then
            ' add item to new list
            J = J + 1
            Areas(AreaIdx).Items(J) = Areas(AreaIdx).Items(I)
        End If
    Next I

    ' reset count of items in inventory
    Areas(AreaIdx).NumItems = J
End Sub
```

When an item is placed in a container, the SetCurAreaContainer routine is called. This routine is also called when an item is removed from a container. In this latter case, the routine is passed an empty string (""), effectively deleting the item from the container.

```
Sub SetCurAreaContainer (ItemName As String)
'------------------------------------------------------------
' Sets the item that's in the current container
'------------------------------------------------------------
    Dim AreaIdx As Integer ' current area

    ' current index
    AreaIdx = AreaIndex(CurArea)

    ' if this is the trigger item
    If UCase(ItemName) = UCase(Areas(AreaIdx).ItemContainer.TriggerItem) Then
        ' make the item disappear
        ItemName = ""

        ' make stuff happen
        ActionExecuteLow Areas(AreaIdx).ItemContainer.Code

        ' show all items
        RedrawAreaItems

        ' give success message
        MsgBox Areas(AreaIdx).ItemContainer.SuccessText
    End If

    ' save item name
    Areas(AreaIdx).ItemContainer.HoldingItem = ItemName
End Sub
```

The last two routines in the AREA.BAS module are simple wrappers around the Windows API wave audio routine, sndPlaySound. The first routine, PlaySound, loads a .WAV file from disk and plays it asynchronously. The second routine, StopSound, stops any currently playing sound. This latter routine is used when moving to a room that has no specified sound file and when exiting the program.

```
Sub PlaySound (SoundName As String, Exclusive As Integer)
'---------------------------------------------------------------
' Play a sound
'---------------------------------------------------------------
Dim TempResult As Integer

    If Exclusive Then
        TempResult = sndPlaySound(App.Path & "\" & SoundName, SND_NODEFAULT)
    Else
        TempResult = sndPlaySound(App.Path & "\" & SoundName, SND_NODEFAULT + SND_ASYNC)
    End If
End Sub

Sub StopSound ()
'---------------------------------------------------------------
' Stop any currently playing .WAV file.
'---------------------------------------------------------------
Dim TempResult As Integer

    TempResult = sndStopSound(0, 0)

End Sub
```

The routines that handle maintaining the player's inventory of items are in a separate .BAS module. Create a new module called INVENTOR.BAS. Add the following Declarations section to this module.

```
Option Explicit
'---------------------------------------------------------------
' INVENTOR.BAS
'---------------------------------------------------------------

' list of items the player has
Dim NumInventory As Integer
Dim Inventory(1 To 20) As String

' for moving items around
Declare Function SetParent Lib "User" (ByVal hWndChild As Integer, ByVal hWndNewParent
As Integer) As Integer
```

The routines in this module are very straightforward. The first, AddInventory, adds an item, specified in the ItemName parameter, to the player's inventory. This inventory is maintained in an array of strings called Inventory.

```
Sub AddInventory (ItemName As String)
'--------------------------------------------------------------
' Add item to inventory
'--------------------------------------------------------------

    ' if not currently in the inventory,
    If Not IsInInventory(ItemName) Then
        ' add the item
        NumInventory = NumInventory + 1
        Inventory(NumInventory) = Trim(ItemName)
    End If
End Sub
```

The GetInventoryCount function returns the number of items currently in the Inventory array by accessing the NumInventory variable.

```
Function GetInventoryCount () As Integer
'--------------------------------------------------------------
' Retrieve the number of items in the inventory.
'--------------------------------------------------------------
    GetInventoryCount = NumInventory
End Function
```

The VB Adventure program calls the IsInInventory function when it needs to determine if a specific item is in the player's inventory. This function returns True if the item given in the ItemName parameter is found in the Inventory array.

```
Function IsInInventory (ItemName As String) As Integer
'--------------------------------------------------------------
' Check to see if an item is in the inventory
'--------------------------------------------------------------
Dim I

    ' scan inventory
    For I = 1 To NumInventory
        If UCase(ItemName) = UCase(Inventory(I)) Then
            ' found it!
            IsInInventory = True
            Exit Function
        End If
    Next I

    ' didn't find it
    IsInInventory = False
End Function
```

Finally, the program calls the RemoveInventory routine when an item is removed from inventory. This will happen when the player drops an item on the ground or into a container.

```
Sub RemoveInventory (ItemName As String)
'---------------------------------------------------------------
' Removes item from inventory
'---------------------------------------------------------------
Dim I As Integer
Dim J As Integer

    J = 0

    ' scan inventory and remove item
    For I = 1 To NumInventory
        If UCase(Inventory(I)) <> UCase(ItemName) Then
            ' add item to new list
            J = J + 1
            Inventory(J) = Inventory(I)
        End If
    Next I

    ' reset count of items in inventory
    NumInventory = J
End Sub
```

That wraps up the code needed to build the VB Adventure game. Now you should be ready to run it.

Where Do You Go From Here?

The great thing about adventure games is their infinite extensibility. Without any changes to the program at all, you can extend the world of this adventure simply by modifying the ADVEN.DSC file. You may want to create your own bitmaps and wave audio files. If you want, you can even ditch this file and start from scratch.

Likewise, you have the source code, so you can expand, modify, and hack the game to your own tastes. Here are some suggestions you might want to try.

- Add a new section called Creature Definitions to the ADVEN.DSC file. Change the program to handle creatures that can freely or randomly roam the adventure world.
- Change the program so that it can remember a player's location when he or she quits the game. Let the player resume the game at this saved location when he or she next plays.
- Modify the ADVEN.DSC file to include an Initialization Definitions section. This section would define a new player's initial room location and inventory. This would make the game more generic, and easily allow for multiple ADVEN.DSC files.

- Add the ability to display .AVI video or animation clips in addition to the current bitmaps.

I want to give many thanks to James Shields for developing VB Adventure and letting me use it in this book. If you enjoyed this game, then be sure to take a look at the role-playing game James developed for the next chapter!

16

Role Playing Games: RPG

16

Role-playing Games: RPG

Computer role-playing games (RPGs) share a long history that intersects with the history of adventure games discussed in the last chapter. Computer RPGs are a natural step from their noncomputerized counterparts, such as the now-classic Dungeons and Dragons.

Playing VB-RPG

When the player starts VB-RPG, he or she is presented with a short sequence of dialog box forms (see Figure 16-1) that sets up the situation the character is in. The player's character has been bitten by a snake, and must travel through the woods to seek out a friendly Sylph who can provide a cure.

The program then displays the main form, as seen in Figure 16-2. The form shows a large map on the left. Character status and text information are displayed on the right, and a compass is shown near the center of the form.

The map is built by combining smaller bitmaps, or *tiles*, to create a view of the player's immediate area. Characters and objects are themselves displayed as tiles on top of the map tiles.

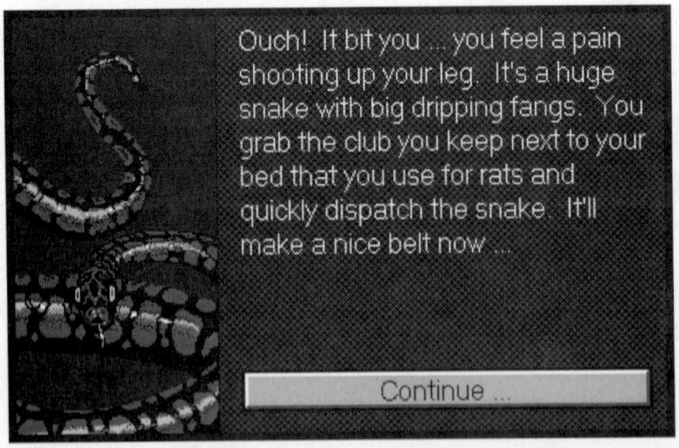

FIGURE 16-1

The Dialog sequence at the start of the game

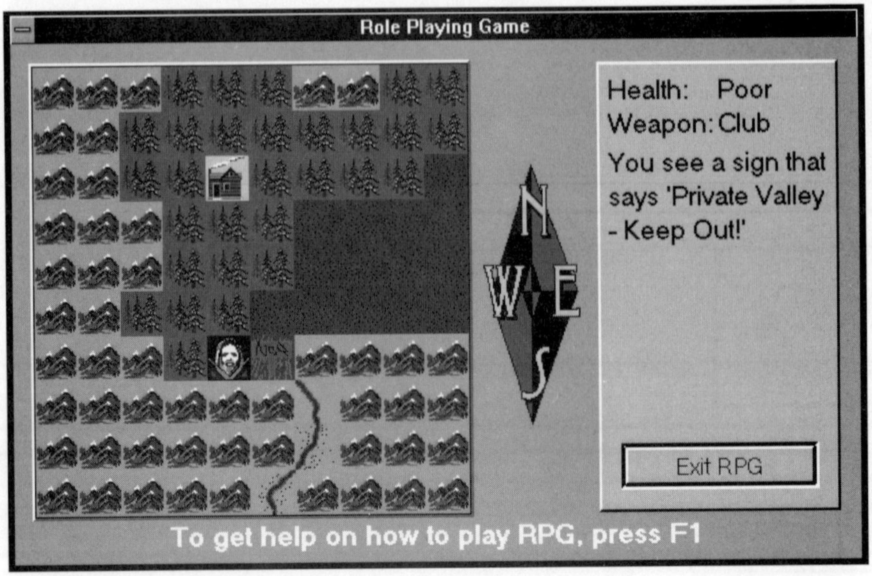

FIGURE 16-2

The VB-RPG main form

The player moves by pressing the directional keys (up, down, left, right, etc.) on the keyboard or by clicking the desired direction on the compass. The player will encounter monsters and other assorted characters as he or she journeys through this unknown land.

The player cannot pass over mountains or water; hidden areas on the map may not be what they first appear.

A player can pick up a found object simply by moving onto the square the object occupies. Likewise, to attack a monster, the player attempts to move onto the monster's tile.

The game ends when the player finds a jeweled chalice or dies, whichever comes first.

Building VB-RPG

At the center of VB-RPG is the map that defines the world the player will explore. On-screen, a portion of this map is displayed as a series of bitmap tiles. The program needs a more compact and easily changed representation of the entire map. This is supplied by a map file that describes the entire world as a collection of text characters. A portion of the map file is shown below.

```
22222222222222222222222222222222222
22222222222222222222222222222222222
22211221122222222222222222222222222
22111111111222222222222222222222222
22117111133222222222222222222222222
22211133333222222222222222222222222
22211133332222222222222222222222222
22111333332222222222222222222222222
22211822222222222224444442222222222
222222A2222222222444444444222222222
222222G2222222224444444444444222222
22222B222222224444444444144444422222
22222H22222224444444444444444444422
222222A2222222224444444444444445422
222222G2222222222244444444444000022
22222B2222222222222444444444402222
22222G2222222222222444444440022222
2222B22222222222224444444402222222
2222G22222222222222444440022222222
222B22222222222222244402222222222222
```

Each character represents a single tile as displayed on the screen. In the section above, the character 2 represents a mountain tile, 1 represents a forest, and 4 depicts water (in this case, a lake).

The first step in creating VB-RPG is to create this map. The map file can be found on the accompanying CD in the directory for this chapter.

Next, you'll need to create a new VB project, called RPG.MAK. To this project add a new .BAS module, named RPG.BAS. This module is needed to hold a data structure used to define game characters. The module also declares a global variable used to communicate between forms, and a support routine that draws a 3D border around controls.

First, add the code in Listing 16-1 to RPG.BAS's Declarations section.

Listing 16-1 RPG.BAS Declarations section

```
Option Explicit
'-----------------------------------------------------------
' Define the character data structure and the globals used
' to communicate between the main Map form and the Display
' form.
'-----------------------------------------------------------

Type Character
    X As Integer
    Y As Integer
    Symbol As Integer
    Health As Integer
    Weapon As Integer
    MinX As Integer 'used for monsters
    MaxX As Integer 'used for monsters
    MinY As Integer 'used for monsters
    MaxY As Integer 'used for monsters
End Type

' result of user choice from the Display form
Global DisplayChoice As Integer

' Constants for 3D Borders
Global Const BORDER_INSET = 0
Global Const BORDER_RAISED = 1

' ScaleMode constants
Global Const TWIPS = 1
Global Const PIXELS = 3
```

Next, add the routine in Listing 16-2, Make3D, to the module. Make3D draws a raised or inset three-dimensional border around a control on a form.

Listing 16-2 Make3D routine

```
Sub Make3D (AForm As Form, ctl As Control, ByVal BorderStyle As Integer, ByVal
BorderWidth As Integer)
'-----------------------------------------------------------------
' Wrap a 3D effect around a control on a form.
'-----------------------------------------------------------------
' Color Constants
Const DARK_GRAY = &H808080
Const WHITE = &HFFFFFF
Const BLACK = &H0

Dim RightSide As Single
Dim BW As Integer
```

```
Dim LeftTopColor As Long, RightBottomColor As Long
Dim i As Integer
Dim SaveMode As Integer

    If Not ctl.Visible Then Exit Sub

    SaveMode = AForm.ScaleMode
    AForm.ScaleMode = PIXELS

    Select Case BorderStyle
        Case 0: ' Inset
            LeftTopColor = DARK_GRAY
            RightBottomColor = WHITE
        Case 1: ' Raised
            LeftTopColor = WHITE
            RightBottomColor = DARK_GRAY
    End Select

    ' Set the top shading line.
    For BW = 1 To BorderWidth
        ' Top
        AForm.CurrentX = ctl.Left - BW
        AForm.CurrentY = ctl.Top - BW
        AForm.Line -(ctl.Left + ctl.Width + (BW - 1), ctl.Top - BW), LeftTopColor
        ' Right
        AForm.Line -(ctl.Left + ctl.Width + (BW - 1), ctl.Top + ctl.Height + (BW -
        1)), RightBottomColor
        ' Bottom
        AForm.Line -(ctl.Left - BW, ctl.Top + ctl.Height + (BW - 1)), RightBottomColor
        ' Left
        AForm.Line -(ctl.Left - BW, ctl.Top - BW), LeftTopColor
    Next

    AForm.ScaleMode = SaveMode
End Sub
```

At various places in the game, you'll want to give the player a choice to make. The game will present a dialog box-style form that describes the player's choice. This form will have a button for each possible choice, and may show a picture that helps illustrate the player's situation. You'll build this "choice" form in a moment. First, though, you need a simple way to display these bitmap illustrations when you need them. One method would be to load them from .BMP files on disk as needed. This is quite easy to do using the Visual Basic LoadPicture function. For example, you might load the bitmap file VAMPIRE.BMP from the application's directory using this line of code:

```
Picture1.Picture = LoadPicture (App.Path & "\VAMPIRE.BMP")
```

The technique above works fine, but may introduce an unwanted delay as the image is loaded from disk. Use an alternative approach by creating a form that's loaded, but never displayed. This form will contain no executable code, just the illustrations you need. When needed, the program can load the bitmaps from the invisible form using a line of code such as

```
FormA.Picture1.Picture = FormB.Pictures(i).Picture
```

Because the bitmaps are already loaded into memory, there is virtually no delay. Create a new form called PICTUREF.FRM. This form will contain the objects and properties described in Table 16-1.

TABLE 16-1

Objects and properties of the PICTUREF.FRM form

Object	Property	Setting
Form	FormName	PictureForm
	Caption	"Picture Storage Form"
	Height	8475
	Left	2655
	Top	240
	Width	6315
PictureBox	Name	Picture1
	Height	3875
	Index	0
	Left	60
	Picture	(set at design time in Properties window)
	ScaleMode	3 'Pixel
	Top	60
	Width	1945
PictureBox	Name	Picture1
	Height	3875
	Index	1
	Left	2100
	Picture	(set at design time in Properties window)
	ScaleMode	3 'Pixel
	Top	60
	Width	1945

Object	Property	Setting
PictureBox	Name	Picture1
	Height	3875
	Index	2
	Left	4140
	Picture	(set at design time in Properties window)
	ScaleMode	3 'Pixel
	Top	60
	Width	1945
PictureBox	Name	Picture1
	Height	3875
	Index	3
	Left	60
	Picture	(set at design time in Properties window)
	Top	4020
	Width	1945
PictureBox	Name	Picture1
	Height	3875
	Index	4
	Left	2100
	Picture	(set at design time in Properties window)
	Top	4020
	Width	1945
PictureBox	Name	Picture1
	Height	3875
	Index	5
	Left	4140
	Picture	(set at design time in Properties window)

continued on next page

continued from previous page

Object	Property	Setting
	ScaleMode	3 'Pixel
	Top	4020
	Width	1945

When it's finished, the form will look like Figure 16-3, with a separate image displayed in each PictureBox control. The six PictureBoxes are actually a control array.

So how do you make a form invisible? Actually, a better question would be, how do you make a form visible? Normally you do this by calling its Show method. The

FIGURE 16-3

The invisible PICTUREF.FRM at design time

first time it is called, the Show method loads the specified form by calling its Load event. You can, however, simply call the Load event in a program *without* calling the Show method. When the form loads, all its resources are available (including PictureBoxes and other controls) even though the form cannot be seen.

This form requires no code, it just needs to have the appropriate bitmaps assigned to each PictureBox control. These bitmaps are used by the next form, called DISPLAY.FRM.

Create this new form, and add to it the objects and properties described in Table 16-2.

TABLE 16-2

Objects and properties of the DISPLAY.FRM form

Object	Property	Setting
Form	FormName	Display
	BackColor	&H00404000&
	BorderStyle	3 'Fixed Double
	ControlBox	0 'False
	Height	4080
	Left	465
	MaxButton	0 'False
	MinButton	0 'False
	Top	1335
	Width	6075
Label	Name	Description
	BackColor	&H00FFFFFF&
	BackStyle	0 'Transparent
	Caption	"Description"
	FontBold	0 'False
	FontSize	12
	ForeColor	&H00FFFFFF&
	Height	3015
	Left	2040
	Top	60
	Width	3735
PictureBox	Name	Pict

continued on next page

continued from previous page

Object	Property	Setting
	AutoRedraw	-1 'True
	AutoSize	-1 'True
	Height	3875
	Left	-60
	Top	-60
	Width	1945
CommandButton	Name	Choice
	BackColor	&H00404000&
	Caption	"Choice(0)"
	FontBold	0 'False
	FontSize	12
	Height	375
	Index	0
	Left	2040
	Top	2640
	Visible	0 'False
	Width	3735
CommandButton	Name	Choice
	BackColor	&H00404000&
	Caption	"Choice(1)"
	FontBold	0 'False
	FontSize	12
	Height	375
	Index	1
	Left	2040
	Top	3120
	Visible	0 'False
	Width	3735

Very little code is required for this form. The position of its controls are adjusted at runtime, but this is done by the main form. The form must simply pass back information on which button was pressed. This is handled in the form's single event, Choice_Click. Add this event, as shown below.

```
Sub Choice_Click (Index As Integer)
'----------------------------------------------------------
' Return the user's choice via the global DisplayChoice.
'----------------------------------------------------------

    ' return choice to calling routine
    DisplayChoice = Index

    ' remove display form
    Display.Hide
End Sub
```

Now let's move to the main form, which you'll name MAP.FRM. This form contains all the objects described in Table 16-3.

TABLE 16-3
Objects and properties of the MAP.FRM form

Object	Property	Setting
Form	FormName	Map
	BackColor	&H00C0C0C0&
	BorderStyle	3 'Fixed Double
	Caption	"Role Playing Game"
	ForeColor	&H00000000&
	Height	7920
	KeyPreview	-1 'True
	Left	1050
	Top	1200
	Width	9480
Label	Name	Label2
	Alignment	2 'Center
	BackStyle	0 'Transparent
	Caption	"To get help on how to play RPG, press F1"
	FontSize	13.5
	ForeColor	&H00FFFFFF&

continued on next page

continued from previous page

Object	Property	Setting
	Height	375
	Left	240
	Top	5100
	Width	8895
Label	Name	lblStatus
	BackColor	&H00000000&
	BackStyle	0 'Transparent
	Caption	"lblStatus"
	FontBold	0 'False
	FontSize	13.5
	ForeColor	&H00000000&
	Height	2955
	Left	6720
	Top	1080
	Width	2415
Label	Name	Label1
	BackColor	&H00000000&
	BackStyle	0 'Transparent
	Caption	"Health:"
	FontBold	0 'False
	FontSize	13.5
	ForeColor	&H00000000&
	Height	375
	Left	6720
	Top	300
	Width	975
Label	Name	lblHealth
	BackColor	&H00C0C0C0&
	BackStyle	0 'Transparent

Object	Property	Setting
	Caption	"Excellent"
	FontBold	0 'False
	FontSize	13.5
	ForeColor	&H00000000&
	Height	375
	Left	7920
	Top	300
	Width	1215
Label	Name	lblWeapon
	BackColor	&H00000000&
	BackStyle	0 'Transparent
	Caption	"Club"
	FontBold	0 'False
	FontSize	13.5
	ForeColor	&H00000000&
	Height	435
	Left	7920
	Top	660
	Width	1215
Label	Name	Label3
	BackColor	&H00000000&
	BackStyle	0 'Transparent
	Caption	"Weapon:"
	FontBold	0 'False
	FontSize	13.5
	ForeColor	&H00000000&
	Height	435
	Left	6720
	Top	660

continued on next page

continued from previous page

Object	Property	Setting
	Width	1155
Label	Name	lblFrame
	BackStyle	0 'Transparent
	Height	4875
	Left	6480
	Top	180
	Width	2715
PictureBox	Name	Picture2
	AutoSize	-1 'True
	BorderStyle	0 'None
	Height	3000
	Left	5160
	Picture	(set at design time in Properties window)
	Top	1200
	Width	1200
PictureBox	Name	Terrain
	AutoRedraw	-1 'True
	AutoSize	-1 'True
	BorderStyle	0 'None
	Height	480
	Index	(create multiple copies, indexed 0 to 8, 10 to 17, and 33 to 35)
	Picture	(set at design time in Properties window)
	Width	480
PictureBox	Name	Picture1
	Height	4830
	Left	180

Object	Property	Setting
	ScaleMode	3 'Pixel
	Top	180
	Width	4830
PictureBox	Name	Characters
	AutoRedraw	-1 'True
	AutoSize	-1 'True
	BorderStyle	0 'None
	Height	480
	Index	(create 4 controls, indexed 0 to 3)
	Picture	(set at design time in Properties window)
	Width	480
PictureBox	Name	picMapCanvas
	AutoRedraw	-1 'True
	Height	4830
	Left	4980
	ScaleMode	3 'Pixel
	Top	5760
	Width	4830
CommandButton	Name	ExitButton
	Caption	"Exit RPG"
	FontBold	0 'False
	FontSize	9.75
	Height	435
	Left	6960
	Top	4140
	Width	1875

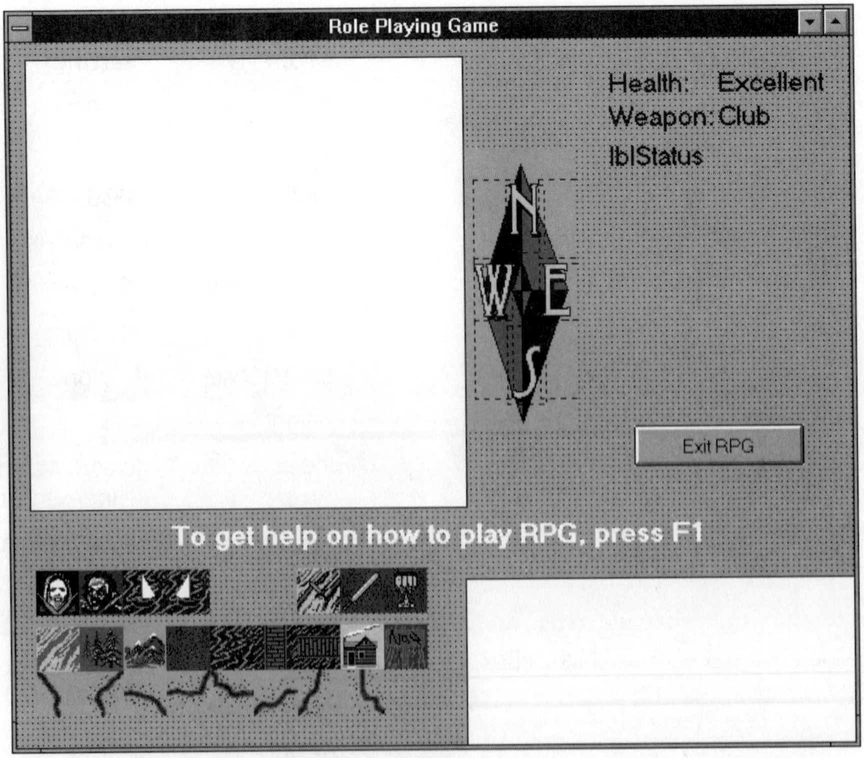

FIGURE 16-4

The main map form, MAP.FRM, at design time

When completed, the map form will look similar to Figure 16-4. A compass dial is displayed in the Picture2 PictureBox. You need to place eight Image controls inside Picture2, positioned over the eight compass directions. These Image controls won't be assigned any bitmaps, but will let the program intercept and handle mouse Click events that can be used to move the player's character. Add these controls inside the Picture2 PictureBox control, as shown in Table 16-4, positioning them over the compass directions they are named for.

TABLE 16-4

Objects contained inside MAP.FRM's Picture2 control

Object	Property	Setting
Image	Name	imgNorth
	MousePointer	7 'Size N S
Image	Name	imgNW
	MousePointer	8 'Size NW SE

Object	Property	Setting
Image	Name	imgSW
	MousePointer	6 'Size NE SW
Image	Name	imgSE
	MousePointer	8 'Size NW SE
Image	Name	imgSouth
	MousePointer	7 'Size N S
Image	Name	imgWest
	MousePointer	9 'Size W E
Image	Name	imgNE
	MousePointer	6 'Size NE SW
Image	Name	imgEast
	MousePointer	9 'Size W E

Now you can begin to add code to the form. As always, you'll need to declare some constants, variables, and Windows API functions used in the form. Add the code in Listing 16-3 to the form's Declarations section.

Listing 16-3 MAP.FRM Declarations section

```
Option Explicit
'------------------------------------------------------------
' Declare all the functions, constants, and variables used
' in MAP.FRM.
'------------------------------------------------------------

' Declare Windows API functions.
Declare Function BitBlt Lib "GDI" (ByVal hDestDC As Integer, ByVal X As Integer, ByVal
Y As Integer, ByVal nWidth As Integer, ByVal nHeight As Integer, ByVal hSrcDC As
Integer, ByVal XSrc As Integer, ByVal YSrc As Integer, ByVal dwRop As Long) As Integer

Declare Function sndPlaySound Lib "MMSYSTEM" (ByVal lpSound As String, ByVal Flags As
Integer) As Integer

' constants for sndPlaySound
Const SND_SYNC = (0)
Const SND_ASYNC = (1)
Const SND_NODEFAULT = (2)
Const SND_MEMORY = (4)
```

continued on next page

continued from previous page

```
Const SND_LOOP = (8)
Const SND_NOSTOP = (16)

' constants for keystrokes
Const VK_PRIOR = &H21
Const VK_NEXT = &H22
Const VK_END = &H23
Const VK_HOME = &H24
Const VK_LEFT = &H25
Const VK_UP = &H26
Const VK_RIGHT = &H27
Const VK_DOWN = &H28

' size of displayed map, in tiles
Const MapXSize = 10
Const MapYSize = 10

' size of entire map, in tiles
Const BigMapXSize = 150
Const BigMapYSize = 150

' constant for BitBlt
Const SRCCOPY = &HCC0020

Const WEAPON_CLUB = 0
Const WEAPON_DAGGER = 1
Const WEAPON_SWORD = 2

Dim FlagSylph As Integer ' True if sylph has been visited
Dim FlagHermit As Integer ' True if the hermit has been visited

Dim StepNumber As Integer 'keeps track of wave file to play

Dim StatusCountdown As Integer  ' keeps track of when status display
                                ' should be cleared

' holds map
Dim MapValues(1 To BigMapXSize) As String
Dim MapTopX As Integer
Dim MapTopY As Integer

' characters in game
Dim NumChars As Integer
Dim Chars(0 To 50) As Character

Const DESC_SYLPH_SICK = "Hello there, my old friend.  It's been far too long since you
                                visited.  You look quite ill.  I can help with that
                                ... but, then I must go.  If you want to cure the
                                poison, you should seek out the Golden Chalice.
                                Rumor has it you can find it to the east."
```

```
Const DESC_SYLPH_WELL = "Hello there, my old friend.  It's been far too long since you
                                visited.  I wish I could stick around and talk,
                                but, I must go.  If you want to cure the poison,
                                you should seek out the Golden Chalice.  Rumor has
                                it you can find it to the east."
Const DESC_BOATDOCK = "You're on a dock.  There is a rickety old row boat tied up
                                here.  You can see an island off to the west."
Const DESC_FOUNTAIN = "You see a magnificent fountain.  All of the plants around the
                                fountain are thriving.  The water coming from it
                                practically glows.  The water looks so clean, so
                                good.  What do you do?"
Const DESC_BOAT_SINKS = "As you pull up to the dock, the boat springs a leak.  You
                                manage to leap out before it sinks, but the boat
                                is gone."
Const DESC_CHALICE = "You found it!  Mmmm... you drink from it and feel MUCH better.
                                Time to wander home and return to the 'hard' life
                                of your pipe and your hammock ... The End"
Const DESC_DEAD = "You're dead.  I guess you won't be needing that chalice after all
                                ... thanks for playing."
Const DESC_SLEEPING = "It's late at night, and you're sleeping soundly.  Ahhh, a nice
                                long night's rest is nice after a long day
                                lounging in your hammock smoking your pipe and
                                drinking homebrew.  But, what's that?  Something's
                                in bed with you."
Const DESC_SNAKEBITE = "Ouch!  It bit you ... you feel a pain shooting up your leg.
                                It's a huge snake with big dripping fangs.  You
                                grab the club you keep next to your bed that you
                                use for rats and quickly dispatch the snake.
                                It'll make a nice belt now ..."
Const DESC_BEGIN_PLAY = "Unfortunately, you're feeling very, very weak.  If it wasn't
                                for your strong constitution, you'd probably be
                                dead now.  Maybe it's time to go looking for a
                                cure and get some revenge.  Your friend Sylvia the
                                Sylph can help.  She lives in the forest in the
                                valley to the south."
Const DESC_HERMIT = "Leave me alone!  Can't you see that I'm taking care of Clyde?
                                He's my only friend in the world.  Some nasty
                                ruffians just ran through here and uprooted him.
                                Now before you go asking a bunch of questions,
                                I'll just tell you what I know ... there's some
                                treasure to the northwest ... and the big evil guy
                                ran straight north.  That's all!  Go away!"
```

The text constants in the section above (the constants whose names begin with DESC_) are used to display text when the choice form, DISPLAY.FRM, is displayed.

The game really gets started when the map form is loaded, so let's start by adding a Form_Load event to MAP.FRM, as shown in Listing 16-4.

Listing 16-4 Load event

```
Sub Form_Load ()
'------------------------------------------------------------
' Load the map information and run the opening sequence.
'------------------------------------------------------------

    ' set up help file
    App.HelpFile = App.Path & "\RPG.HLP"

    ' make sure that things are random
    Randomize

    ' set the height
    Map.Height = 6000

    ' load picture form, but don't show
    Load PictureForm
    Load Display

    ' load map from disk
    LoadMap

    ' set current coordinates
    MapTopX = 1
    MapTopY = 1

    ' set initial character position
    Chars(0).X = 5
    Chars(0).Y = 5
    SetHealth 0, 1
    SetWeapon 0, WEAPON_CLUB

    ' start up monsters / NPCs
    FlagSylph = False
    CreateMonsters

    StepNumber = 1

    ' show initial messages
    SetStatus "Your adventure begins ..."
    PlaySound "SNORE", False

    ShowChoice DESC_SLEEPING, "", "Continue ...", 5

    ' show snake screen
    PlaySound "BITE", False

    ShowChoice DESC_SNAKEBITE, "", "Continue ...", 1

    ShowChoice DESC_BEGIN_PLAY, "", "Begin Play", 4
```

```
    ' paint initial map
    PaintMap

    ' Center the main map form.
    Me.Move (Screen.Width - Me.Width) \ 2, (Screen.Height - Me.Height) \ 2
End Sub
```

In the Load event, you initialize everything needed to run the game. The game map must be loaded into memory, and this is handled by calling the LoadMap routine. Remember that the map, although displayed on the screen as a collection of bitmap tiles, is actually stored on disk as a text file. This file, MAP.TXT, contains a single character for each tile that will be displayed on the screen. Of course, only a small part of this map can be seen by the player at any one time. Add the following LoadMap routine to the form.

```
Sub LoadMap ()
'----------------------------------------------------------
' Read the map file and store in MapValues string array.
'----------------------------------------------------------
Dim FileHandle As Integer ' file handle for read
Dim YIndex                ' index for map read

    ' get handle to use
    FileHandle = FreeFile

    On Error Resume Next
    Open App.Path & "\MAP.TXT" For Input As #FileHandle

    If Err = 0 Then
        For YIndex = 1 To BigMapYSize
            Line Input #FileHandle, MapValues(YIndex)
        Next YIndex
    End If

    Close #FileHandle

    On Error GoTo 0
End Sub
```

There are monsters lurking about in this game, and these characters must be created. The CreateMonsters routine in Listing 16-5 builds the data structures that describe these nefarious creatures.

Listing 16-5 CreateMonsters routine

```
Sub CreateMonsters ()
'----------------------------------------------------------
' Initialize the monster character structures.
'----------------------------------------------------------
```

continued on next page

continued from previous page

```
    ' first monster
    Chars(1).X = 84
    Chars(1).Y = 15
    Chars(1).Health = 1
    Chars(1).Weapon = WEAPON_CLUB
    Chars(1).Symbol = 1
    Chars(1).MinX = 78
    Chars(1).MaxX = 88
    Chars(1).MinY = 12
    Chars(1).MaxY = 16

    ' second monster
    Chars(2).X = 84
    Chars(2).Y = 16
    Chars(2).Health = 1
    Chars(2).Weapon = WEAPON_CLUB
    Chars(2).Symbol = 1
    Chars(2).MinX = 78
    Chars(2).MaxX = 88
    Chars(2).MinY = 12
    Chars(2).MaxY = 16

    ' third monster
    Chars(3).X = 97
    Chars(3).Y = 33
    Chars(3).Health = 2
    Chars(3).Weapon = WEAPON_DAGGER
    Chars(3).Symbol = 1
    Chars(3).MinX = 90
    Chars(3).MaxX = 103
    Chars(3).MinY = 31
    Chars(3).MaxY = 34

    ' final monster
    Chars(4).X = 126
    Chars(4).Y = 4
    Chars(4).Health = 4
    Chars(4).Weapon = WEAPON_DAGGER
    Chars(4).Symbol = 1
    Chars(4).MinX = 127
    Chars(4).MaxX = 127
    Chars(4).MinY = 6
    Chars(4).MaxY = 6

    NumChars = 4
End Sub
```

The program must also create the player's character. Information about all the characters is stored in an array of Character data structures called Char, with the player's information stored in the array's first element, Char(0). In the Load event, the program must designate the player's starting position on the map, as well as set the player's health level and what weapon he or she possesses. The routines SetHealth and SetWeapon are used to set these attributes for any character. Add these routines, as shown in Listing 16-6.

Listing 16-6 SetHealth and SetWeapon routines

```
Sub SetHealth (CharNum As Integer, NewHealth As Integer)
'--------------------------------------------------------------
' Modify a character's health value.
'--------------------------------------------------------------

    ' set the new health
    Chars(CharNum).Health = NewHealth

    ' this creature is dead ...
    If Chars(CharNum).Health <= 0 Then
        ' make it scream
        PlaySound "DEAD", True
        Chars(CharNum).Health = 0

        ' if this is the player, end the game
        If CharNum = 0 Then
            Dead
        End If
    End If

    ' if this is the user
    If CharNum = 0 Then
        ' display the new health
        DisplayHealth
    End If
End Sub

Sub SetWeapon (CharNum As Integer, Weapon As Integer)
'--------------------------------------------------------------
' Assign a new weapon to a character.
'--------------------------------------------------------------

    ' set the new weapon type
    Chars(CharNum).Weapon = Weapon

    ' if this is the user, display it
    If CharNum = 0 Then
        DisplayWeapon
    End If
End Sub
```

In the Load event, before the map form is actually displayed, the player is shown a sequence of three dialog box forms. These are presented using the DISPLAY.FRM form you created earlier. This sequence serves as an introduction to the game. The DISPLAY.FRM form is used throughout the game, whenever a choice must be presented to the player. To set up this form, the program must assign various properties and adjust the location of certain controls on DISPLAY.FRM. This work is encapsulated in the routine called ShowChoice.

```
Sub ShowChoice (Description As String, ChoiceA As String, ChoiceB As
String, PicNum As Integer)
'-------------------------------------------------------------
' When the player encounters something (a monster or object,
' for example), the player may be asked to make a choice.
' This choice is presented in the Display form.  This routine
' sets property values and shows the Display form.
'-------------------------------------------------------------

    If PicNum >= 0 Then
        Display.Pict.Picture = PictureForm.Picture1(PicNum)

        Display.Tag = "SHOW"
    Else
        Display.Tag = ""
    End If

    Display.Description.Caption = Description
    Display.Choice(0).Caption = ChoiceA
    Display.Choice(1).Caption = ChoiceB
    AdjustDisplay
    Display.Show 1

End Sub
```

The ShowChoice routine calls another routine, AdjustDisplay, whose sole purpose is to resize the DISPLAY.FRM form based on whether or not it contains a picture. This is shown in Listing 16-7.

Listing 16-7 AdjustDisplay routine

```
Sub AdjustDisplay ()
'-------------------------------------------------------------
' Adjust the Display form's controls based on the value of
' its Tag property.  The Tag property indicates if a bitmap
' will be displayed on the form or just text.
'-------------------------------------------------------------
Dim margin As Integer
Dim BW As Integer

    margin = (9 * Screen.TwipsPerPixelX)
```

```
    BW = Display.Width - Display.ScaleWidth

    ' Make room for a bitmap
    If UCase$(Display.Tag) = "SHOW" Then
        Display.Pict.Visible = True

        Display.Width = BW + Display.Pict.Width + (margin * 2) + Display.Description.Width
        Display.Description.Left = margin + Display.Pict.Width
        Display.Choice(0).Left = margin + Display.Pict.Width
        Display.Choice(1).Left = margin + Display.Pict.Width

    ' Just show the text
    Else
        Display.Pict.Visible = False

        Display.Width = BW + (margin * 2) + Display.Description.Width
        Display.Description.Left = margin
        Display.Choice(0).Left = margin
        Display.Choice(1).Left = margin
    End If

    ' hide choice button(s) if needed
    Display.Choice(0).Visible = (Len(Display.Choice(0).Caption) <> 0)
    Display.Choice(1).Visible = (Len(Display.Choice(1).Caption) <> 0)

    ' center form on screen
    Display.Move (Screen.Width - Display.Width) / 2, (Screen.Height - Display.Height) / 2
End Sub
```

Before the map form is initially displayed, the map must be constructed and displayed in the Picture1 PictureBox control. This is handled via the PaintMap routine. This routine uses the BitBlt API function to copy individual tile images onto the PictureBox control the player sees on-screen. Actually, PaintMap constructs the bitmap in an off-screen PictureBox called picMapCanvas, then BitBlts picMapCanvas into the on-screen Picture1 PictureBox. This creates much smoother rendering, as the player cannot see the individual tiles being drawn.

```
Sub PaintMap ()
'--------------------------------------------------------------
' Build a new map bitmap in memory (using Windows API calls),
' then BitBlt this new bitmap into the on-screen PictureBox.
'--------------------------------------------------------------
Dim X
Dim XIndex, YIndex
Dim CharacterIndex As Integer

    For XIndex = 0 To MapXSize - 1
        For YIndex = 0 To MapYSize - 1
            X = BitBlt(picMapCanvas.hDC, XIndex * 32, YIndex * 32, 32, 32,
                Terrain(TerrainVal(Mid(MapValues(YIndex + MapTopY), XIndex + MapTopX,
                1))).hDC, 0, 0, SRCCOPY)
```

continued on next page

continued from previous page

```
        Next YIndex
    Next XIndex

    For CharacterIndex = 0 To NumChars
        If (Chars(CharacterIndex).X >= MapTopX) And (Chars(CharacterIndex).X < MapTopX +
        MapXSize) And (Chars(CharacterIndex).Y >= MapTopY) And (Chars(CharacterIndex).Y <
        MapTopY + MapYSize) And (Chars(CharacterIndex).Health > 0) Then
            ' paint character
            X = BitBlt(picMapCanvas.hDC, (Chars(CharacterIndex).X - MapTopX) * 32,
                (Chars(CharacterIndex).Y - MapTopY) * 32, 32, 32,
                Characters(Chars(CharacterIndex).Symbol).hDC, 0, 0, SRCCOPY)
        End If
    Next CharacterIndex

    X = BitBlt(Picture1.hDC, 0, 0, MapXSize * 32, MapYSize * 32, picMapCanvas.hDC, 0, 0,
     SRCCOPY)

End Sub
```

On many occasions, the PaintMap routine is overkill. PaintMap redraws the entire visible map area, but many times the program needs only to update a single tile. In these instances, the PaintMapSquare routine is used. PaintMapSquare BitBlts a single tile onto a specified map location.

```
Sub PaintMapSquare (X As Integer, Y As Integer)
'------------------------------------------------------------
' Redraw just a single tile on the map.
'------------------------------------------------------------
Dim Temp

    If (X <> Chars(0).X) Or (Y <> Chars(0).Y) Then
        Temp = BitBlt(Picture1.hDC, (X - MapTopX) * 32, (Y - MapTopY) * 32, 32, 32,
                Terrain(TerrainVal(Mid(MapValues(Y), X, 1))).hDC, 0, 0, SRCCOPY)
    Else
        Temp = BitBlt(Picture1.hDC, (X - MapTopX) * 32, (Y - MapTopY) * 32, 32, 32,
                Characters(0).hDC, 0, 0, SRCCOPY)
    End If
End Sub
```

The game progresses as the player explores the mysterious new world. Moving through this world is quite easy. The player can simply press the arrow keys on the keyboard's numeric keypad. The game processes all these keys in the form's KeyDown event. This event contains the core of the game's logic. Add the Form_KeyDown event, as shown in Listing 16-8.

Listing 16-8 Form_KeyDown event

```
Sub Form_KeyDown (KeyCode As Integer, Shift As Integer)
'------------------------------------------------------------
' Handle the player's request to move to another tile.
'------------------------------------------------------------
```

```
Dim OldX As Integer
Dim OldY As Integer
Dim OldMapX As Integer
Dim OldMapY As Integer
Dim NewTerrain As Integer

    ' save the old position of the character / screen
    OldX = Chars(0).X
    OldY = Chars(0).Y
    OldMapX = MapTopX
    OldMapY = MapTopY

    ' get the new position of the character
    Select Case KeyCode
        Case VK_DOWN:
            If Chars(0).Y < BigMapYSize Then
                Chars(0).Y = Chars(0).Y + 1
            End If
        Case VK_UP:
            If Chars(0).Y > 1 Then
                Chars(0).Y = Chars(0).Y - 1
            End If
        Case VK_LEFT:
            If Chars(0).X > 1 Then
                Chars(0).X = Chars(0).X - 1
            End If
        Case VK_RIGHT:
            If Chars(0).X < BigMapXSize Then
                Chars(0).X = Chars(0).X + 1
            End If
        Case VK_HOME:
            If Chars(0).X > 1 Then
                Chars(0).X = Chars(0).X - 1
            End If

            If Chars(0).Y > 1 Then
                Chars(0).Y = Chars(0).Y - 1
            End If
        Case VK_PRIOR:
            If Chars(0).X < BigMapXSize Then
                Chars(0).X = Chars(0).X + 1
            End If

            If Chars(0).Y > 1 Then
                Chars(0).Y = Chars(0).Y - 1
            End If
        Case VK_NEXT:
            If Chars(0).X < BigMapXSize Then
                Chars(0).X = Chars(0).X + 1
            End If

            If Chars(0).Y < BigMapYSize Then
```

continued on next page

continued from previous page

```
                Chars(0).Y = Chars(0).Y + 1
            End If
        Case VK_END:
            If Chars(0).X > 1 Then
                Chars(0).X = Chars(0).X - 1
            End If

            If Chars(0).Y < BigMapYSize Then
                Chars(0).Y = Chars(0).Y + 1
            End If
    End Select

    NewTerrain = TerrainVal(Mid(MapValues(Chars(0).Y), Chars(0).X, 1))

    ' if this is water or mountain, don't move
    If NewTerrain = 2 Or NewTerrain = 4 Then
        Chars(0).X = OldX
        Chars(0).Y = OldY
    ' is there a live monster at this location?
    ElseIf IsMonster(Chars(0).X, Chars(0).Y) Then
        Dim MonsterIndex As Integer

        ' get the index to the monster
        MonsterIndex = MonsterAt(Chars(0).X, Chars(0).Y)

        ' we don't need to move
        Chars(0).X = OldX
        Chars(0).Y = OldY

        ' attempt to hit the monster
        Attack 0, MonsterIndex
        ' move monsters
        MoveMonsters
        PaintMap
        Exit Sub
    End If

    If (Chars(0).X <> OldX) Or (Chars(0).Y <> OldY) Then
        Dim TempResult As Integer

        ' move monsters
        MoveMonsters

        ' check to see if we should clear the status
        If StatusCountdown = 1 Then
            ' clear status label
            lblStatus = ""
            StatusCountdown = 0
        ' if we're still counting down, decrement
        ElseIf StatusCountdown > 0 Then
            ' count down
```

```
            StatusCountdown = StatusCountdown - 1
        End If

        ' if they found a dagger
        If NewTerrain = 33 Then
            NewTerrain = 0
            StrOverwrite MapValues(Chars(0).Y), "0", Chars(0).X
            SetStatus "You found a dagger!"
            SetWeapon 0, WEAPON_DAGGER
        ' check for a sword
        ElseIf NewTerrain = 34 Then
            NewTerrain = 3
            StrOverwrite MapValues(Chars(0).Y), "3", Chars(0).X
            SetStatus "You found a sword!"
            SetWeapon 0, WEAPON_SWORD
        ElseIf NewTerrain = 35 Then
            Chalice
        End If

        ' play the step sound
        Select Case NewTerrain
            Case 0: ' step sound for sand / desert
                PlaySound "STEPDES" & Format(StepNumber, "0"), False
            Case 1: ' step sound for forest
                PlaySound "STEPFOR" & Format(StepNumber, "0"), False
            Case 3, 8: ' step sound for plains
                PlaySound "STEPGRE" & Format(StepNumber, "0"), False
            Case 5, 6: ' step sound for bridge
                PlaySound "STEPBRI" & Format(StepNumber, "0"), False
            Case Else: ' generic step sound
                PlaySound "STEP" & Format(StepNumber, "0"), False
        End Select

        ' move to the next step sound
        StepNumber = 3 - StepNumber

        ' recompute x position of screen
        If ((Chars(0).X - MapTopX) < 3) And (Chars(0).X > 3) Then
            MapTopX = Chars(0).X - 3
        ElseIf ((Chars(0).X - MapTopX) > 6) And (Chars(0).X < 198) Then
            MapTopX = Chars(0).X - 6
        End If

        ' recompute y position of screen
        If ((Chars(0).Y - MapTopY) < 3) And (Chars(0).Y > 3) Then
            MapTopY = Chars(0).Y - 3
        ElseIf ((Chars(0).Y - MapTopY) > 6) And (Chars(0).Y < 198) Then
            MapTopY = Chars(0).Y - 6
        End If

        PaintMap
    End If
```

continued on next page

continued from previous page

```
    ' check for special stuff
    If (Chars(0).X = 41) And (Chars(0).Y = 18) Then
        LakePath
    ElseIf (Chars(0).X = 66) And (Chars(0).Y = 52) Then
        SecretCave
    ' check for sign at entrance to player's valley
    ElseIf (Chars(0).X = 6) And (Chars(0).Y = 9) Then
        SetStatus "You see a sign that says 'Private Valley - Keep Out!'"
    ElseIf ((Chars(0).X = 62) And (Chars(0).Y = 70)) Or ((Chars(0).X = 78) And
    (Chars(0).Y = 63)) Then
        SetStatus "You see a sign that says 'Big Valley - Nothing Happens Here ... And
        We Like It That Way'"
    ElseIf (Chars(0).X = 7) And (Chars(0).Y = 32) Then
        SylviaTheSylph
    ' check for boat/island
    ElseIf (Chars(0).X = 32) And (Chars(0).Y = 14) Then
        BoatDock
    ' check for hermit
    ElseIf (Chars(0).X = 126) And (Chars(0).Y = 57) Then
        Hermit
    ElseIf (Chars(0).X = 127) And (Chars(0).Y = 6) Then
        SetStatus "There's the chalice!  Boy, that guy guarding it sure looks big.
        I hope you're well armed!"
    ElseIf (Chars(0).X = 127) And (Chars(0).Y = 5) Then
        SetStatus "The closer you get, the bigger he is.  Good luck!  You'll need
        it ..."
    End If

End Sub
```

In the course of the game, the player encounters various situations, some good, some bad, and some downright deadly. Most of these encounters are tied to the player landing on a particular map tile. Major encounters, such as finding the sylph, or stumbling upon the secret cave, are handled by their own routines. Add these routines, as described in Listing 16-9.

Reaching the Boat Dock is handled by the BoatDock and BoatDockRow routines.

Listing 16-9 BoatDock and BoatDockRow routines

```
Sub BoatDock ()
'------------------------------------------------------------
' Handle choice at the Boat Dock.
'------------------------------------------------------------
Static IslandCount As Integer

    ' if the boat has sunk ... can't go to island '
    If IslandCount >= 5 Then
        Exit Sub
    End If
```

```
' play the harbor sounds
PlaySound "BOATDOCK", False

ShowChoice DESC_BOATDOCK, "Row To Island", "Stay Here", -1

' ensure proper repaint
DoEvents

' if the user wants to go to the island
If DisplayChoice = 0 Then
    ' row to island
    BoatDockRow 31, 26, -1, 2

    ' finally at the island
    Chars(0).Symbol = 0
    Chars(0).Y = 12
    Chars(0).X = 25
    CenterMap
    PaintMap

    ' handle fountain
    PlaySound "FOUNTAIN", False

    ShowChoice DESC_FOUNTAIN, "Drink Water and Leave", "Just Leave", -1

    ' handle user choice of drinking
    If DisplayChoice = 0 Then
        ' increment drinks from the fountain
        IslandCount = IslandCount + 1

        ' if the user needs healing, do it
        If Chars(0).Health < 3 Then
            ' ensure map repaints
            DoEvents
            PlaySound "CURE", True
            SetHealth 0, Chars(0).Health + 1

            ' ensure health level repaints
            DoEvents
        End If
    End If

    ' row to dock
    BoatDockRow 26, 31, 1, 3

    ' finally at the dock
    Chars(0).Symbol = 0
    Chars(0).Y = 14
    Chars(0).X = 32
    CenterMap
    PaintMap
```

continued on next page

continued from previous page

```
        ' check to see if island is used up
        If IslandCount = 5 Then
            ShowChoice DESC_BOAT_SINKS, "", "Continue ...", -1
        End If
    End If
End Sub

Sub BoatDockRow (XStart As Integer, XEnd As Integer, XInc As Integer, Symbol As Integer)
'-------------------------------------------------------------------
' Handle journey across the lake.
'-------------------------------------------------------------------
Dim I As Integer
Dim TimeTemp As String

    ' play boat rowing sound
    PlaySound "BOAT", False

    ' row to island
    Chars(0).Y = 13

    ' use west headed boat for char
    Chars(0).Symbol = Symbol

    ' move across the lake
    For I = XStart To XEnd Step XInc
        Chars(0).X = I
        CenterMap
        PaintMap

        ' wait a second before moving
        TimeTemp = Time$
        Do While TimeTemp = Time$
        Loop
    Next I

    ' return symbol to normal
    Chars(0).Symbol = 0
End Sub
```

During the adventure, the player might encounter a hermit, though the meeting will probably be less than enlightening. This befuddled character is handled in the Hermit routine.

```
Sub Hermit ()
'-------------------------------------------------------------------
' The player encounters the Hermit.
'-------------------------------------------------------------------

    ' if we've been here before, don't do it again
    If FlagHermit Then
        Exit Sub
```

```
        End If

        ' play the Hermit's Theme
        PlaySound "HERMIT", False

        ' make sure we don't come back here again
        FlagHermit = True

        ' give hermit's message to player
        ShowChoice DESC_HERMIT, "", "Continue ...", 3

    End Sub
```

The resourceful player may stumble upon a hidden path to an otherwise inaccessible lake. This discovery is handled by the LakePath routine (Listing 16-10).

Listing 16-10 LakePath routine

```
Sub LakePath ()
'--------------------------------------------------------------
' The player has encountered a secret lake path.
'--------------------------------------------------------------

    ' check to see if we've done this before
    If Mid(MapValues(17), 40, 1) = "C" Then
        ' already done, get out
        Exit Sub
    End If

    PlaySound "LAKEPATH", False

    ' tell user they found a path
    SetStatus "You found a secret path!"

    ' show the path to the user - This actually modifies the map.
    StrOverwrite MapValues(17), "C", 40
    PaintMap

    StrOverwrite MapValues(17), "E", 39
    PaintMap

    StrOverwrite MapValues(16), "C", 38
    PaintMap

    StrOverwrite MapValues(16), "F", 37
    PaintMap

    StrOverwrite MapValues(17), "D", 36
    PaintMap

    StrOverwrite MapValues(17), "E", 35
```

continued on next page

continued from previous page

```
    PaintMap

    StrOverwrite MapValues(16), "C", 34
    PaintMap

    StrOverwrite MapValues(16), "E", 33
    PaintMap
End Sub
```

An object of considerable use can only be found when the intrepid player discovers the location of the secret cave. This lucky happenstance is controlled by the SecretCave routine.

```
Sub SecretCave ()
'------------------------------------------------------------
' Reveal the Secret Cave.
'------------------------------------------------------------

    ' check to see if we've done this before
    If Mid(MapValues(51), 66, 1) = "A" Then
        ' already done, get out
        Exit Sub
    End If

    ' play sound
    PlaySound "SECCAVE", False

    ' tell user they found a cave
    SetStatus "You found a secret cave!"

    ' show the cave to the user - This actually modifies the map.
    StrOverwrite MapValues(51), "A", 66
    PaintMap

    StrOverwrite MapValues(50), "H", 65
    PaintMap

    StrOverwrite MapValues(49), "O", 65
    StrOverwrite MapValues(48), "O", 64
    StrOverwrite MapValues(48), "X", 65
    StrOverwrite MapValues(48), "O", 66
    StrOverwrite MapValues(47), "O", 65
    PaintMap
End Sub
```

When the player begins the game, the character has just been bitten by a snake, so his or her health is somewhat poor. A quick recuperation is possible if the player can find Sylvia the Sylph, who lives somewhere in the woods. The SylviaTheSylph routine controls this encounter.

```
Sub SylviaTheSylph ()
'-------------------------------------------------------------
' Handle visiting Sylvia the Sylph
'-------------------------------------------------------------

    ' if we've been here before, get out
    If FlagSylph Then
        Exit Sub
    End If

    ' play the Sylvia's Theme
    PlaySound "SYLPH", False

    ' make sure we don't come back here again
    FlagSylph = True

    ' if the character is wounded
    If Chars(0).Health < 3 Then
        ShowChoice DESC_SYLPH_SICK, "Accept Sylvia's Help", "Refuse Her Help", 0

        If DisplayChoice = 0 Then
            ' play the healing sound
            PlaySound "CURE", False

            ' increase the character's health
            SetHealth 0, Chars(0).Health + 1
        End If
    Else
        ' the character is fully healed already
        ShowChoice DESC_SYLPH_WELL, "", "Continue Your Adventure", 0
    End If

End Sub
```

Of course, finding the sylph and restoring the player to full health is only one adventure in this game. The ultimate goal is the acquisition of a golden chalice. This momentus discovery is handled by the Chalice routine.

```
Sub Chalice ()
'-------------------------------------------------------------
' The player has found the Chalice!
'-------------------------------------------------------------

    PlaySound "CHALICE", False

    ' display the chalice and winning message
    ShowChoice DESC_CHALICE, "", "Exit", 2

    ' exit the program
    End
End Sub
```

Of course, as in all challenges, there are risks. Although with fortitude, cunning, and wits the player may achieve the goal, the player also will likely run into the following routine.

```
Sub Dead ()
'--------------------------------------------------------------
' Uh-oh. You're dead!
'--------------------------------------------------------------

    ' display the chalice and winning message
    ShowChoice DESC_DEAD, "", "Exit", 4

    ' exit the program
    End
End Sub
```

Every program must have its support subroutines—routines that encapsulate frequent occurrences into manageable little packages. VB-RPG has several of these, some of which fall into categories.

Monster Support Routines

The following four routines, IsMonster, MonsterAt, MoveMonster, and MoveMonsters, all simplify handling the player's encounters with monsters. Add these routines, as shown in Listing 16-11.

Listing 16-11 Handling Monster encounters

```
Function IsMonster (X As Integer, Y As Integer) As Integer
'--------------------------------------------------------------
' Is there a monster at this location?
'--------------------------------------------------------------

    IsMonster = (MonsterAt(X, Y) <> -1)
End Function

Function MonsterAt (X As Integer, Y As Integer) As Integer
'--------------------------------------------------------------
' What is the index of the monster at this location?
'--------------------------------------------------------------
Dim I As Integer

    ' scan monsters
    For I = 1 To NumChars
        ' found the monster, return the index
        If (Chars(I).Health > 0) And (Chars(I).X = X) And (Chars(I).Y = Y) Then
            MonsterAt = I
            Exit Function
        End If
```

```
    Next I

    ' couldn't find monster, return -1
    MonsterAt = -1
End Function

Sub MoveMonster (MonsterIndex As Integer)
'--------------------------------------------------------------
' Move this monster, try to move towards character.
'--------------------------------------------------------------
Dim NewX As Integer
Dim NewY As Integer
Dim NewTerrain As Integer

    ' get attempted new X position
    If Chars(0).X < Chars(MonsterIndex).X Then
        NewX = Chars(MonsterIndex).X - 1
    ElseIf Chars(0).X > Chars(MonsterIndex).X Then
        NewX = Chars(MonsterIndex).X + 1
    Else
        NewX = Chars(MonsterIndex).X
    End If

    ' get attempted new Y position
    If Chars(0).Y < Chars(MonsterIndex).Y Then
        NewY = Chars(MonsterIndex).Y - 1
    ElseIf Chars(0).Y > Chars(MonsterIndex).Y Then
        NewY = Chars(MonsterIndex).Y + 1
    Else
        NewY = Chars(MonsterIndex).Y
    End If

    ' get value of current terrain
    NewTerrain = TerrainVal(Mid(MapValues(NewY), NewX, 1))

    ' if this is where the character is, attack!
    If (NewX = Chars(0).X) And (NewY = Chars(0).Y) Then
        Attack MonsterIndex, 0
        Exit Sub
    ' if there's no monster here, try to move
    ElseIf (MonsterAt(NewX, NewY) = -1) And (NewTerrain <> 2) And (NewTerrain <> 4) Then
        ' if this is within bounds for this monster
        If (NewX >= Chars(MonsterIndex).MinX) And (NewX <= Chars(MonsterIndex).MaxX) And
           (NewY >= Chars(MonsterIndex).MinY) And (NewY <= Chars(MonsterIndex).MaxY)
           Then
            ' move the monster
            Chars(MonsterIndex).X = NewX
            Chars(MonsterIndex).Y = NewY
        End If
    End If
End Sub

Sub MoveMonsters ()
```

continued on next page

continued from previous page

```
'------------------------------------------------------------
' Move all of the monsters
'------------------------------------------------------------
Dim I As Integer ' used for monster index

    ' scan monsters and move the ones that can
    For I = 1 To NumChars
        If Chars(I).Health > 0 Then
            MoveMonster I
        End If
    Next I
End Sub
```

Updating the Screen

Several routines are used to handle updating various parts of the map form. Two important ones, PaintMap and PaintMapSquare, were presented earlier. The screen also displays the player's character's health, what weapon he or she is carrying, and some brief status information. This information is displayed using the DisplayHealth, DisplayWeapon, and SetStatus routines (Listing 16-12).

Listing 16-12 DisplayHealth, DisplayWeapon, and SetStatus subroutines

```
Sub DisplayHealth ()
'------------------------------------------------------------
' Display health to user
'------------------------------------------------------------

    Select Case Chars(0).Health
        Case 0:
            lblHealth.ForeColor = RGB(0, 0, 0)
            lblHealth.Caption = "Dead"
        Case 1:
            lblHealth.ForeColor = RGB(255, 0, 0)
            lblHealth.Caption = "Poor"
        Case 2:
            lblHealth.ForeColor = RGB(255, 255, 0)
            lblHealth.Caption = "Average"
        Case 3:
            lblHealth.ForeColor = RGB(0, 255, 0)
            lblHealth.Caption = "Excellent"
    End Select
End Sub

Sub DisplayWeapon ()
'------------------------------------------------------------
' Display the player's current weapon.
'------------------------------------------------------------
```

```
        Select Case Chars(0).Weapon
            Case 0:
                lblWeapon = "Club"
            Case 1:
                lblWeapon = "Dagger"
            Case 2:
                lblWeapon = "Sword"
        End Select
    End Sub

    Sub SetStatus (NewStatus As String)
    '--------------------------------------------------------------
    ' Set status and countdown
    '--------------------------------------------------------------

        lblStatus.Caption = NewStatus
        StatusCountdown = 5
    End Sub
```

Attacked!

When a character is attacked, VB-RPG must decide if the attack was successful, and if so, how much damage was incurred. The attack itself is handled by the following Attack routine.

```
Sub Attack (Attacker As Integer, Defender As Integer)
'--------------------------------------------------------------
' Compute the results of an attack.
'--------------------------------------------------------------

    ' if the weapon hits, apply damage
    If WeaponHit(Chars(Attacker).Weapon) Then
        PlaySound "HIT", True

        ' compute damage and apply to defender
        SetHealth Defender, Chars(Defender).Health -
        WeaponDamage(Chars(Attacker).Weapon)

        ' display result if not player
        If Attacker <> 0 Then
            SetStatus "He hit you!  Ouch!"
        End If
    Else
        ' play swish (miss) sound
        PlaySound "MISS", True
    End If
End Sub
```

The Attack routine first calls a function, WeaponHit, that returns True if the weapon actually made contact. This is handled by generating random values based on the type of weapon used.

```
Function WeaponHit (Weapon As Integer) As Integer
'------------------------------------------------------------
' Did the weapon make a hit?
'------------------------------------------------------------

    Select Case Weapon
        Case WEAPON_CLUB:
            WeaponHit = (Rnd < .4)
        Case WEAPON_DAGGER:
            WeaponHit = (Rnd < .35)
        Case WEAPON_SWORD:
            WeaponHit = (Rnd < .65)
    End Select
End Function
```

If the weapon did hit the character, the Attack routine then calculates the injury's effect on the character's health. This is calculated by calling the WeaponDamage routine, which also uses generated random numbers to return the extent of the injury.

```
Function WeaponDamage (Weapon As Integer) As Integer
'------------------------------------------------------------
' Calculate damage based on type of weapon.
'------------------------------------------------------------

    Select Case Weapon
        Case WEAPON_CLUB:
            WeaponDamage = 1
        Case WEAPON_DAGGER:
            WeaponDamage = 1 + Int(Rnd + .5)
        Case WEAPON_SWORD:
            WeaponDamage = 1 + Int(2 * Rnd + .5)
    End Select
End Function
```

Odds and Ends

The following support routines don't fall easily into any general category. For example, the CenterMap routine is used by the BoatDock and BoatDockRow routines to keep the player's location centered on the map.

```
Sub CenterMap ()
'------------------------------------------------------------
' Keep player centered in map display.
'------------------------------------------------------------

    MapTopX = Chars(0).X - (MapXSize / 2)
    MapTopY = Chars(0).Y - (MapYSize / 2)
End Sub
```

The PlaySound routine is a simple wrapper around the sndPlaySound Windows API routine.

```
Sub PlaySound (SoundName As String, Exclusive As Integer)
'------------------------------------------------------------
' Play a wave audio file.
'------------------------------------------------------------
Dim TempResult As Integer

    If Exclusive Then
        TempResult = sndPlaySound(App.Path & "\" & SoundName & ".WAV", SND_NODEFAULT)
    Else
        TempResult = sndPlaySound(App.Path & "\" & SoundName & ".WAV", SND_NODEFAULT + SND_ASYNC)
    End If
End Sub
```

The StrOverwrite routine overwrites a section of one string with the contents of another string. This routine is generic and could be used in any program that required this type of string replacement. It is used in VB-RPG to modify the character strings that define the map. This routine modifies the map at runtime to reveal hidden paths and caves.

```
Sub StrOverwrite (InputStr As String, OverStr As String, Offset As Integer)
'------------------------------------------------------------
' Used to modify a specified location (or locations) in the
' map array.
'------------------------------------------------------------

    InputStr = Left(InputStr, Offset - 1) & OverStr & Mid(InputStr, Offset + Len(OverStr))
End Sub
```

Finally, the TerrainVal function returns a numeric value associated with a map location.

```
Function TerrainVal (C As String) As Integer
'------------------------------------------------------------
' Returns a terrain value.
'------------------------------------------------------------

    TerrainVal = InStr("0123456789ABCDEFGHIJKLMNOPQRSTUVWXYZ", C) - 1
End Function
```

Handling Map Form Events

In addition to the Load and KeyDown events described earlier, several other event handlers are required to take care of various occurrences. For example, when the form is redisplayed, you want to make sure the map is redisplayed properly. This is handled by adding a simple Paint event to the Picture1 control.

```
Sub Picture1_Paint ()
'-------------------------------------------------------------
' Repaint the map as necessary.
'-------------------------------------------------------------

    ' ensure we've got a good map
    PaintMap
End Sub
```

Likewise, the program must redraw the three-dimensional borders around certain form controls. This can be handled easily with the addition of a Paint event for the form.

```
Sub Form_Paint ()
    Make3D Me, Picture1, BORDER_RAISED, 2
    Make3D Me, lblFrame, BORDER_RAISED, 2
    Make3D Me, ExitButton, BORDER_INSET, 2
End Sub
```

Although the VB-RPG game was originally designed to be controlled by the keyboard, the addition of a few simple Image controls over the compass bitmap makes adding mouse support trivial. These eight Image controls create hot spots over the compass at each of the eight compass directions. Each Image control has a simple Click event that calls the form's KeyDown event, passing it the value of an appropriate directional key. For example, when the imgNorth control is clicked, it calls Form_KeyDown, passing it the VK_UP key value. In this way, the program thinks the player actually pressed the up arrow key! Add all eight event handlers, as shown in Listing 16-13.

Listing 16-13 Mouse event handlers

```
Sub imgEast_Click ()
'-------------------------------------------------------------
' Move east via mouse click.
'-------------------------------------------------------------

    Form_KeyDown VK_RIGHT, 0
End Sub

Sub imgNE_Click ()
'-------------------------------------------------------------
' Move northeast via mouse click.
'-------------------------------------------------------------

    Form_KeyDown VK_PRIOR, 0
End Sub

Sub imgNorth_Click ()
```

```
'---------------------------------------------------------------
' Move north via mouse click.
'---------------------------------------------------------------

    Form_KeyDown VK_UP, 0
End Sub

Sub imgNW_Click ()
'---------------------------------------------------------------
' Move northwest via mouse click.
'---------------------------------------------------------------

    Form_KeyDown VK_HOME, 0
End Sub

Sub imgSE_Click ()
'---------------------------------------------------------------
' Move southeast via mouse click.
'---------------------------------------------------------------

    Form_KeyDown VK_NEXT, 0
End Sub

Sub imgSouth_Click ()
'---------------------------------------------------------------
' Move south via mouse click.
'---------------------------------------------------------------

    Form_KeyDown VK_DOWN, 0
End Sub

Sub imgSW_Click ()
'---------------------------------------------------------------
' Move southwest via mouse click.
'---------------------------------------------------------------

    Form_KeyDown VK_END, 0
End Sub

Sub imgWest_Click ()
'---------------------------------------------------------------
' Move west via mouse click.
'---------------------------------------------------------------

    Form_KeyDown VK_LEFT, 0
End Sub
```

The player can terminate the game either by pressing the Exit RPG button or by selecting Close from the system menu. To handle both these situations, add the two events shown below.

```
Sub ExitButton_Click ()
'-------------------------------------------------------------
' Exit the program
'-------------------------------------------------------------

    End
End Sub

Sub Form_Unload (Cancel As Integer)
'-------------------------------------------------------------
' End the program.
'-------------------------------------------------------------

    End
End Sub
```

Enhancements and Improvements to VB-RPG

This game was constructed to be easy to extend and change. Changing the map is as easy as changing the MAP.TXT file, though you need to be careful to take into account the current location of characters and objects. This program lends itself to enhancements as well. Here are a few ideas to get you started.

- Define the locations and attributes of objects and characters in a separate text file, independent of the game itself.
- Build more intelligence, perhaps even a personality, into each character.
- Extend the character attributes to include such things as skill and experience. For example, the more a player uses a sword, the better the player should become with that weapon.

I'm indebted to James Shields for creating this wonderful game, as well as the Adventure game in the last chapter. These examples really exploit the possibilities of Visual Basic and Windows for building intriguing and captivating games.

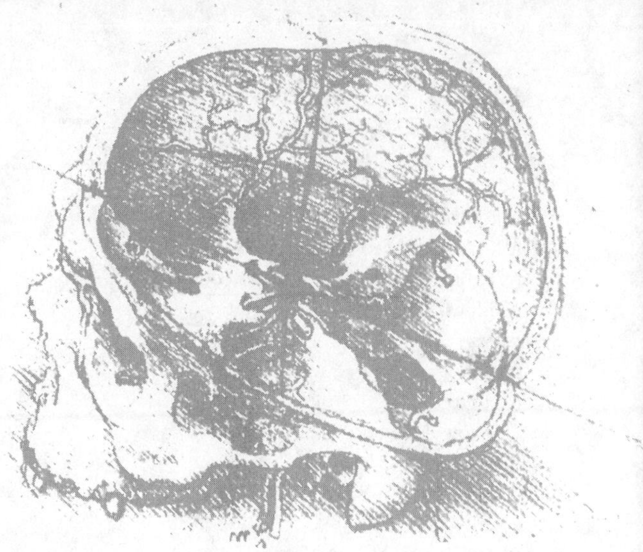

Index

T

X

Y

Z

NOTES

NOTES

NOTES

NOTES

NOTES

NOTES

NOTES

NOTES

NOTES

NOTES

NOTES

ENVIRONMENTAL AWARENESS

Books have a substantial influence on the destruction of the forests of the Earth. For example, it takes 17 trees to produce one ton of paper. A first printing of 30,000 copies of a typical 480-page book consumes 108,000 pounds of paper, which will require 918 trees!

Waite Group Press™ is against the clear-cutting of forests and supports reforestation of the Pacific Northwest of the United States and Canada, where most of this paper comes from. As a publisher with several hundred thousand books sold each year, we feel an obligation to give back to the planet. We will therefore support organizations which seek to preserve the forests of planet Earth.

WAITE GROUP PRESS™

GARDENS OF IMAGINATION

Christopher Lampton

Learn to program sophisticated animated maze games with ray casting and other techniques. Disk includes a high-speed maze game with code, and utilities for designing new mazes.

Available now
580 pages
ISBN: 1-878739-59-X
U.S. $34.95 Can. $50.95
1 - 3.5″ disk

THE BLACK ART OF WINDOWS GAME PROGRAMMING

Eric R. Lyons

The Black Art of Windows Game Programming makes it easy to use the WinG DLL to write high-performance Windows games, even if you've never developed Windows programs before. This book teaches real-world game programming techniques, featuring practical examples, hints, and code.

Available now
650 pages
ISBN: 1-878739-95-6
U.S. $34.95 Can. $50.95
1 - CD-ROM

RAY TRACING WORLDS WITH POV-RAY

Alexander Enzmann, Lutz Kretzschmar, and Chris Young

Bundled with the POV-Ray 2.0 ray tracer and Moray 2.0 wireframe modeler, this intermediate-level book details how to create sophisticated ray tracing scenes on your PC.

Available now
600 pages
ISBN: 1-878739-64-6
U.S. $44.95 Can. $62.95
1 - 3.5″ disk

TO ORDER TOLL FREE CALL 1-800-368-9369

TELEPHONE 415-924-2575 • FAX 415-924-2576

OR SEND ORDER FORM TO: WAITE GROUP PRESS, 200 TAMAL PLAZA, CORTE MADERA, CA 94925

Qty	Book	US/Can Price	Total
___	Black Art of 3D Game Programming	$49.95/72.95	_____
___	Black Art of Windows Game Programming	$34.95/50.95	_____
___	Gardens of Imagination	$34.95/50.95	_____
___	Image Lab, Second Edition	$39.95/57.95	_____
___	Ray Tracing Worlds with POV-Ray	$44.95/62.95	_____
___	Visual Basic 4.0 Multimedia How-To	$36.95/53.95	_____
Calif. residents add 7.25% Sales Tax			_____

Shipping

USPS ($5 first book/$1 each add'l) _____

UPS Two Day ($10/$2) _____

Canada ($10/$4) _____

TOTAL _____

Ship to

Name ____________________

Company ____________________

Address ____________________

City, State, Zip ____________________

Phone ____________________

Payment Method

☐ Check Enclosed ☐ VISA ☐ MasterCard

Card# ____________________ Exp. Date ________

Signature ____________________

SATISFACTION GUARANTEED OR YOUR MONEY BACK.

This is a legal agreement between you, the end user and purchaser, and The Waite Group®, Inc., and the authors of the programs contained in the disk. By opening the sealed disk package, you are agreeing to be bound by the terms of this Agreement. If you do not agree with the terms of this Agreement, promptly return the unopened disk package and the accompanying items (including the related book and other written material) to the place you obtained them for a refund.

SOFTWARE LICENSE

1. The Waite Group, Inc. grants you the right to use one copy of the enclosed software programs (the programs) on a single computer system (whether a single CPU, part of a licensed network, or a terminal connected to a single CPU). Each concurrent user of the program must have exclusive use of the related Waite Group, Inc. written materials.

2. The program, including the copyrights in each program, is owned by the respective author and the copyright in the entire work is owned by The Waite Group, Inc. and they are therefore protected under the copyright laws of the United States and other nations, under international treaties. You may make only one copy of the disk containing the programs exclusively for backup or archival purposes, or you may transfer the programs to one hard disk drive, using the original for backup or archival purposes. You may make no other copies of the programs, and you may make no copies of all or any part of the related Waite Group, Inc. written materials.

3. You may not rent or lease the programs, but you may transfer ownership of the programs and related written materials (including any and all updates and earlier versions) if you keep no copies of either, and if you make sure the transferee agrees to the terms of this license.

4. You may not decompile, reverse engineer, disassemble, copy, create a derivative work, or otherwise use the programs except as stated in this Agreement.

GOVERNING LAW

This Agreement is governed by the laws of the State of California.

LIMITED WARRANTY

The following warranties shall be effective for 90 days from the date of purchase: (i) The Waite Group, Inc. warrants the enclosed disk to be free of defects in materials and workmanship under normal use; and (ii) The Waite Group, Inc. warrants that the programs, unless modified by the purchaser, will substantially perform the functions described in the documentation provided by The Waite Group, Inc. when operated on the designated hardware and operating system. The Waite Group, Inc. does not warrant that the programs will meet purchaser's requirements or that operation of a program will be uninterrupted or error-free. The program warranty does not cover any program that has been altered or changed in any way by anyone other than The Waite Group, Inc. The Waite Group, Inc. is not responsible for problems caused by changes in the operating characteristics of computer hardware or computer operating systems that are made after the release of the programs, nor for problems in the interaction of the programs with each other or other software.

THESE WARRANTIES ARE EXCLUSIVE AND IN LIEU OF ALL OTHER WARRANTIES OF MERCHANTABILITY OR FITNESS FOR A PARTICULAR PURPOSE OR OF ANY OTHER WARRANTY, WHETHER EXPRESS OR IMPLIED.

EXCLUSIVE REMEDY

The Waite Group, Inc. will replace any defective disk without charge if the defective disk is returned to The Waite Group, Inc. within 90 days from date of purchase.

This is Purchaser's sole and exclusive remedy for any breach of warranty or claim for contract, tort, or damages.

LIMITATION OF LIABILITY

THE WAITE GROUP, INC. AND THE AUTHORS OF THE PROGRAMS SHALL NOT IN ANY CASE BE LIABLE FOR SPECIAL, INCIDENTAL, CONSEQUENTIAL, INDIRECT, OR OTHER SIMILAR DAMAGES ARISING FROM ANY BREACH OF THESE WARRANTIES EVEN IF THE WAITE GROUP, INC. OR ITS AGENT HAS BEEN ADVISED OF THE POSSIBILITY OF SUCH DAMAGES.

THE LIABILITY FOR DAMAGES OF THE WAITE GROUP, INC. AND THE AUTHORS OF THE PROGRAMS UNDER THIS AGREEMENT SHALL IN NO EVENT EXCEED THE PURCHASE PRICE PAID.

COMPLETE AGREEMENT

This Agreement constitutes the complete agreement between The Waite Group, Inc. and the authors of the programs, and you, the purchaser.

Some states do not allow the exclusion or limitation of implied warranties or liability for incidental or consequential damages, so the above exclusions or limitations may not apply to you. This limited warranty gives you specific legal rights; you may have others, which vary from state to state.

SATISFACTION REPORT CARD

Please fill out this card if you wish to know of future updates to *Black Art of Visual Basic Game Programming,* or to receive our catalog.

SATISFACTION CARD

Company Name: ____________ **Division/Department:** ____________

Last Name: ____________ **First Name:** ____________ **Middle Initial:** ____________

Street Address: ____________

City: ____________ **State:** ____________ **Zip:** ____________

Daytime Telephone: (   )

Date product was acquired: **Month** ______ **Day** ______ **Year** ______ **Your Occupation:** ____________

Overall, how would you rate *Black Art of Visual Basic Game Programming?*

- ☐ Excellent
- ☐ Very Good
- ☐ Good
- ☐ Fair
- ☐ Below Average
- ☐ Poor

What did you like MOST about this book? ____________

What did you like LEAST about this book? ____________

Please describe any problems you encountered using the CD: ____________

How did you use this book (problem-solver, tutorial, reference...)? ____________

What is your level of computer expertise?

- ☐ New
- ☐ Dabbler
- ☐ Hacker
- ☐ Power User
- ☐ Programmer
- ☐ Experienced Professional

What computer languages are you familiar with? ____________

Please describe your computer hardware:

Computer ______ Hard disk ______

5.25" disk drives ______ 3.5" disk drives ______

Video card ______ Monitor ______

Printer ______ Peripherals ______

Sound board ______ CD-ROM ______

What online services do you subscribe to?

- ☐ CompuServe
- ☐ BIX
- ☐ America Online
- ☐ Internet Provider
- ☐ Delphi
- ☐ GEnie

Where did you buy this book?

- ☐ Bookstore (name): ____________
- ☐ Discount store (name): ____________
- ☐ Computer store (name): ____________
- ☐ Catalog (name): ____________
- ☐ Direct from WGP
- ☐ Other ______

What price did you pay for this book? ____________

What influenced your purchase of this book?

- ☐ Recommendation
- ☐ Advertisement
- ☐ Magazine review
- ☐ Store display
- ☐ Mailing
- ☐ Book's format
- ☐ Reputation of Waite Group Press
- ☐ Other

How many computer books do you buy each year? ______

How many other Waite Group books do you own? ______

What is your favorite Waite Group book? ____________

Is there any program or subject you would like to see Waite Group Press cover in a similar approach? ____________

Additional comments? ____________

Please send to: **Waite Group Press**
Black Art of Visual Basic Game Programming
200 Tamal Plaza
Corte Madera, CA 94925

☐ **Check here for a free Waite Group catalog**

STOP!

BEFORE YOU OPEN THE DISK OR CD-ROM PACKAGE ON THE FACING PAGE, CAREFULLY READ THE LICENSE AGREEMENT.

Opening this package indicates that you agree to abide by the license agreement found in the back of this book. If you do not agree with it, promptly return the unopened disk package (including the related book) to the place you obtained them for a refund.